I0897114

AI-Enhanced Assistive Technologies for Accessible Classrooms

Filipe T. Moreira
https://orcid.org/0000-0002-3461-9827
inED, ESE, Instituto Politécnico do Porto, Portugal

Sara Martins
https://orcid.org/0009-0001-5335-6241
Universidade de Aveiro, Portugal

IGI Global
Scientific Publishing
Publishing Tomorrow's Research Today

Vice President of Editorial Melissa Wagner
Director of Acquisitions Mikaela Felty
Director of Book Development Jocelynn Hessler
Production Manager Mike Brehm
Cover Design Jose Rosado

Published in the United States of America by
IGI Global Scientific Publishing
701 East Chocolate Avenue
Hershey, PA, 17033, USA
Tel: 717-533-8845 | Fax: 717-533-7115
Website: https://www.igi-global.com E-mail: cust@igi-global.com

Copyright © 2027 by IGI Global Scientific Publishing. All rights reserved. No part of this publication may be reproduced, stored or distributed in any form or by any means, electronic or mechanical, including photocopying, without written permission from the publisher. Use of this publication to train generative artificial intelligence (AI) technologies is expressly prohibited. The publisher reserves all rights to license its use for generative AI training and machine learning model development.

Product or company names used in this set are for identification purposes only. Inclusion of the names of the products or companies does not indicate a claim of ownership by IGI Global Scientific Publishing of the trademark or registered trademark.

Library of Congress Cataloging-in-Publication Data

LCCN: 2026032012 (CIP Data Pending)
ISBN13: 9798260027165
Isbn13Softcover: 9798260027172
EISBN13: 9798260027189
British Cataloguing in Publication Data
A Cataloguing in Publication record for this book is available from the British Library.

All work contributed to this book is new, previously-unpublished material.
The views expressed in this book are those of the authors, but not necessarily of the publisher.
This book contains information sourced from authentic and highly regarded references, with reasonable efforts made to ensure the reliability of the data and information presented. The authors, editors, and publisher believe the information in this book to be accurate and true as of the date of publication. Every effort has been made to trace and credit the copyright holders of all materials included. However, the authors, editors, and publisher cannot assume responsibility for the validity of all materials or the consequences of their use. Should any copyright material be found unacknowledged, please inform the publisher so that corrections may be made in future reprints.

Table of Contents

Detailed Table of Contents

the study explores selected AI-driven assistive technologies, including Microsoft Immersive Reader, OrCam MyEye and Floreo VR. The findings indicate that these technologies enhance accessibility through adaptive functionalities such as AI-enabled text-to-speech, computer vision and immersive virtual environments that foster personalised learning experiences. The study provides critical insights for educators and policymakers and underscores the significance of AI-powered assistive technologies in mitigating learning barriers and promoting equitable participation.

This chapter reframes AI-mediated mobile, wearable, and XR assistive systems as justice-critical educational infrastructure rather than peripheral accommodation. It integrates capability realization, recognition justice, and procedural fairness with cognitive load governance, self-regulated learning, and person-environment fit, then advances a socio-technical ecosystem model using affordance theory and distributed cognition across interface, content, pedagogy, assessment, and governance. A function taxonomy positions AI assistance as adaptive mediation shaping epistemic access, scaffold calibration, and construct fidelity. Risk governance operationalizes contextual integrity, data minimization, contestability, and auditability, addressing accessibility bias. The chapter yields policy grammars for interoperability, accommodation continuity, and dignity-preserving participation in multilingual, low-resource schooling ecologies.

This chapter explores how artificial intelligence is reshaping assistive technologies to improve access to education by visually impaired students. It specifically tends to analyze the global context of visual impairment, review key international frameworks such as the CRPD 2006, Marrakesh Treaty 2016, and SDGs 2015, and evaluate the role and potential of AI based technologies in promoting inclusive education. Understanding the global burden of visual impairment and the functional aspect of the eye provides essential context for these developments.AI based innovations such as intelligent screen readers, text to speech systems, audio navigation tools, smart white canes, wearable devices, and real time object recognition applications support

Preface

Over the past few decades, the field of assistive technology for education has undergone a profound transformation, driven in large measure by the steady advance of digital tools. Each new generation of device has reshaped what teachers and learners are able to do. The personal computer greatly expanded the range of resources available to students with disabilities. The tablet, more portable and more intuitive, brought many of those resources closer to everyday classroom use. The smartphone, in turn, placed an extraordinary amount of functionality in the palm of the hand. For some categories of need, and particularly for blind and low vision users, the smartphone at times appeared poised to replace a large share of dedicated assistive devices altogether, consolidating magnifiers, screen readers, navigation aids and reading machines into a single mainstream product.

More recently, a new wave of technologies has begun to reshape the landscape once again. Wearable devices, augmented and virtual reality, immersive learning environments and, above all, Artificial Intelligence (AI) are opening possibilities that would have seemed remote only a short time ago. When these technologies are combined with one another, and especially when they are coupled with artificial intelligence, a whole world of possibility appears to be taking shape. Real-time object recognition, intelligent text to speech, computer vision, adaptive content and personalised scaffolding are no longer confined to specialised laboratories. They are increasingly embedded in tools that learners can use directly, in ordinary classrooms, on devices they already own.

This promise, however, arrives accompanied by genuine challenges, many of which the scientific community has not yet resolved. We do not always know which of these innovations produce durable learning gains, for whom, and under what conditions. Questions of privacy, algorithmic bias, digital inequality, teacher preparedness and the ethics of data use remain open, and the pace of technological change frequently outstrips the pace of rigorous validation.

All these questions matter because the need is both vast and varied. The World Health Organization estimates that some 1.3 billion people, roughly one in six of the world's population, live with a significant disability (World Health Organization, 2022). Accessibility, then, reaches far beyond any single condition. It concerns learners with sensory, cognitive, developmental, physical and emotional needs alike, and the barriers they encounter are as diverse as the learners themselves. That diversity is mirrored in the chapters of this volume, which range from visual impairment to autism spectrum disorder, and from immersive learning to mental wellbeing.

International instruments have begun to frame the expectations that should govern this terrain. The United Nations Convention on the Rights of Persons with Disabilities (United Nations, 2006), the Marrakesh Treaty (World Intellectual Property Organization, 2013) and the 2030 Agenda for Sustainable Development, in particular the commitment to inclusive and equitable quality education expressed in Goal 4 (United Nations, 2015), together establish a normative horizon against which these tools must be measured. Established design frameworks such as Universal Design for Learning (Rose & Meyer, 2002; CAST, 2024) and the XR Accessibility User Requirements published by the World Wide Web Consortium (W3C, 2021) offer principled foundations on which accessible experiences can be built, while UNESCO's guidance on artificial intelligence in education (UNESCO, 2023) cautions that the promise of these technologies must be tempered by a human centred and equity oriented approach.

It is into this unsettled and rapidly evolving terrain that the present volume seeks to make a contribution. AI-Enhanced Assistive Technologies for Accessible Classrooms does not claim to offer final answers. Its purpose is to advance the discussion, bringing together researchers and practitioners from a wide range of countries and disciplines to examine, from complementary points of view, how emerging technologies can be designed and deployed in the service of genuinely inclusive education. The breadth of the contributing authors, who write from Indonesia, India, Jordan, Oman, the Philippines and elsewhere, is itself a reminder that accessibility is a global concern, and that meaningful solutions must be sensitive to diverse linguistic, cultural and resource contexts.

The book is organised into two complementary sections.

The first section, Mobile, Wearable, and Immersive (AR/VR/XR) Solutions, turns to the technologies that are most visibly redefining the field. The opening chapter examines the philosophical underpinnings, design principles, development methodologies and evaluation techniques associated with accessible educational technologies, showing how inclusive design, multimodal interaction and intelligent learning environments can work together towards sustainable and inclusive ecosystems. A second chapter draws on international case studies, including Microsoft Immersive Reader, OrCam MyEye and Floreo VR, to identify the adaptive functionalities through which such tools enhance accessibility, and to distil best practices for educators and policymakers. The section then deepens its conceptual ambition by reframing AI mediated mobile, wearable and extended reality systems as justice critical educational infrastructure rather than peripheral accommodation, advancing a socio technical model attentive to capability, recognition, procedural fairness and responsible governance. A further chapter sets out a roadmap for augmented, virtual and extended reality in inclusive learning, proposing an immersive learning framework grounded in Universal Design for Learning while candidly acknowledging the accessibility gaps that remain. The section closes with a quantitative study of printable and projectable augmented reality materials in preschool English education, demonstrating the potential of low cost, print based augmentation in teacher led early years settings.

The second section, Designing for Diverse Learners: Applications and Inclusive Practices, shifts the focus from technologies to the learners they are intended to serve. One chapter explores how artificial intelligence is reshaping assistive technologies for visually impaired students, from intelligent screen readers and audio navigation tools to smart canes and real time object recognition, weighing their promise against the ethical and practical challenges that condition equitable adoption. Another offers a systematic review of technology supported interventions for children with autism spectrum disorder, finding that evidence based practices such as game-based learning, multisensory instruction and structured literacy yield stable academic and developmental gains. The section then widens the very notion of assistive technology, reframing the smartphone, so often regarded as a distraction, as a potential ally of school mental health, and reminding us that the barriers learners face are not only informational but also emotional. A concluding chapter examines the integration of gamification and game-based learning with accessibility principles, surveying empirical findings on inclusive practice and making a case for interdisciplinary collaboration and equitable design in the creation of games that include rather than exclude.

Taken together, these contributions neither overstate the capabilities of the technologies they examine nor dismiss their potential. They model the kind of careful, evidence attentive and ethically grounded inquiry that the field now requires. If this volume helps educators, designers, researchers and policymakers to ask better questions, and to approach AI enhanced assistive technologies with both imagination and prudence, it will have served its purpose.

Filipe T. Moreira
inED, ESE, Instituto Politécnico do Porto, Portugal

Sara Martins
DigiMedia, DeCA, Universidade de Aveiro, Portugal

REFERENCES

CAST. (2024). *Universal Design for Learning guidelines version 3.0*. Lynnfield, MA: CAST. Retrieved from https://udlguidelines.cast.org

Rose, D. H., & Meyer, A. (2002). *Teaching every student in the digital age: Universal Design for Learning*. Association for Supervision and Curriculum Development.

UNESCO. (2023). *Guidance for generative AI in education and research*. UNESCO.

United Nations. (2006). *Convention on the Rights of Persons with Disabilities*. United Nations.

United Nations. (2015). *Transforming our world: The 2030 Agenda for Sustainable Development*. United Nations.

World Health Organization. (2022). *Global report on health equity for persons with disabilities*. World Health Organization.

World Intellectual Property Organization. (2013). *Marrakesh Treaty to Facilitate Access to Published Works for Persons Who Are Blind, Visually Impaired or Otherwise Print Disabled*. WIPO.

World Wide Web Consortium. (2021). *XR Accessibility User Requirements (XAUR)*. J. O'Connor, J. Sajka, J. White, S. Hollier, & M. Cooper (Eds.). W3C Working Group Note. Retrieved from https://www.w3.org/TR/xaur/

Acknowledgment

The preparation of this volume has been a collective endeavour, and it would not have reached completion without the generosity and commitment of many people.

Our first thanks go to all those who responded to the call for chapters and contributed proposals for the book. The breadth and quality of the submissions reflected a shared conviction that accessible, AI enhanced learning environments deserve sustained scholarly attention, and the volume owes much of its richness to that collective response.

We are equally grateful to everyone who helped to make the book known, sharing the call among colleagues, networks and institutions, and supporting its dissemination across academic and professional communities. Their efforts ensured that the project reached a wide and diverse circle of contributors and readers.

In particular, we wish to express our sincere gratitude to all those who took part in the double blind peer review of the chapters. The reviewers gave their time, their expertise and their careful judgement without recognition or reward, and their thoughtful and constructive feedback strengthened every contribution and safeguarded the scholarly integrity of the volume. Their work, often unseen, lies at the heart of what this book has become.

To all of these contributors, named and unnamed, we offer our heartfelt thanks.

Filipe T. Moreira
inED, ESE, Instituto Politécnico do Porto, Portugal

Sara Martins
DigiMedia, DeCA, Universidade de Aveiro, Portugal

[illegible]

To all of these contributors, named and unnamed, we offer our heartfelt thanks.

Filipe T. Moreira
[illegible], Porto, Portugal

Sara Marques
[illegible], Portugal

Chapter 1
Advancing Inclusive Education Through Artificial Intelligence and Assistive Innovation

Rajinder Kumar
http://orcid.org/0009-0001-4129-0388
Guru Kashi University, Talwandi Sabo, India

Manpreet Kaur
http://orcid.org/0000-0003-1027-9239
Guru Kashi University, Talwandi Sabo, India

ABSTRACT

The intervention of AI and assistive technologies is a new paradigm shift in inclusive education that preconditions new opportunities to personalize learning, improve accessibility, and fulfil the needs of learners with disabilities, special educational needs, and linguistic diversity. The chapter gives an in-depth analysis of the theoretical background, technological use, empirical studies, ethical aspects, and implementation issues related to AI-based inclusive education. Based on recent international research and case studies from seven countries, speech and language processing tools, adaptive learning platforms, multimodal interaction systems, and learning analytics can significantly improve academic performance, engagement, and emotional regulation when implemented with appropriate teacher training, ethical frameworks, and infrastructure support. It concludes with the evidence-based policy that can be embraced by the policymakers, educators and developers of technology to facilitate equitable, ethical and pedagogically viable AI implementation in diverse learning environments.

DOI: 10.4018/979-8-2600-2716-5.ch001

2027, IGI Global Scientific Publishing. Copying or distributing in print or electronic forms without written permission of IGI Global Scientific Publishing is prohibited. Use of this chapter to
ative artificial intelligence (AI) technologies is expressly prohibited. The publisher reserves all rights to license its use for generative AI training and machine learning model development.

INTRODUCTION

The international policy towards education has been interested since the 20th century in ensuring that inclusive education, which involves educational systems accommodative of all learners regardless of their physical, cognitive, linguistic, and socio-economic capabilities, is realized. The fourth United Nations Sustainable Development Goal (SDG 4) explicitly mentions the fact that in 2030, the element of inclusive and equitable quality education to everyone should be present (Tegon, 2021). However, the traditional educational approaches have failed to meet the requirements of different learners with a disability, special educational needs (SEN) and learners with a language and culturally diverse background. Traditional curricula and instructional programs often have barriers to learning especially among students with autism spectrum disorder (ASD), cerebral palsy (CP), Down syndrome (DS), dyslexia, dyscalculia, attention deficit hyperactivity disorder (ADHD) and physical impairments (Ebrahimian, 2025), (Devadas, 2025), (Omosunlade, 2025).

The development of artificial intelligence (AI) and high-level assistive technologies can be transformative in solving these long-standing problems. These technologies include a broad area of activities, such as intelligent tutoring systems (ITS), adaptive learning platforms, speech-to-text and text-to-speech systems, natural language processing (NLP), computer vision, learning analytics, virtual and augmented reality (VR/AR), and AI-related assistive devices (Ebrahimian, 2025), (Devadas, 2025), (Roy et al., 2025), (Sarkar & Madhu, 2025), (Stelea et al., 2025).

Recent empirical studies indicate that in the case of proper pedagogical designs, teacher training and ethical precautions, AI-based assistive technologies can contribute to the significant improvement in academic achievement, engagement and emotional regulation among a variety of learners (Ebrahimian, 2025), (Gayosso Mexia et al., 2024), (Omosunlade, 2025), (Opesemowo, 2024). A cross-national sample of 75 special education teachers in seven countries reported that AI training hours had a positive significant relationship ($r = 0.62$, $p < 0.01$) with perceived tool effectiveness with teachers having more than 10 hours of training rating AI tools as 31% more effective (Ebrahimian, 2025). In Ecuador, adaptive AI systems led to advancements for 85% of students with disabilities, while in Mexico, AI-supported collaborative environments increased participation by 60% (Gayosso Mexia et al., 2024).

Nevertheless, there are major challenges and risks involved in the implementation of AI within inclusive education. Disparities in infrastructure, especially those in schools which are under-resourced or developing countries, make equitable access challenging. There is also a shortage of teacher training, institutionalization, and digital divide between urban and rural population that make things worse during implementation (Devadas, 2025), (Akhter, 2025), (Opesemowo, 2024). Besides, the cultural incompatibility of AI tools that are developed mostly in the Western world also casts doubt on their suitability and usefulness in various international environments (Ebrahimian, 2025).

This chapter seeks to present an evidence-based, critical, and interdisciplinary baseline of advancing inclusive education by AI and assistive innovation by combining interdisciplinary understanding across the fields of education, computer science, disability studies and policy research. The analysis draws on recent systematic reviews, empirical studies, and case studies published between 2021 and 2025, offering timely insights into both the transformative potential and the persistent challenges of this rapidly evolving field.

Table 1. Comparative Analysis of AI-Enabled Inclusive Education (2021–2025)

Year	Key AI Technologies Used	Target Learners	Major Benefits Reported	Challenges Identified	Research Highlights
2021	Speech-to-text, screen readers, basic assistive software	Visual & physical disabilities	Improved accessibility & participation	Limited personalization	Early adoption of assistive AI tools
2022	Adaptive learning platforms, NLP translation	Learning disabilities & multilingual learners	Personalized learning & language support	Teacher training gaps	Growing use of AI for differentiated instruction
2023	Intelligent Tutoring Systems (ITS), learning analytics	SEN, dyslexia, ADHD	Better engagement & performance tracking	Data privacy concerns	AI used for predictive learning support
2024	AI collaborative learning platforms, real-time captioning	Inclusive classrooms & multilingual learners	Increased participation & communication	Digital divide & infrastructure issues	Mexico & Ecuador studies show participation gains
2025	Generative AI tutors, VR simulations, multimodal AI, AAC tools	Autism, CP, Down syndrome, non-verbal learners	Improved academic performance, emotional regulation & communication	Algorithmic bias & ethical concerns	Cross-national study shows strong impact & need for training

THEORETICAL BASES OF INCLUSION AND ASSISTIVE EDUCATIONAL TECHNOLOGIES

A successful use of AI and assistive technologies in inclusive education must be based on solid theoretical frameworks to support the design, implementation, and evaluation processes. The five main theoretical underpinnings that guide current research and practice are explored, namely Universal Design for Learning (UDL), inclusive pedagogy and equity frameworks, human centered design and co-design models, constructivist and socio-cultural learning theories, and accessibility theories and digital equity principles.

Figure 1. Conceptual Framework for AI-Driven Inclusive Education

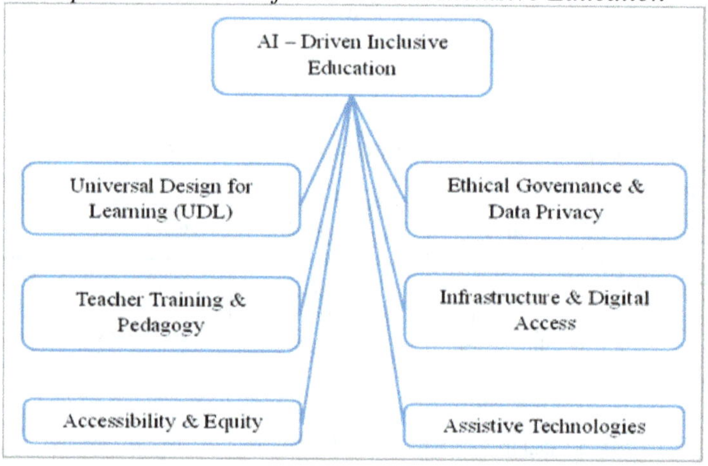

The conceptual model of inclusive education with AI is presented in figure 1 and features the key elements of an inclusive learning environment which incorporate technology, access and equity. AI-Driven Inclusive Education is the core component, leveraging artificial intelligence to cater to the needs of all learners and enhance learning experiences. The six major dimensions of the framework are: Universal Design for Learning (UDL) – flexible and personalized learning, Teacher Training and Pedagogy – effective ways of using AI in teaching, and Accessibility and Equity – equal learning opportunities for all students. It also indicates the significance of Infrastructure and Digital Access to ensure access to the technology required and Assistive Technologies (ATs) to assist learners with special needs. Lastly, Ethical Governance and Data Privacy highlight responsible AI practices, such as fairness, transparency, and student data protection.

Universal Design for Learning (UDL)

The concept of Universal Design of Learning (UDL) has become the most used design framework of inclusive educational technology and curriculum. UDL was originally designed by CAST (Center of Applied Special Technology), and it is based on neuroscience research on the process of learning and offers a roadmap to developing flexible learning environments that can support the needs of diverse learners (Devadas, 2025), (Vortia, 2025), (Roy et al., 2025), (Arias-Flores et al., 2025), (Koranteng, 2025). The three key principles of the framework are multiple means of representation (what of learning), multiple means of action and expression (how of learning) and multiple means of engagement (Devadas, 2025), (Vortia, 2025).

AI-enabled assistive technologies align particularly well with UDL principles by offering unprecedented flexibility in content presentation, learner interaction, and engagement strategies (Devadas, 2025), (Vortia, 2025), (Roy et al., 2025), (Arias-Flores et al., 2025). The intelligent tutoring systems may offer various options of presenting knowledge through text-based answers to learners to speech, gesture, or visual display (Roy et al., 2025), (Sarkar & Madhu, 2025).

Recent studies show that the principles of UDL can be implemented in AI-assisted curriculum design. This approach resulted in substantial improvements: an 18% literacy gain among Down syndrome learners, reduced task completion times and increased accuracy for cerebral palsy learners, and improved attention and social engagement for autism spectrum disorder students. The study's design-based research framework demonstrated how UDL can guide the systematic development and evaluation of AI-enhanced inclusive curricula (Omosunlade, 2025).

Similarly, a narrative review of AI applications in mathematics education for students with learning disabilities in the United States found that tools like Photomath, Mathway, Socratic, Century, and the MACS Curriculum were most effective when grounded in UDL and Constructivist Learning Theory. These frameworks provided a theoretical basis for evaluating AI's role in enhancing accessibility and personalization through differentiated instruction, automated feedback, and early screening for conditions such as dyscalculia and dysgraphia (Vortia, 2025).

Nevertheless, opponents observe that the application of AI systems to implement UDL should be done with care to prevent the framework being applied superficially. The mere offering of various formats of content delivery is not a guarantee of meaningful accessibility, when the pedagogical design behind the offering of such visualizations is unable to meet the cognitive, emotional, and social needs of learners (Devadas, 2025).

Inclusive Pedagogy and Equity Frameworks

Outside of UDL, more comprehensive systems of inclusive pedagogy focus on the social, cultural, and political aspects of education. Inclusive pedagogy acknowledges that learning obstacles are not situated only in individual learners and are built up through the educational system and the educational curriculum and teaching practices that legitimize some modes of knowing and being (Ebrahimian, 2025),

(Devadas, 2025), (Gayosso Mexia et al., 2024). This is similar to the social model of disability that perceives disability as a result of interaction between the individual and the environmental barriers and not a deficit (Devadas, 2025).

AI-driven inclusive education initiatives increasingly incorporate these equity-oriented frameworks. A cross-national study of AI-driven assistive technologies in special needs classrooms across seven countries (Iran, Italy, Philippines, USA, India, Brazil, South Africa) explicitly grounded its analysis in UNESCO's AI in Education initiative and IFIP's digital equity agenda. This human-centered approach to technology integration reflects a commitment to equity that extends beyond technical accessibility to encompass cultural responsiveness and participatory design (Ebrahimian, 2025).

Educación Inclusiva Potenciada por Tecnología (EIPT), conceptual model developed in Ecuador and Mexico, is based on the combination of advanced technologies and inclusive pedagogical principles and ethics. This framework highlights the need for AI tools to personalize learning and increase accessibility while also empowering students to participate and take agency over their learning. Ethical and responsible implementation tailored to the context and/or user-centred approaches that respect the cultural context and lived experiences of learners are emphasized in EIPT (Gayosso Mexia et al., 2024).

Equity frameworks also provide the basis for critical analysis of the ways in which AI systems can reinforce and/or mitigate current educational disparities. AI's transformative potential for STEM education highlights the need to acknowledge the opportunity for equity and access, yet implement AI in a way that accounts for systemic barriers that marginalized learner's encounter. This requires moving Beyond individualized accommodation, the focus is on how AI systems can influence the educational structures, curricula, and assessment systems and practices to be more inclusive by design (Kohnke & Zaugg, 2025).

Human-Centered Design and Co-Design Models

Human-centered design (HCD) and participatory co-design approaches have become increasingly prominent in the development of AI-enabled assistive technologies. These approaches place the needs, tastes and skills of end-users, such as learners with disabilities, educators, and families, at the centre of both the design, development and evaluation process (Ebrahimian, 2025), (Sarkar & Madhu, 2025), (Wells, 2025). The principles of HCD are in line with the disability rights movement focus on nothing about us without us where the assistive technologies are actually effective in meeting the needs of those the technology is being designed to serve (Wells, 2025).

Co-design models build upon HCD by placing users as active participants of the design process instead of the passive consumers of technology. The cross-national research of AI in special needs classrooms discovered that the involvement of teachers in design and evaluation of AI tools was a key to successful implementation. Those teachers that underwent co-design processes, stated that they had more ownership of the technologies as well as were more capable of modifying the technology to meet the needs of their students. The study recommended mandatory AI literacy for teachers and culturally adaptive AI design processes that involve educators from diverse contexts (Ebrahimian, 2025).

A proposed framework for AI-driven symbolic text prediction for non-verbal individuals explicitly incorporates participatory design principles. The framework recommends prototyping and ethical audit and longitudinal case studies to be carried out to non-verbal users, speech-language pathologists, special educators, and AAC (augmentative and alternative communication) developers. This cooperation model is geared towards making AI-AAC systems fair, transparent, and actually personalized to the needs of users in terms of communication (Wells, 2025).

However, implementing genuine co-design in AI development faces practical challenges. Technical complexity of AI systems, power imbalances between technology developers and end-users, time and resource constraints, and the significance of meaningful participation may be restricted (Wells, 2025). Furthermore, the co-design processes should overcome the tensions between customization at an individual level and scalability, because highly personalized solutions can prove hard to transfer to various settings (Ebrahimian, 2025).

Constructivist and Socio-Cultural Learning Theories

The theory of constructivist and socio-cultural learning theories offers significant underpinnings on how artificial intelligence-driven assistive technologies can be used to facilitate purposeful learning. Constructivism, especially in the way of Piaget and subsequent authors, insists on the active process of knowledge building in a learner as he/she interacts with the surrounding world instead of being a passive receiver of information. This view guides the design of AI systems which offer scaffolded support to enable learners to develop knowledge in bits as they explore and attempt to solve problems under guided guidance (Vortia, 2025), (Salendab et al., 2025).

The socio-cultural theory of Vygotsky and especially the notion of the Zone of Proximal Development (ZPD) have been considered specifically impactful in the AI-assisted inclusive education (Ebrahimian, 2025), (Devadas, 2025). The ZPD is the difference between the things that a learner is capable of doing on his/her own and the things that they can accomplish with the help of the proper support (Devadas, 2025). The cross-national examination of AI in special needs classrooms discovered that the results of the research were consistent with the theory of mediated learning according to Vygotsky, according to which AI is a scaffold to the cognitive development. Speech-to-text systems, generative AI tutors, and VR simulations were found to provide the kind of mediated support that enables learners with disabilities to access content and demonstrate understanding that would otherwise be beyond their independent capabilities (Ebrahimian, 2025).

The idea of distributed cognition, which further develops the thoughts of Vygotsky by focusing on the distributed nature of cognitive processes between people, technology, and setting is especially applicable to the study of AI-assisted learning. In this view, AI systems are not just the peripheral aid but rather become a part of the cognitive framework of learners, and they can be extended to something beyond the scope of a human or technological intelligence. This has significant consequences to assessment and evaluation in that it creates the concern of what authentic demonstration of learning entails when AI tools are involved with the learning process (Devadas, 2025).

Accessibility Theories and Digital Equity

Accessibility theories and digital equity frameworks provide critical lenses for examining how AI-enabled assistive technologies can either reduce or reproduce barriers to educational participation. Legal requirements on accessibility in educational institutions exist in the United States in the Americans with Disabilities Act (ADA) and Section 504 of the Rehabilitation Act and in other nations with comparable legislation (Wells, 2025).

Recent AI-driven platforms explicitly incorporate these accessibility standards. AccessiLearnAI, an accessibility-first, AI-powered e-learning platform, is designed with compliance to semantic HTML5 and ARIA (Accessible Rich Internet Applications) standards, ensuring compatibility with assistive technologies like screen readers.

Nevertheless, compliance related to accessibility is not enough to get true digital equity. According to the scholars of critical disability studies, although necessary, technical accessibility standards tend to represent a medical model of disability, which centers on the individual accommodation of disability instead of the structural change. To strengthen the concept of digital equity one must consider how artificial intelligence systems might be used to oppose ableist values within the design of educational systems and design learning spaces that celebrate neurodiversity and other forms of knowing (Devadas, 2025), (Kohnke & Zaugg, 2025).

AI-ENABLED ASSISTIVE TOOLS AND APPLICATIONS IN DIVERSE EDUCATIONAL CONTEXTS

The AI assistive technologies landscape in inclusive education is not a homogenous set of tools and applications, but rather a wide range of tools and applications that are meant to meet particular obstacles to learning and participation. This subchapter discusses six key fields of AI applications, including adaptive content delivery and personalised learning platforms, intelligent tutoring systems, speech and language technologies, multimodal interaction and immersive technologies, learning analytics and predictive systems, and AI-based assistive technologies to particular disabilities.

Figure 2. AI-Driven Inclusive Learning Process Model

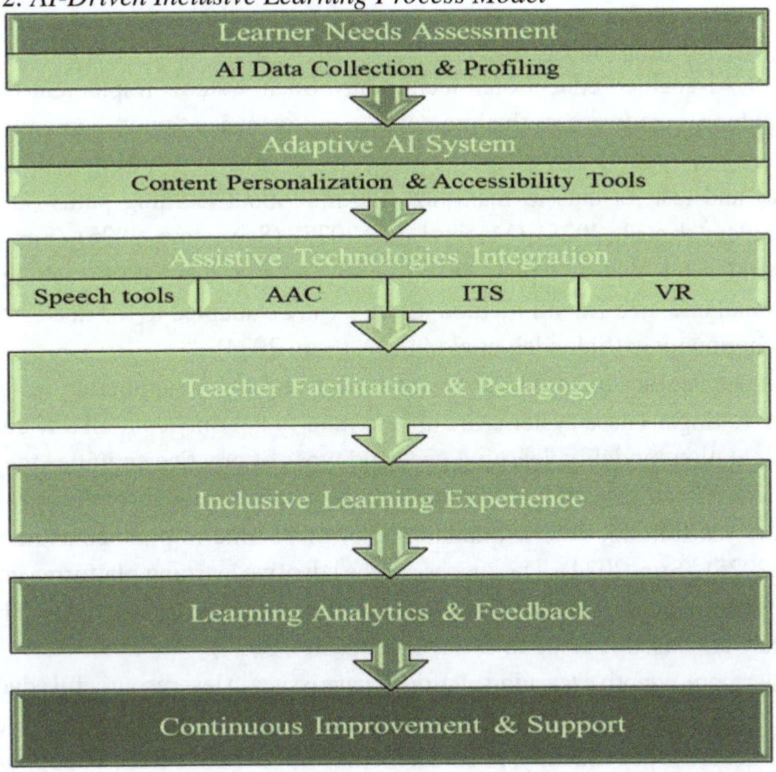

The AI-driven inclusive learning process model in Figure 2 shows the way AI can be used to provides personalized and accessible learning. It starts with Learner Needs Assessment using AI to collect and profile data to grasp individual learning needs. Based on this information, an Adaptive AI System provides content personalization and accessibility support. The model also incorporates Assistive Technologies (speech tools, Augmentative and Alternative Communication (AAC), Intelligent Tutoring Systems (ITS) and VR (Virtual Reality) which are intended to increase learning participation and engagement. The Teacher Facilitation and Pedagogy is essential in directing and assisting students in the AI supported environment. All of these elements are integrated to provide an Inclusive Learning Experience, which is then followed by Learning Analytics and Feedback to track student progress and enhance learning outcomes. Lastly, Continuous Improvement and Support are highlighted to ensure continued improvement of the accessibility, effectiveness, and inclusiveness of education.

Adaptive Content Delivery and Personalized Learning Platforms

Adaptive learning platforms represent one of the most widely implemented categories of AI-enabled educational technology. Such systems implement machine learning algorithms to assess the interactions, performance trends, and preferences of learners and dynamically adapt the difficulty of content, learning rate, teaching strategies and test formats to maximize the individual learning paths (Devadas, 2025), (Salendab et al., 2025), (Macias Leon, 2025), (Srivastava, 2025), (Sun, 2024). The general idea is that such platforms may offer a better method of teaching than a conventional one-size-fits-all method, as they can be adapted to the needs of every learner continuously (Salendab et al., 2025), (Sun, 2024).

The recent studies indicate how adaptive learning can be applied in various educational settings. These systems are able to modify not only content difficulty but also presentation modality, learning pace and types of practice activities they offer (Sun, 2024). This is especially useful to students with learning disabilities, who can have more scaffolding, other explanations, or more time to practice as necessary (Vortia, 2025), (Sun, 2024). The success of the adaptive learning platforms however relies heavily on quality of the underlying algorithms and pedagogical models upon which they are based (Salendab et al., 2025), (Sun, 2024).

Furthermore, adaptive learning platforms have issues in less resourceful educational institutions. This study's findings confirm that adaptive learning platforms cannot be implemented independently, but must include a system of extensive support such as teacher training, technical facilities and ethical controls (Salendab et al., 2025).

Intelligent Tutoring Systems for Diverse Learners

Intelligent Tutoring Systems (ITS) are a more advanced application of AI in personalized learning, offering individualized tutoring sessions that respond to students' knowledge levels, learning styles, and emotional reactions (Devadas, 2025), (Akhter,

2025), (Aarthi et al., 2025), (Sun, 2024). Unlike simpler adaptive learning platforms that typically modify the difficulty level of the content, ITS leverage detailed learner models, domain models, and pedagogical models to deliver personalized instruction, feedback, and support (Akhter, 2025; Sun, 2024).

The systematic literature review of 110 studies investigating the use of ITS in the secondary education of multilingual learners showed that systems that used complex learner models, linguistically-sensitive feedback and multimodal delivery significantly improved understanding, memory, learner confidence, and engagement. The literature review uncovered several elements of successful ITS for diverse learners: Bayesian Knowledge Tracing and Performance Factor Analysis for modeling students' cognitions, adaptation of instruction for the individual student's learning trajectory, multimodal instructional resources for supporting diverse learners, and culturally responsive adaptation of instruction for supporting culturally relevant domain knowledge (Akhter, 2025).

Nevertheless, there are a number of challenges associated with the introduction of ITS. The systematic review of ITS highlighted the crucial importance of teachers' preparation, infrastructure and ethical handling of data in implementing the project. The high bandwidth internet and computing power associated with complex ITS may be limited by the problem with infrastructure, particularly under-resourced schools (Akhter, 2025).

New opportunities of ITS are introduced by emerging technologies such as generative artificial intelligence, but it should also be carefully looked at to avoid bias, preserve privacy, and maintain cultural diversity. The AI can be advanced to allow more natural language interactions and personalization, although such advances require strong ethical protection. The review represents a framework of inclusive, adaptive and pedagogically based ITS design that compromises between technological innovation and equity and ethical considerations (Akhter, 2025).

Speech and Language Technologies

Speech and language technologies represent a critical category of AI-enabled assistive tools, particularly for learners with communication disabilities, language-based learning disabilities, and those from linguistically diverse backgrounds. These technologies include speech-to-text (automatic speech recognition), text-to-speech (speech synthesis), natural language processing for language translation and simplification, and AI-driven augmentative and alternative communication (AAC) systems (Ebrahimian, 2025), (Devadas, 2025), (Roy et al., 2025), (Sarkar & Madhu, 2025), (Stelea et al., 2025), (Wells, 2025), (Arias-Flores et al., 2025).

Speech-to-text systems enable learners with physical disabilities, dysgraphia, or motor impairments to produce written text through voice input, removing barriers to written expression (Ebrahimian, 2025), (Roy et al., 2025), (Sarkar & Madhu, 2025). The cross-national study of AI in special needs classrooms found that speech-to-text systems were among the most widely used AI-driven assistive technologies, enhancing inclusive pedagogy for students with disabilities such as autism spectrum disorder, dyslexia, ADHD, and physical impairments. Teachers reported that these systems improved students' ability to participate in writing activities and demonstrate their knowledge without being limited by fine motor challenges (Ebrahimian, 2025).

Text-to-speech systems also facilitate the complementary role of text to speech conversion to assist visual impaired, dyslexic, or readers with reading comprehension challenges learners (Devadas, 2025), (Roy et al., 2025), (Sarkar & Madhu, 2025), (Stelea et al., 2025). Studies of AI-based assistive technologies to support students with disabilities have discovered that text-to-speech, screen readers, and real-time captioning greatly enhanced accessibility and engagement. These technologies enable the learner to receive the written material in the form of sound, which can be adjusted with the required reading pace and voice tone to fit the preferences of the individual learner (Sarkar & Madhu, 2025), (Stelea et al., 2025).

NLP technologies are not limited to speech-to-text and text-to-speech and offer more advanced language assistance. Language translation with AI allows language learners to receive educational materials in their acquiring language, eliminating language barrier to learning (Stelea et al., 2025), (Srivastava, 2025). An example of such an AI is AccessiLearnAI which uses Large Language Models to translate in real-time as well as automatically create alt-text, summaries and text-to-speech features. It is a comprehensive strategy that supports many accessibility requirements at the same time, including students with disabilities, diverse language orientation, or bandwidth constraints (Stelea et al., 2025).

AAC systems based on AI are one of the most innovative uses of speech and language technologies in the field of non-verbal people. The suggested system would be beneficial to all children, adults, and multilingual individuals and gauge cognitive load, prediction accuracy, individual responsiveness, and user satisfaction (Wells, 2025).

Multimodal Interaction and Immersive Technologies

The newest AI applications in inclusive education are multimodal interaction systems and immersive technologies, such as the virtual reality (VR), augmented reality (AR), and mixed reality (MR). These technologies deliver multisensory experiences in learning that can support various learning styles and meet certain accessibility requirements (Ebrahimian, 2025), (Devadas, 2025), (Akhter, 2025).

VR simulations have shown particular promise for students with autism spectrum disorder and other developmental disabilities. The cross-national study of AI in special needs classrooms found that VR simulations, alongside speech-to-text systems and generative AI tutors, enhanced inclusive pedagogy and improved academic performance, engagement, and emotional regulation (Ebrahimian, 2025).

The multimodal instructional materials, that is, the information presented through a visual, auditory, kinesthetic, and textual mode, align with the concept of UDL as they offer different means of representation. In the case of learners with sensory impairments, multimodal systems can highlight the modalities that are available to them and offer alternative representations to the content that cannot be accessed (Akhter, 2025).

Nevertheless, immersive technologies are associated with serious difficulties of implementation. VR/AR hardware may be too expensive, and technical knowledge needed to create and maintain immersive learning environments can be too high especially in under-resourced schools (Srivastava, 2025). The mentioned cross-national study has begged the question of overstimulation in certain AI-enhanced learning settings, where the regulation of the level of sensoreceptivity is required (Ebrahimian, 2025), (Omosunlade, 2025).

Learning Analytics and Predictive Systems

AI and learning analytics can be applied to educational data to uncover learning patterns, forecast student outcomes, and facilitate personalized teaching and learning (Devadas, 2025), (Sun, 2024), (Salendab et al., 2025). The systems enable teachers to pinpoint students who may be at risk, track their learning progress, and implement timely interventions based on data analysis and automated reporting features (Ebrahimian, 2025). Predictive analytics using AI can enhance inclusive education by monitoring students' strengths, weaknesses, and engagement. Despite these benefits, there are some ethical issues to consider when using these technologies in education, such as privacy, consent, and the potential for misuse of sensitive student information (Wells, 2025), (Chakraborty et al., 2025). Researchers also emphasize that historical data can be skewed and adversely impact the opportunities of marginalized learners (Sun, 2024).

AI-Powered Assistive Technologies for Specific Disabilities

In addition to general-purpose adaptive learning and tutoring systems, AI provides the creation of disabilities and learning-specific assistive technologies. This part examines the AI uses in motor impairment, hearing impairment, learning disability and neurodevelopmental conditions, and the visual impairment.

For learners with visual impairments, AI-powered assistive technologies include smart glasses with object recognition and navigation assistance, screen readers with natural language processing for improved context understanding, and automatic alt-text generation for images (Roy et al., 2025), (Stelea et al., 2025), (Ferebee, 2025). AccessiLearnAI's automatic alt-text generation using Large Language Models demonstrates how AI can reduce the manual labor required to make visual content accessible while improving the quality and contextual relevance of descriptions (Stelea et al., 2025).

In the case of learners with hearing impairment, the AI-based real-time captioning and sign language recognition systems are essential in offering the spoken language material to them. These systems employ natural language processing and speech recognition to produce correct and timed captions of live lectures, discussions, and the multimedia content (Sarkar & Madhu, 2025).

For learners with autism spectrum disorder, cerebral palsy, and Down syndrome, AI-assisted curriculum models have demonstrated significant impact. A study on digital inclusion in special education found that AI-assisted curriculum models applied in literacy, numeracy, social-emotional learning, and motor responsiveness resulted in an 18% literacy gain among Down syndrome learners, reduced task completion times and increased accuracy for cerebral palsy learners, and improved attention and social engagement for autism spectrum disorder students. The study emphasized that AI should be integrated as a core curricular design principle, not merely an assistive tool, to address barriers in conventional curricula (Omosunlade, 2025).

Table 2. Comparative Impact of AI Assistive Technologies on Learning Outcomes

AI Tool	**Learning Improvement**	**Accessibility Support**	**Engagement Level**	**Best Use Case**
Adaptive Learning Platforms	High	Medium	High	Personalized instruction
Intelligent Tutoring Systems	Very High	Medium	Very High	Individual tutoring
Speech-to-Text & TTS	Medium	Very High	Medium	Physical & visual disabilities
AI Translation & NLP	Medium	High	High	Multilingual learners
VR & Multimodal Systems	High	Medium	Very High	Autism & experiential learning
AAC & Symbol Prediction	High	Very High	High	Non-verbal communication

EMPIRICAL EVIDENCE AND INTERNATIONAL CASE STUDIES

The theoretical promise of AI-enabled inclusive education must be evaluated against empirical evidence of its impact in real-world educational settings. This section analyzes the empirical research and case studies of AI-based assistive technologies conducted in various settings that support their effectiveness, challenges and implementation models.

Cross-National Implementation Studies

Cross-national research would offer a useful understanding of the way AI-based inclusive education would operate in various cultural, economic, and policy settings. The latest study that is most comprehensive investigated the implementation of AI-based assistive technologies in special needs classrooms in seven countries: Iran, Italy, Philippines, USA, India, Brazil, and South Africa. It was a mixed-methods study that comprised a 25-item survey, that was Likert scale, semi-structured interviews with 20 teachers, and classroom observations consisting of 75 teachers of special education (Ebrahimian, 2025).

The authors of the research have discovered considerable academic performance, engagement, and emotional regulation gains in seven countries with the introduction of AI-based assistive technologies, such as speech-to-text systems and generative AI tutors and VR simulations, provided with relevant teacher training. The quantitative analysis revealed that the perceived effectiveness of the tool is strongly positively correlated ($r = 0.62, p < 0.01$) with the number of the hours spent training AI (Ebrahimian, 2025). Teachers with more than 10 hours of training rated AI tools to be 31% more effective than those with little training and this underlines the importance of professional development (Ebrahimian, 2025).

Nevertheless, the paper has equally found considerable cross-national differences in implementation problems. Forty-two percent of teachers mentioned infrastructure gaps as one of the ongoing obstacles to fair adoption of AI, and this problem is especially strong in Brazil, India, and South Africa. Cultural mismatch of AI tools designed mainly in the Western world was an issue in all the countries, but specifically in Iran and the Philippines, when teachers stated that most of the examples of content, language models, and interface designs did not reflect the local cultural contexts (Ebrahimian, 2025).

Impact on Academic Performance and Engagement

Empirical research proves over and over again that AI-based assistive technologies may be used to enhance academic achievement and engagement in case of proper pedagogical framework and provisioning. The cross-national research revealed positive effects on academic performance, involvement, and emotional regulation between the various types of disabilities such as autism spectrum disorders, dyslexia, ADHD, and physical disabilities (Ebrahimian, 2025).

The research used design-based research framework to carry out needs analysis, prototype modules development and pilot testing within inclusive classrooms. Quantitative findings revealed significant improvements: an 18 percent literacy improvement in Down syndrome learners, shorter task completion time and higher accuracy in cerebral palsy learners and better attention and social interactions in autism spectrum disorder learners. Teacher and parent qualitative feedback showed that learner independence and engagement had improved, but overstimulation problems were mentioned (Omosunlade, 2025).

Nevertheless, the results of not all studies are equally positive. The AI systematic review about the personalized learning revealed that although AI-driven adaptive-learning systems have the potential to improve the learning results, the concerns regarding the algorithmic discrimination and privacy are still the issues of significant concern. The review has highlighted that the success of AI systems is critically dependent on their design, context of implementation, and support systems around them (Sun, 2024).

Case Studies in Specific Disability Contexts

Cases that concentrate on the individual disability groups offer a perspective of the practicality of AI-based assistive technologies. The research on AI-assisted curriculum models in the context of autism, cerebral palsy, and Down syndrome is particularly educative. The study employs a design-based research model that is in line with the Universal Design of Learning theory, and AI was incorporated as a fundamental design principle in the curricula but not one that was used as an aide (Omosunlade, 2025).

The adaptive reading materials, phonological support, and vocabulary building activities were offered in the AI-assisted curriculum that worked on the literacy development of the students with Down syndrome. The 18% literacy improvement testified to the fact that AI can be useful in working with the unique learning profile of the learners with Down syndrome, who tend to respond to repetition, visuals, and more time in practice (Omosunlade, 2025).

In the case of students with autism spectrum disorder, the curriculum was social-emotional learning and attention control based on the use of AI to create routines, visual schedules, and predictable interactions. The enhanced attention and socializing skills proved that AI could help the executive function, as well as socialization-related difficulties typical of autism (Omosunlade, 2025).

The examples provided by Georgia Tech and the University of Michigan suggest that AI has a transformative potential in both K-12 and higher education environments. The chapter that analyzed these instances discussed adaptive learning systems, emotional recognition systems, and chatbots that are based on AI to support diversity, equity, and inclusion (Le, 2025).

Implementation Models Across Educational Settings

Empirical studies indicate that there is various implementation paradigm on AI-enabled inclusive education that is applied in formal, non-formal and technology-mediated learning settings. In institutionalized K-12, the cross-national study observed that successful implementation was normally characterized by introducing it in stages, with pilot projects in some classes first before it could be extended to other schools or districts on a larger scale. This incremental process enabled the process of refinement with the help of teacher and students' response, technical troubleshooting, and revision of professional development programs (Ebrahimian, 2025).

The analysis of AI-assisted curriculum models, in special education, showed the implementation model that incorporated AI in the early stages as an integral curricular design idea. The model offered an expandable plan through which IDEA (Individuals with Disabilities Education Act) requirements and enhancing obligations to digital equity in special education could be improved (Omosunlade, 2025).

This is because in non-formal and under-resourced educational settings, there are severe infrastructure and resource bottlenecks that need to be tackled by the implementation models. The example of the phenomenological study conducted in Nigerian communities revealed that the implementation of such solutions was possible only under the condition of creativity to address the lack of infrastructures, such as offline-capable AI applications, mobile-first design with support of the low-end devices, and community-based support mechanisms that would offset the insufficient formal technical assistance. The paper has highlighted the relevance of policy framework, investment in infrastructure, and partnership to establish equitable access and integration of AI (Opesemowo, 2024).

The studies of AI strategies to support inclusive education resources and support highlight the role of collaborative strategies with educators, students, families, technology developers, and policymakers. The chapter comments on the application of practical examples and case studies to provide actionable information on how AI can be used to enhance inclusive education, especially in relation to enhancing resources, accessibility, and mental health of students with special needs (Al-Rashaida et al., 2025).

Systematic Reviews and Meta-Analyses

Systematic reviews and meta-analyses summarise evidence in more than one study and offer more comprehensive information on the efficacy and difficulties of AI-assisted inclusive education. The ITS systematic review of multilingual learners reviewed 110 peer-reviewed articles, which are a comprehensive evaluation of the effectiveness in different contexts. The review established that ITS contributed immensely to the understanding, memorization, confidence of the learners, and their engagement when they used complex learner models, linguistically sensitive feedback, and multimodal delivery. The significance of teacher training, infrastructure preparedness, and ethical data management to make the implementation effective were also manifested in the review (Akhter, 2025).

The systematic review of AI in personalized learning reviewed 46 studies published between 2018-2024 in accordance with the PRISMA 2020 Checklist. The learning outcomes discussed in the review were centered on the use of artificial intelligence and its ethics. Results reported that AI-based custom adaptive-learning systems provide educational content based on the needs of a particular student, and ITS improve communication with the students by providing custom feedback, which is especially helpful with technical subject matter. Nevertheless, other issues such as algorithmic discrimination, privacy, and the necessity to pursue fairness and bias to make all learners beneficent and not discriminated were also found in the review (Sun, 2024).

A literature review on artificial intelligence and assistive technologies in education application to disabilities assessed the method of integrating AI-enabled assistive technology to promote inclusive education. Specific technologies mentioned in the review, including the speech-to-text, captioning, and adaptive interfaces, and analyzed personalization strategies referring to such a framework as Universal Design of Learning. The review however, observed that there was no empirical data or in-depth data on the policies or implementation, thus there were gaps in the existing research base (Arias-Flores et al., 2025).

A methodical analysis of the application of digital technologies in the promotion of inclusive education focused on existing tendencies in the field of various types of technologies. Although the available metadata does not provide specific results, the review adds to the emerging body of literature on the topic of digital inclusivity and presents implications to policymakers, educators, and researchers who want to enhance accessibility and learning outcomes in various educational settings.

Figure 3. Comparative Impact of AI Tools on Student Learning Outcomes

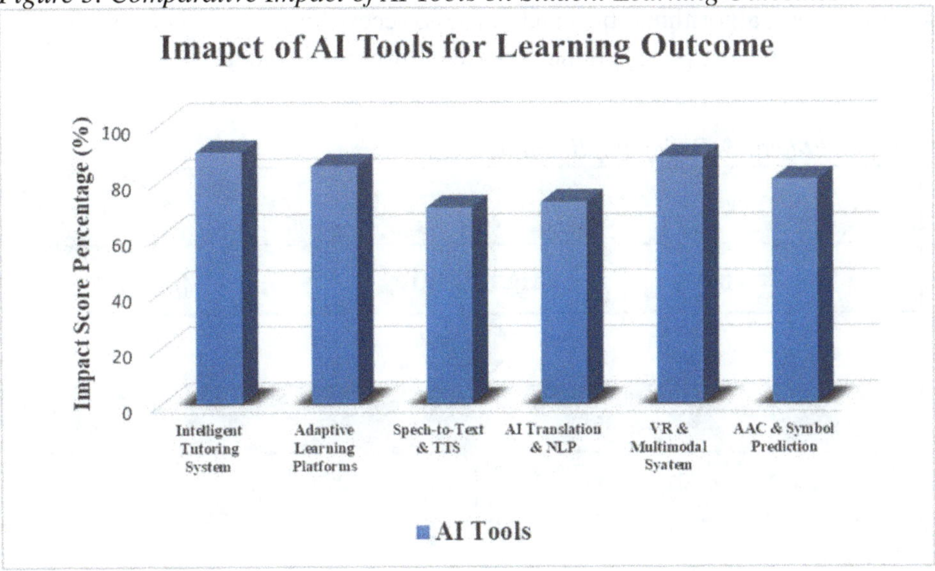

As presented in the bar graph, ITS are most effective in terms of learning outcomes (≈90%), providing feedback that is tailored for students and adaptive support and individualised pathways. VR and multimodal learning environments are just behind (≈88%) as they provide engagement through immersion and physical or experience-based learning spaces are relevant to a variety of learners. One of the highest rates of effectiveness for adaptive learning platforms (≈85%) is the ability to tailor content difficulty, pacing and instructional strategies to learner profiles. Successful communication and participation is also achieved by using AAC and symbol prediction (around 80%), especially for non-verbal learners and pupils with speech impairments. However, there are also tools, AI translation and natural language procession, which help in overcoming the language barrier and make learning content accessible across languages, making the option of cross-lingual inclusion possible (72%). Last but not least, speech-to-text and text-to-speech technologies (≈70%) strongly enhance accessibility and participation for learners with visual, physical or reading disabilities, albeit doing so to a lesser extent than more interactive/personalized AI offerings.

ETHICAL, LEGAL, AND POLICY IMPLICATIONS

The integration of AI into AT for inclusive education raises a number of ethical, legal and policy questions that must be considered to ensure the process is fair, responsible and effective. Five important dimensions are discussed: data privacy and security issues, algorithmic bias and fairness, accessibility compliance standards, equitable access, and policy frameworks and governance model.

Figure 4. Ethical & Policy Implications

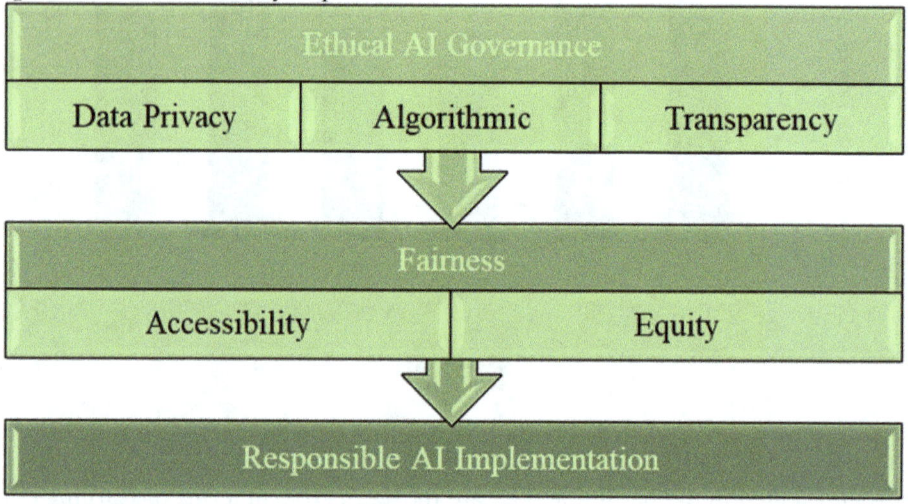

AI's ethical and policy implications in education are demonstrated in Figure 4. It outlines important aspects of Ethical AI Governance, such as Data Privacy, Algorithmic Fairness, and Transparency, that are crucial for building trustworthy AI systems. The principles support the practice of Fairness by supporting Equal Opportunities, Accessibility and Equity for all learners. Finally, ethical governance, equitable and fair decision making and inclusive policies are essential to the responsible use of AI in education, the safeguarding of learners' rights and the equitable access to educational technologies.

Data Privacy and Security Concerns

AI-driven education systems, like those used in student performance tracking, behavior monitoring, biometric, health, and disability data collection, are able to collect vast quantities of sensitive student information (Ebrahimian, 2025), (Devadas, 2025), (Sun, 2024), (Chakraborty et al., 2025). This poses significant privacy and security issues, especially for students with disabilities who could otherwise be discriminated against by the misuse of their information (Wells, 2025; Chakraborty et al. 2025). Studies have shown that transparency and GDPR-compliant systems have helped alleviate some privacy concerns, while there are challenges in areas with weak data protection regulations (Ebrahimian, 2025) (Stelea et al., 2025). The principles of data governance and informed consent, secure data handling, and responsible AI utilization are crucial in ensuring the protection of student privacy and accountability.To uphold student privacy and accountability, it is crucial to establish robust data governance, ensure informed consent, manage data securely, and practice responsibly using AI (Sun, 2024).

Accessibility Compliance Standards

The legal frameworks and technical standards of accessibility offer valuable checks and balances to AI-enabled inclusive education. Accessibility in educational institutions is legally required in the United States by the Americans with Disabilities Act of 1990 (ADA), Section 504 of the Rehabilitation Act and the Individuals with Disabilities Education Act of 1997 (IDEA) (Wells, 2025), (Omosunlade, 2025).

AccessiLearnAI illustrates a clear focus on accessibility conforming through the design based on semantic HTML5 and ARIA codes, ensuring that it is compatible with assistive technologies such as the screen reader. This active attitude to accessibility compliance is the opposite of retrofitting features of accessibility after the initial development, which in most cases leads to the insufficient or incomplete accessibility (Stelea et al., 2025).

The discussion of AI-supported curriculum models with students with autism, cerebral palsy, and Down syndrome showed that the integration of AI can support the IDEA requirements and reinforce the promises of the digital equity in special education. The study offered a scalable model of access to education by design through the incorporation of AI as a central design principle of UDL to address legal demands of accessible education (Omosunlade, 2025).

Studies of AI-based AAC systems observe that such legal requirements as Section 504 and the ADA apply to accessibility. The paper recommends the use of more robust regulations and transparency requirements so that AI-AAC systems comply with the accessibility requirements. Nevertheless, the research also says that the current criteria of accessibility might be insufficient to overcome the specific impact of AI systems, which may bring new inaccessibility into being despite its claim to bring greater accessibility (Wells, 2025).

The systematic review of assistive technologies and AI reviewed technologies used to address disabilities based on the speech-to-text, captioning, and adaptive interface technology. Nevertheless, the review did mention that there was not a specific policy or implementation analysis of adherence to certain standards, such as WCAG, ADA or Section 508. This disconnect shows the necessity of paying more clear attention to accessibility compliance in the development and evaluation of AI (Arias-Flores et al., 2025).

It has been observed that just the compliance of accessibility is not enough to attain actual inclusion. Such standards of technical accessibility are essential, but they also tend to uphold a medical paradigm of disability that looks towards accommodations of the individual and not the systemic change. To develop a stronger solution, we need to look at how AI systems can disrupt ableist assumptions in educational design, and provide learning environments that represent neurodiversity and different ways of knowing (Devadas, 2025), (Kohnke & Zaugg, 2025).

Equitable Access and the Digital Divide

The digital divide, i.e. the difference between those who are and are not equipped to access digital technologies, is a key obstacle to inclusive education using AI (Ebrahimian, 2025), (Devadas, 2025), (Salendab et al., 2025), (Sarkar & Madhu, 2025), (Kooli & Chakraoui, 2025), (Al-Rashaida et al., 2025), (Srivastava, 2025), (Opesemowo, 2024). This gap overlaps with the current education disparities that occur due to socio-economic status, geographic position, race, and disability, resulting in increased disadvantages of disadvantaged learners (Srivastava, 2025), (Opesemowo, 2024).

The study on the use of AI to create sustainable and inclusive education points out that urban-rural digital divide, high costs of adoption, and the lack of technological infrastructure in developing countries are major challenges. The paper highlights the importance of stringent control and access controls to deal with these problems. Absent a focus on equal access, AI-driven education will only widen the current disparities by giving the already-privileged students better access to learning (Srivastava, 2025).

The works on AI-based assistive technologies in students with disabilities underline that the infrastructural inequalities are an important issue. The chapter deals with such ethical issues as algorithmic bias and data privacy and infrastructure gaps, which require thorough needs evaluations, collaborative ecosystems, and emphasis on both affordability and accessibility to foster equity (Sarkar & Madhu, 2025).

According to the case studies in Ecuador and Mexico, inadequacy in technological infrastructure was a persistent problem. The EIPT model focuses on the significance of infrastructure investment and intersectoral cooperation to overcome these impediments. The study gives a guidance on how to use emerging technologies to promote inclusive education and at the same time manage equity issues (Gayosso Mexia et al., 2024).

Policy Frameworks and Governance Models

Robust governance models and policy frameworks are essential for the successful integration of AI into inclusive education, with considerations for ethical, legal, technical, and pedagogical aspects (Ebrahimian, 2025), (Devadas, 2025), (Kooli & Chakraoui, 2025). Such frameworks need to find a balance between innovation and equity, and protect students. The following principles are recommended for ethical AI, culturally responsive design, investing in infrastructure, teacher's AI competence, and stakeholders' involvement in decision making (Ebrahimian, 2025): The significance of universal access policies, transparency demands, bias audits, data protection and public-private partnerships for responsible adoption of AI are also underlined (Kooli &Chakraoui, 2025). Furthermore, the methods for its implementation need to focus on human values, teacher training, accessibility and affordability, and collaborative governance, to foster inclusive and ethical education (Devadas, 2025), (Sarkar & Madhu, 2025).

CHALLENGES, GAPS, AND FUTURE RESEARCH DIRECTIONS

Although AI-enabled inclusive education has a great potential, there are still massive challenges and research gaps. This part discusses five areas of critical concern, including institutional preparedness and infrastructure constraints, professional growth and teacher education, the digital divide and socio-cultural factors, technical constraints and scalability aspects, and research gaps and priorities in the future.

Institutional Readiness and Infrastructure Barriers

Institutional readiness—the capacity of educational institutions to effectively adopt, implement, and sustain AI-enabled technologies—varies dramatically across contexts and represents a significant barrier to equitable implementation. These are compounded by infrastructure obstacles such as poor internet connectivity, insufficient computer equipment, lack of technical support and poor financing (Ebrahimian, 2025), (Srivastava, 2025), (Opesemowo, 2024).

The cross-national research has concluded that 42 percent of teachers reported a lack of infrastructure as a long-standing obstacle to equitable AI implementation. This issue was especially severe in the schools that lack resources, and in the developing world, where the technological infrastructure can be primitive (Ebrahimian, 2025).

The phenomenological research conducted in Nigerian societies revealed that infrastructural inadequacy i.e. absence of high-speed internet and insufficient funds was a significant obstacle. Nevertheless, such workarounds can in many cases offer lower functionality than full-fledged AI systems, which forms a two-tier system in which under-resourced schools can only access limited versions of AI systems (Opesemowo, 2024).

Research on leveraging AI for sustainable and inclusive education highlights that limited technological infrastructure in developing regions is a significant barrier. The cost of adoption of AI is also high, which restricts its accessibility, especially among schools that represent low-income communities. The paper underlines the fact that strategic investments in infrastructure are needed to maximize digital inclusiveness (Srivastava, 2025).

The study on the use of AI to support inclusive education resources and tools tackles the inequality in resources as a challenge. The chapter suggests collaborative strategies to make AI solutions inclusive and productive since institutional preparedness needs not only to provide technologies but also organizational change, policy formulation, and cultural transformation (Al-Rashaida et al., 2025).

Professional Development and Teacher Training

While there is great potential for the use of AI in inclusive education, teacher training and professional development remain critical areas of concern, as many teachers are not adequately prepared (Ebrahimian, 2025), (Devadas, 2025), (Sarkar & Madhu, 2025). Research indicates that teachers who have received more AI training generally found AI tools to be much more effective, underscoring the need for ongoing professional development (Ebrahimian, 2025). AI literacy courses for technical proficiency, ethical concerns, data analysis, and pedagogical application are recommended. Teachers also need to know how to tailor the finding of AI-generated recommendations to student needs, in addition to human oversight (Akhter, 2025). Further, gradual professional growth, peer support, and collaborative learning spaces need to be constructed, enabling teachers to shift their focus from being instructors to facilitators and mentors for the use of AI in classrooms (Devadas, 2025), (Sarkar & Madhu, 2025).

The Digital Divide and Socio-Cultural Challenges

The digital divide and socio-cultural challenges continue to be significant obstacles to inclusive education through the use of AI, especially in under-resourced communities (Ebrahimian, 2025) (Wells, 2025) (Opesemowo, 2024). The challenges range from access to technology, inadequate Internet connectivity, cost, language barriers, and the absence of culturally relevant AI tools. Many studies have revealed that the AI systems created in Western societies fail to address the local culture and language in other countries, including Iran and the Philippines, thus reducing their effectiveness (Ebrahimian, 2025). Barriers mentioned in Nigeria, Ecuador, and Mexico included infrastructure constraints, teacher resistance, and socio-political challenges, underlining the importance of developing user-centric, culturally responsive, and participatory approaches to implementing AI in education (Gayosso Mexia et al., 2024; Opesemowo, 2024).

Technical Limitations and Scalability Issues

Although AI for inclusive learning has seen significant progress, it is still burdened with significant technical challenges, such as speech recognition, natural language processing, personalization, and scalability (Ebrahimian, 2025), (Akhter, 2025), (Wells, 2025). Another area of concern is the potential for AI to create overly stimulating environments and the ongoing necessity of human oversight (Ebrahimian, 2025). AI tools like real-time translation, text-to-speech, and AI-generated alt-text enhance accessibility, while systems which can completely adapt and be accessible for everyone are still being developed (Stelea et al., 2025). Moreover, there is a significant requirement for the extensive computing power needed to support large-scale personalized AI tutoring, which can be costly and unfeasible for many educational institutions (Salendab et al., 2025).

Research Gaps and Future Priorities

Although there is a significant amount of research conducted in the field of inclusive education enabled by AI, there are still some drawbacks which can be the direction of future studies (Devadas, 2025), (Roy et al., 2025), (Sarkar &Madhu, 2025), (Akhter, 2025), (Kooli &Chakraoui, 2025), (Wells, 2025), (Arias-Flores et al., 2025). These gaps encompass methodological limitations, underexplored populations and contexts, insufficient attention to long-term outcomes, and limited understanding of implementation processes (Ebrahimian, 2025), (Akhter, 2025), (Wells, 2025), (Arias-Flores et al., 2025).

Studies of AI-based AAC systems mention that there are research gaps in assessing the use of metaliteracy in non-verbal intellectually disabled persons. The paper will give future directions of the research which include prototype testing where ethical audits are practiced, longitudinal case studies and participatory design to provide equitable, transparent, and personalized AI-AAC solutions. These suggestions highlight that the research should go beyond proof-of-concept tests to actual assessment of performance in practice (Wells, 2025).

The systematic review of the AI and assistive technologies in disabilities identified the absence of primary empirical data and descriptions of policy or implementation analysis. The review established that the extant literature did not sufficiently address the institutional readiness, professional development, socio-cultural contexts, digital-divide contexts, future research directions, and cross-disciplinary collaboration. This puts the emphasis on the necessity of research that would investigate not technological capabilities, but organizational, social, and policy contexts that influence implementation (Arias-Flores et al., 2025).

The studies of AI-based assistive technology with students with disabilities focus on the necessity of the continued research, interdisciplinary cooperation, and humanistic design. The research verifies the significance of analytic needs assessment, step-by-step application, and the collaborative ecologies, but points out that additional research is required to comprehend how to develop and maintain such environments (Sarkar & Madhu, 2025).

Figure 5. Major Barriers to AI-Enabled Inclusive Education

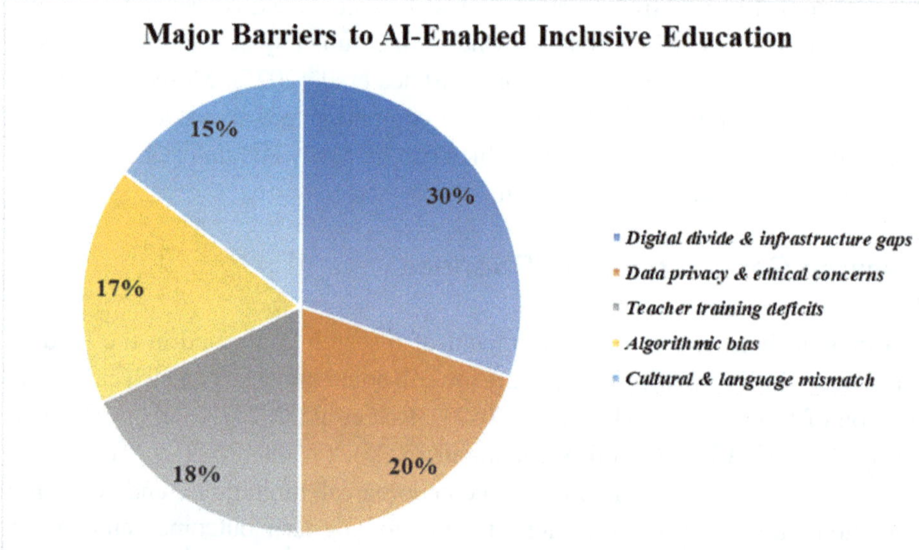

It is also clear from the pie chart that the digital divide and infrastructure challenges (30%) are still in fact emerging as main obstacles causing inertia to curricular innovation with AI for inclusive education, which indicates there exist lingering disparities in accessibility to sustainable internet, devices, and technological tools. Data privacy and ethical concerns (20%) Privacy - Ethical (policy), as institutions need to be able to demonstrate secure management of sensitive student data and encourage trustworthy, responsible AI use. Another obstacle to the effective implementation of artificial intelligence is the lack of teachers' skills in implementing AI, with 18% of respondents pointing to a lack of in-service training for teachers. In addition, algorithmic bias (17%) is a challenge to fairness and inclusiveness, as biased input data and system design can marginalize students with disabilities and/or from different linguistic and cultural backgrounds. Culture and language mismatch hits global adoption (15%) highlighting the demand for conversational AI systems which are culturally sensitive, reflect local culture/language specifics, and can accommodate linguistic diversity.

Table 3. Traditional vs AI-Enabled Inclusive Education

Feature	Traditional Inclusive Education	AI-Enabled Inclusive Education
Personalization	Limited	Highly adaptive & real-time
Accessibility	Manual accommodations	Automated & multimodal
Assessment	Standardized	Continuous & data-driven
Language Support	Teacher-dependent	AI translation & NLP
Engagement	Passive methods	Interactive & immersive
Teacher Role	Instructor	Facilitator & learning guide
Monitoring	Periodic	Real-time analytics
Scalability	Resource intensive	Scalable with technology

CONCLUSION

The adoption of Artificial Intelligence (AI) and assistive technologies in the context of inclusive education is an innovative opportunity to break down the existing barriers to access, participation and achievement for learners with a disability, SEN and linguistic variation. This chapter has offered an in-depth analysis of the theoretical background, technological uses, empirical research, ethical implications, and the implementation issues that are linked to AI-powered inclusive education.

The diverse range of AI-based assistive tools explored, from adaptive learning platforms and intelligent tutoring systems to speech and language technologies, multimodal interaction systems, learning analytics, and special assistive technologies for specific disabilities highlights the versatility of technological innovation in this area. The results of this cross-national study showed a significant positive correlation between the number of hours teachers spend training with AI and their perceived effectiveness of the tools ($r = 0.62$, $p < 0.01$), highlighting the critical need for teacher professional development when implementing AI tools (Ebrahimian, 2025).

Nevertheless, the chapter has also raised major challenges and dangers that should be taken into consideration to make the AI-enabled inclusive education delivery true to its promise. In a study that determined that the digital divide was a key issue

(Ebrahimian, 2025), 42 percent of teachers noted that inadequate infrastructure was a consistent problem in promoting equitable AI use. The cultural inappropriateness of AI tools that are designed in the West and used in other parts of the world casts doubts on the suitability and efficacy of the AI-based tool (Ebrahimian, 2025), (Akhter, 2025). Higher training needs among teachers, institutional capital, and technological issues complicate further.

To sum up, AI-based assistive technologies have more potential than ever to enhance the inclusive education process, yet the potential would not translate into practice without leaving the technological solutionism and addressing the multifaceted interaction of pedagogical, ethical, social, cultural, and political determinants of the educational inclusiveness. The evidence discussed in this chapter shows that AI may be a strong instrument of equity in a situation where it is thoughtfully applied, but it might also replicate or magnify already existing inequalities when applied without due consideration of ethics, equity and context. The path forward would require ongoing investment in human-centred design, participatory governance, teacher professional development, investment in infrastructure, and critical examination of the promises and risks of AI in education. Incorporating AI into education requires a solid theoretical foundation, practical evidence, and insights gained from international experiences, as well as considering the ethical and policy implications early in the process and keeping the focus on the ultimate agenda: achieving universal education and social justice.

REFERENCES

Aarthi, S., Ravikumar, R. N., Khudayberganov, S., Ismailov, A., & Khujaniyozova, O. R. (2025). Using Intelligent Tutoring Systems to Enhance Student Engagement. *Advances in Computational Intelligence and Robotics Book Series*, 155–188. DOI: 10.4018/979-8-3373-1827-1.ch008

Akhter, E. (2025). *Ai in the classroom: evaluating the effectiveness of intelligent tutoring systems for multilingual learners in secondary education. 01*(01), 532–563. https://doi.org/DOI: 10.63125/gcq1qr39

Al-Rashaida, M., Aishan, H., Moustafa, A., Abuwatfa, R., Mohsen, W., & Khan, A. G. Y. (2025). AI Strategies for Inclusive Education Resources and Support. In *AI in Learning, Educational Leadership, and Special Education: Innovations and Ethical Dilemmas* (pp. 349-380). IGI Global. DOI: 10.4018/979-8-3373-0573-8.ch012

Arias-Flores, H., Valencia-Aragón, K., Calle-Jimenez, T., & Sanchez-Gordon, S. (2025). *Artificial Intelligence and Assistive Technologies: A Systematic Review of Educational Applications for Disabilities.* 283–292. DOI: 10.1007/978-3-031-93848-1_19

Chakraborty, D., Ray, D., & Nair, S. (2025). Ethical Considerations In Deploying AI And Data-Driven Technologies For Adaptive Education. *International Journal of Environmental Sciences*, •••, 8291–8299. DOI: 10.64252/cef9cs80

Devadas, V. (2025). *AI augmented education for children with special needs: A scholarly perspective.* World Journal of Advanced Engineering Technology and Sciences., DOI: 10.30574/wjaets.2025.15.3.1125

Ebrahimian. (2025). *Empowering Inclusive Pedagogy: Teacher's Experiences with AI-Driven Assistive Technologies in Special Needs Classrooms.* DOI: 10.21203/rs.3.rs-7408910/v1

Ferebee, S. (2025). *AI and Accessibility: Breaking Barriers for People with Disabilities.* DOI: 10.70389/PJAI.100012

Gayosso Mexia, S., Servín Gómez, A., de la Paz Hernández García, L. M., & Sánchez Granados, J. M. (2024). EIPT: Innovación Tecnológica y Ética para la Transformación de la Educación Inclusiva. *Latinskaia Amerika = América Latina*, *5*(6). Advance online publication. DOI: 10.56712/latam.v5i6.3223

Kohnke, S., & Zaugg, T. (2025). Artificial Intelligence: An Untapped Opportunity for Equity and Access in STEM Education. *Education Sciences*, *15*(1), 68. DOI: 10.3390/educsci15010068

Kooli, C., & Chakraoui, R. (2025). AI-driven assistive technologies in inclusive education: Benefits, challenges, and policy recommendations. *Sustainable Futures : An Applied Journal of Technology, Environment and Society*, *10*, 101042. DOI: 10.1016/j.sftr.2025.101042

Koranteng, U. (2025). *Designing the AI-Inclusive Framework (AIF): Integrating artificial intelligence, assistive technology, and universal design for learning in inclusive education. SSRN*. https://doi.org/DOI: 10.2139/ssrn.6088026

Le, R. (2025). Transformative AI Tools for Inclusive and Holistic Learning Environments. *Advances in Computational Intelligence and Robotics Book Series*, 469–492. DOI: 10.4018/979-8-3373-5097-4.ch017

Macias Leon, H. A. (2025). *Estrategias de enseñanza basadas en inteligencia artificial para lograr un aprendizaje personalizado, inclusivo y centrado en las necesidades individuales de cada estudiante. 4*(3), 81–93. https://doi.org/DOI: 10.64041/riidg.v4i3.50

Omosunlade, O. S. (2025). Digital inclusion in special education with AI-assisted curriculum models for Autism, Cerebral palsy, and Down syndrome. *World Journal Of Advanced Research and Reviews*, *25*(2), 2793–2804. DOI: 10.30574/wjarr.2025.25.2.0501

Opesemowo, O. A. G. (2024). Artificial Intelligence in Education, Bridging Community Gap: A Phenomenological Approach. *International Journal of Nursing Education*, *14*(14). Advance online publication. DOI: 10.24310/ijne.14.2024.20505

Roy, B., Ghosh, S., Sarkar, S. K., Sen, A., & Choudhury, N. R. (2025). Implications of Artificial Intelligence for Special Education Technology. In Walters, A. (Ed.), *Transforming Special Education Through Artificial Intelligence* (pp. 401–430). IGI Global Scientific Publishing., DOI: 10.4018/979-8-3693-5538-1.ch015

Salendab, F. A., Cogo, D. A., Catipay, A. Z., & Millendez, G. J. T. (2025). The Role of Artificial Intelligence (AI) in Personalized Learning and Adaptive Assessments. *Advances in Computational Intelligence and Robotics Book Series*, 93–122. DOI: 10.4018/979-8-3373-2185-1.ch004

Sarkar, R., & Madhu, R. (2025). Ensuring Equity and Access for Students With Disabilities. *Advances in Computational Intelligence and Robotics Book Series*, 93–138. https://doi.org/DOI: 10.4018/979-8-3373-5097-4.ch004

Srivastava, K. (2025). *Leveraging Artificial Intelligence for Sustainable and Inclusive Education: Opportunities, Challenges, and Recommendations*. 361–376. DOI: 10.1201/9781998511471-18

Stelea, G. A., Robu, D., & Sandu, F. (2025). AccessiLearnAI: An Accessibility-First, AI-Powered E-Learning Platform for Inclusive Education. *Education Sciences*, *15*(9), 1125. DOI: 10.3390/educsci15091125

Sun, J. (2024). The Impact of Artificial Intelligence on Personalized Learning in Education: A Systematic Review. *Pakistan Journal of Life and Social Sciences*, *22*(2). Advance online publication. DOI: 10.57239/PJLSS-2024-22.2.00560

Tegon, R. (2021). Toward the 4th Agenda 2030 Goal. *Handbook of Research on Teaching With Virtual Environments and AI*. DOI:DOI: 10.4018/978-1-7998-7638-0.ch025

Vortia, W. (2025). Use of AI in teaching mathematics to persons living with disabilities: The Context of the United States. *Magna Scientia Advanced Research and Reviews*, *14*(2), 112–120. DOI: 10.30574/msarr.2025.14.2.0096

Wells, M. B. (2025). Empowering non-verbal individuals through AI-driven symbolic text prediction: A metaliteracy approach to communication and inclusion. *Discover Education*, *4*(1), 360. Advance online publication. DOI: 10.1007/s44217-025-00809-8

Chapter 2
Emerging AI-Assisted Mobile, Wearable, and Immersive Assistive Technologies:
International Case Studies and Best Practices for Inclusive Education

Sonam Tripathi
http://orcid.org/0009-0002-0617-0556
Banasthali Vidyapith, Niwai, India

Samiksha Vyas
http://orcid.org/0009-0000-1479-4065
Vivekananda Global University, Jaipur, India

Jitendra Singh Rathore
http://orcid.org/0000-0002-8237-019X
Banasthali University, Jaipur, India

ABSTRACT

In the contemporary digital education landscape, assistive technologies have emerged as pivotal enablers of accessibility and inclusive learning. This chapter examines the integration of artificial intelligence (AI)-assisted mobile, wearable and immersive technologies to support learners with diverse cognitive, sensory and developmental needs. Employing a qualitative multiple case study design and thematic analysis, the study explores selected AI-driven assistive technologies, including Microsoft

DOI: 10.4018/979-8-2600-2716-5.ch002

2027, IGI Global Scientific Publishing. Copying or distributing in print or electronic forms without written permission of IGI Global Scientific Publishing is prohibited. Use of this chapter to ative artificial intelligence (AI) technologies is expressly prohibited. The publisher reserves all rights to license its use for generative AI training and machine learning model development.

Immersive Reader, OrCam MyEye and Floreo VR. The findings indicate that these technologies enhance accessibility through adaptive functionalities such as AI-enabled text-to-speech, computer vision and immersive virtual environments that foster personalised learning experiences. The study provides critical insights for educators and policymakers and underscores the significance of AI-powered assistive technologies in mitigating learning barriers and promoting equitable participation.

1. INTRODUCTION

Ever wondered if the rapid progress of intelligent technologies truly makes education more inclusive for all learners? It is no longer just about integrating digital tools into classrooms or improving instructional delivery. The real challenge lies in creating learning environments that are accessible, adaptive, and meaningful for students with diverse needs. In today's tech-driven educational world, where institutions increasingly adopt Artificial Intelligence (AI), mobile apps, wearable devices, and immersive virtual platforms, ensuring equitable participation has become more complex than ever (Kumar, 2025; Mais & Yauma, 2026). This is where AI-assisted assistive technologies play a crucial role. These technologies are not just supplementary tools supporting learning; they represent a transformative shift in how accessibility is understood and applied within education. By integrating intelligent features into mainstream learning environments, they can go beyond traditional accommodation methods and foster more inclusive and equitable educational experiences (Toyokawa et al., 2023).

Human learning has always evolved alongside technological advancement. From printed texts to digital interfaces, and now to AI-powered systems, each transition has reshaped how knowledge is accessed, processed, and understood. In this evolving landscape, AI-assisted assistive technologies such as real-time speech recognition, computer vision, adaptive text systems, and immersive virtual simulations are fundamentally transforming how learners with disabilities engage with educational content (Kumar, 2025). These technologies enable learners to access information in personalised formats, communicate more effectively, and participate more independently within both formal and informal learning contexts. Much like structured narratives make complex information more accessible and meaningful, these intelligent systems translate educational content into adaptable and user-centred experiences. This integration of advanced technological capabilities with pedagogical intent reflects a broader shift towards inclusive design, where accessibility is embedded within the learning process itself rather than added as a corrective measure. As a result, assistive technologies are increasingly recognised as essential components of inclusive digital education systems (Mais & Yauma, 2026).

As digital education continues to expand globally, Artificial Intelligence (AI)-assisted assistive technologies are increasingly transforming the landscape of inclusive learning and accessibility. However, existing studies largely focus on individual technologies or specific educational contexts, with limited cross-case analytical understanding of how these technologies support cognitive, communicative, sensory, and immersive learning experiences. Furthermore, implementation challenges, infrastructural barriers, affordability concerns, and ethical considerations remain insufficiently explored across diverse educational settings (Li et al., 2025). Addressing this gap, this chapter provides a cross-case analytical understanding of technologies such as Microsoft Immersive Reader, Texthelp Read&Write, Ava, Eye-D, OrCam MyEye, Floreo VR, and DIKSHA to examine their role in promoting accessibility, learner participation, and inclusive education. The findings offer important insights for educators, researchers, policymakers, practitioners, and EdTech developers interested in advancing technology-enabled inclusive learning environments.

However, despite the growing prominence and perceived transformative potential of AI-assisted assistive technologies, it is important to critically examine how effectively these innovations are realised within real-world educational contexts. While existing discourse frequently highlights their capabilities and anticipated benefits, such representations often present an idealised view that may not fully capture the complexities of practical implementation. Educational environments are inherently diverse, shaped by variations in infrastructure, learner needs, institutional readiness, and socio-economic conditions. Yet, much of the current literature adopts a broad perspective, often focusing on accessibility frameworks and adoption trends while paying limited attention to how individual technologies function across different contexts. There remains a lack of integrative and comparative case-based research that systematically examines how these technologies address diverse cognitive, sensory, and learning challenges in practice. Furthermore, the mechanisms through which features such as speech recognition, computer vision, immersive simulations, and real-time captioning translate into meaningful learning experiences remain insufficiently explored. At the same time, existing studies often imply the effectiveness of these technologies without adequately considering contextual variability and implementation constraints. Consequently, it cannot be conclusively claimed that these technologies consistently produce measurable improvements in learning outcomes for students with disabilities without further independent empirical investigation. These limitations highlight the need for a more critical and context-sensitive exploration of AI-assisted assistive technologies in inclusive education (Toyokawa et al., 2023).

1.1 Assistive Technologies: Enabling Accessibility in Digital Education

Assistive technologies offer a transformative way to enhance accessibility in contemporary digital education environments. Designed to support learners with diverse needs, they enable alternative ways to access information, interact with content, and participate in learning activities. In today's increasingly technology-mediated classrooms, learners with disabilities often face barriers to perception, communication, and comprehension. AI-assisted assistive technologies address these challenges by serving as an interface between the learner and the learning environment, facilitating more inclusive and responsive educational experiences. In essence, these technologies serve as a bridge connecting learners with digital content in ways that are adaptable, personalised, and accessible, thereby supporting meaningful participation across diverse educational contexts (Assistive Technology Industry Association, 2023).

According to the Assistive Technology Industry Association (ATIA), assistive technology refers to any item, equipment, software program, or product system used to increase, maintain, or improve the functional capabilities of individuals with disabilities (ATIA, 2023).

Assistive technologies represent the transformation of conventional educational content into adaptive and user-centred formats through the integration of intelligent systems. Rather than relying on static modes of content delivery, these technologies employ functionalities such as text-to-speech conversion, speech recognition, real-time captioning, and computer vision to dynamically respond to individual learner needs (Krasniqi et al., 2022). For instance, tools such as Ava enable learners with hearing impairments to participate more actively in classroom discussions through real-time AI-generated captions, while Eye-D and OrCam Eye assist visually impaired learners by converting surrounding visual information into spoken descriptions and supporting object recognition. Similarly, immersive platforms such as Floreo VR create safe virtual environments where neurodivergent learners can practice social, behavioural, and communication skills in interactive settings. Texthelp Read&Write and Microsoft Immersive Reader further enhance accessibility by supporting learners with reading difficulties through text-to-speech, reading assistance, translation, and personalised comprehension features. Collectively, these technologies illustrate how AI-assisted assistive systems are transforming accessibility from passive accommodation into adaptive, learner-centred, and participatory educational engagement. This evolution signifies a transition from traditional instructional models—where learners are required to fixed pedagogical structures—towards more flexible and responsive learning environments. By integrating the analytical capabilities of artificial intelligence with the principles of inclusive design, assistive technologies enhance not only accessibility but also learner engagement, autonomy, and overall learning effectiveness. Consequently, AI-assisted assistive technologies are increasingly recognised as a critical component in advancing inclusive, equitable, and technology-enabled educational systems (Fitas, 2025).

1.2 *Artificial Intelligence and Assistive Technologies in Inclusive Education*

In the contemporary pursuit of inclusive and accessible education, learners increasingly seek environments that enable meaningful participation and accommodate diverse needs. In today's digital landscape, accessibility is strengthened through the integration of artificial intelligence, data-driven systems, and immersive technologies. This convergence transforms complex learning processes into adaptive formats, enabling learners with disabilities to engage more effectively. In technology-mediated environments, intelligent systems have become critical enablers of inclusive education (Pagliara et al., 2024). The integration of adaptive technologies with structured learning enhances engagement and supports informed educational practices. AI-assisted assistive technologies improve the clarity and accessibility of learning content while enabling monitoring of learner interaction and engagement. These systems capture learner needs and support personalised, inclusive learning experiences (Chalkiadakis et al., 2024), allowing institutions to design strategies that better respond to diverse learner requirements.

In the Information Age, education is shifting toward technology-enabled and data-informed learning, driven by advancements in artificial intelligence, big data, and digital platforms. This transition moves away from traditional approaches toward structured, evidence-based methods guiding teaching and learning. By analysing learner data, institutions can generate actionable insights that enhance instructional effectiveness (Lata, 2024). Although often associated with technical processes such as algorithmic analysis and data processing, these capabilities alone are insufficient without the ability to translate insights into meaningful learning experiences. The value of assistive technologies lies in communicating insights in clear, engaging, and accessible ways. The integration of intelligent systems with inclusive design transforms static content into adaptive and interactive experiences, enhancing engagement and participation (Shireesha & Jeevan, 2024). Without effective implementation, even advanced technologies may fail to achieve their intended impact. By situating assistive technologies within real educational contexts, AI-enabled systems reduce the complexity and uncertainty associated with diverse learning needs, making content more accessible. For effectiveness, these systems must ensure that learning experiences are engaging and meaningful. AI-assisted technologies simplify complex processes by emphasising key insights and presenting them in formats that support cognitive clarity and retention. Human interaction and contextual understanding remain essential to the effective application of these in education.

The potential of inclusive education is realised when intelligent systems align with diverse learner needs. This alignment enhances accessibility and engagement, improving learning outcomes. Accurately identifying learner needs improves the effectiveness of interventions through continuous data analysis and adaptive system design. By leveraging such insights, educational systems can create accessible and meaningful learning experiences. At the same time, integrating data with assistive technologies requires ethical considerations, including privacy, bias, and equitable access (Ahmed et al., 2025; Melo-López et al., 2025). As institutions increasingly rely on data-driven systems, balancing innovation with ethical responsibility is essential. From an educational perspective, AI-assisted assistive technologies enhance engagement, accessibility, and participation, enabling adaptive and evidence-based learning environments (Pagliara et al., 2024).

Using intelligent technologies to support accessibility represents a powerful approach to fostering inclusive education. This approach not only enables learners to access information but also supports deeper engagement and participation within learning environments. The unique strength of AI-assisted assistive technologies lies in their ability to transform complex educational processes into meaningful and adaptive learning experiences. While learners may access information through traditional means, they engage more effectively when learning is personalised and responsive to their needs. By presenting content in ways that address both cognitive and experiential dimensions of learning, these technologies help overcome barriers that learners may face in conventional educational systems (Fortis et al., 2025).

In essence, the integration of intelligent systems and adaptive approaches positions AI-assisted assistive technologies as a critical component of inclusive education. Educational systems adopting these technologies gain advantages in accessibility, engagement, and equity. By leveraging intelligent, data-driven solutions, institutions can better support diverse learners and create more inclusive and effective educational environments (Bi, 2025).

1.2.1 Objectives

To examine the role of AI-assisted technologies in enhancing accessibility and fostering inclusive learning for diverse learners.

To analyse selected case studies of AI-enabled assistive technologies in supporting accessibility, personalised learning, and learner participation in digital education.

1.2.2 Research Methodology

This observational study examines the role of AI-assisted assistive technologies in promoting inclusive education, with a focus on how intelligent systems enhance accessibility and learner engagement. A multiple case study approach was adopted as the research design to analyse seven assistive technologies selected based on their widespread use, innovative integration of artificial intelligence, and relevance in supporting diverse learner needs (Piyathanavong et al., 2024; Zangiacomi et al., 2020). This approach is particularly suitable for examining real-world educational contexts and enables cross-case comparison to identify patterns across different technological solutions (Vyas et al., 2025). The analysis is based on secondary data sources, including platform documentation, user interaction features, empirical research studies, and industry reports. A thematic content analysis was conducted to identify key dimensions, including accessibility, personalisation, learner engagement, and inclusivity. These themes were systematically analysed to understand how different technologies contribute to enhancing learning outcomes in inclusive educational environments. However, the study is limited by its reliance on secondary data, which may not fully capture user experiences or contextual variations across diverse educational settings.

1.3 Cases of AI-Assisted Assistive Technologies in Inclusive Education

Our digital education landscape is rapidly evolving, characterised by the increasing integration of advanced technologies and digital learning platforms. While these developments have expanded access to educational resources, they have also highlighted the growing need to ensure that learning environments remain accessible and inclusive for students with diverse abilities. As educational institutions continue to adopt innovative technologies, an important question emerges: how can these technological advancements be effectively utilised to support learners with varying cognitive, sensory, and physical needs?

The answer lies in artificial intelligence–assisted assistive technologies. These technologies enable learners with disabilities to engage with educational content through adaptive tools such as intelligent reading systems, speech recognition software, and immersive learning environments. By providing alternative modes of interaction and personalised learning experiences, AI-enabled assistive technologies help reduce accessibility barriers and foster meaningful participation in digital education. Through selected case studies, this chapter explores how emerging assistive technologies contribute to the development of more inclusive and accessible learning ecosystems.

1.4 AI-Enabled Reading Support Tools: Microsoft Immersive Reader

Imagine a classroom where a student opens a digital text but struggles to move beyond the first paragraph. The words appear dense, unfamiliar, and difficult to process. For many learners, especially those studying in a second language or facing reading difficulties, this experience is not unusual. Reading, although considered one of the most fundamental academic skills, often becomes a barrier rather than a gateway to learning. In an educational landscape increasingly shaped by digital technologies, an important question emerges: can intelligent tools transform the reading experience and make learning more accessible for everyone? The answer, for many educators and researchers, lies in the development of assistive technologies such as Microsoft Immersive Reader. Interestingly, the story behind Immersive Reader itself began with a simple but powerful idea. During a Microsoft hackathon in 2015, developers and designers explored how reading technologies could be redesigned to support learners with diverse abilities. What started as an experimental idea soon evolved into a widely used educational tool built on principles of inclusive design. The goal was clear -create a reading experience that allows learners to interact with text in ways that suit their individual needs (Darrow, 2025).

Microsoft Immersive Reader integrates several accessibility features, including text-to-speech narration, adjustable text spacing, line focus, syllable separation, grammar highlighting, and translation support (Microsoft, 2024). These features enable learners to engage with text through multiple sensory channels, combining auditory and visual processing to support comprehension. By offering these adaptive options, the tool aims to make reading less overwhelming and more accessible for learners who struggle with traditional text formats (Dewi et al., 2021). Research exploring the use of Immersive Reader in language learning environments suggests that such features may help learners strengthen listening comprehension and phonemic awareness. For instance, allowing students to listen to a passage while simultaneously reading its transcript can help them recognise pronunciation patterns and linguistic structures that may otherwise be difficult to identify through listening alone (Bairaqdar, 2025). Similarly, classroom-based studies investigating the use of Immersive Reader in reading instruction have reported encouraging outcomes. In one study involving Grade 4 pupils, learners who used Immersive Reader achieved higher post-test reading comprehension scores than those in the control group.

A demonstration of Microsoft Immersive Reader and its accessibility features—such as read-aloud narration, line focus, grammar highlighting, and translation tools—is available online (see https://www.youtube.com/watch?v=wHJJCLV-DNg).

Despite its effectiveness in supporting reading comprehension for learners with dyslexia and ADHD, Microsoft Immersive Reader has several functional and contextual limitations. The tool is not a replacement for screen readers, making it less suitable for users with severe visual impairments who require advanced navigation of complex interfaces, images, and structured documents. Its performance may also be limited when dealing with complex layouts, such as tables or visually rich content, reducing its effectiveness for comprehensive academic materials. Additionally, certain features are restricted in secure or confidential documents, while platform inconsistencies and partial offline functionality may affect accessibility across different environments. From a usability perspective, the range of customization options may be overwhelming for some users, particularly those with cognitive challenges. These constraints indicate that while Immersive Reader is a valuable assistive tool, its effectiveness depends on context, content type, and complementary accessibility support systems (Santos, 2025). Despite these mixed findings, several studies highlight positive perceptions among both educators and students when Immersive Reader is integrated into classroom activities. Teachers have reported that the tool can enhance teaching quality and support learner motivation; students, on the other hand, have indicated that its features help them better understand reading assignments and participate more actively in learning tasks (Dewi et al., 2021). Ultimately, Microsoft Immersive Reader exemplifies how artificial intelligence can be used to reimagine the reading experience. Rather than replacing traditional instruction, the tool functions as a supportive assistive technology that complements teaching strategies and helps create more inclusive learning environments. While research continues to explore its long-term educational impact, the growing interest in tools such as Immersive Reader reflects a broader shift towards designing technologies that place accessibility and learner diversity at the centre of digital education.

1.5 Assistive Literacy Technologies: Texthelp Read&Write

For many students, reading and writing are not just academic tasks but daily challenges that shape their educational experiences. Imagine a learner opening a digital document and struggling to follow the text, unable to decode unfamiliar words or organise ideas into meaningful sentences. For students with dyslexia, learning disabilities, or limited language proficiency, this is often a reality. Difficulties in processing written information can affect confidence, participation, and engagement. As digital learning environments expand, an important question arises: how can technology transform literacy challenges into opportunities for inclusive learning?

One response is Texthelp Read&Write, a literacy support software designed to help individuals read, write, and communicate more effectively in digital environments. It functions as a toolbar integrated with documents, web pages, PDFs, and online platforms. Features such as text-to-speech, speech-to-text dictation, word prediction, spell checking, picture dictionaries, and screen masking provide multiple ways to interact with text. These tools enable learners to listen while reading, receive writing support, and organise ideas, reducing cognitive barriers (Texthelp, 2025). The story of Read&Write began in Northern Ireland in 1996, when Martin McKay founded Texthelp to make technology more accessible. Recognising that text-heavy interfaces posed challenges for learners with dyslexia, he aimed to develop tools that promote independence and inclusion. What began as a small initiative has evolved into a global literacy support platform used by millions (Everway, 2023).

Over time, Texthelp Read&Write has developed from a basic text-to-speech tool into a comprehensive assistive literacy system. It now incorporates speech recognition, word prediction, and optical character recognition (OCR), enabling users to read text within images or scanned documents. These features support processing through multiple sensory channels, combining auditory and visual input to enhance comprehension (Texthelp, 2025). Research indicates that assistive literacy tools can improve accessibility for students with dyslexia by offering alternative ways to engage with written information (Dawson et al., 2019; Svensson, 2021).

Educational research further suggests that such technologies enhance engagement and confidence in academic tasks. Studies show that combining visual text with audio narration improves comprehension by supporting multiple cognitive pathways (Wood, 2017). Similarly, classroom-based research indicates that Read&Write tools help dyslexic learners organise ideas, correct spelling, and improve written communication (Foisy, 2024).

In recent years, Texthelp has rebranded as "Everway", reflecting a broader mission to expand assistive technologies. Despite this shift, Read&Write remains a central product, supporting users across schools, universities, and workplaces. By combining accessibility, literacy development, and inclusive design, the software continues to enable more independent interaction with digital content.

A demonstration of Texthelp Read&Write, highlighting its literacy support features, is available online (https://www.youtube.com/watch?v=R7lQ4U5C3cE).

Despite its comprehensive literacy support capabilities, the effectiveness of Texthelp Read&Write is shaped by several technical and operational constraints. Its dependence on stable internet connectivity limits access to core features such as grammar checking, translation, and vocabulary tools, while occasional performance issues and software instability may disrupt user workflow. The platform's extensive feature set can also present a steep learning curve, particularly for new users, affecting ease of adoption. Additionally, its functionality is contingent on the quality of the original content, as it cannot resolve deeply embedded accessibility issues in poorly structured materials. Constraints related to limited offline functionality, PDF editing capabilities, and inconsistencies in certain features may further affect usability. Moreover, subscription costs and hardware requirements may influence accessibility, particularly for users in resource-constrained environments (Svensson, 2021).

Ultimately, Read&Write illustrates how assistive technologies can reshape literacy support in digital education. Integrating reading and writing assistance into a single platform enables learners to approach tasks with greater confidence and independence. While such tools do not replace foundational literacy skills, they complement traditional instruction by reducing barriers and promoting inclusive participation.

1.6 Immersive Learning Technologies for Autism: Floreo VR

Step into a classroom where learning is not confined to textbooks or lectures but unfolds within immersive digital environments where students can practise real-world interactions. For many learners on the "autism spectrum", navigating everyday social situations—such as initiating conversations, interpreting facial expressions, or responding appropriately—can be challen ging. While traditional approaches attempt to address these difficulties, replicating authentic social experiences within classrooms remains limited. As educators explore innovative ways to support diverse learners, an important question arises: Can immersive technologies enable students to develop social and communication skills more effectively than conventional methods?

One response to this challenge is Floreo VR, an "immersive virtual reality platform", designed to support "neurodivergent learners", particularly individuals with autism spectrum disorder (ASD). Floreo provides structured virtual environments where learners can practise social and behavioural skills through guided simulations (Wang, 2023). The platform was founded by Vijay Ravindran, motivated by his son's autism diagnosis and early observations of engagement with virtual environments. Floreo operates through a co-pilot learning model, where learners use a "VR headset", while a teacher, therapist, or parent monitors the session via a connected tablet. This interface allows instructors to observe the learner's experience and guide interactions in real time. Through interactive modules, learners practise skills such as greeting others, recognising emotions, navigating public spaces, and responding in classroom settings (Floreo, 2024). By offering a safe and repeatable environment, Floreo enables practice without the unpredictability of real-world interactions.

Empirical studies provide early insights into its potential. A pilot study on the Floreo Joint Attention Module found the system safe and good with preliminary improvements in joint attention and social communication skills (Ravindran et al., 2019). Similarly, feasibility studies suggest that VR-based simulations can support communication and behavioural learning when integrated into structured programs (Floreo VR Feasibility Study, 2025). Ongoing clinical trials are further examining whether immersive VR interventions can improve social communication and behavioural outcomes among children with autism (ClinicalTrials.gov, 2024). Broader research also indicates that virtual environments offer structured opportunities for practising social interactions (Kellems, 2025).

Despite its potential in supporting neurodivergent learners, the effectiveness of Floreo VR is influenced by several physical, technical, and pedagogical constraints. Users may experience discomfort such as dizziness, sensory overload, or difficulty tolerating the headset, particularly among individuals with heightened sensory sensitivities. Its effectiveness also varies based on individual cognitive and emotional readiness, with some users showing resistance or limited engagement. Additionally, the requirement for specialized hardware and supervision may limit accessibility in resource-constrained settings. Technical issues such as connectivity and device performance can further affect usability. From a pedagogical perspective, questions remain regarding the transferability of virtual learning to real-world contexts, along with the limited scope of available content, which may restrict its broader application. However, despite these promising findings, the effectiveness of immersive technologies should be approached with caution (Shapiro et al., 2025). Research indicates that VR interventions function best as complementary tools rather than "standalone solutions", as outcomes vary based on instructional design, learner characteristics, and integration with broader educational or therapeutic strategies (Kellems, 2025). Consequently, while Floreo VR demonstrates strong potential, it does not guarantee universal outcomes for all learners.

Collaborations with research institutions further highlight the growing interest in evaluating immersive technologies for autism intervention. Floreo VR has partnered with organisations such as the "Children's Hospital of Philadelphia" and has been implemented in schools, clinics, and therapy programs as a research-informed tool supporting social skill development and inclusive learning practices.

A demonstration of Floreo VR, illustrating its immersive learning applications, is available online (https://www.youtube.com/watch?v=FloreoVRdemo).

Ultimately, Floreo VR illustrates how immersive technologies can expand inclusive education by enabling learners to practise real-world interactions within safe and structured environments. While further research is needed to determine long-term outcomes, existing studies suggest that immersive technologies may play an important role in supporting inclusive and accessible learning environments.

1.7 Wearable Assistive Vision Technologies: OrCam MyEye

Consider a simple everyday situation—reading a restaurant menu, identifying a street sign, or recognising a familiar face in a crowded room. For individuals who are blind or visually impaired, these routine activities present significant challenges. Accessing printed information or interpreting visual cues often requires external assistance, limiting independence in daily life. As technology advances, an important question emerges: can artificial intelligence transform visual information into accessible formats that enable more independent interaction with the surrounding environment?

One response to this challenge is OrCam MyEye, a "wearable artificial intelligence" driven vision device designed to assist individuals who are blind, visually impaired, or who experience reading difficulties. Developed by OrCam Technologies, the device attaches magnetically to the frame of a user's glasses and uses a "miniature camera" with computer vision and machine learning algorithms to interpret visual information. Through a small speaker near the user's ear, it converts visual inputs into spoken audio, enabling users to read text, recognise objects, and identify people in real time (OrCam, 2024). The device originated in 2010 in Jerusalem, Israel, when Professor Amnon Shashua and entrepreneur Ziv Aviram founded OrCam Technologies. Building on their experience with Mobileye, they aimed to apply artificial intelligence to address accessibility challenges by translating visual information into auditory feedback (Zero Project, 2018).

The development of OrCam MyEye has evolved significantly. The prototype was introduced in 2013, followed by its commercial launch in 2015. Later advancements led to OrCam MyEye 2.0 in 2017, which reduced device size and removed the need for a separate processing unit. The latest version, OrCam MyEye 3 Pro, incorporates advanced AI features, including conversational interaction that enables users to identify objects and summarise text through voice commands. The device offers key functionalities including instant text recognition from books, menus, screens and facial recognition for identifying familiar individuals, and object identification for recognising products, currency and colours. Interaction is intuitive, as users can activate functions by pointing at text or objects or directing their gaze (Zero Project, 2018).

A demonstration of OrCam MyEye is available at https://www.youtube.com/watch?v=zxO2Tis_NSE, showing its AI-powered text reading, face recognition, and object identification features.

Research indicates that wearable artificial vision devices such as OrCam MyEye provide meaningful support for individuals with severe visual impairments. A multicentre study reported improvements in users' ability to perform tasks such as reading, object identification, and face recognition, contributing to increased independence and satisfaction (Amore et al., 2023). Similarly, clinical studies suggest that converting visual information into audio feedback supports reading and object recognition among individuals with retinal conditions (Nguyen et al., 2022). Comparative research further highlights that AI-driven wearable devices enable users to access printed information and environmental cues more independently (Granquist, 2021), while broader studies indicate that smart vision technologies enhance accessibility through real-time auditory feedback (Udayakumar et al., 2025).

Despite its advanced capabilities, the effectiveness of the OrCam MyEye device is shaped by several technical, economic, and usability constraints. Its high cost significantly limits accessibility, particularly for users in resource-constrained settings, while reliance on adequate lighting conditions may affect performance in low-light environments. The device may also exhibit occasional inaccuracies in text and object recognition, along with processing delays and limited battery life, restricting prolonged use. From a usability perspective, factors such as physical mounting, gesture-based controls, and required motor coordination may present challenges, especially for elderly or first-time users. Furthermore, functional limitations, including restricted facial recognition capacity and the inability to support navigation or text sharing, constrain its broader applicability (OrCam, 2024). Environmental dependencies, such as lighting interference and the need for internet connectivity during setup and updates, further influence its real-world effectiveness (Lavric et al., 2024). OrCam MyEye 2 was recognised as one of "*TIME Magazine's Best Inventions* in 2019", reflecting its technological and social impact. Today, the device is used in more than 30 countries and supports multiple languages, making it accessible to a global user base (American Foundation for the Blind, 2019).

Ultimately, OrCam MyEye demonstrates how wearable artificial intelligence can transform accessibility by converting visual information into spoken language. While further research is needed to evaluate long-term effectiveness, such technologies highlight the potential of computer vision and machine learning to support inclusive ecosystems and enable individuals with visual impairments to engage more independently with their environment.

1.8 AI-Based Visual Assistance Technologies: Eye-D

Imagine trying to navigate a busy street, read a signboard, or identify everyday objects without being able to see clearly. For individuals who are blind or visually impaired, such situations present barriers to independence and mobility. While traditional assistive tools such as white canes and guide dogs provide essential support, interpreting visual information—such as recognising objects, reading text, or identifying surroundings—often requires assistance. As artificial intelligence and mobile technologies advance, an important question emerges: can smartphones themselves function as assistive tools that help visually impaired individuals interpret their surroundings through intelligent audio feedback?

One response to this challenge is Eye-D, an artificial intelligence–powered "mobile application" designed to assist individuals with visual impairments by converting visual information into spoken descriptions. Developed in Bengaluru, India, the technology uses computer vision and machine learning to analyse images captured through a smartphone camera and translate them into audio feedback (GingerMind

Technologies, 2024). The initiative was founded between 2014 and 2015 by Gaurav Mittal, Vaibhav Deep Asthana, and Subodh Mittal, inspired by Mittal's experience at a National Association for the Blind event in 2012. Observing how assistive tools enabled independence motivated the development of affordable solutions. Launched as Eye-D Pro in 2016, the application utilises smartphones rather than specialised hardware. It allows users to capture images of objects, documents, or their surroundings, which are then processed and described via audio output. The platform supports multiple languages and provides descriptions of objects, signs, and printed materials, enabling users to understand their environment effectively (YourStory, 2022).

A demonstration of the Eye-D application is available at https://www.youtube.com/watch?v=Y5Sx0kY8m0U, showing its real-time object recognition and navigation support for visually impaired users.

Developing Eye-D required overcoming several challenges, particularly understanding the real-world needs of visually impaired users. The team engaged directly with users to design practical and accessible solutions. The startup also faced initial funding constraints, which were later addressed by grants from the Karnataka government. Over time, Eye-D evolved into a broader accessibility ecosystem, reaching more than 70,000 users across over 160 countries by 2022. The company also explored hardware solutions, such as the Eye-D Cam, a smart-glasses system developed with the Barcelona City Council to support safer navigation (YourStory, 2022).

Research supports the effectiveness of such technologies. Studies indicate that mobile assistive applications supporting object recognition, navigation, and text recognition can help users perform tasks more independently (Pundlik, 2023). Similarly, computer-vision systems can detect objects and provide real-time audio guidance, enabling users to interpret their surroundings (Bai et al., 2019). Additional research shows that AI-based object recognition, combined with audio feedback, reduces the time required to locate objects and navigate environments. For instance, the NaviSense study demonstrated improved object retrieval among visually impaired users (Sridhar et al., 2025), while smartphone-based systems using real-time image analysis and text-to-speech enhance independent interaction with visual information (Rhouma & Silva, 2026). However, limitations remain. Smartphone usability, camera positioning, and interface navigation can be challenging without visual cues, while environmental factors such as lighting, noise, and camera constraints may affect accuracy.

A distinction can also be observed when comparing Eye-D with wearable devices such as OrCam MyEye. While both rely on computer vision, OrCam operates as a specialised wearable device attached to glasses, whereas Eye-D functions as a smartphone-based application. This difference highlights two approaches to assistive innovation: specialised hardware versus accessible software built on widely available devices.

The effectiveness of the Eye-D application is shaped by several technical and contextual constraints. Its dependence on stable internet connectivity may restrict usability in low-connectivity environments, while performance can decline in complex or crowded settings, affecting the accuracy of object recognition and navigation. The tool also relies on users capturing appropriate visual input, which can be challenging for visually impaired individuals. Furthermore, device variability, battery consumption, and occasional inaccuracies in interpretation may reduce overall reliability. Issues related to affordability, regional adaptability, and interface usability may additionally influence its adoption across diverse user groups, highlighting the need for continuous refinement to enhance real-world effectiveness (Udayakumar et al., 2025).

Consequently, applications such as Eye-D should be viewed as supportive tools that complement traditional mobility aids and human assistance rather than as replacements.

1.9 Digital Learning Platforms for Inclusive Education: DIKSHA

India, a nation known for its immense cultural diversity, linguistic richness, and vast geographical landscape, faces a unique challenge in ensuring equitable access to quality education for every learner. From bustling metropolitan cities to remote rural villages, the education system must serve millions of students and teachers across varied socio-economic and technological environments. In such a dynamic context, digital innovation has emerged as a powerful tool to bridge educational disparities and democratize access to knowledge. One such transformative initiative is "DIKSHA" (https://diksha.gov.in/) (Digital Infrastructure for Knowledge Sharing), launched by the Ministry of Education on September 5, 2017, as a national digital platform to strengthen India's educational ecosystem (Ministry of Education, 2023). Conceived as part of a vision for "Teacher-First Digitalization", DIKSHA was inspired by the Strategy and Approach Paper for the National Teacher Platform, which emphasised the need for a centralised digital infrastructure to support teachers with lesson plans, professional development resources, and collaborative learning opportunities (UNESCO, 2021). The initiative addressed a long-standing challenge in India's education system—fragmented learning resources and significant disparities in educational quality between rural and urban schools, as well as across different states (Awareness and utilization of DIKSHA..., 2020). Built on the open-source Sunbird technology framework, the platform was designed to be scalable and adaptable, enabling state governments to customize content according to their regional curricula and languages while maintaining a unified national digital learning ecosystem (UNESCO, 2021).

A demonstration of the DIKSHA platform is available at https://www.youtube.com/watch?v=hFCg3Qb-Ljk, highlighting its digital resources and unified learning infrastructure.

Over time, DIKSHA evolved from a teacher-centric repository into a comprehensive national education platform that supports both teachers and students nationwide. During the "Transformation into a National Hub (2018–2019)", the platform introduced innovative features such as "Energized Textbooks (ETBs)", which incorporated QR codes into school textbooks, allowing students to scan the codes and access audio-visual learning materials directly related to their lessons. This approach enabled learners to combine traditional textbooks with interactive digital resources, even in environments with limited internet connectivity. The platform also emphasized inclusivity by supporting more than 30 Indian languages, ensuring that educational content could reach learners in their regional languages and reducing linguistic barriers to learning (Kumar & Rao, 2025). Later, during the COVID-19 pandemic, DIKSHA played a crucial role in maintaining educational continuity through the "PM eVidya Initiative", under which the platform was designated the "One Nation, One Digital Platform" as part of the "Atma Nirbhar Bharat Programme" (Ministry of Education, 2023). During this period of school closures, DIKSHA experienced exponential growth, becoming the primary digital repository for learning resources across India (Verma, 2025). The platform also hosted large-scale teacher training programmes, such as "NISHTHA 1.0 (National Initiatives for School Heads and Teachers' Holistic Advancement)", enabling educators to participate in online professional development programmes (Kumar & Rao, 2025). Complementing these initiatives were several key pillars that strengthened DIKSHA's inclusive approach, including "VidyaDaan", a national programme encouraging individuals, NGOs, and corporations to contribute educational content; "Offline Accessibility", which allowed users to download learning materials for use without internet connectivity; and "Children with Special Needs (CWSN)" resources, which include audiobooks, Indian Sign Language (ISL) videos, and specialized dictionaries to support learners with disabilities (Roul & Mohalik, 2025). Through these initiatives, DIKSHA has emerged as a cornerstone of India's digital education strategy, demonstrating how technology can foster a more inclusive, accessible, and collaborative learning environment for millions of learners across the country (Digital India, 2023).

As digital education initiatives gained momentum globally, India introduced DIKSHA (Digital Infrastructure for Knowledge Sharing) as a pioneering platform to build a unified national digital learning ecosystem. According to UNESCO (2021), DIKSHA was initially designed as a teacher-centric digital infrastructure that provides educators with access to lesson plans, teaching resources, and professional development modules through a centralised platform. The platform later expanded its role in strengthening teacher capacity by implementing initiatives such as NISHTHA, which enabled large-scale teacher training via digital modules (Kumar & Rao, 2025). During the COVID-19 pandemic, DIKSHA emerged as a critical platform for ensuring educational continuity, serving as a central repository of digital learning resources that enabled millions of students to continue learning from home (Verma, 2025).

Despite its large-scale impact, the effectiveness of DIKSHA is shaped by several infrastructural and contextual constraints. The platform's reliance on stable internet connectivity and digital devices limits its accessibility in rural and resource-constrained settings, thereby reinforcing existing digital divides. Additionally, much of its content is designed for self-paced learning, which restricts its applicability in interactive, real-time classroom environments. The lack of robust monitoring and reporting mechanisms further complicates the evaluation of user engagement and learning outcomes. Moreover, variations in content quality, regional adaptability, and accessibility for learners with disabilities may affect its inclusiveness. Collectively, these limitations highlight that while DIKSHA serves as a powerful digital repository, its effectiveness depends significantly on contextual readiness, institutional support, and technological infrastructure (Agarwal, 2025).

Recognising its growing significance, the Ministry of Education (2023) integrated DIKSHA into the PM "eVidya" initiative, declaring it "One Nation, One Digital Platform" for school education in India. In addition to its scale and policy support, the platform also promotes inclusive digital learning by offering multilingual educational resources and accessibility features designed to reach learners from diverse socio-economic and linguistic backgrounds (Roul & Mohalik, 2025).

1.10 AI-Assisted Communication Technologies: Ava

In classrooms, workplaces, and everyday interactions, spoken communication often presents significant challenges for individuals who are deaf or hard of hearing. While assistive devices such as hearing aids and cochlear implants offer partial support, they do not always ensure full participation in group discussions or fast-paced conversations. In response to these limitations, artificial intelligence–driven communication tools have emerged to enhance accessibility.

One such innovation is Ava, an "AI-powered speech-to-text application" that provides real-time captions, enabling individuals with hearing impairments to follow conversations and participate more effectively in educational, social, and professional settings. Ava was founded in 2016 by Thibault Duchemin, Quentin Abadie, and Serena Chaudhry, inspired by Duchemin's personal experience of growing up with "deaf parents" and witnessing communication barriers in group interactions.

Designed as a "mobile application", Ava uses artificial intelligence and automatic speech recognition (ASR) to transcribe spoken language into real-time captions on digital devices. The platform allows multiple participants to join shared conversations, identifies speakers, and displays live captions, thereby facilitating inclusive communication. Additional features such as conversation history, speaker identification, and vocabulary customization enhance its usability in dynamic environments such as classrooms and workplaces (Initialized Capital, 2020; UC Berkeley News, 2024).

A demonstration of the Ava captioning platform can be viewed at https://www.youtube.com/watch?v=MgKVPcJE6Ds, which illustrates its real-time captioning capabilities.

Research indicates that AI-based speech-to-text systems significantly improve communication accessibility for individuals with hearing impairments by enabling greater participation and comprehension in collaborative settings (Cavender et al., 2020). Studies further suggest that captioning technologies support inclusive learning by providing immediate visual representations of spoken dialogue. At the same time, advancements in AI-driven speech recognition continue to expand their applicability across educational and professional contexts (Stinson et al., 2020). However, these systems are not without limitations, as factors such as background noise, accents, rapid speech, and technical vocabulary can affect transcription accuracy.

Ava's effectiveness is constrained by several practical and technical limitations. Factors such as background noise, overlapping speech, strong accents, and technical jargon can reduce transcription accuracy, particularly in dynamic environments. Additionally, the system is highly dependent on stable internet connectivity, and prolonged usage may lead to device-related constraints such as battery drain. Limitations in speaker identification during informal group interactions and restricted offline functionality further affect usability. Moreover, cost-related barriers, including subscription requirements for extended usage, and data privacy concerns due to cloud-based processing, may influence its adoption in sensitive or resource-constrained contexts (Cunningham, 2024).

Consequently, while tools like Ava enhance communication accessibility, they are generally considered supportive technologies rather than complete replacements for human interpreters. Nevertheless, ongoing advancements in artificial intelligence are steadily improving their performance and reliability. Today, Ava is widely used across educational institutions, workplaces, and public environments, demonstrating how AI-assisted technologies can transform communication by making it more accessible, inclusive, and participatory for individuals with hearing impairments.

2. DISCUSSION AND CONCLUSION

Accessibility and inclusion have always been fundamental to meaningful education. Since the earliest forms of organised learning, educational systems have continuously evolved to reduce barriers and expand participation for diverse learner populations. Although the methods and technologies used to support accessibility have transformed significantly over time, the core objective remains unchanged, enabling learners to communicate, participate, comprehend, and engage effectively within educational environments. In contemporary digital learning ecosystems, where education is increasingly mediated through intelligent technologies and online platforms, AI-assisted assistive technologies possess the potential to transform conventional educational experiences into more adaptive, personalised, and inclusive forms of learning. In an era characterised by rapid digital transformation and increasing dependence on technology-mediated instruction, the strategic integration of assistive technologies has become increasingly important for ensuring equitable and meaningful educational participation. (Fitas, 2025). An analysis of AI-assisted assistive technologies across Microsoft Immersive Reader, textHelp Read&Write, Floreo VR, OrCam MyEye, Eye-D, DIKSHA, and Ava reveal a shared commitment to enhancing accessibility through technological innovation. Yet, each tool reflects distinct functional priorities and learner needs. While Microsoft Immersive Reader and textHelp Read&Write emphasise literacy-focused accessibility through text-to-speech, grammar assistance, and translation, OrCam MyEye and Eye-D prioritise real-world visual assistance by enabling object recognition, text reading, and navigation. Ava, in contrast, focuses on communication accessibility by converting speech into real-time text, facilitating inclusive interaction for individuals with hearing impairments. Floreo VR and DIKSHA adopt a broader approach, using immersive environments and scalable platforms to support behavioural learning and enable widespread access to educational resources.

An essential principle of inclusive educational technology is recognising that assistive technologies are not intended to replace the learner's educational journey, but rather to support and enhance accessibility, participation, and engagement within learning environments (Kooli and Chakraoui, 2025). The cross-case thematic analysis identified several interconnected patterns that demonstrate how AI-assisted assistive technologies operate across diverse educational contexts. Accessibility and personalisation emerged as central themes, with tools such as Microsoft Immersive Reader and Texthelp Read&Write enabling adaptive interaction through features including text-to-speech conversion, grammar assistance, translation, and customised reading formats that respond to individual learner needs. This personalised support was frequently designed to reduce cognitive overload and improve learner comprehension, particularly among students with dyslexia and other learning difficulties

(Ogoshi et al., 2023). Communication accessibility formed another significant pattern, most notably reflected in Ava, where real-time speech-to-text captioning facilitated inclusive interaction and participation for individuals with hearing impairments in classroom and collaborative settings. Sensory and real-world assistance also emerged as a prominent dimension through technologies such as OrCam MyEye and Eye-D, which utilised artificial intelligence, computer vision, and object recognition to support navigation, environmental awareness, and independent interaction for visually impaired users. Immersive and experiential learning represented an additional theme, particularly evident in Floreo VR, where simulated virtual environments enabled neurodivergent learners to practice social communication, behavioural responses, and life skills within structured and controlled settings. Finally, scalability and inclusive access were reflected in platforms such as DIKSHA, which utilised digital infrastructure and mobile-based accessibility to provide educational resources to diverse learner populations across varied socio-economic and geographical contexts. Collectively, these patterns illustrate that AI-assisted assistive technologies operate across cognitive, communicative, sensory, and experiential dimensions to promote more inclusive, adaptive, and accessible educational environments.

The longstanding educational principle that accessibility enhances participation remains highly relevant within contemporary digital learning environments; however, the emergence of Artificial Intelligence (AI), Virtual Reality (VR), computer vision, immersive environments, machine learning, and adaptive analytics has significantly transformed how accessibility is conceptualised and implemented within education. Rather than functioning as static assistive mechanisms, modern AI-assisted technologies increasingly operate as intelligent, responsive, and context-aware systems capable of continuously adapting to diverse learner profiles and interaction patterns. The growing integration of behavioural analytics, adaptive feedback mechanisms, real-time accessibility systems, and learner interaction data has further reshaped the role of assistive technologies by enabling more personalised, inclusive, and responsive educational experiences (Kirongo et al., 2022). Advancements in artificial intelligence, immersive environments, computer vision, and real-time processing technologies have transformed how accessibility is experienced in educational settings. AI-assisted assistive technologies are now shaped by emerging priorities such as personalisation, inclusivity, adaptability, and learner-centred engagement. Tools incorporating text-to-speech systems, speech recognition, object detection, immersive simulations, and real-time captioning enable learners to interact with educational content through multiple sensory and communicative pathways. At the same time, integrating behavioural insights, accessibility analytics, and adaptive feedback mechanisms enhances not only functional accessibility but also learner confidence, autonomy, and participation. This convergence of intelligent systems and inclusive educational design positions AI-assisted assistive technologies as transformative enablers capable of supporting equitable, engaging, and accessible learning experiences across diverse educational ecosystems (Kooli and Chakraoui, 2025).

As a result, there is a noticeable shift not only from viewing accessibility as a supplementary support mechanism toward recognising it as a central component of inclusive educational design, but also in how educational technologies interact with diverse learner needs and experiences. The integration of Artificial Intelligence (AI), Virtual Reality (VR), computer vision, speech recognition, immersive environments, and data-driven adaptive systems is reshaping the landscape of assistive technologies within contemporary education by creating intelligent ecosystems that merge accessibility, pedagogy, and technological innovation. These technological advancements are transforming assistive tools into intelligent, responsive, and learner-centred, capable of dynamically adapting to learners' cognitive, sensory, communicative, and behavioural requirements. Consequently, accessibility is increasingly evolving beyond functional accommodation toward a more holistic framework that promotes autonomy, participation, engagement, and equitable learning opportunities across diverse educational settings (Chung-Shing et al., 2025).

These findings carry significant implications for both national and global educational practices. The contextual adaptability of AI-assisted assistive technologies emerges as a critical factor for broader implementation, demonstrating that accessibility solutions can be tailored to diverse languages, cultural contexts, socio-economic realities, and educational infrastructures without compromising educational effectiveness. At the same time, the scalability of advanced assistive systems remains constrained in bandwidth-limited and resource-constrained environments highlighting the continuing need for affordable, lightweight, mobile-first, and infrastructure-sensitive technological solutions. The findings further suggest that the effectiveness of assistive technologies is maximised when technological innovation is strategically aligned with pedagogical objectives, learner readiness, institutional support, and inclusive instructional practices. Positioned at the intersection of intelligent technology, accessibility, and learner-centred educational design, AI-assisted assistive technologies increasingly engage not only the cognitive dimensions of learning but also the emotional, behavioural, and social experiences of learners. Technologies such as real-time captioning systems, immersive simulations, adaptive text-to-speech platforms, object recognition tools, and AI-driven communication support contribute to greater learner confidence, independence, and participation within digital learning environments. This convergence of intelligent systems and inclusive pedagogy therefore represents a transformative movement capable of strengthening both accessibility and human connection within contemporary education ecosystems (Li et al., 2025).

The future of AI-assisted assistive technologies holds substantial transformative potential as emerging technologies continue to shape more personalised, adaptive, and context-aware educational experiences. Through the integration of machine learning, predictive analytics, immersive environments, and intelligent accessibility systems, educational platforms can increasingly deliver tailored support that responds dynamically to diverse learner profiles and educational challenges (Kooli & Chakraoui, 2025). However, the long-term success of these technologies depends on balancing technological sophistication with accessibility, affordability, usability, ethical considerations, and pedagogical intentionality. While advanced AI and immersive technologies can significantly enhance learner engagement and interaction, their educational value is most effectively realised when supported by inclusive design principles, adaptive feedback mechanisms, teacher readiness, and sustainable implementation strategies (Dumitru et al., 2026).

This chapter provides important insights for educators, researchers, edtech developers, practitioners, special education teachers and policymakers by highlighting the emerging role of AI-assisted assistive technologies in advancing accessibility, inclusion, learner empowerment, and educational participation. In conclusion, AI-assisted assistive technologies should not be understood as isolated technological innovations but rather as part of a broader interdisciplinary transformation that integrates educational technology, cognitive science, accessibility studies, behavioural understanding, and human-centred design. The evidence presented across the selected case studies suggests that when intelligent technologies, inclusive pedagogy and contextual implementation strategies are effectively aligned they can create scalable and meaningful educational environments capable of reducing barriers and supporting diverse learner populations across global educational contexts. From a policy and implementation perspective, educational institutions and policymakers must prioritise equitable access to digital infrastructure, inclusive educational software, teacher training, and accessibility-focused technological integration to ensure sustainable adoption of AI-assisted assistive technologies. Similarly, AI developers and EdTech providers should prioritise inclusive and ethical design practices by incorporating accessibility standards, adaptive language support, transparent data practices, and interoperability with existing educational and assistive systems. Ethical considerations related to learner privacy, algorithmic bias, data security, and responsible AI implementation must also remain central to future technological development. Future research should therefore continue to investigate the cognitive, behavioural, ethical, socio-technical, and long-term educational dimensions of assistive technologies through longitudinal and context-specific studies (Kooli and Chakraoui, 2025). Such efforts are essential to ensure that emerging AI-powered accessibility solutions contribute not only to functional access but also to sustainable educational inclusion, learner well-being, and equitable participation across diverse educational ecosystems.

REFERENCES

Agarwal, A. (2025). *DIKSHA-based smart classroom setups – What's missing?* iDream Education. https://www.idreameducation.org/blog/diksha-based-smart-classroom/

Ahmed, S., Rahman, M. S., Kaiser, M. S., & Hosen, A. S. (2025). Advancing personalized and inclusive education for students with disability through artificial intelligence: Perspectives, challenges, and opportunities. *Digital*, *5*(2), 11. DOI: 10.3390/digital5020011

American Foundation for the Blind. (2019). *An evaluation of OrCam MyEye 2.0. AccessWorld*. https://www.afb.org/aw/19/8/15066

Amore, F., Silvestri, V., Guidobaldi, M., Sulfaro, M., Piscopo, P., Turco, S., De Rossi, F., Rellini, E., Fortini, S., Rizzo, S., Perna, F., Mastropasqua, L., Bosch, V., Oest-Shirai, L. R., Haddad, M. A. O., Higashi, A. H., Sato, R. H., Pya, Y., Daibert-Nido, M., & Markowitz, S. N. (2023). Efficacy and patients' satisfaction with the OrCam MyEye device among visually impaired people: A multicenter study. *Journal of Medical Systems*, *47*(1), 11. DOI: 10.1007/s10916-023-01908-5 PMID: 36645535

Assistive Technology Industry Association. (2023). *What is assistive technology?* https://www.atia.org/home/at-resources/what-is-at/

Bairaqdar, M. (2025). Using Microsoft's immersive reader tool to enhance students' listening comprehension. *Dialog on Language Instruction*, 35(1).

Bi, N. B. D. N. (2025). Inclusive and equitable education with AI: Addressing the needs of diverse learners through AI solutions, ensuring quality and accessibility. *International Journal of Humanities and Social Science Invention*, *14*(4), 69–74. DOI: 10.35629/7722-14046974

Cavender, A., Ladner, R., & Riskin, E. (2020). Automated captioning technologies and accessibility for people who are deaf or hard of hearing. *ACM Transactions on Accessible Computing*.

Chalkiadakis, A., Seremetaki, A., Kanellou, A., Kallishi, M., Morfopoulou, A., Moraitaki, M., & Mastrokoukou, S. (2024). Impact of artificial intelligence and virtual reality on educational inclusion: A systematic review of technologies supporting students with disabilities. *Education Sciences*, *14*(11), 1223. DOI: 10.3390/educsci14111223

Chung-Shing, C. H. A. N., Wong, S. Y., Agapito, D., & Veleda, T. A. M. (2025). The effect of pre-trip virtual reality and on-site smart device use on accessible tourism experiences. *Sustainable Futures : An Applied Journal of Technology, Environment and Society*, *10*, 100811. DOI: 10.1016/j.sftr.2025.100811

Cunningham, E. (2024). *Assistive technology: Ava*. IXD@Pratt. https://ixd.prattsi.org/2024/09/assistive-technology-ava/

Darrow, A. (2025). *The UX journey of reading products at Microsoft Education. UX of EdTech*. Medium.

Dawson, K., Antonenko, P., Lane, H., & Zhu, J. (2019). Assistive technologies to support students with dyslexia. *Teaching Exceptional Children*, *51*(3), 226–239. DOI: 10.1177/0040059918794027

Dewi, S. R., Fatmawati, S., & Widodo, A. (2021). Integrating Microsoft immersive reader in SMAR model to promote students' reading comprehension. *Refleksi Edukatika: Jurnal Ilmiah Kependidikan*, *11*(2), 190–196. DOI: 10.24176/re.v11i2.5354

Digital India. (2023). *DIKSHA: Digital infrastructure for knowledge sharing*. Government of India.

Dumitru, C., Muttashar Abdulsahib, G., Ibrahim Khalaf, O., & Bennour, A. (2026). Integrating artificial intelligence in supporting students with disabilities in higher education: An integrative review. *Technology and Disability*, *38*(1), 3–24. DOI: 10.1177/10554181251355428

Fitas, R. (2025). Inclusive education with AI: Supporting special needs and tackling language barriers. *AI and Ethics*, *5*(6), 5729–5757. DOI: 10.1007/s43681-025-00824-3

Fitas, R. (2025). Inclusive education with AI: Supporting special needs and tackling language barriers. *AI and Ethics*, *5*(6), 5729–5757. DOI: 10.1007/s43681-025-00824-3

Floreo. (2024). *Virtual reality learning for neurodivergent learners*.

Foisy, L. (2024). *Boosting writing skills in K-12 dyslexic students using Read&Write*. The Alt Text Project.

Fortiş, A. E., Gaudo, M. V., Fazendeiro, P., Exposito, E., & Pedro, N. (2025). *Inclusive education with AI: Supporting special needs and overcoming language barriers*. In *AI in early education: Integrating artificial intelligence for inclusive and effective learning* (pp. 173–200). DOI: 10.1002/9781394352821.ch11

GingerMind Technologies. (2024). *Eye-D: AI-powered assistance for visually impaired users.*

Granquist, C. (2021). OrCam MyEye 1 and Seeing AI: Text recognition technologies for individuals with severe visual impairment. *Journal of Visual Impairment & Blindness.*

Initialized Capital. (2020). *Transcribing the online and offline world for the deaf and hard-of-hearing community and beyond with Ava.* https://blog.initialized.com/2020/12/transcribing-the-online-and-offline-world-for-the-deaf-hard-of-hearing-community-and-beyond-with-ava/

Kellems, R. O. (2025). *A systematic review of immersive virtual reality interventions for autism spectrum disorder.* Information Journal.

Kirongo, A. C., Huka, G., Bundi, D., Kitaria, D., & Muchiri, G. (2022). Implementation of AI-based assistive technologies for learners with physical disabilities in areas of innovation and special schools: A practical design thinking approach. African Journal of Science. *Technology and Social Sciences, 1*(2), 73–76. DOI: 10.58506/ajstss.v1i2.124

Kooli, C., & Chakraoui, R. (2025). AI-driven assistive technologies in inclusive education: Benefits, challenges, and policy recommendations. *Sustainable Futures : An Applied Journal of Technology, Environment and Society, 10*, 101042. DOI: 10.1016/j.sftr.2025.101042

Krasniqi, V., Zdravkova, K., & Dalipi, F. (2022). Impact of assistive technologies on inclusive education and independent life of Down syndrome persons: A systematic literature review and research agenda. *Sustainability (Basel), 14*(8), 4630. DOI: 10.3390/su14084630

Kumar, P., & Rao, S. (2025). Empowering educators: Evaluating DIKSHA and SWAYAM for digital teacher training and economic inclusion in India.

Kumar, S. (2025). AI and inclusive education: Opportunities and challenges. *International Journal of Scientific Research in Modern Science and Technology, 4*(9), 92–100. Advance online publication. DOI: 10.59828/ijsrmst.v4i9.375

Lata, P. (2024). Towards equitable learning: Exploring artificial intelligence in inclusive education. *SSRN, 7*, 416. DOI: 10.2139/ssrn.4987156

Lavric, A.. (2024). A comprehensive survey on emerging assistive technologies for visually impaired individuals. *Sensors (Basel).* Advance online publication. DOI: 10.3390/s24154834

Li, J., Yuyang, Y., & Xiaojun, Z. (2025). Exploring artificial intelligence in inclusive education: A systematic review of empirical studies. *Applied Sciences (Basel, Switzerland), 15*(23), 12624. DOI: 10.3390/app152312624

Li, W., Song, R., Zhang, B., & Yu, K. (2025). AI creativity and legal protection for AI-generated works in posthuman societal scenarios. *Sustainable Futures : An Applied Journal of Technology, Environment and Society, 9*, 100749. DOI: 10.1016/j.sftr.2025.100749

Mais, A., & Yauma, L. A. (2026). Inclusive education in the digital age: A systematic literature review on assistive technology development. *Multidisciplinary Reviews, 9*(5), e2026223. DOI: 10.31893/multirev.2026223

Melo-López, V. A., Basantes-Andrade, A., Gudiño-Mejía, C. B., & Hernández-Martínez, E. (2025). The impact of artificial intelligence on inclusive education: A systematic review. *Education Sciences, 15*(5), 539. DOI: 10.3390/educsci15050539

Microsoft. (2024). *Microsoft Immersive Reader overview*. Microsoft Learn.

Ministry of Education. (2023). *DIKSHA: Digital infrastructure for knowledge sharing*. Government of India.

Ogoshi, S., Ogoshi, Y., Saitoh, T., Tanaka, K., Itoh, Y., Wakamatu, M., & Nakai, A. (2023). Individual Education Support System Using ICT for Developmental Disabilities. In *Cognitive Behavioral Therapy-Basic Principles and Application Areas*. IntechOpen. DOI: 10.5772/intechopen.106065

OrCam. (2024). *OrCam MyEye assistive technology for people with visual impairments*.

Pagliara, S. M., Bonavolontà, G., Pia, M., Falchi, S., Zurru, A. L., Fenu, G., & Mura, A. (2024). The integration of artificial intelligence in inclusive education: A scoping review. *Information (Basel), 15*(12), 774. DOI: 10.3390/info15120774

Piyathanavong, V., Huynh, V. N., Karnjana, J., & Olapiriyakul, S. (2024). Role of project management on sustainable supply chain development through Industry 4.0 technologies and circular economy during the COVID-19 pandemic. *Operations Management Research : Advancing Practice Through Research, 17*(1), 13–37. DOI: 10.1007/s12063-022-00283-7

Ravindran, V., Osgood, M., Sazawal, V., Solorzano, R., & Turnacioglu, S. (2019). Virtual reality support for joint attention using the Floreo joint attention module: Usability and feasibility pilot study. *JMIR Pediatrics and Parenting, 2*(2), e14429. DOI: 10.2196/14429 PMID: 31573921

Roul, R., & Mohalik, R. (2025). Quality of e-content on DIKSHA platform. *International Education and Research Journal.*

Santos, C. M. (2025). Improving reading comprehension skills in English for Grade 4 pupils through Microsoft immersive reader. *Asia Pacific Higher Education Research Journal, 12*(1), 1–17. DOI: 10.56278/apherj.v12i1.3198

Shapiro, K., Ravindran, V., Downing, G., Stepensky, M. R., Mak-Parisi, S., Solorzano, R., Barbayannis, G., & Turnacioglu, S. (2025). Children with Autism Using the Floreo Virtual Reality Building Social Connections Module: A Feasibility Study. *Autism-Open Access, 15*(2), 436. DOI: 10.35248/2165-7890.25.15.436

Shireesha, M., & Jeevan, J. (2024). The role of artificial intelligence in personalized learning: A pathway to inclusive education. *Library of Progress – Library Science, Information Technology & Computer*, 44(3).

Stinson, M., Elliot, L., & Kelly, R. (2020). Captioning and speech-to-text technologies in education for deaf and hard-of-hearing students. *Journal of Special Education Technology.*

Svensson, I. (2021). Effects of assistive technology for students with reading and writing difficulties. *Disability and Rehabilitation. Assistive Technology.* Advance online publication. DOI: 10.1080/17483107.2019.1646821 PMID: 31418305

Texthelp. (2025). *Read&Write for education.* Texthelp.

Toyokawa, Y., Horikoshi, I., Majumdar, R., & Ogata, H. (2023). Challenges and opportunities of AI in inclusive education: A case study of data-enhanced active reading in Japan. *Smart Learning Environments, 10*(1), 67. DOI: 10.1186/s40561-023-00286-2

Udayakumar, D., Gopalakrishnan, S., Raghuram, A., Kartha, A., Krishnan, A. K., Ramamirtham, R., Muthangi, R., & Raju, R. (2025). Artificial intelligence-powered smart vision glasses for visually impaired individuals. *Indian Journal of Ophthalmology, 73*(Suppl 3), S492–S497. DOI: 10.4103/IJO.IJO_1621_24

UNESCO. (2021). *DIKSHA: Digital infrastructure for knowledge sharing.*

University of California. Berkeley News. (2024). *This company's mission is to make the world accessible to deaf people.* https://news.berkeley.edu/2024/11/08/this-companys-mission-is-to-make-the-world-accessible-to-deaf-people-it-all-started-at-berkeleys-big-ideas-contest/

Verma, R. (2025). Access and use of DIKSHA for school teachers and students amid [*Indian Journal of Educational Technology.*]. *COVID*, •••, 19.

Wang, X. (2023). Utilizing virtual reality to assist social competence in children with autism. *Computers & Education*. Advance online publication. DOI: 10.1016/j.compedu.2023.104815

WIRED. (2023). *Data vulnerability concerns in India's DIKSHA platform.*

Wood, S. G. (2017). Does use of text-to-speech and related read-aloud tools improve reading comprehension? *Journal of Learning Disabilities*. PMID: 28112580

Zangiacomi, A., Pessot, E., Fornasiero, R., Bertetti, M., & Sacco, M. (2020). Moving towards digitalization: A multiple case study in manufacturing. *Production Planning and Control, 31*(2–3), 143–157. DOI: 10.1080/09537287.2019.1631468

Zero Project. (2018). *OrCam MyEye: Vision device to understand texts and identify objects*. Essl Foundation. https://zeroproject.org/view/project/8b8f3fb8-9a17-eb11-a813-0022489b3a6d

Chapter 3

Human-Centered AI-Mediated Mobile, Wearable, and XR Assistive Systems for Inclusive Education:

Conceptual Framework for Multimodal Intelligence

Ashraf Alam
http://orcid.org/0000-0001-6178-1187
Department of Education, National Institute of Technology Calicut, India

ABSTRACT

This chapter reframes AI-mediated mobile, wearable, and XR assistive systems as justice-critical educational infrastructure rather than peripheral accommodation. It integrates capability realization, recognition justice, and procedural fairness with cognitive load governance, self-regulated learning, and person-environment fit, then advances a socio-technical ecosystem model using affordance theory and distributed cognition across interface, content, pedagogy, assessment, and governance. A function taxonomy positions AI assistance as adaptive mediation shaping epistemic access, scaffold calibration, and construct fidelity. Risk governance operationalizes contextual integrity, data minimization, contestability, and auditability, addressing accessibility bias. The chapter yields policy grammars for interoperability, accommodation continuity, and dignity-preserving participation in multilingual, low-resource schooling ecologies.

DOI: 10.4018/979-8-2600-2716-5.ch003

2027, IGI Global Scientific Publishing. Copying or distributing in print or electronic forms without written permission of IGI Global Scientific Publishing is prohibited. Use of this chapter to tive artificial intelligence (AI) technologies is expressly prohibited. The publisher reserves all rights to license its use for generative AI training and machine learning model development.

1. INTRODUCTION

1.1 Rationale and Problem Statement

Inclusive education now operates inside a digital architecture that routinely presumes a default learner, a default language, and a default body-mind interface. This presumption becomes structurally exclusionary when scaled platforms standardize interaction grammars, assessment formats, and engagement metrics that cannot flex to learner variability. The global magnitude of the challenge is not marginal. An estimated 1.3 billion people experience significant disability, around 16 percent of the world's population, and more than 2.5 billion people need at least one assistive product while nearly one billion are denied access, with access levels in some low-income contexts reported in the low single digits. This chapter's central problem is therefore an equity-availability paradox, digital schooling expands reach while intensifying misfit through uniform content pipelines, rigid modality defaults, and data-driven decision regimes that can penalize atypical communication, sensory profiles, or executive-function variability. This chapter contributes by repositioning assistive technologies as educational justice infrastructure that must be designed for dignity, autonomy, and belonging.

1.2 Scope, Definitions, and Conceptual Boundary Conditions

This chapter treats mobile, wearable, and XR assistive systems as multimodal mediation infrastructures that shape what learners can perceive, express, and meaningfully participate in, across formal classrooms, blended environments, and home-school boundary spaces. Assistive technology is defined broadly as any toolchain that reduces functional barriers in perception, communication, interaction, participation, and assessment, including accessibility features embedded in mainstream devices. AI-mediated assistance is defined as adaptive mediation that can infer context, translate across modalities, generate alternative representations, recommend supports, and scaffold self-regulation, while remaining agency-preserving and contestable (Riyat et al., 2025; Carreon et al., 2025; Tohănean et al., 2025). Inclusion is defined as meaningful participation and learning under conditions of dignity, autonomy, and belonging, rather than physical presence or compliance with minimum access checklists. Accessibility is operationalized as functional equivalence of learning opportunity, not identical experience. Multimodal intelligence is treated as the coordinated orchestration of text, speech, image, gesture, gaze, haptics, and context signals with user control and cognitive-load governance. The chapter is conceptual-theoretical, and it intentionally avoids empirical evaluation claims.

1.3 Chapter Aims, Conceptual Contribution, and Integrative Framework

The chapter aims to deliver a unified conceptual map that links normative obligations to design requirements and governance constraints for AI-mediated assistive ecosystems across mobile, wearable, and XR modalities. The integrative framework is built from five cross-cutting constructs. First, rights-and-justice logics that define non-negotiable inclusion thresholds, treating access as an entitlement rather than discretionary support. Second, learning-sciences translation that connects cognitive architecture, motivation, self-regulation, and participation theory to concrete accessibility decisions, including modality selection, pacing, and scaffold fading. Third, socio-technical ecosystem analysis that locates accessibility breakdowns at boundaries between interface, content, pedagogy, assessment, and governance layers. Fourth, an AI assistive function taxonomy that treats translation, transformation, and tutoring mediation as instructional design choices that reshape epistemic access and assessment validity. Fifth, responsible innovation logic that frames privacy, accountability, bias control, and professional capacity as inclusion prerequisites rather than add-on compliance. This chapter contributes by specifying actionable design and governance principles that remain legible across disciplines.

1.4 Chapter Organization and Reader-Use Pathways

The chapter proceeds in seven sections with a deliberate progression from foundations to ecosystem dynamics, then to AI-mediated assistance, followed by design and governance, concluding with synthesis and implications. Section 2 establishes normative, disability-model, learning-sciences, and instructional design foundations that translate inclusion commitments into design-relevant criteria. Section 3 reframes assistive technologies as a socio-technical learning ecosystem across mobile, wearable, and XR modalities, using relational and distributed perspectives to explain why accessibility fails in practice despite feature availability. Section 4 conceptualizes AI assistance as adaptive mediation rather than automation, detailing how personalization can either expand capability or codify constraint. Section 5 converts theory into design grammars through UDL, participatory design, and standards-as-quality infrastructure. Section 6 specifies governance, ethics, and policy alignment, treating procurement, privacy, accountability, and educator capacity as system-level determinants of inclusion. Across Sections 2 to 6, one table per section functions as a synthesis device that compresses complex theory into implementable mappings, enabling rapid diagnosis and design alignment without diluting conceptual rigor.

2. FOUNDATIONS AND CONCEPTUAL FRAMEWORKS FOR ASSISTIVE TECHNOLOGIES IN EDUCATION

2.1 Normative and Philosophical Foundations for Inclusion as Justice-Linked Infrastructure

This chapter contributes by recoding assistive technologies as educational justice infrastructure, meaning a socio-institutional obligation that stabilizes dignity, autonomy, and belonging rather than a discretionary accommodation. A rights-and-entitlements framing treats accessibility as an enforceable baseline for participation, not a compensatory add-on after exclusion has already been produced by standardized curricula and platform logics (Desmarchelier et al., 2025; Richelli et al., 2025). Within this normative architecture, *capability realization* specifies real freedoms to learn and to participate, while *adequacy thresholds* specify non-negotiable minimum conditions of access across content, classroom discourse, and assessment formats. *Recognition justice* foregrounds stigma reduction, status equality, and identity-safe participation, particularly where disability intersects with language, gender, poverty, and migration. *Procedural justice* demands fair governance in eligibility, accommodation allocation, platform rulemaking, and recourse. These lenses become operational when translated into design obligations, later condensed in Table 1, which functions as a high-density bridge between moral claims and implementable requirements.

2.2 Disability Models, Barrier Ontologies, and Design-Sensitive Problem Formulations

A robust conceptual foundation requires a barrier ontology that distinguishes impairment-centric framing from environment-centric and interactional framing, because each model generates different design priorities and different failure modes. The medicalized model privileges impairment correction and diagnostic gatekeeping, which can harden deficit narratives and normalize surveillance (Daineko & Seitnur, 2025; Hicks et al., 2025). The social model privileges barrier removal and accessible environments, but can under-specify embodied fatigue, sensory dysregulation, and fluctuating conditions that demand adaptive supports. The *biopsychosocial* model supports dynamic provisioning across contexts, aligning to multi-tier support logic and contextual adaptation. Interactional approaches, including *person-environment fit* and task-tool-context alignment, treat accessibility as relational and emphasize that learning barriers emerge at interface-pedagogy-assessment boundaries, not inside the learner. This chapter contributes by treating these models as design heuristics rather than metaphysical claims, and Table 1 synthesizes how each conceptual lens specifies what counts as harm, what counts as support, and what counts as responsible institutional conduct.

Table 1. Conceptual Lenses Mapped to Inclusive Assistive Design Implications

Conceptual Lens and Core Theory Frame	Barrier Definition and Injustice Signature	Design Imperatives for Mobile-Wearable-XR Ecosystems	Pedagogic and Assessment Alignment Logic	Foreseeable Risks if Misapplied
Capability Realization and Freedom-to-Learn Logic	Conversion failures where resources cannot become functionings, producing participation deprivation and opportunity foreclosure	Prioritize user-controlled modality switching, scaffold fading, and continuity of accommodations across contexts and platforms	Maintain construct relevance through functional equivalence, preserving learning goals while removing irrelevant access friction	Over-personalization that narrows pathways, creating benevolent restriction and lowered expectation loops
Recognition Justice and Dignity-Preserving Participation Frame	Status harm through stigma, misrecognition, and identity threat that degrades belonging and discursive legitimacy	Design for social acceptability, discreet assistive affordances, and identity-safe defaults that avoid forced disclosure	Embed collaboration accessibility, turn-taking supports, and non-humiliating participation norms within classroom workflows	Cosmetic inclusion that hides exclusion, producing quiet marginalization and performative accessibility
Procedural Justice and Contestable Governance Logic	Unfair decision processes, opaque rules, and lack of recourse that institutionalize exclusion through administrative arbitrariness	Implement auditability, explainability for educators, appeals pathways, and policy-aware configuration controls	Align tool use rules with assessment boundaries, specifying accommodation versus modification without ambiguity	Compliance theater where documentation replaces lived accessibility, weakening trust and increasing disengagement
Biopsychosocial and Context-Sensitive Support Provisioning	Dynamic barriers arising from fluctuating capacity, fatigue, stress load, and environmental triggers	Enable adaptive pacing, sensory load regulation, and context-aware prompts with strict data minimization	Couple supports to self-regulation routines, feedback timing, and differentiated instruction logic	Surveillance drift through continuous sensing, producing coercive support and privacy erosion
Person-Environment Fit and Activity-System Alignment	Misfit across learner-task-tool-environment relations, amplified at layer boundaries between interface, pedagogy, and policy	Engineer interoperability, low-friction setup, and robust failure-safe behavior across devices and modalities	Treat assistive functions as instructional design decisions, ensuring coherence with curricular sequencing and participation practices	Fragmented toolchains that increase switching costs and cognitive overhead, intensifying access friction

Table 1 should be read as a translation engine that connects normative commitments to concrete design constraints and governance duties, allowing institutions to specify non-negotiable requirements while preserving pedagogic flexibility and learner agency.

2.3 Learning Sciences Foundations for Assistive Design as Cognitive-Relational Engineering

Learning-sciences translation is required because assistive mediation alters cognitive work allocation, attentional economics, and self-regulation demands, so design must track cognitive architecture and participation dynamics rather than only interface compliance. *Cognitive load governance* demands segmentation, signaling, pacing controls, and user-managed redundancy so multimodality becomes a choice architecture rather than a forced overload. *Working memory* and *executive function* constructs justify externalized planning, checklists, time supports, and error-tolerant interaction grammars that reduce volatility in task initiation and completion (Alam & Mohanty, 2024; Fong et al., 2025). *Self-regulated learning* emphasizes metacognitive prompts, progress visibility, and scaffold fading to avoid dependency formation. Motivation is stabilized through *autonomy-supportive assistance*, competence-calibrated feedback, and relatedness-preserving participation pathways, aligning with dignity and recognition commitments signposted in Table 1. Participation theory reframes inclusion as legitimate engagement in classroom discourse and collaborative problem-solving, requiring assistive supports that protect epistemic agency, not merely content access.

2.4 Instructional Design and Accessibility Frameworks as Pedagogy-to-Technology Translation Layers

Instructional design frameworks operationalize inclusion by specifying how learning goals, participation structures, and assessment rules can remain stable while access pathways diversify. *Universal Design for Learning* functions as a translation grammar that turns variability into planned options across representation, action-expression, and engagement, while *differentiated instruction* localizes these options to classroom constraints and instructional pacing (Liginlal & Al-Emadi, 2026; Hamid et al., 2025). Multi-tier support architectures provide a governance-compatible logic for graduated assistance intensity, yet must be insulated from deficit tracking through recognition-oriented norms. Inclusive assessment requires *validity preservation* and construct fidelity, meaning accommodations remove irrelevant barriers without changing what is being inferred about learning, and this boundary-setting must be explicit in institutional rules. Linguistic inclusion is strengthened by *translanguaging* and culturally sustaining design, preventing assistive tools from becoming assimilation instruments that erase community repertoires. This chapter contributes by insisting that instructional coherence, not feature abundance, is the primary criterion for inclusive assistive ecosystems, and Table 1 remains the anchor for aligning pedagogy, design, and governance.

3. ASSISTIVE TECHNOLOGY AS A SOCIO-TECHNICAL LEARNING ECOSYSTEM ACROSS MOBILE, WEARABLE, AND XR MODALITIES

3.1 Layered Ecosystem Architecture and Accessibility as Systemic Coherence

Assistive technologies in inclusive education must be conceptualized not as discrete tools but as interdependent components within a layered socio-technical ecosystem that spans interface, interaction, content, pedagogy, assessment, and governance. Accessibility breakdowns frequently occur at boundary points where one layer satisfies compliance criteria while another silently reintroduces exclusion, such as an accessible interface embedded within an inflexible assessment policy (Chamola et al., 2025; Ghugar et al., 2025). The construct of *accommodation continuity* becomes critical in this layered view, denoting whether supports persist across platforms, grade transitions, teacher practices, and home-school boundary spaces. Drawing from *ecological systems theory* and *implementation climate* constructs, ecosystem performance depends on institutional readiness, role clarity, and workflow alignment, not merely feature presence. Accessibility thus becomes a property of relational coherence, where tools, norms, schedules, procurement clauses, and classroom discourse patterns align to reduce *access friction* and prevent cumulative participation debt across educational trajectories.

3.2 Relational Affordances, Distributed Cognition, and Activity-System Diagnostics

Accessibility is fundamentally relational, a proposition grounded in *affordance theory*, where the functional meaning of a device emerges from the dynamic coupling between user capacities, task demands, environmental constraints, and social norms. Assistive systems redistribute cognitive labor through *distributed cognition*, offloading memory, planning, and representational transformation to artifacts, peers, and AI-mediated prompts. This redistribution reshapes epistemic authority and participation hierarchies, making governance of cognitive offloading ethically salient. *Activity theory* provides a diagnostic grammar, mapping subject, tool, rules, community, division of labor, and outcomes, revealing contradictions such as rule sets that prohibit assistive use during high-stakes evaluation (Ashour & Elkhawaga, 2026; Naik, 2024). *Sociomateriality* further clarifies how dashboards, seating layouts, bandwidth variability, and device form factors co-produce participation conditions. The ecosystem mapping in Table 2 synthesizes these theoretical constructs, translating them into modality-specific affordances, integration requirements, and risk profiles that institutional actors can operationalize.

Table 2. Modality Affordances and Ecosystem Risk Mapping

Modality Configuration	Primary Accessibility Affordances and Cognitive Redistribution	Pedagogic Integration and Workflow Alignment Requirements	Layer Boundary Failure Patterns	Equity, Privacy, and Dignity Risk Vectors
Mobile Ubiquitous Computing Ecosystem	Context-aware scaffolding, multimodal input-output switching, microlearning sequencing, cognitive offloading through reminders and adaptive prompts	Alignment with lesson pacing, offline-first design, low-bandwidth optimization, and accommodation continuity across home-school interfaces	Interface accessibility paired with inaccessible assessment policy or fragmented login regimes that disrupt support persistence	Surveillance drift through location-context sensing, stigmatization if device visibility signals difference, data retention creep
Wearable Embodied Mediation Systems	Haptic cueing, auditory augmentation, biosignal-informed pacing, discreet feedback loops that regulate attention and arousal	Classroom norm-setting for legitimacy, sensory-load calibration, opt-out without penalty, integration with teacher interpretive routines	Sensory overload despite feature richness, teacher misinterpretation of biosignal data, policy ambiguity on acceptable use	Biometric data exposure, coercive normalization through constant monitoring, erosion of autonomy via always-on sensing
XR Immersive Simulation Environments	Embodied interaction, spatialized multimodal representation, experiential rehearsal of abstract concepts and social scripts	Equivalent interaction grammars, motion-sensitivity safeguards, alternative pathways that preserve construct validity	Presence-rich experience coupled with inaccessible narrative design, fatigue accumulation, exclusion in high-sensory contexts	Identity misrepresentation, stereotyping in virtual narratives, capture of gaze and behavioral telemetry without clear governance

continued on following page

Table 2. Continued

Modality Configuration	Primary Accessibility Affordances and Cognitive Redistribution	Pedagogic Integration and Workflow Alignment Requirements	Layer Boundary Failure Patterns	Equity, Privacy, and Dignity Risk Vectors
Hybrid Cross-Platform Assistive Mesh	Interoperable data flows, synchronized accommodations, cross-device state persistence, adaptive modality handoff	Interoperability standards, unified identity management, teacher-facing dashboards that preserve agency and interpretive discretion	Fragmented toolchains increasing switching costs, cognitive overload from redundant notifications, inconsistent scaffold fading	Vendor lock-in creating structural exclusion, opaque algorithmic mediation, differential degradation for marginalized users
Low-Resource and Intermittent Connectivity Contexts	Offline content caching, SMS-based prompts, lightweight multimodal compression, device-sharing protocols	Community-based charging infrastructure, culturally responsive workflow design, caregiver-inclusive communication loops	Feature collapse under bandwidth constraints, inaccessible updates, reliance on unstable connectivity	Digital divide amplification, unequal update cycles, infrastructural precarity undermining accommodation continuity

Table 2 demonstrates that accessibility is a multi-layer governance problem rather than a feature checklist, requiring systemic coherence across modalities, institutional routines, and socio-economic contexts.

3.3 Mobile Assistive Systems as Boundary-Crossing Continuity Infrastructures

Mobile assistive systems operate as boundary-crossing infrastructures that link classroom, household, transit, and informal learning ecologies, thereby mitigating context collapse and supporting continuity of scaffolds. Through *microlearning architectures* and temporal spacing logic, mobile devices can reduce cognitive volatility by distributing learning episodes across manageable intervals, benefiting learners with executive-function variability or caregiving responsibilities (Wild et al., 2025; Gowrishankar et al., 2025). Context-aware mediation can adjust language simplification, prompt intensity, or reminder frequency based on temporal and situational cues, yet such adaptability must be constrained by *contextual integrity* to prevent mission creep in data collection. Low-bandwidth optimization, offline caching, and energy-aware design become equity determinants in resource-constrained settings, where infrastructure fragility can otherwise negate assistive intent. Social acceptability also matters, as visible device use can produce stigma or misrecognition, demanding discreet interaction grammars and norm-setting practices that preserve dignity while maintaining pedagogic transparency.

3.4 Wearables and XR as Embodied Participation and Sensory Ecology Reconfigurations

Wearable and XR systems extend assistive mediation into embodied and spatial dimensions, transforming participation through *embodied cognition* and *phenomenology of perception*. Haptic signaling, auditory overlays, and gaze-responsive prompts can regulate attention and support self-regulation, yet they must respect sensory ecology and avoid overstimulation (Chen et al., 2024; Yao, 2025). XR environments enable immersive simulation for conceptual abstraction and social rehearsal, yet require motion-sensitivity safeguards, fatigue monitoring, and alternative interaction grammars to preserve inclusivity. The construct of *equivalent learning pathways* is central, ensuring that alternative modalities preserve construct meaning and assessment validity. Narrative design within immersive spaces must align with recognition justice, preventing stereotyping and identity harm (Alam & Mohanty, 2023; Girhe et al., 2024). Institutional legitimacy depends on explicit classroom norms that authorize assistive use without stigmatization, reinforcing that embodied mediation is a pedagogic instrument rather than a marker of deficiency. In sum, socio-technical ecosystem coherence across mobile, wearable, and XR modalities determines whether assistive innovation expands freedom-to-learn or reproduces exclusion under new technological guises.

4. AI-DRIVEN ASSISTIVE TECHNOLOGIES AS ADAPTIVE MEDIATION RATHER THAN AUTOMATION

4.1 Human-Centered AI and Intelligence-Augmentation Paradigms in Inclusive Education

AI-mediated assistive systems must be conceptualized within a *human-centered AI* paradigm that prioritizes agency, contestability, proportionality, and dignity-preserving mediation rather than efficiency-maximizing automation. Within an *intelligence-augmentation* frame, AI functions as a capability amplifier that redistributes cognitive effort while preserving learner intentionality and teacher professional judgment (Thabet et al., 2025; Rybenská et al., 2024). This chapter contributes by differentiating automation from augmentation, personalization from manipulation, and convenience from equitable accessibility. *Calibrated scaffolding* becomes the core design imperative, meaning supports must be adjustable, fade-able, and aligned with learning goals to avoid deskilling or dependency loops. Motivation theory reinforces the requirement for *autonomy-supportive assistance*, where learners retain control over modality selection, prompt intensity, and disclosure visibility (Ahuja et al., 2025; Liu et al., 2024). Without such calibration, adaptive systems risk encoding low expectations, narrowing epistemic exposure, and generating benevolent constraint architectures that quietly restrict access to advanced conceptual work.

4.2 AI Assistive Function Taxonomy as Epistemic Mediation Architecture

AI-driven assistive technologies operate across multiple mediation layers that reshape what can be perceived, expressed, evaluated, and socially negotiated in educational settings. Linguistic mediation includes speech-to-text, text-to-speech, translation, simplification, and semantic summarization, each affecting discourse access and meaning fidelity (Perry et al., 2024; Malviya & Rajput, 2025). Representational mediation encompasses image description, diagram narration, layout transformation, and symbolic substitution, influencing cognitive load and inferential pathways. Interaction mediation incorporates voice input, gesture recognition, gaze alternatives, predictive text, and error-tolerant interfaces, redefining participation grammars. Metacognitive mediation supports planning, time management, goal tracking, and error-aware hints, altering self-regulatory architectures (Santos et al., 2025; Abrar et al., 2026). Social participation mediation includes captioned dialogue, accessible collaboration artifacts, and turn-taking orchestration, influencing belonging and epistemic authority. These functions are not neutral utilities but instructional design decisions that modify assessment boundaries and participation hierarchies. Table 3 systematizes this taxonomy, aligning function categories with theoretical anchors, validity risks, and governance safeguards.

Table 3. AI Assistive Functions Aligned with Theoretical Anchors and Safeguards

Assistive Function Domain	Educational and Epistemic Purpose	Theoretical Anchor and Cognitive Framework	Validity and Equity Distortion Risks	Governance and Design Safeguards
Linguistic Mediation Systems	Expand access to oral and written discourse through multimodal translation and semantic compression	*Dual coding, cognitive load governance, translanguaging* as epistemic resource rather than deficit	Construct shift if simplification alters inferential demand, accent misrecognition leading to testimonial injustice	User-controlled granularity, accent-robust modeling, audit logs enabling contestation and correction
Representational Transformation Engines	Convert diagrams, visuals, and symbolic structures into alternative sensory modalities for functional equivalence	*Multimedia learning theory, functional equivalence*, perceptual load regulation	Over-description increasing cognitive load, distortion of spatial reasoning constructs	Adjustable description depth, teacher-facing validation checkpoints, alignment with assessment construct definitions
Interaction Mediation Interfaces	Enable alternative input-output grammars for diverse motor and sensory profiles	*Person-environment fit*, distributed cognition, error-tolerant interface theory	Predictive bias narrowing expressive diversity, exclusion of atypical gesture or gaze patterns	Inclusive training datasets, manual override capacity, transparent performance metrics for educators
Metacognitive and Executive Scaffolds	Externalize planning, pacing, and feedback to stabilize self-regulation and task persistence	*Self-regulated learning, zone of proximal development*, scaffold fading logic	Dependency formation, diminished intrinsic motivation through over-prompting	Scaffold intensity sliders, time-bound prompts, explicit fading algorithms tied to mastery indicators
Social Participation Orchestrators	Facilitate equitable turn-taking, captioned dialogue, and collaborative artifact accessibility	Participation theory, recognition justice, dialogic pedagogy constructs	Status stratification if assistive cues mark difference, algorithmic prioritization bias	Discreet interaction modes, policy alignment with classroom norms, regular bias audits and stakeholder review

Table 3 demonstrates that AI-mediated assistance reconfigures epistemic access and participation architectures rather than merely accelerating existing processes. Each function domain intersects with construct validity, motivational climate, and relational equity. The safeguards enumerated above are not optional add-ons but structural constraints that preserve dignity and prevent algorithmic benevolence from morphing into epistemic paternalism (Katke & Pacharaney, 2024; Gholizadeh HamlAbadi et al., 2024). By embedding adjustable controls, contestability mechanisms, and teacher-facing interpretive transparency, institutions can ensure that adaptive mediation amplifies freedom-to-learn without introducing construct drift or expectation suppression. This synthesis reinforces the principle that AI assistance must be pedagogically intentional and governance-bound, aligning with the justice-based commitments articulated in earlier sections.

4.3 Adaptive Personalization, Measurement Integrity, and Pathway Governance

Adaptive systems rely on progression logic that must remain pedagogically coherent and normatively defensible. *Mastery-based sequencing* and learning progression constructs can calibrate scaffold intensity and task complexity, yet must avoid closed-loop personalization that narrows exposure to advanced tasks (Wang, 2024; Xu et al., 2025). The *zone of proximal development* provides a dynamic calibration heuristic, positioning assistance as contingent and collaborative rather than static level assignment. Measurement integrity requires *construct fidelity*, ensuring that accommodations remove irrelevant barriers without altering inferential targets. *Differential item functioning* concepts highlight how assistive mediation may inadvertently advantage or disadvantage subgroups if algorithmic adaptation is misaligned. Without explicit pathway governance, recommender architectures can entrench deficit-coded expectations, restricting epistemic mobility (Adako et al., 2025; Alam & Mohanty, 2022). Therefore, adaptive mediation must incorporate pathway audits, expectation monitoring, and scaffold-fading triggers linked to demonstrated competence, preserving opportunity breadth and resisting algorithmic stratification.

4.4 Fairness, Epistemic Justice, Privacy, and Accountability as Inclusion Preconditions

Fairness in AI-mediated assistive systems extends beyond statistical parity into *equity of opportunity to demonstrate learning*, a normative benchmark grounded in recognition and capability realization. *Accessibility bias* arises when models degrade for the very populations they intend to support, such as non-standard dialect speakers, AAC users, or individuals with atypical gaze patterns (Giuliano, 2024; Alsamh et al., 2024). Epistemic justice frameworks illuminate testimonial and interpretive harms that occur when misrecognition undermines credibility or when educators over-trust algorithmic output. Accountability must therefore include human-in-the-loop governance, explainability that is pedagogically legible, and contestability protocols that allow correction without stigma (Liu et al., 2025; Baheti et al., 2025). Privacy is an inclusion precondition, not merely regulatory compliance, particularly in wearable and XR contexts where biometric, voice, and behavioral telemetry can expose sensitive traits. *Contextual integrity*, data minimization, purpose limitation, and retention constraints anchor responsible deployment. In aggregate, these governance commitments ensure that adaptive mediation remains emancipatory rather than extractive, sustaining dignity and trust within inclusive educational ecosystems.

5. DESIGNING INCLUSIVE ASSISTIVE TECHNOLOGIES THROUGH UDL, PARTICIPATORY DESIGN, AND STANDARDS-AS-INFRASTRUCTURE

5.1 Universal Design for Learning as Multimodal Design Grammar and Cognitive Governance Architecture

Inclusive assistive ecosystems require a design grammar that converts learner variability into planned optionality without generating cognitive overload or stigmatizing differentiation, and *Universal Design for Learning* operates as that translational meta-framework. Within this grammar, representation is not mere format substitution but *functional equivalence engineering*, where text, speech, image, haptics, and symbolic supports are orchestrated under *cognitive load governance* principles to maintain inferential rigor. Action and expression demand alternative performance pathways that align with construct fidelity, integrating voice input, AAC interfaces, multimodal submission formats, and error-tolerant authoring tools without altering epistemic targets (Elsadig et al., 2024; Ramalakshmi et al., 2026). Engagement becomes autonomy-supportive architecture, embedding relevance cues, adjustable challenge calibration, predictable routines, and affect-sensitive pacing. This chapter contributes by reframing UDL as multimodal systems engineering, where optionality is structured through progressive disclosure and scaffold fading, thereby preventing choice overload while preserving agency, competence, and relational belonging across mobile, wearable, and XR modalities.

5.2 Participatory Design, Co-Production, and Design Justice as Epistemic Inclusion Methodologies

User-centered design is insufficient when inclusion is treated as moral infrastructure rather than market differentiation, therefore *participatory design* and *co-production* become epistemic commitments that redistribute authority to lived-experience expertise. Within a *design justice* paradigm, marginalized learners, caregivers, interpreters, and special educators are not test users but co-architects whose experiential knowledge recalibrates problem definitions and usability assumptions (Alam, 2023a; Hong et al., 2024). Such co-production addresses power asymmetries embedded in procurement, vendor dominance, and technocratic governance, aligning with recognition and procedural justice commitments articulated earlier. *Stigma-sensitive design* demands discreet assistive affordances, opt-in visibility controls, and classroom norm-setting to prevent forced disclosure (Toto et al., 2024; Pieriboni et al., 2026). Cultural-linguistic diversity further requires *translanguaging-informed co-design*, treating multilingual repertoires as epistemic assets rather than deviation from a standardized norm. Table 4 consolidates these theoretical commitments into implementable design principles mapped across modalities, revealing how justice-oriented constructs translate into concrete mobile, wearable, and XR design constraints.

Table 4. Theory-Informed Design Principles for Inclusive Assistive Ecosystems

Design Principle and Justice Frame	Theoretical Justification and Cognitive-Ethical Anchor	Mobile Implementation Characteristics	Wearable and XR Implementation Characteristics	Anti-Patterns and Mitigation Logics
Functional Equivalence and Construct Fidelity	*Validity preservation*, *evidence-centered design*, capability realization ensuring removal of irrelevant barriers without altering epistemic targets	Multimodal content switching, semantic compression controls, offline caching aligned with curricular sequencing	Alternative interaction grammars, motion-sensitivity safeguards, sensory load modulation preserving task integrity	Superficial format substitution that alters inferential demand, mitigated by teacher-facing construct alignment checkpoints
Autonomy-Supportive Optionality Architecture	*Self-determination theory*, scaffold fading, autonomy-preserving personalization	Adjustable prompt intensity, progressive disclosure menus, user-controlled modality toggles	Intensity sliders for haptic or auditory cues, opt-out without penalty in immersive sessions	Over-prompting leading to dependency, mitigated by time-bound fading algorithms and mastery-linked recalibration
Recognition and Dignity-Preserving Interaction	Recognition justice, identity-safe participation, stigma-sensitive interface theory	Discreet accessibility features, neutral iconography, customizable visibility settings	Private feedback channels, non-public cueing, avatar customization reflecting diverse identities	Visible labeling or forced disclosure, mitigated by configurable privacy layers and classroom norm codification

continued on following page

Table 4. Continued

Design Principle and Justice Frame	Theoretical Justification and Cognitive-Ethical Anchor	Mobile Implementation Characteristics	Wearable and XR Implementation Characteristics	Anti-Patterns and Mitigation Logics
Interoperability and Accommodation Continuity	*Person-environment fit*, socio-technical coherence, path-dependency avoidance	Cross-platform state persistence, unified identity management, low-friction authentication	Synchronized accommodation data across immersive sessions and wearable feedback systems	Fragmented toolchains increasing cognitive overhead, mitigated by standards-aligned procurement and API harmonization
Culturally Sustaining and Translanguaging Integration	Culturally sustaining pedagogy, funds-of-knowledge framework, epistemic pluralism	Bilingual interface layers, community language lexicons, adaptive vocabulary scaffolds	Multilingual narration tracks, gesture-language mapping diversity, culturally contextualized immersive narratives	Linguistic assimilation bias, mitigated by community co-design and dynamic language repertoire toggles

Table 4 demonstrates that inclusive design is not a feature checklist but a justice-aligned systems architecture that integrates cognitive theory, sociological recognition constructs, and governance foresight. Each principle functions as a constraint on design exuberance, preventing technological overreach that might undermine autonomy, privacy, or construct validity. The anti-pattern column clarifies that misapplication often arises from good intentions executed without epistemic calibration, such as adding redundant modalities that inflate cognitive load or embedding culturally narrow narratives within immersive spaces. By embedding mitigation logics directly into design protocols, institutions can operationalize inclusion as structured coherence rather than ad hoc accommodation. This table thus serves as a normative-technical bridge linking participatory epistemology with engineering practice, ensuring that assistive innovation remains anchored to dignity, capability expansion, and assessment integrity.

5.3 Accessibility Standards, Interoperability Regimes, and Procurement as Pedagogic Governance

Accessibility standards must be reframed from compliance artifacts into pedagogic infrastructure that determines whether assistive affordances persist across institutional layers. Accessible authoring becomes a lifecycle commitment, integrating captioning, alternative text, semantic markup, and navigational coherence from content creation through archival retrieval (Kchaou et al., 2025; Dhouib et al., 2025). Interoperability is not merely technical compatibility but *socio-technical alignment*, ensuring that accommodation data, scaffold intensity settings, and modality preferences persist across devices, grade levels, and assessment platforms. Procurement thus becomes pedagogic governance in disguise, where contractual clauses mandate auditability, remediation timelines, documentation transparency, and low-friction teacher workflows (Irigoyen et al., 2024; Thakur et al., 2024). *Total cost of ownership* emerges as an equity determinant, as underfunded maintenance or training gaps produce de facto exclusion. Standards-aligned procurement mitigates vendor lock-in and path dependency, ensuring that assistive ecosystems remain adaptable, future-proof, and coherent with evolving curricular and regulatory landscapes.

5.4 Inclusive Assessment Integrity, Neurodiversity-Affirming Constraints, and Trauma-Informed Design Parameters

Inclusive assistive design must converge with *assessment validity theory* to delineate the boundary between accommodation and modification, preserving construct fidelity while removing irrelevant barriers. Fairness is conceptualized as equitable opportunity to demonstrate learning, requiring explicit institutional articulation of which supports are construct-neutral (Alam, 2023b; Bonanno et al., 2025). *Neurodiversity-affirming paradigms* challenge normalization pressures by validating sensory variance, divergent attention profiles, and alternative communication pathways as legitimate human variation rather than pathology. Trauma-informed design adds safety, predictability, and user-controlled pacing as ethical constraints, particularly salient in XR environments where immersive stimuli may trigger distress or cognitive fatigue (Jagatheesaperumal et al., 2024; Navas-Bonilla et al., 2025). Sensory ecology calibration, including adjustable contrast, auditory intensity, and motion parameters, protects dignity and agency. When these constraints are embedded within standards-aligned procurement and participatory co-design, assistive ecosystems evolve into stable infrastructures of belonging, preserving epistemic agency while sustaining rigor across mobile, wearable, and immersive educational contexts.

6. GOVERNANCE, ETHICS, AND POLICY ALIGNMENT FOR ASSISTIVE ECOSYSTEM SUSTAINABILITY

6.1 Institutional Strategy, Organizational Readiness, and Implementation Science Logics

Inclusive assistive ecosystems cannot be sustained through device acquisition alone, they require institutional strategy grounded in *implementation science*, *organizational readiness*, and *systems coherence* constructs. Governance must align curriculum authorities, information technology units, disability services, assessment boards, and safeguarding mechanisms into a unified architecture of responsibility (Karageorgou et al., 2024; Shafik, 2025). *Implementation climate* determines whether assistive innovations are normalized within classroom routines or treated as peripheral add-ons subject to discretionary use. Budgetary structures and *total cost of ownership* calculations function as equity determinants, because maintenance cycles, staff training hours, software updates, and device refresh intervals shape long-term access continuity. *Accommodation continuity governance* ensures that modality preferences, scaffold intensities, and assessment accommodations persist across grade transitions and platform migrations (Bhambri, 2025; Al Shami & Nashwan, 2024). Without role clarity and cross-unit coordination, assistive infrastructures degrade into fragmented toolchains that increase cognitive switching costs and institutional mistrust, undermining the justice commitments articulated earlier in the chapter.

6.2 Responsible Innovation, Risk Governance, and Safety Engineering in Educational Contexts

Responsible deployment of AI-mediated assistive systems demands *risk-based governance* calibrated to proportionality, especially where biometric, gaze, or behavioral telemetry are involved. Institutional accountability frameworks must distribute responsibility across vendors, administrators, and educators, clarifying escalation pathways for malfunction, bias, or data breach (Hong et al., 2025; Baxter & Hainey, 2024). *Safety engineering* concepts such as hazard identification, failure containment, redundancy, and post-incident learning are translatable into educational domains where errors can produce exclusion from assessment or reputational harm. Continuous monitoring, bias auditing, and stakeholder review panels operationalize *responsible innovation* as an ongoing process rather than a pre-launch checklist (Alam, 2023c; Creed et al., 2024). Table 5 consolidates governance domains, decision imperatives, and enforcement mechanisms into a coherent accountability matrix, reinforcing that assistive ecosystems are socio-technical infrastructures requiring anticipatory oversight and iterative recalibration.

Table 5. Governance and Accountability for Inclusive Assistive Systems

Governance Domain and Ethical Frame	Required Institutional Decisions and Policy Articulations	Accountable Stakeholder Configuration	Failure Modes and Systemic Risks	Safeguards, Audit Mechanisms, and Enforcement Protocols
Strategic Alignment and Policy Coherence	Formal articulation of inclusion mandates, accommodation continuity policies, interoperability standards, and procurement criteria	Executive leadership, curriculum boards, IT governance councils	Fragmented mandates leading to inconsistent accommodation persistence and cognitive overload	Cross-unit governance committees, annual policy audits, transparent reporting dashboards
Data Protection and Contextual Integrity Safeguards	Data minimization rules, retention schedules, secondary-use restrictions, consent and assent protocols	Data protection officers, legal counsel, platform vendors	Surveillance drift, biometric misuse, erosion of trust and dignity	Encryption standards, role-based access controls, independent compliance reviews
Algorithmic Fairness and Bias Mitigation	Bias testing thresholds, model transparency standards, performance monitoring across demographic groups	Vendor engineering teams, institutional oversight boards	Accessibility bias, testimonial injustice, unequal degradation for marginalized users	Regular bias audits, stakeholder advisory panels, mandatory remediation timelines
Assessment Integrity and Construct Fidelity Governance	Clear delineation of accommodation versus modification, documentation of construct-preserving supports	Assessment authorities, instructional designers, teachers	Construct drift, unfair advantage claims, invalid score interpretation	Validity review panels, teacher-facing guidance documents, appeal mechanisms
Professional Capacity and Ethical Competence Development	Accessibility literacy training, interpretive competence for AI outputs, boundary-setting norms	Human resource units, professional development coordinators	Over-reliance on automation, misinterpretation of adaptive feedback, deskilling	Structured certification programs, reflective practice cycles, peer review protocols

Table 5 operationalizes responsible innovation as a distributed accountability ecosystem rather than a singular compliance task. Each governance domain intersects with normative justice commitments, cognitive integrity, and socio-technical coherence. Strategic alignment ensures that assistive tools remain embedded within curricular and assessment architectures, preventing ad hoc usage that destabilizes equity goals (Beach et al., 2026; Örün & Türk, 2026). Data protection safeguards protect dignity and relational trust, particularly in contexts involving voice, biometric, or gaze data streams. Algorithmic fairness oversight mitigates accessibility bias that could disproportionately degrade performance for marginalized learners. Assessment governance protects construct fidelity and preempts reputational harm from misaligned accommodations (Chiew et al., 2024; Kapralos et al., 2024). Professional capacity development stabilizes human-in-the-loop oversight, ensuring that educators interpret adaptive outputs critically rather than deferring to algorithmic authority. Together, these safeguards convert abstract ethical principles into enforceable institutional practices that sustain inclusive assistive ecosystems across evolving technological landscapes.

6.3 Ethical Frameworks, Relational Autonomy, and Data Justice Imperatives

Ethical governance of assistive AI in education requires a synthesis of *principlism*, *care ethics*, and *relational autonomy* constructs that recognize learners as interdependent agents rather than isolated decision-makers. Recognition justice mandates stigma-sensitive deployment and identity-safe defaults, preventing labeling harms that undermine belonging (Memisevic & Hadžić, 2025; Hutson & Hutson, 2024). *Data justice* reframes privacy as distributive fairness, addressing disproportionate surveillance of marginalized populations and ensuring equitable burden-sharing in data extraction. Ethical tensions arise between personalization and profiling, support and control, safety and privacy, necessitating proportionality analysis and contestability mechanisms (Srivathsa et al., 2025; Sharma et al., 2025). Institutional trust functions as a mediating construct, because learners and caregivers must believe that assistive systems operate in their interest. Transparent recourse pathways, meaningful consent practices, and participatory oversight boards stabilize this trust ecology, reinforcing that ethical legitimacy is sustained through procedural fairness and inclusive deliberation rather than technological sophistication alone.

6.4 Policy Ecosystems, Interoperability Futures, and Scalable Equity Architecture

Scalable inclusion depends on policy ecosystems that harmonize accessibility standards, data protection regimes, inclusive education mandates, and procurement governance into a coherent regulatory lattice. *Interoperability* must extend beyond technical compatibility to encompass semantic alignment of accommodation data and cross-platform state persistence, preventing vendor lock-in that recreates exclusion through path dependency (Ursachi et al., 2025; Alam, 2022). Child rights principles and contextual integrity norms guide meaningful consent and retention policies, especially for high-sensitivity data streams in wearable and XR environments. Future-proofing requires modular architectures, open standards, and adaptive regulatory clauses capable of evolving alongside technological innovation (Poggianti et al., 2025). Equity impact assessments become routine components of deployment cycles, evaluating distributional effects before scaling. In this governance architecture, assistive ecosystems are stabilized as durable public infrastructures, capable of sustaining dignity, autonomy, and epistemic agency across global educational contexts characterized by technological heterogeneity and socio-economic disparity.

7. CONCLUSION

7.1 Integrative Synthesis of the Conceptual Architecture for Inclusive Assistive Ecosystems

This chapter has advanced a systems-level reconceptualization of AI-mediated mobile, wearable, and XR assistive technologies as justice-anchored, theory-grounded, and governance-bound infrastructures rather than peripheral accommodations. By integrating *capability realization*, *recognition justice*, and *procedural fairness* with *cognitive load governance*, *self-regulated learning*, and *person-environment fit*, the analysis has demonstrated that accessibility is not a feature property but a relational achievement emerging from socio-technical coherence. Assistive mediation reshapes epistemic access, redistributes cognitive labor through *distributed cognition*, and reconfigures participation hierarchies, thereby demanding careful calibration to preserve construct fidelity and autonomy. The ecosystem perspective has clarified that inclusion failures often arise at layer boundaries between interface, pedagogy, assessment, and policy, while the governance matrix has shown that privacy, accountability, and professional competence are preconditions for dignity-preserving deployment. Collectively, these constructs form a unified conceptual architecture in which multimodal intelligence, scaffold calibration, and interoperability operate within a normative envelope that secures belonging and epistemic agency across diverse global contexts.

7.2 Implications for Research, Practice, Industry, and Policy in a Multimodal Future

The implications of this synthesis are multidimensional and transdisciplinary. For research, conceptual refinement is required around *accommodation continuity*, *access friction*, and *epistemic mobility*, ensuring that theoretical models capture participation quality rather than mere access counts. For practice, educators must operationalize UDL as multimodal systems engineering, cultivating interpretive competence for AI outputs and embedding scaffold-fading logics within everyday routines. For industry, human-centered design must be treated as a non-negotiable constraint, with adjustable assistance, explainable mediation, and bias auditing embedded into core architecture rather than appended post hoc. For policy, interoperability mandates, data minimization protocols, and equity impact assessments must converge into scalable governance ecosystems capable of sustaining inclusive infrastructures across heterogeneous technological environments. The future trajectory of inclusive education thus depends on embedding *responsible innovation*, *relational autonomy*, and *data justice* into the design, deployment, and regulation of assistive systems, ensuring that emerging multimodal ecologies expand real freedoms to learn rather than reproduce exclusion through sophisticated digital architectures.

REFERENCES

Abrar, M., Khalid, S., & Ullah, R. (2026). The intersection of artificial intelligence and assistive technologies in the diagnosis and intervention of mental health conditions. *Artificial Intelligence Review*, *59*(2), 40. DOI: 10.1007/s10462-025-11447-9

Adako, O. P., Adeusi, O. C., & Alaba, P. A. (2025). AI in autism education: A review of collaborative and longitudinal approaches. *Disability and Rehabilitation. Assistive Technology*, •••, 1–26. DOI: 10.1080/17483107.2025.2579825 PMID: 41175378

Ahuja, N. J., Dutt, S., Choudhary, S. L., & Kumar, M. (2025). Intelligent tutoring system in education for disabled learners using human–computer interaction and augmented reality. *International Journal of Human-Computer Interaction*, *41*(3), 1804–1816. DOI: 10.1080/10447318.2022.2124359

Al Shami, A., & Nashwan, A. J. (2024). Assistive technology in rehabilitation: exploring historical models, current innovations, and emerging trends. *The Palgrave Encyclopedia of Disability*, 1-8. DOI: 10.1007/978-3-031-40858-8_415-1

Alam, A. (2022). Impact of university's human resources practices on professors' occupational performance: empirical evidence from India's higher education sector. In *Inclusive businesses in developing economies: Converging people, profit, and corporate citizenship* (pp. 107–131). Springer International Publishing., DOI: 10.1007/978-3-031-12217-0_6

Alam, A. (2023a). Media multitasking with M-learning technology in real-time classroom learning: Analysing the dynamics in formal educational settings for the future of E-learning in India. In *2023 2nd International Conference on Smart Technologies and Systems for Next Generation Computing (ICSTSN)* (pp. 1-6). IEEE. DOI: 10.1109/ICSTSN57873.2023.10151509

Alam, A. (2023b). The secret sauce of student success: Cracking the code by navigating the path to personalized learning with educational data mining. In *2023 2nd International Conference on Smart Technologies and Systems for Next Generation Computing (ICSTSN)* (pp. 1-8). IEEE. DOI: 10.1109/ICSTSN57873.2023.10151558

Alam, A. (2023c). Intelligence unleashed: An argument for AI-enabled learning ecologies with real world examples of today and a peek into the future. In *International Conference on Innovations in Computer Science, Electronics & Electrical Engineering*-2022 (Vol. 2717, No. 1, p. 030001). AIP Publishing LLC. DOI: 10.1063/5.0129803

Alam, A., & Mohanty, A. (2022, December). Facial analytics or virtual avatars: competencies and design considerations for student-teacher interaction in AI-powered online education for effective classroom engagement. In *International Conference on Communication, Networks and Computing* (pp. 252-265). Cham: Springer Nature Switzerland. DOI: 10.1007/978-3-031-43145-6_21

Alam, A., & Mohanty, A. (2023, January). Learning on the move: a pedagogical framework for state-of-the-art mobile learning. In *International Conference on Data Management, Analytics & Innovation* (pp. 735-748). Singapore: Springer Nature Singapore. DOI: 10.1007/978-981-99-1414-2_52

Alam, A., & Mohanty, A. (2024). Integrated constructive robotics in education (ICRE) model: A paradigmatic framework for transformative learning in educational ecosystem. *Cogent Education, 11*(1), 2324487. DOI: 10.1080/2331186X.2024.2324487

Alsamh, M. H., Hawbani, A., Kumar, S., & Alsamhi, S. H. (2024). Multisensory metaverse-6G: A new paradigm of commerce and education. *IEEE Access : Practical Innovations, Open Solutions, 12*, 75657–75677. DOI: 10.1109/ACCESS.2024.3392838

Ashour, A., & Elkhawaga, G. O. (2026). Innovations in geriatric care: Leveraging technology to meet the needs of an aging world, a narrative review. *The Journal of the Egyptian Public Health Association, 101*(1), 2. DOI: 10.1186/s42506-025-00203-0 PMID: 41677990

Baheti, M., Tyagi, B., Kumar, V., Prabavathy, M., & Sharma, A. (2025, August). Learning of languages through Computer Assisted technologies & IOT enabled devices. In *2025 World Skills Conference on Universal Data Analytics and Sciences (WorldSUAS)* (pp. 1-6). IEEE. DOI: 10.1109/WorldSUAS66815.2025.11199122

Baxter, G., & Hainey, T. (2024). Using immersive technologies to enhance the student learning experience. *Interactive Technology and Smart Education, 21*(3), 403–425. DOI: 10.1108/ITSE-05-2023-0078

Beach, P., Lytle, B., Ness, N., Leung, S., Lieberman, L., & Peng, C. (2026). Navigating innovation: The lived experiences of orientation & mobility specialists using assistive technology and virtual reality. *Disability and Rehabilitation. Assistive Technology*, •••, 1–13. DOI: 10.1080/17483107.2026.2626466 PMID: 41672743

Bhambri, P. (2025). Virtual and augmented reality for immersive learning experiences: Practical applications and challenges. *Architecting the digital future: Platforms, design, and application*, 17-46. DOI: 10.4018/979-8-3693-2973-3.ch002

Bonanno, M., Saracino, B., Ciancarelli, I., Panza, G., Manuli, A., Morone, G., & Calabrò, R. S. (2025, July). Assistive technologies for individuals with a disability from a neurological condition: A narrative review on the multimodal integration. In *Healthcare* (Vol. 13, No. 13, p. 1580). MDPI. DOI: 10.3390/healthcare13131580

Carreon, A., Mosher, M., Goldman, S., Smith, S., & Smith, B. (2025). A ten-year review of the Journal of Special Education Technology: Innovations and trends for individuals with disabilities. *Journal of Special Education Technology, 01626434251349414*. Advance online publication. DOI: 10.1177/01626434251349414

Chamola, V., Peelam, M. S., Mittal, U., Hassija, V., Singh, A., Pareek, R., Mangal, P., Sangwan, D., de Albuquerque, V. H. C., Mahmud, M., & Brown, D. J. (2025). Metaverse for education: Developments, challenges, and future direction. *Computer Applications in Engineering Education*, *33*(3), e70018. DOI: 10.1002/cae.70018

Chen, J., Yi, C., Du, H., Niyato, D., Kang, J., Cai, J., & Shen, X. (2024). A revolution of personalized healthcare: Enabling human digital twin with mobile AIGC. *IEEE Network*, *38*(6), 234–242. DOI: 10.1109/MNET.2024.3366560

Chiew, T. K., Khoo, S., Ansari, P., & Kiruthika, U. (2024). Mobile and wearable technologies for persons with disabilities: A bibliometric analysis (2000–2021). *Disability and Rehabilitation. Assistive Technology*, *19*(3), 994–1002. DOI: 10.1080/17483107.2022.2138996 PMID: 36306172

Creed, C., Al-Kalbani, M., Theil, A., Sarcar, S., & Williams, I. (2024). Inclusive augmented and virtual reality: A research agenda. *International Journal of Human-Computer Interaction*, *40*(20), 6200–6219. DOI: 10.1080/10447318.2023.2247614

Daineko, Y., & Seitnur, A. (2025). Artificial intelligence for predictive health analytics: Challenges, methods, and immersive system integration. *Procedia Computer Science*, *265*, 636–641. DOI: 10.1016/j.procs.2025.07.232

Desmarchelier, B., Djellal, F., Gallouj, F., & Gallouj, N. (2025). Beyond the reverse product cycle: An exploration of the digital, social and spatial transformation of libraries. *Research Policy*, *54*(8), 105297. DOI: 10.1016/j.respol.2025.105297

Dhouib, A., Fadi Hijab, M. H., Chemnad, K., Al-Thani, D., & Othman, A. (2025). Advancing inclusive smart learning environments: A systematic review of technologies, challenges, and best practices for students with disabilities. *Smart Learning Environments*, *12*(1), 70. DOI: 10.1186/s40561-025-00416-y

Elsadig, M., Alohali, M. A., Ibrahim, A. O., & Abulfaraj, A. W. (2024). Roles of blockchain in the metaverse: Concepts, taxonomy, recent advances, enabling technologies, and open research issues. *IEEE Access : Practical Innovations, Open Solutions*, *12*, 38410–38435. DOI: 10.1109/ACCESS.2024.3367014

Fong, K. N. K., Hai, E. Y. K., Zhang, J. J., & Lam, W. W. T. (2025). Use of advanced technologies in occupational therapy. In *Occupational Therapy in East Asia* (pp. 343–364). Routledge., DOI: 10.4324/9781032721170-18

Gholizadeh HamlAbadi, K., Laamarti, F., & El Saddik, A.Gholizadeh HamlAbadi. (2024). Meta-review on brain-computer interface (BCI) in the metaverse. *ACM Transactions on Multimedia Computing Communications and Applications*, *20*(12), 1–42. DOI: 10.1145/3696109

Ghugar, U., Nayak, R., & Awotunde, J. B. (2025). Enabling technologies for seamless Human-Machine interaction in industry 5.0. In *Computational Intelligence for Analysis of Trends in Industry 4.0 and 5.0* (pp. 215–240). Auerbach Publications., DOI: 10.1201/9781003533023-9

Girhe, T., Pandya, E., & Chacko, A. M. (2024, September). Sahayak: Affordable AI enabled Assistive Technology for Intellectually Disabled. In *2024 IEEE International Conference on Signal Processing, Informatics, Communication and Energy Systems (SPICES)* (pp. 1-5). IEEE. DOI: 10.1109/SPICES62143.2024.10779644

Giuliano, R. (2024). From 5G-advanced to 6G in 2030: New services, 3GPP advances, and enabling technologies. *IEEE Access : Practical Innovations, Open Solutions*, *12*, 63238–63270. DOI: 10.1109/ACCESS.2024.3396361

Gowrishankar, R., Dhaarani, S., Sreejaruhasini, D., & Balavignesh, P. (2025, November). Smart Assistive Wearable Glasses for the Visually Impaired. In *2025 5th International Conference on Evolutionary Computing and Mobile Sustainable Networks (ICECMSN)* (pp. 1-5). IEEE. DOI: 10.1109/ICECMSN68058.2025.11383269

Hamid, M. S., Abo Hamza, E. G., Bedewy, D., Elsiddig, F. M. E., AlShammari, S. A., Bakhiet, S. F., & Mohamed, N. I. A. (2025, August). Impact of digital competencies and assistive technologies on learning outcomes for students with learning disabilities in Kingdom of Saudi Arabia: a systematic review. In *Frontiers in education* (Vol. 10, p. 1640556). Frontiers Media SA. DOI: 10.3389/feduc.2025.1640556

Hicks, E., Park, S., Mavrovounioti, A., Du, W., Hu, J., Na, K., Serrano, N., Munoz, R. C., Ankrah, E., Min, A., Johnson, J., & Hayes, G. R. (2025). Informing the Design of Mobile and Wearable Technology for Noise Sensitivity. *Proceedings of the ACM on Human-Computer Interaction*, *9*(5), 1–26. DOI: 10.1145/3743725

Hong, F., Wang, L., & Li, C. Z. (2024). Adaptive mobile cloud computing on college physical training education based on virtual reality. *Wireless Networks, 30*(7), 6427–6450. DOI: 10.1007/s11276-023-03450-1

Hong, H., Dai, L., & Zheng, X. (2025). Advances in wearable sensors for learning analytics: Trends, challenges, and prospects. *Sensors (Basel), 25*(9), 2714. DOI: 10.3390/s25092714 PMID: 40363153

Hutson, J., & Hutson, P. (2024). Immersive technologies. In *Inclusive smart museums: Engaging neurodiverse audiences and enhancing cultural heritage* (pp. 153–228). Springer Nature Switzerland., DOI: 10.1007/978-3-031-43615-4_5

Irigoyen, E., Larrea, M., & Graña, M. (2024). A narrative review of haptic technologies and their value for training, rehabilitation, and the education of persons with special needs. *Sensors (Basel), 24*(21), 6946. DOI: 10.3390/s24216946 PMID: 39517844

Jagatheesaperumal, S. K., Ahmad, K., Al-Fuqaha, A., & Qadir, J. (2024). Advancing education through extended reality and internet of everything enabled metaverses: Applications, challenges, and open issues. *IEEE Transactions on Learning Technologies, 17*, 1120–1139. DOI: 10.1109/TLT.2024.3358859

Kapralos, B., Uribe-Quevedo, A., & Dubrowski, A. (2024). Immersive technologies for medical education. In *Encyclopedia of computer graphics and games* (pp. 921–928). Springer International Publishing., DOI: 10.1007/978-3-031-23161-2_130

Karageorgou, E., Adam, S., Doukakis, S., & Vlamos, P. (2024). Digital Accessibility for Students with Disabilities and Inclusive Learning in Education. In *International Genomics, Neuroscience, Therapeutics and Data Innovation Summit* (pp. 417-424). Cham: Springer Nature Switzerland. DOI: 10.1007/978-3-032-03402-1_44

Katke, S. R., & Pacharaney, U. (2024, November). Smart Solutions for Visual Impairment by AI-Based Assistive Devices. In *2024 2nd DMIHER International Conference on Artificial Intelligence in Healthcare, Education and Industry (IDICAIEI)* (pp. 1-5). IEEE. DOI: 10.1109/IDICAIEI61867.2024.10842872

Kchaou, M., Munusamy, Y., Alharthi, K. A., & Al-Mahmodi, A. F. (2025). Industry 5.0 adaptation for disability-inclusive healthcare: A review of emergent and AI technologies for assistive digital health. *Digital Health, 11*, 20552076251395558. DOI: 10.1177/20552076251395558 PMID: 41229932

Liginlal, D., & Al-Emadi, S. (2026). Digital accessibility and equity: The need for stronger regulations and the imperative of innovation. *Universal Access in the Information Society, 25*(2), 37. DOI: 10.1007/s10209-025-01305-4

Liu, J., Bleakney, A. W., Cheung, W. C., Yu, H., Cao, C., & Jan, Y. K. (2025). Emerging assistive technologies in paralympic sports: A systematic review. *Disability and Rehabilitation. Assistive Technology*, •••, 1–28. DOI: 10.1080/17483107.2025.2597408 PMID: 41403368

Liu, Z., He, Y., Demian, P., & Osmani, M. (2024). Immersive technology and building information modeling (BIM) for sustainable smart cities. *Buildings (Basel, Switzerland)*, *14*(6), 1765. DOI: 10.3390/buildings14061765

Malviya, R., & Rajput, S. (2025). AI-driven innovations in assistive technology for people with disabilities. In *Advances and Insights into AI-Created Disability Supports* (pp. 61–77). Springer Nature Singapore., DOI: 10.1007/978-981-96-6069-8_4

Memisevic, H., & Hadžić, S. (2025). Assistive Technology in Inclusive Education. In *The Palgrave Encyclopedia of Disability* (pp. 1–8). Springer Nature Switzerland., DOI: 10.1007/978-3-031-40858-8_508-1

Naik, A. S. (2024, June). Assistive Technology in Banking. In *2024 15th International Conference on Computing Communication and Networking Technologies (ICCCNT)* (pp. 1-6). IEEE. DOI: 10.1109/ICCCNT61001.2024.10724888

Navas-Bonilla, C. D. R., Guerra-Arango, J. A., Oviedo-Guado, D. A., & Murillo-Noriega, D. E. (2025, February). Inclusive education through technology: a systematic review of types, tools and characteristics. In *Frontiers in Education* (Vol. 10, p. 1527851). Frontiers Media SA. DOI: 10.3389/feduc.2025.1527851

Örün, Ö., & Türk, M. (2026). Bridging the Gap: The Role of Immersive Technologies for Learners With Disabilities. In *Practical Perspectives on Inclusive and Immersive Learning Environments* (pp. 27-58). IGI Global Scientific Publishing. DOI: 10.4018/979-8-3373-5188-9.ch002

Perry, N., Sun, C., Munro, M., Boulton, K. A., & Guastella, A. J. (2024). AI technology to support adaptive functioning in neurodevelopmental conditions in everyday environments: A systematic review. *NPJ Digital Medicine*, *7*(1), 370. DOI: 10.1038/s41746-024-01355-7 PMID: 39702672

Pieriboni, G., Buzzi, M., & Leporini, B. (2026). Stem education and ICT-enhanced tools for students with disabilities: A five-year review. *Universal Access in the Information Society*, *25*(1), 3. DOI: 10.1007/s10209-025-01282-8

Poggianti, C., Chessa, S., Pelagatti, S., & Kocian, A. (2025). Immersive technologies for inclusive digital education: A systematic survey. *Human Behavior and Emerging Technologies*, *2025*(1), 8888303. DOI: 10.1155/hbe2/8888303

Ramalakshmi, K., Kumari, L. K., Mohan, B., Gunturi, S. K., Santhoshkumar, S. P., Krishnan, R. S., & Raj, J. R. F. (2026). Harnessing Immersive Technologies: Insights Into Augmented and Virtual Reality Applications. In *AI Applications in Instructional Education Strategies* (pp. 171-188). IGI Global Scientific Publishing. DOI: 10.4018/979-8-3373-0598-1.ch007

Richelli, A., Stocchetti, N., Gasparini, C., Montanari, S., Rozzini, L., & Gringoli, F. (2025, November). Towards Fully Accessible Digital Content: A Haptic-VR Workflow for Blind Users. In *Proceedings of the 3rd ACM Workshop on Mobile Immersive Computing, Networking, and Systems* (pp. 9-14). DOI: 10.1145/3742889.3768346

Riyat, M. K., Kakkar, R. K., & Kakkar, A. (2025). Creating Immersive Learning Experiences in Education Domain Through Virtual and Augmented Reality. In *Enhancing Learning Experiences With Digital Tools: AI, ChatGPT, and Virtual and Augmented Reality* (pp. 123–156). IGI Global Scientific Publishing., DOI: 10.4018/979-8-3693-9811-1.ch006

Rybenská, K., Knapová, L., Janiš, K., Kühnová, J., Cimler, R., & Elavsky, S. (2024). SMART technologies in older adult care: A scoping review and guide for caregivers. *Journal of Enabling Technologies*, *18*(4), 200–222. DOI: 10.1108/JET-05-2023-0016

Santos, J., Vieira, M., Fernandes, D., Félix, J., Rodrigues, W., Soares, F., & Nascimento, T. H. (2025, November). Low-Cost Immersive Molecule Visualization from Hand-Drawn Smartwatch Input for Virtual Reality Learning. In *International Symposium on Visual Computing* (pp. 236-246). Cham: Springer Nature Switzerland. DOI: 10.1007/978-3-032-14495-9_18

Shafik, W. (2025). Emerging Trends and Technological Innovations and People with Disabilities and the Marginalized. *Global Sustainable Transition with Inclusion: A Focus on the People with Disabilities and the Marginalized*, 293-325. DOI: 10.1007/978-981-96-6557-0_11

Sharma, S., Dureja, S., Saini, D., Jose, R., Pant, R., & Singh, A. (2025). Empowering impaired learners: Technological advancements in higher education. *Technology and Disability*, *37*(2), 123–136. DOI: 10.1177/10554181251313711

Srivathsa, B. S., Pandey, H., & Naganandini, G. (2025). Future Trends in Education: The Impact of AI, Data Science, and Immersive Technologies. In *Driving Quality Education Through AI and Data Science* (pp. 139-164). IGI Global Scientific Publishing. DOI: 10.4018/979-8-3693-8292-9.ch007

Thabet, S., Ateya, A. A., ElAffendi, M., & Abo-Zahhad, M. (2025). MEC and SDN Enabling Technologies, Design Challenges, and Future Directions of Tactile Internet and Immersive Communications. *Future Internet, 17*(11), 494. DOI: 10.3390/fi17110494

Thakur, N., Chouskey, P., Bansal, N., & Chopra, M. (2024). Systematic review of recent trends of Industry 5.0 with assistive technologies in higher education and smart healthcare. *Applied assistive technologies and informatics for students with disabilities*, 277-299. DOI: 10.1007/978-981-97-0914-4_16

Tohănean, D. I., Vulpe, A. M., Mijaica, R., & Alexe, D. I. (2025). Embedding digital technologies (AI and ICT) into physical education: A systematic review of innovations, pedagogical impact, and challenges. *Applied Sciences (Basel, Switzerland), 15*(17), 9826. DOI: 10.3390/app15179826

Toto, G. A., Marinelli, C. V., Cavioni, V., Di Furia, M., Traetta, L., Iuso, S., & Petito, A. (2024). What is the role of technologies for inclusive education? A systematic review. In *International conference on higher education learning methodologies and technologies online* (pp. 533-565). Springer, Cham. DOI: 10.1007/978-3-031-67351-1_36

Ursachi, T. M., Brezoaie, R. E., & Dascalu, M. I. (2025, June). Emerging Technologies in Immersive Learning: A Systematic Review of Trends, Challenges, and Opportunities. In *2025 IEEE 2nd International Conference on Blockchain, Smart Healthcare and Emerging Technologies (SmartBlock4Health)* (pp. 1-9). IEEE. DOI: 10.1109/SmartBlock4Health64843.2025.11189574

Wang, Z. (2024). Artificial intelligence in dance education: Using immersive technologies for teaching dance skills. *Technology in Society*, *77*, 102579. DOI: 10.1016/j.techsoc.2024.102579

Wild, G., Nanyonga, A., Iqbal, A., Bano, S., Somerville, A., & Pollock, L. (2025). Lightweight and mobile artificial intelligence and immersive technologies in aviation. *Visual Computing for Industry, Biomedicine, and Art*, *8*(1), 21. DOI: 10.1186/s42492-025-00203-z PMID: 40900374

Xu, J., Zhai, X., Chen, N. S., Ghani, U., Istenic, A., & Xin, J. (2025). Integrating AI-Driven Wearable Metaverse Technologies into Ubiquitous Blended Learning: A Framework Based on Embodied Interaction and Multi-Agent Collaboration. *Education Sciences*, *15*(7), 900. DOI: 10.3390/educsci15070900

Yao, L. (2025). The role of technology in supporting communication and learning in children with autism. In *Connecting Ideas, Cultures, and Communities* (pp. 473-478). Routledge. DOI: 10.1201/9781003591511-74

Chapter 4
Assistive and AI-Driven Technologies for Visually Impaired Students

Chinna Suresh
http://orcid.org/0000-0002-3389-1116
SASTRA (Deemed to be) University, India

Lalithabala Boopathi
http://orcid.org/0009-0005-1152-0006
SASTRA (Deemed to be) University, India

Devaki Varadharajan
http://orcid.org/0000-0002-7109-0205
SASTRA (Deemed to be) University, India

Murathoti Rajendra Nath Babu
http://orcid.org/0000-0001-8904-383X
Nagaland University, India

ABSTRACT

This chapter explores how artificial intelligence is reshaping assistive technologies to improve access to education by visually impaired students. It specifically tends to analyze the global context of visual impairment, review key international frameworks such as the CRPD 2006, Marrakesh Treaty 2016, and SDGs 2015, and evaluate the role and potential of AI based technologies in promoting inclusive education. Understanding the global burden of visual impairment and the functional aspect of the eye provides essential context for these developments.AI based innovations such as intelligent screen readers, text to speech systems, audio navigation tools, smart white canes, wearable devices, and real time object recognition applications support

DOI: 10.4018/979-8-2600-2716-5.ch004

2027, IGI Global Scientific Publishing. Copying or distributing in print or electronic forms without written permission of IGI Global Scientific Publishing is prohibited. Use of this chapter to ative artificial intelligence (AI) technologies is expressly prohibited. The publisher reserves all rights to license its use for generative AI training and machine learning model development.

independence and personalized learning. Despite their promise, they pose ethical, social, and implementation challenges relating to privacy, bias, digital inequality, safety and teacher preparedness. This chapter synthesizes global data, and policy frameworks to highlight the opportunities and challenges for equitable adoption.

INTRODUCTION

The introduction of artificial intelligence into assistive technologies offers a profound paradigm on improving education delivery and achievement among the students with a visual impairment. With the changing nature of digital ecosystems, AI powered applications are transforming the way learners with visual impairments engage with information, navigate the learning process, and engage in academic tasks (Elshaer et al., 2025). These inventions are much wider than conventional accommodations as they are dynamic, adaptable, and multisensory learning experience that could not have been imagined before. In the modern educational systems where the digital material has become a principal of the teaching process, the contribution of the AI empowered assistive technologies has become vital to guarantee equal participation (Devaki et al., 2025).

Visual impairment is one of the major public health and educational concerns that are experienced globally. Regardless of medical care and technological advancements, many millions of people suffer preventable or untreated vision loss, which has a direct impact on their learning possibilities, self-sufficiency, and social engagement. Schools, especially in the low and middle income countries, are sometimes not able to offer easily available materials, qualified staff and accommodating learning facilities for visually impaired students (Anokye et al., 2025; Fitas, 2025). This disparity brings out the urgency of scalable and technology driven solutions that can assist learners despite geographical and socioeconomic limitations.

Table 1. Data of Visual Impairment Personals Across the Global up to 2023-2024

Indicator	Global Estimate	Reported Year
People with near or distance vision impairment	Minimum 2.2 billion	2023
Preventable or Unaddressed Vision impairment	1 billion Cases	2023
Leading global causes of vision impairment	Cataract (94 million) Refractive errors (88.4 million) Age related muscular degeneration (8 million) Glaucoma (7.7 million) Diabetic retinopathy (826 million)	2023

continued on following page

Table 1. Continued

Indicator	Global Estimate	Reported Year
Effective coverage of refractive error correction (Received Pair of spectacles)	36 per cent	2023
Effective coverage of cataract treatment (Received quality surgery)	17 per cent	2023
Global blindness prevalence (modelled)	43 million	2020-2021
Moderate to severe vision impairment (MSVI)	295 million	2020-2021
Mild vision impairment	258 million	2020-2021
Near vision impairment (presbyopia)	510 million people	2019-2023
Highest burden regions	South Asia and Sub Saharan Africa	2020-2023
Projected global sight loss by 2050	Over 1.7 billion people by 2050	2019
Preventable or treatable proportion of vision loss	90 per cent	2021-2023
Gender Distribution	Higher prevalence in women across all severity levels	2020

(Sources: World Health Organization Fact Sheet-Blindness and Vision Impairment (2023); WHO World Report on Vision (2019); International Agency for the Prevention of Blindness (IAPB) Vision Atlas (2021); Vision Loss Expert Group global estimates (2021); Lancet Global Health Commission on Global Eye Health (2021)).

Table 1 is a summarized version of the latest international statistics on visual impairment, which points to the magnitude and sophistication of the problem. The above statistics indicate the world eye health situation that is characterized by intense and significant inequalities in terms of access to basic treatment (Que et al., 2025). These global trends also have a direct impact on educational disadvantage, as children begin their educational journey with untreated vision problems that hinder their ability to read and participate in the classroom. While the extent of vision impairment is significant, it is important to note that it is a preventable issue. Although vision impairment is very extensive, from the above statistics it is learned that most of the cases can be avoided which highlights systemic failures and not inevitable factors. The differences in time zone of the region and gender inequalities highlight how differences in social, cultural, geographical and economic factors influence access to timely eye care. Overall, the statistics support the seriousness of enhancing early intervention, equal service provision, and technology based support particularly in the field of education where visual access is critical.

These international statistics are also directly translated to disadvantages in education. The fact that high numbers of children are going to school with undiagnosed or uncorrected problems with their vision leads to late acquisition of literacy, poor classroom performance and academic accomplishment. Students in areas where there is a poor access to eye care find it difficult to read regular print, to copyboard, to get around school.

The artificial intelligence empowered assistive technologies for instance *intelligent screen readers*, *real time object recognition systems*, *tactile graphics generators*, and *voice interactive* learning application are proving to be able to fill the above highlighted gaps. These technologies add to the access of electronic learning resources, and autonomy, confidence, and active engagement of visually impaired students in individualised or personalised learning environments as per their pace of learning and educational needs (Pamuji et al., 2023).

International Frameworks that Safeguard the Rights of Visually Impaired

International frameworks like **UN Convention on the Rights of Persons with Disabilities (CRPD, 2006)** and the **Marrakesh Treaty (2016)** have played a major role in support of rights of visually impaired persons and their principles are closely ailed with Sustainable Development Goals (SDGs) (Hassan et al., 2025).

CRPD articles on accessibility, education, employment, health, and access to information do support directly SDGs (2015) including ***SDG 4 (Quality Education), SDG 8 (Decent Work), SDG 10 (Reduced Inequalities),*** and ***SDG 11 (Sustainable Cities).*** The *Marrakesh Treaty* is in line with SDG 4 because it facilitates the development and cross-national distribution of accessible books, which wards off the progression of reading materials among learners with visual disabilities to resolve the issue of inadequate supply of reading material internationally (Ferri & Rossello, 2023).

Together these frameworks advocate a world in which the visually impaired individuals may be fully engaged in the realm of education, work, civil life and culture so that no one is left behind, the very principle of the SDGs.

Table 2. Combined Data on CRPD Articles Supporting Rights of Visually Impaired Person Aligned with SDGs

CRPD Article	Right for Visually Impaired Persons	Linked SDGs	Articles Align with SDGs
Article 5: Equality before the law & prohibit discrimination because of disability	Equal protection, Guarantees reasonable accommodation regardless of disability and socio-economic background.	SDG 10 (Reduced Inequalities)	Ensuring equal access to education, employment, and public services.
Article 9: Accessibility to physical environment, transportation, information, communication, and digital technologies.	Accessible ICT (Screen Reader cum friendly websites and Mobile apps), Inclusive transport systems, Accessible buildings (Braille Signage, tactile Maps)	SDG 11 (Sustainable Cities) & SDG 9 (Industry, Innovation & Infrastructure)	Promotes inclusive safe, resilient and sustainable cities, with a focus on innovation and infrastructure.
Article 12: Legal Capacity on equal basis with others	Equal rights to open bank accounts, marriage, vote and own property	SDG 16 (Peace, Justice & Strong Institutions)	Ensures legal systems are accessible and supports rule of law for persons with disabilities
Article 13: Access to Justice for person with disabilities	Accessible courts, documents, Audio based legal information, Training the police, lawyers, and judges on disability inclusion	SDG 16	Strengthens justice systems for persons with disabilities, promotes equal access to legal remedies and strengthens institutional accountability
Article 21: Freedom of Expression & Access to Information in Accessible formats	Braille, audio, large print, accessible to Digital Platforms, e-learning platforms, Screen reader friendly government websites	SDG 4 (Quality Education) SDG 9 (Innovation)	Ensures accessible learning materials and digital inclusion
Article 24: Inclusive Education at all levels	Inclusive education and Pedagogy, Accessible to Braille textbooks, audio books, Assistive technology or Assistive devices, Accessible Examinations and Trained special educators	SDG 4 (Quality Education)	Promotes inclusive, equitable education for all and supports teacher training in inclusive pedagogy
Article 25: Same quality of healthcare as others	Accessible medical information (audio, Braille), Accessible hospitals and Clinics, informed consent	SDG 3 (Good Health & Well-Being)	Ensures Universal access to health services, promotes disability inclusive health polices, and supports mental and physical well being
Article 26: Habilitation & Rehabilitation	Assistive devices, (White cane, braille displays, Screen readers), orientation and mobility training, skills training for daily living	SDG 3	Supports functional independence and rehabilitation and assistive services

continued on following page

Table 2. Continued

CRPD Article	Right for Visually Impaired Persons	Linked SDGs	Articles Align with SDGs
Article 27: Ensure Equal Employment Opportunities	Non-discrimination in hiring, workplace accommodation, Equal opportunity policies, Vocational training	SDG 8 – Decent Work & Economic Growth	Promotes inclusive labour markets, supports economic development, and encourages workplace accessibility
Article 29: Participation in Political and Public life	Accessible voting, be elected, join political parties	SDG 16	Strengthens democratic participation, Braille ballots, Audio Assisted voting machines
Article 30: Participation in Culture Life, Recreation, Leisure & Sports	Audio described films, Accessible Museums and libraries, Enjoy sports and recreation,	SDG 11	Ensures inclusive cultural & public spaces, community participation
Marrakesh Treaty: Access to Published Works	Accessible books (Braille, audio, large print, DAISY). international sharing of accessible formats, Removal of copyright barriers of accessibility	SDG 4	Reduces the "book famine" (Severe shortage of learning materials in accessible format for disabled persons like blind and low vision) supports lifelong learning by the disability personals

(Source: UN Convention on the Rights of Persons with Disabilities (CRPD, 2006); UN 2030 Agenda for Sustainable Development (SDGs, 2015).

The Table 2 synthesizes the CRPD and Marrakesh treaty frameworks to illustrate how the CRPD and the SDGs intersect in supporting inclusive education, emphasizing the importance of accessible leaning materials, assistive technologies and AI tools for the rights of the visually impaired (Ferri & Donnellan, 2022).

SECTION 1: VISUAL IMPAIRMENT AND EDUCATIONAL CONTEXT

This section will lay the conceptual and contextual foundation for the chapter by focusing on visual impairment in relation to education.

1.1 Background of Visual Impairment in Education

Visual impairment is a problem that affects about 2.2 billion individuals across the world with a good percentage of such cases being preventable or treatable, and hence, the necessity of innovative solutions in all aspects of life including in education. The conventional method of education has been a major challenge for the visually impaired learners, who in most cases have been deprived of the interactive and flexible facilities that would allow them to participate on equal terms. But recent developments multisensory AI technologies have proven to be good in addressing accessibility disparities, offering adaptable solutions which incorporate multiple sensory capabilities such as sight, hearing, and touch to enhance the educational inclusiveness. These technologies which include screen readers, Braille displays, and voice assistants would be important in helping visually impaired students gain access to digital content, navigate online, and interact with educational content without the need to have another person. As an example, screen readers such as Job Access with Speech (JAWS) (Prakash et al., 2023) and Non Visual Desktop Access (NVDA) which are powered by AI use text-to-speech (TTS) synthesis to make digital software accessible to blind students and help them to engage with digital content and navigate digital settings. In addition to these underpinning tools, new applications of AI are transforming learning the English language by offering real-time feedback on pronunciation and grammar and gearing up to produce students with virtual English worlds using extended reality (Yan et al., 2025). The objective of this integration is to examine listening and speaking skills with the help of AI algorithms, which will provide individuals with individual learning paths and simulated real-life situations to improve oral expression.

1.2 Structure of the Eye and Its Educational Relevance

The eye receives light through the cornea, which bends and directs it toward the lens. The lens further focuses the light onto the retina, where it is converted into electrical impulses by cones and rods. These impulses pass across the optic nerve to the brain where visual interpretation is possible. Any obstruction of this route in the cornea, lens, retina or optic nerve may result in impaired sharpness, narrow visual fields, or a lack of ability to see differences and details.

These functional restrictions directly affect access to learning materials among students in learning institutions. To provide an example, the central vision impairment has an impact on reading and writing activities, whereas peripheral field impairment influences the ability to move and find the information on a page or a screen. It is through these functional effects that teachers will be able to select appropriate assistive technologies like magnifiers, screen readers, high contrast displays, or tactile materials.

Such limitations of the anatomy also affect certain learning outcomes. As an illustration, students with central vision loss can more commonly read more slowly and find it harder to comprehend using regular print materials, whereas students with peripheral field loss can find it difficult to locate information on a worksheet or digital interface.

Figure 1. Pictorial representation of An Eye

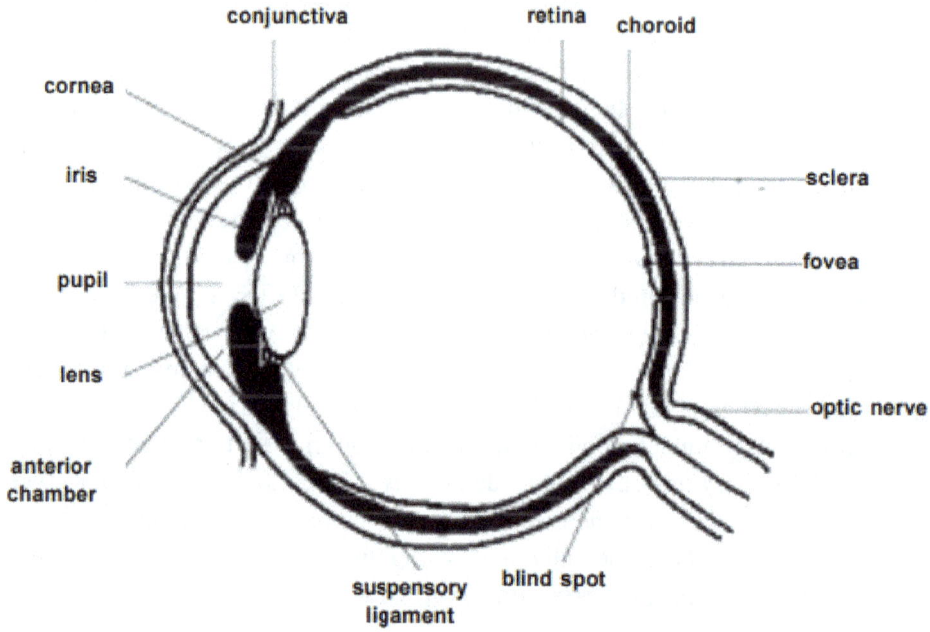

Figure 1 presents the internal structure of the human eye, showing key structures involved in the process of vision. It gives a labelled cross sectional view that helps in comprehending of how light is received, concentration and transmission of the light to the brain.

1.3 Understanding and Types of Visual Impairments

The idea of visual impairment is very general as it includes different levels of visual problems (Reiss, 2021; Wang et al., 2023), including partial visual loss and complete blindness. Blindness is the total absence of sight (Wang et al., 2023) or a highly limited one that is usually described as the inability to see light or any visual elements. Visual impairment may equally include a marked decline in the eyesight which cannot be fixed using just an ordinary pair of glasses, contact lenses and medical interventions. It can cause problems with vision, face recognition, or low light operation (Reiss, 2021). These differences have a direct influence on the manner in which students learn, which is why it is critical to make sure that teachers choose the right assistive technologies and teaching methods.

1.4 Types of Visual Impairments

Figure 2. Types of Visual Impairments

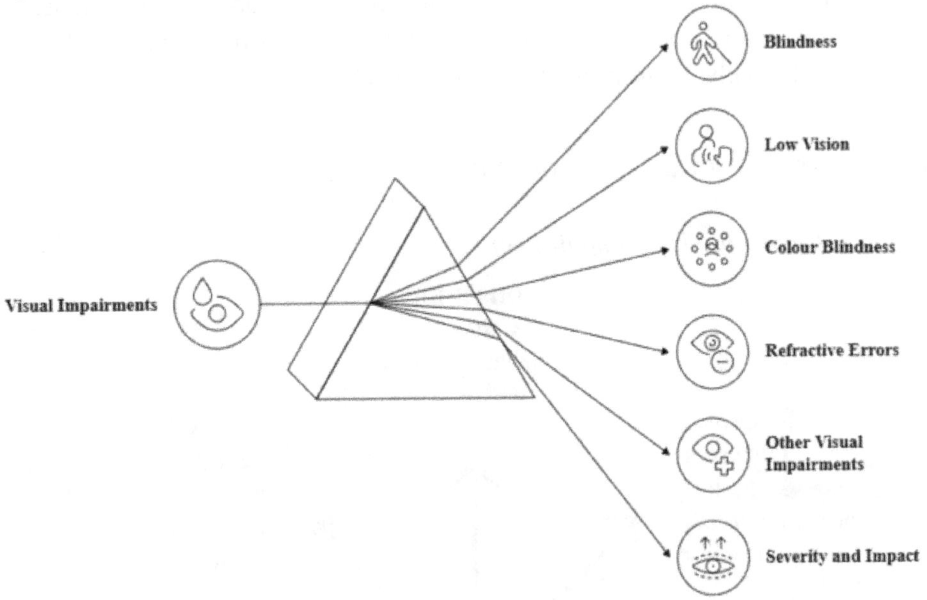

Figure 2 illustrates classifies the major types of visual impairments, offering a structured overview that facilitate both clinical knowledge as well as educational clarity helping educators match students with suitable assistive technologies. It differentiates between *blindness, low vision, colour blindness, refractive errors, other visual impairments,* and the different levels of severity and effect of these conditions.

Blindness: The students lack any use of vision or have very low acuity (= 6/60 or 20/200) or a visual field of less than 20. They are dependent on Braille, tactile resources, audio texts and screen readers.

Low Vision: Students retain some vision but need magnification, high-contrast materials, enlarged print, or adapted layouts. They may struggle with reading speed, board work, and diagrams (Pundlik et al., 2024; Wang et al., 2023).

Colour Blindness: The inability to differentiate some colours (red and green). Impairs reading of colour coded charts, maps, diagrams and lab assignments. Needs other prompts (Reiss, 2021).

Refractive Errors: Myopia affects distance tasks; hyperopia affects near tasks; astigmatism affects both; presbyopia reduces near focus. Uncorrected errors impact reading and copying.

Other Visual Impairments: Incorporates the double vision, tunnel vision and visual field loss (e.g. hemianopia). Students can lose peripheral information, and they have a problem with moving or searching text (Wang et al., 2023).

Severity and Impact: Minor impairments need simple adjustments; moderate impairments require specialised tools; severe/profound impairments require adaptive devices or alternative sensory methods (Wang et al., 2023).

1.5 Causes of Visual Disabilities

Figure 3. Causes of Visual Impairment

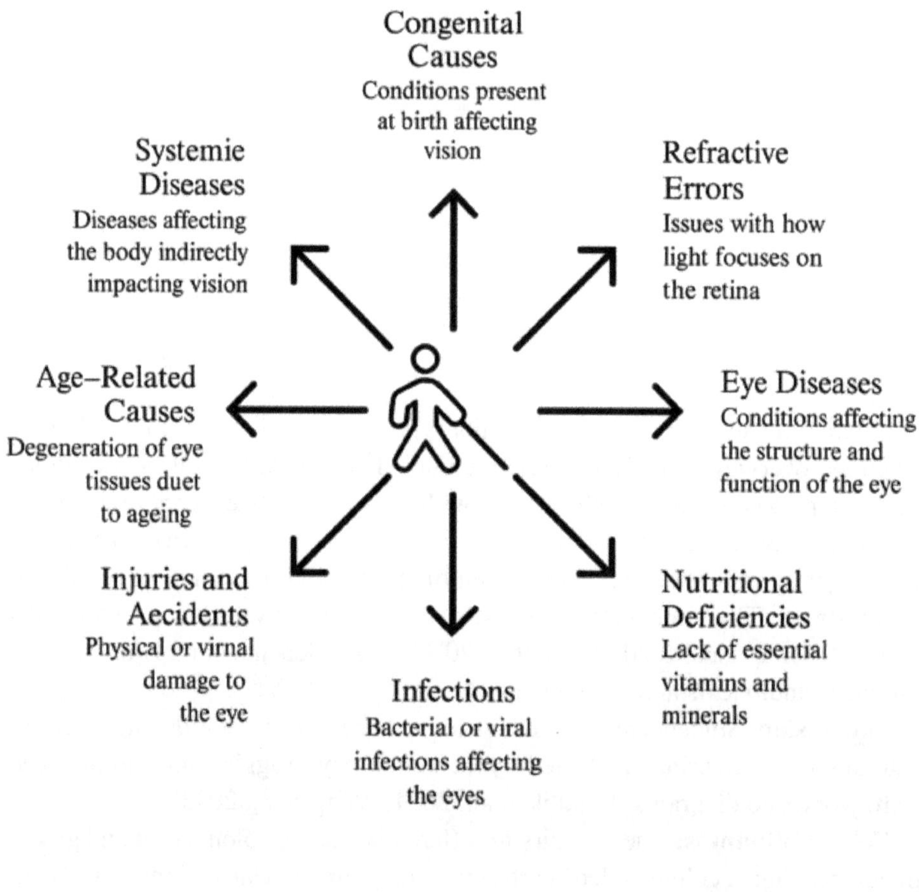

The visual impairment may be caused by the types of damage, underdevelopment or disruption of any part of the visual system and Figure 3 indicates the presence of various underlying causes that result in this loss of functioning. Congenital disorders can disrupt the development of the eye or optic tract resulting in visual impairment throughout life. Refractive errors are errors that happen when the shape of the eye cannot allow light to reach the retina in a proper way hence leading to the vision being blurred or distorted. The infections can damage the key structures and gradually deteriorate the vision of the affected individuals. Nutritional deficiencies also undermine the ocular tissues and decrease their resistance to infection or recovery. Infections may end up scarring or inflaming the eye whereas injuries lead to direct trauma which can permanently alter the vision (Milde et al., 2024) . The changes which come with age degrade retinal and neural tissues and systemic illnesses like diabetes damages blood vessels and nerves which aid in healthy vision. A combination of any of these mechanisms proves the point that irrelevant biological and environmental factors affect the sensitive processes that require clear and functional sight. The causes of the impairments are relevant to the field of education because the nature of the impairments differs with regard to how they affect the student's capability to read, move around, and so on, thereby requiring the relevant assistive tools, especially the use of AI technology.

1.6 Challenges Faced by Visually Impaired Students

Visual impairments students are faced with a lot of challenges that influence their lives, social life and even education. The physical environmental navigation can be complicated, and the mobility aid may be in the form of a *white cane* or *guide dogs*. The other significant barrier is reading printed information which is extremely difficult to achieve (Girish & Vaidyanathan, 2021); hence other formats such as *oversized print books*, *audio books* and *screen readers* are required in order to study on their own. Social interaction and adaptive communication methods can also be affected by visual impairments and assistive technologies can be used to reduce such interventions.

As an example, a low vision student might not be able to read diagrams during a science class, which means that he/she will fail to grasp the most important points. With AI-based OCR programs like Microsoft Seeing AI, the learner is instantly able to visualise an actual description of these diagrams, allowing them to contribute equally. In the same light, learners with mobility difficulties on the school campuses enjoy AI-powered navigation systems, such as Aira, which assist them by offering real-time directions and alleviating stress related to the process of moving around the classrooms.

Figure 4. Challenges faced by Visually impaired Students

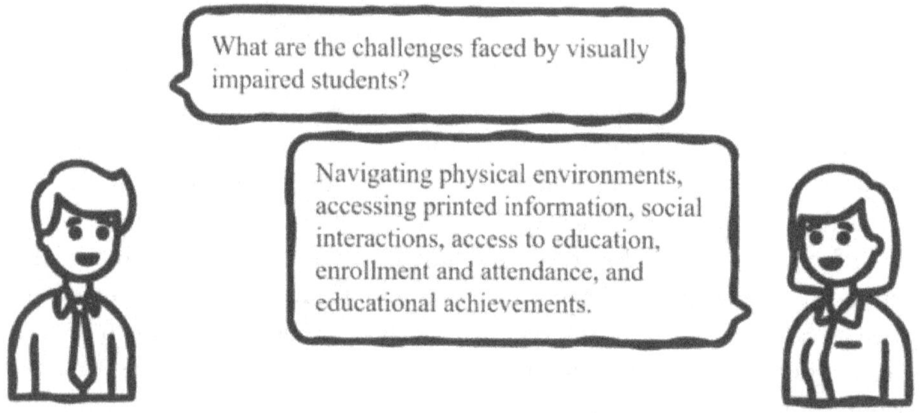

Figure 4 highlights key challenges faced by visually impaired students, such as mobility, access to information, and educational inclusion.

Impact on Education.

1. **Access to Education**: Learners with visual impairments usually experience challenges in accessing high quality education (Panda & Kaur, 2024). According to UNESCO nearly 90 per cent of children with disabilities in less developed nations are out of school (Anokye et al., 2025). In contrast in more affluent regions, inclusive educational policies and tailored programmes are more common, but still, they encounter certain obstacles.
2. **Enrollment and Attendance:** Reports from the *World Blind Union* indicates that learners with visual impairment are markedly underrepresented within education systems around the world. In particular in less developed countries, around 10 per cent of children with visual impairments only are enrolled in school (Anokye et al., 2025).
3. **Educational Achievements:** Individuals with visual disabilities often face challenges that impact their academic attainment, such as limited access to specialised educational (Zaraii Zavaraki, 2024) materials, technologies, as well as qualified teaching staff.

1.7 Regional Differences for Visually Impaired Students

1. **Developed Countries:** In highly developed countries, visual impairments students tend to be enrolled in regular schools or special education programmes. For instance, in the United States (US), around 1.2 per cent of students receive

special education services for visual disabilities, according to national education statistics.

2. **Developing Countries:** Educational provisions for visual impairments students in low and middle income nations (Zaraii Zavaraki, 2024) often fall short. The obstacles encompass (Hamideh Kerdar et al., 2024) a dearth of specialised educational facilities, insufficient teacher preparation, and limited financial resources.
3. **Under Developed Countries:** In the underdeveloped countries, children with visual impairments have an even worse educational condition than the developing countries. In most of the low and middle income nations, especially in the parts of Sub Saharan Africa region, children with visual disabilities find it extremely difficult to access the basic schooling. Such challenges are very limited access to specialised schools, the formulation or poor implementation of education policy, and lack of trained teachers who would effectively deal with learners with visual impairments. Due to poverty, discrimination, and lack of certain vital services like vision check, eyeglasses, or support gadgets, many children fail to attend school or drop out of school. This has left children with visual impairments in underdeveloped countries to have some of the largest disparities on school attendance, educational performance, and future prospects (Anokye et al., 2025).

1.8 Overview of Assistive Technology and Artificial Intelligence in Education

Definition and Scope of Artificial Intelligence:

Assistive technologies (AT) and artificial intelligence (AI) have become the focus of an notable amount of scholarly activity and practice in the education field over recent years. The technologies have currently been significant in assisting various learners and improving teaching learning processes in various learning environments (Fitas, 2025; Kooli & Chakraoui, 2025). Assistive technologies are defined as tools, devices, and software that has been created to enhance the functional abilities of handicapped or learning disabled learners so that they can equally access learning opportunities. Further broadening the opportunities of personalized and inclusive education, AI, which is frequently described as the capacity of a system to process external information, learn based on it, and use the acquired learning to achieve certain objectives through adaptive behaviour.

The progress of computing technologies since the middle of the 20th century was the basis of the AT as well as AI innovations (Kathiria et al., 2024) . The current high tech AI systems like *intelligent tutoring systems*, *adaptive learning environ-*

ments, and *language processing systems* are used alongside assistive technologies to make learning processes more receptive and accessible. Machine Learning (ML) (McIntyre, 2022) and Natural Language Processing (NLP) are two key subfields of AI that have a disproportionate impact on education (Daher, 2025). ML can be used to instruct students based on their data and NLP can be used to build learning tools, such as speech-to-text, text-to-speech, and conversational agents, that help students with reading, writing, and communication.

The vision of AI in education has both limited implementations (including automated score markers and voice assisted learning devices) and a larger vision of general AI that can be used to accomplish more complex learning processes(Pamuji et al., 2023). Although superintelligent AI is speculative, there are already major changes that can be achieved in inclusive education with the current development. Collectively, AT and AI are transforming the classroom through facilitating accessibility, customisation, and purposeful engagement among all students.

1.9 Application of Assistive Technology and AI in Education

Assistive Technology and Artificial Intelligence are transforming the contemporary education system through the development of an inclusive, personalized, and accessible learning experience. These tools are useful in helping diverse learners particularly the disabled learners by eliminating barriers and allowing them to participate meaningfully in the classroom. Intelligent tutoring platforms enable the adaptability of content, real time responses and better student interaction with AI driven platforms (Dong et al., 2024; Kooli & Chakraoui, 2025).

Figure 5: Application of Assistive Technology and AI in Education

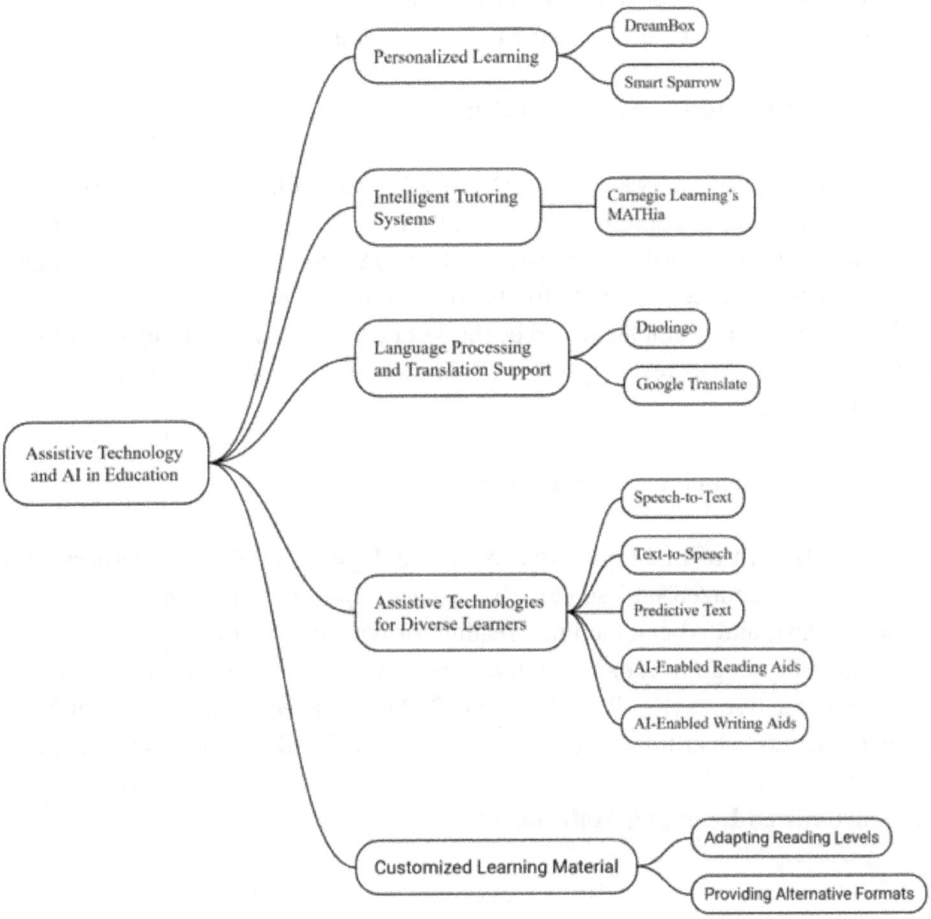

Figure 5 highlights key applications of assistive technology and AI in education, such as personalized learning, tutoring, translation, accessibility tools, and adaptive materials for different learners.

1. **Personalized Learning:**

AI powered and assistive technologies based learning platforms adjust the educational content, activities, and assistance in accordance with the needs, preferences, and learning speeds of individual learners (Kooli & Chakraoui, 2025). These systems identify the learning patterns of students and the level of improvement they are making, which allows teachers to notice strengths, weakness and the gaps that the students need extra attention. Tools like **DreamBox** and **Smart Sparrow** can be used to make learning environments more inclusive and responsive through the adjustment of difficulty and the provision of customized feedback.

2. **Intelligent Tutoring Systems (ITS):**

Intelligent Tutoring Systems, which are AI, based offer learners personalized instruction parallel to one-on-one human tutoring. These systems provide personalized instructions, real-time feedback, and customized learning routes, including those students who need more scaffolding or enrichment (Kathiria et al., 2024). One of the most popular examples would be the ***MATHia*** created by Carnegie Learning and which modifies its teaching approach in accordance with the performance and needs of each learner.

3. **Assistive Technologies for Diverse Learners:**

AI is a benefit of traditional assistive technologies providing to learners with disabilities customized and adaptive assistance. ***Speech to text, text to speech, predictive text***, and AI can facilitate reading or writing activities to students with visual, auditory, cognitive, or motor impairments to help them engage more actively in classroom activities (Kooli & Chakraoui, 2025). Such technologies guarantee the equitable access to learning since support gets personalized to the needs of a learner .

4. **Customized Learning Materials:**

The AI systems can be used to create customized learning content, adjust teaching materials, and suggest ways of correcting the individual learning problems of the students. This involves modifying the reading levels, offering alternative formats or recommending targeted interventions and, thus, supporting differentiated instructions and inclusive education (Kathiria et al., 2024).

SECTION 2: THE ROLE OF TECHNOLOGY IN EDUCATION FOR STUDENTS WITH DISABILITIES:

The application of technology has been very radical and significant in the learning environment amongst disabled learners. These inventions offer invaluable tools and solutions which make it invaluable to their learning experiences, increase their level of accessibility, and make it more participatory (Dumitru et al., 2026).

2.1. Applications of Assistive and AI Technologies for Visually Impaired Students

Assistive and AI systems such as screen readers, voice assistants, and OCR systems assist visually impaired students in gaining more independently and participate more fully in learning environments.

These tools are directly applied to quantifiable learning in a classroom setting. Screen readers can help students to read digital textbooks at the same speed as other students, whereas AI enhanced TTS engines allow students to understand the text in reading tasks. OCR products enable students to get printed worksheets by themselves, and they do not have to be dependent on teachers or classmates. Combined, the technologies foster self-efficiency, boost involvement, and enhance academic success in subjects.

2.1.1 Description of Screen Readers and How They Utilize AI.

Figure 6: Illustrates Screen Readers

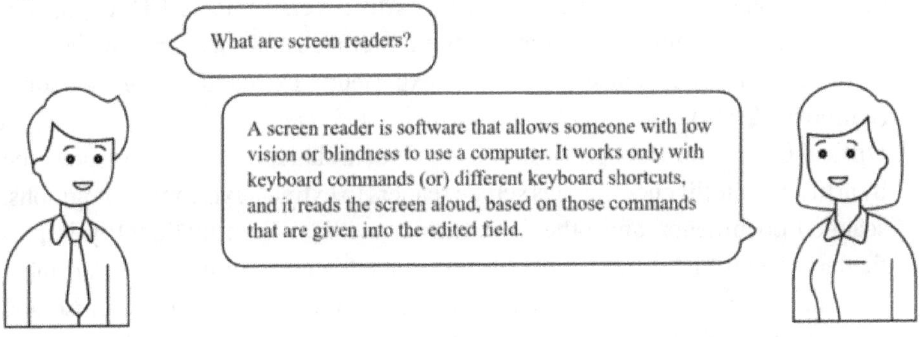

This figure 6 illustrates the core idea behind the existence of the screen readers by demonstrating how the devices help blind people by converting the text and interface elements on the screen into audible sounds. They simulate text and visual materials on the screen into audible sound or braille to enable users to use computers without depending on their eyes (Phutane et al., 2023). Artificial intelligence also enhances the functionality of these tools by enabling them to find and explain the visual content and provide specific audio feedback that should be offered to the users based on their needs and interests (Alimović, 2024). A combination of these improvements ensures that screen readers are more precise, more intuitive, and more responsive, which greatly increases the level of digital access among visually impaired learners.

Utilisation of AI in Screen Readers

The AI assisted screen readers increase accessibility in that they allow more streamlined navigation, which is more intuitive and contributes to achieving the CRPD Article 9 objectives, as well as promoting SDG 9 and SDG 11 in their objective of inclusive digital accessibility.

1. **Language Processing and Translation Support:** Natural Language Processing (NLP) applications are crucial in facilitating multilingual classrooms as well as diverse classrooms. Such tools as ***Duolingo*** apply AI to achieve the learning of a language with interactive exercises and adaptive feedback. AI based translation systems such as the ***Google Translate*** can be used to minimize language obstacles and facilitate better communication as well as enhance the availability of learning resources among students with diverse language groups (Lee et al., 2024) .
2. **Enhanced Text-to-Speech (TTS) Voices:** The AI improves the TTS engines by creating more natural sounding voices which may be customised in pitch, speed and accent. Modern TTS systems use deep learning methods to produce natural intonations and human like voices. Moreover, AI helps TTS engines to customise voice output according to the preferences of users and the context of the content and, hence, makes the experience of reading more personal (Alimović, 2024) .
3. **Optical Character Recognition (OCR):** Optical character recognition powered by artificial intelligence enables screen readers to extract text from photographs, scanned documents, and other non-textual media. This functionality is particularly beneficial when accessing text embedded within images or portable document format files (Alimović, 2024). Additionally, AI can recognise and convert handwritten content into digital text, thereby expanding the range of materials accessible to screen readers (Kooli & Chakraoui, 2025).

Popular AI-driven Screen Readers (e.g., JAWS, NVDA).

Many prominent AI-enabled screen readers are helping to improve the accessibility of disabled individuals with visual impairments by incorporating innovative technologies to improve text-to-speech conversion, navigation, and user experience. In this section of the chapter, researchers are presenting a brief overview of several prominent screen readers and their use of AI technology.

1. Job Access with Speech (JAWS)

Job Access with Speech (JAWS) is a popular screen reader that enables blind or low-sight persons to use speech or Braille technology to read digital material. JAWS used together with Microsoft Outlook allows users to customize communication through email use, calendars and address book features on their own using on-screen elements and translating them into audible information. The software is all keyboard operated and users can utilise the software to move around in Outlook without necessarily having to input anything visually (Prakash et al., 2023).

AI Integration: AI systems will have the capability to identify the context of text and other web materials, which will improve the accuracy and relevance of the verbal output. There is also the capability to do customised settings and user specific modification which has resulted in a more personalised experience based on the individual preferences through AI technology.

2. Non Visual Desktop Access (NVDA)

NVDA is a highly powerful and adaptable screen reader that provides essential accessibility features for blind and visually impaired users. NDVA is a free and open source screen reader for Microsoft windows developed by NV Access and Contributions. It was initiated by Michael Curran in 2006 to provide an affordable alternative to commercial screen readers. NVDA supports a wide range of applications and functionalities, including Microsoft office applications, web browsers, braille displays and various speech synthesizers. NVDA's support for WAI (Web Accessibility Initiative) and ARIA (Accessible Rich Internet Applications) standard enhances the accessibility of web applications for blind users (Kooli & Chakraoui, 2025). In addition, it utilises high quality TTS engines and supports braille displays, allowing for customisable speech and braille output .

AI Integration: Advancements in AI powered text-to-speech technology have produced more natural and expressive voice output. Users can customise speech qualities to their preferences. The screen reader NVDA leverages AI to manage dynamic content and updates, ensuring that users receive accurate and timely information on changes to web sites.

2.1.2 Integration of Text-to-Speech (TTS) in Educational Materials:

Figure 7: illustrates Text-to-Speech Software

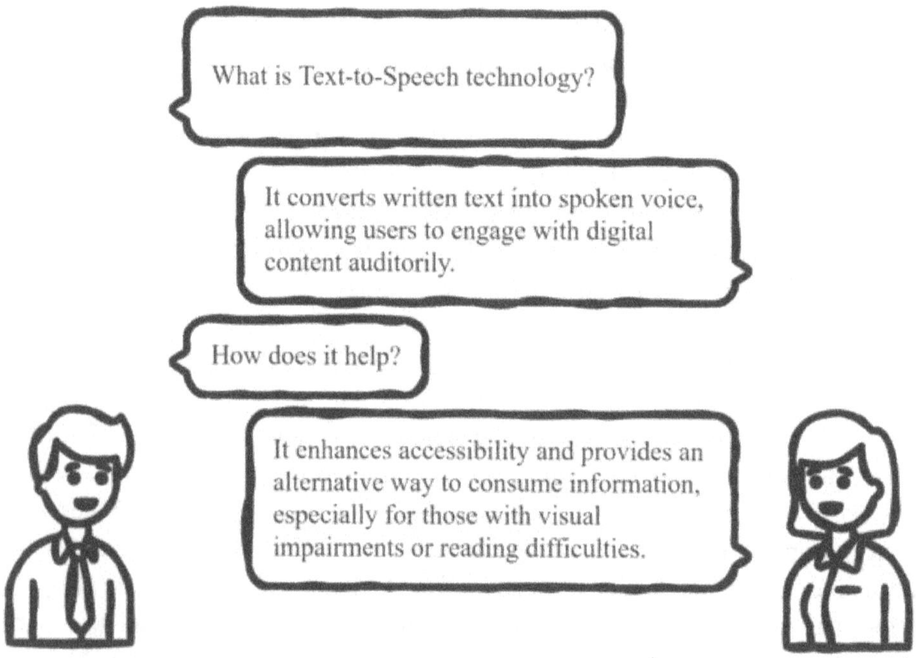

Figure 7 illustrates what is Text-to-speech software is and what purpose it is developed. It is essential for making educational materials accessible to visually impaired pupils. TTS improves the learning experience for visual impairments students and other reading issues by translating written material into spoken words. Here's how TTS fits into educational resources to support varied learning demands.:

1. Reading and Accessibility

Access to reading is an important element in the inclusive education. The article 24 of CRPD recommends that the learning material format should support all types of learners, while the Marrakesh Treaty allows the creation and sharing of accessible books across the boarders, which reduces the concept "Book Famine". Together with SDG 4's emphasis on equitable quality education, these frameworks ensure that every learner, irrespective of their disabilities, can access knowledge without any discrimination.

a. **Textbooks and Reading Materials:** Text-to-speech technology allows transforming the textbooks, articles, and other printed text materials into audio formats (Yang & Taele, 2025)so that visual impairments students can get the content through auditory means. This conversion process may be done on both digital files and scanned physical documents with the use of optical character recognition methods. The different voice parameters, including speed, pitch, and volume, can be adjusted by the user to suit the listening experience to their own tastes and understandability requirements (Panda & Kaur, 2024).
b. **Web Content:** The text-to-speech support can be easily applied to the web browsers either by the extensions or add-ons allowing the visually impaired students to read and interact with a broad amount of online publications, learning resources, and interactive offers.
c. **Accessible Websites:** Educational websites and Internet may include the TTS feature instantly, and the information can become more accessible to the TTS users.

2. Interactive Learning Tools
    a. **E-Learning Platforms:** E-learning platforms have an opportunity to use a text-to-speech technology to deliver course materials via the oral presentation of lectures, quizzes and teaching content. This makes it easy to approach the information in a context that is convenient to the visually impaired students. In addition, TTS may be utilized in interactive capabilities like (Mina et al., 2023) virtual laboratories or simulations, where the instructions and feedback are spoken, which makes the learning process more complete.
    b. **Educational Apps:** Text-to-speech functionality is regularly incorporated into educational technology, such as language learning tools, reading apps, and study guides. This allows students to train pronunciation and grasp new vocabulary and revisit information. Most of these applications allow a user to tailor the text-to-speech experience to fit their unique needs as a learner (i.e. choosing one of a variety of voices or increasing or decreasing reading pace).

2.1.3 Challenges and Considerations With respect to TTS:

a. Accuracy and Naturalness:

Voice Quality: Although text-to-speech technology has advanced, it is crucial that the synthesized speech maintains intelligibility, natural sounding quality, and ease of comprehension to facilitate effective learning.

Pronunciation The correct pronunciation of complicated terminology, names, and technical vocabulary is essential for comprehension, and therefore text-to-speech systems must be designed to address these concerns effectively.

b. Integration and Compatibility:

System Compatibility: An important feature to ensure is the compatibility of the text-to-speech functionality. Text-to-speech functionality may be used on a wide range of systems, and hence its compatibility is vital for ensuring a smooth user interface.

Customisation: Users can adjust TTS settings to personalise the experience and meet their needs.

2.1.4 Difference between Screen Readers and Text to Speech:

Figure 8: Illustrates the Difference Between Screen Readers and Text to Speech Software's

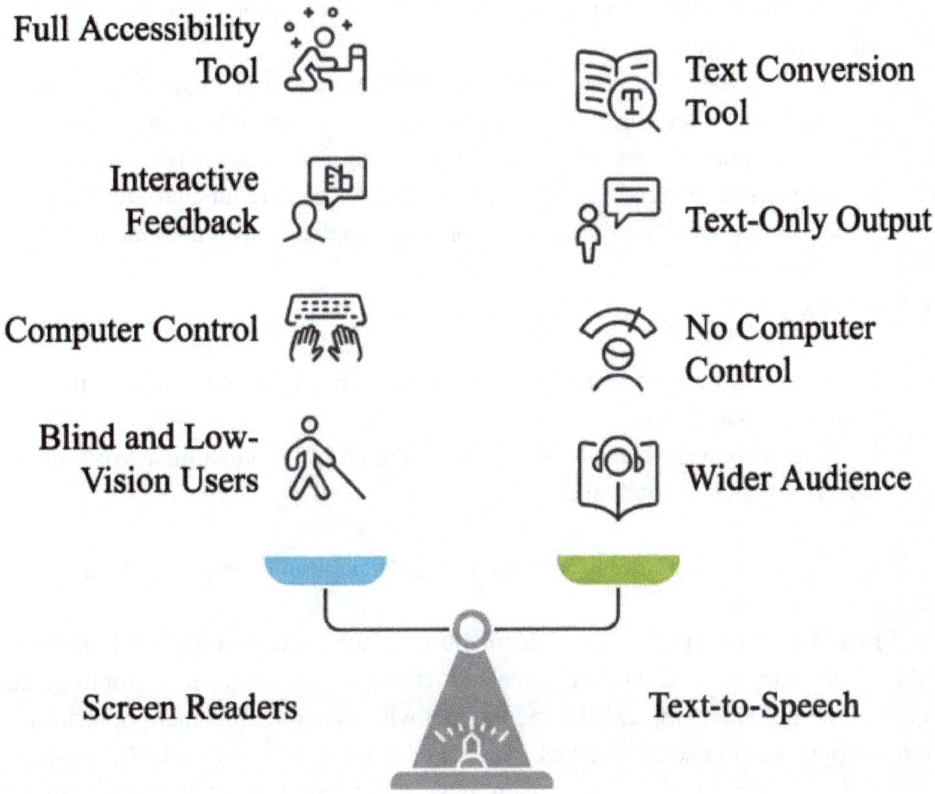

The figure 8 presents the clear difference between the screen readers and the Text to Speech (TTS) software is in the level of interaction, control by the user and targeted audience. Although screen readers can be said to be fully accessible due to their ability to provide navigation and control over the digital environments, TTS tools are only aimed at converting written information into spoken one. These differences are also clearly brought out in the infographic and indicate how the various technologies are applicable to various access needs.

2. 2: Voice Assistants

a. Voice-Over:

Voice-Over is built into macOS and iOS, allowing smooth use of Apple devices and software.
Advanced text-to-speech uses AI to produce high quality, customisable voices. The Voice-over voice can be adjusted in terms of pitch, speed, and tone.
Braille Support: Works with braille displays to generate real-time braille.
Gesture based Navigation and Controls: Enables gesture navigation on touchscreens and provides easy controls for using applications and content.

b. Narrator

Narrator is a built in screen reader for Windows that does not require any additional installation.
It offers AI powered text-to-speech with the ability to customise voice characteristics such as pitch and speed.

Narrator provides functionality for reading and navigating web pages, documents, and system interfaces.

AI Integration: AI driven enhancements enhance the naturalness and intelligibility of Narrator's text-to-speech voices. Furthermore, AI assists Narrator to make sense of the website complexities and interact with dynamic information, resulting in more precise and useful feedback. Screen readers such as JAWS, NVDA, Voice over and Narrator, which are AI driven, have significantly increased accessibility by visually impaired people, by offering them a advanced speech synthesizer, the ability to manage dynamic content and creating user specific experiences. Such tools are not only more helpful to make digital content usable but also contribute to more autonomy and inclusivity in many educational and professional settings.

2.2.1 Role of Voice Assistants in Aiding Visually Impaired Students.

Voice assistants such as ***Siri*** and ***Google Assistant*** can offer their assistance to visually impaired students by ensuring that they do not have to use their hands to access information and services but only speak. This facilitates their learning and acquiring what they require.

1. Accessibility and Navigation

a. **Hands Free Interaction**: The voice assistants allow visually impaired students to do tasks and access information without ever having to have visual inputs. This hands free ability is very useful in multitasking and in navigation through different environments.
b. **Location Based Guidance:** Voice assistants can provide directions, be useful in navigating campuses, and find individual rooms and other facilities with the help of GPS and mapping technology.

2. **Educational Support:** Voice assistants may enable visually impaired students to find information quickly about all types of topics, which may include finding answers to the questions or checking the definition and explanation for certain topics. This enhances research and learning. Voice assistants can assist students in managing their homework tasks, setting deadline alerts, and giving clarifications or other materials on academic subjects. Moreover, voice assistants can read materials in books, documents or websites, which can allow the sightless students to access and understand the materials.
3. **Accessibility Features**: Voice assistants have the capability of managing a large number of smart devices and apps, such as volume, lighting, and electronic devices in the classroom. This improves the overall accessibility and convenience. A great number of voice assistants can be configured into individualised voices, speaking speed, language, and accent, which means that students can personalise the voice assistant to fit their needs.

2.2.2 Challenges and Considerations with Respect to Voice over:

a. **Privacy and Security:** Voice assistants collect and process voice data, which raises concerns around privacy and security. Ensuring appropriate and secure management of student data is critical.
b. **Accuracy and Context:** Although voice assistants are becoming more accurate, they might not be able to understand context and give accurate answers in some scenarios.
c. **Requirement for Internet Connectivity:** Most voice assistants are Internet enabled and can only be used effectively once they are connected to the internet. It is vital to have stable internet connectivity to their effective functioning. The voice assistants like *Siri, Google assistant*, and *Alexa* offer significant service to the visually impaired students, allowing them to access information without using their hands, they can converse, and they can receive instructional support (Baguma & Wolters, 2021).

2.3 The Role of AI in Enhancing Optical Character Recognition (OCR) for Visually Impaired Learners

The application of the Optical Character Recognition (OCR) technology is essential to visually impaired learners since it allows them to combine the printed or handwritten text into digital form with accuracy, efficiency, and functionality that can be read aloud or translated into braille.

1. Improved Text Recognition
   a. **Enhanced Accuracy:** The use of AI algorithms, especially those are based on deep learning and neural networks, has greatly improved the accuracy of text recognition in OCR technology.
   b. **Contextual Understanding:** AI technology improves the use of OCR by utilizing natural language processing to understand the text in context. This makes it simple to understand the words that can be confused due to the use of different font styles or deficiencies.
2. Enhanced Handling of Diverse Text Formats
   a. **Complex Layouts:** AI based OCR systems would support complex document designs, which include multi column text, tabular and embedded content. This gives access to a wider scope of learning content among the visually impaired learners as they will be able to have access to textbooks, articles, and academic materials.
   b. **Handwriting Recognition:** The technological advancements in artificial intelligence have improved the level of OCR systems to identify and decode written handwriting. This can be especially useful in regard to working with handwritten notes, assignments, and paper based documents which cannot be accessed digitally.
3. Real Time Text Extraction
   a. **Live Text Extraction:** OCR strengthened with artificial intelligence can be used to extract real time texts in live video feeds or camera shots. As an example, students with visual deficiencies can take advantage of smartphone cameras to snap and scan the text of books, white boards or documents immediately and translate it into an electronic format so that students can enjoy learning materials on the move.
   b. **Image-to-Text Conversion:** Sophisticated artificial intelligence technologies will allow converting text images into digitized values in real-time, which will give students access to tangible materials and educational resources.
4. Integration with Assistive Technologies
   a. **Braille Translation:** AI enhanced OCR systems can convert recognised text into braille formats for use with braille displays or embossers. This

integration ensures that visually impaired students who utilise braille technology have access to a wider range of educational resources.

b. **Educational Apps and Platforms:** AI enhanced OCR is usually integrated into educational applications and digital platforms, to enable users to easily access the learning materials. This includes the software solutions of text book reading, the use of web based resources, and interaction with educational materials.

Examples of AI Enhanced OCR Tools

a. **Google Lens:** Leverages artificial intelligence to enable real time optical character recognition on photographs captured by a smartphone camera, extracting and interpreting text from a diverse range of sources, such as books, signage, and documents.

b. **Microsoft Seeing AI:** Leverages artificial intelligence to interpret text from photos, describe visual scenes, and recognise objects. It is specially designed and optimized to suit the requirements of people with visual impairments and it has real time optical character recognition and voice based feedback. The application of artificial intelligence has significantly improved the accuracy, flexibility, and usability of the OCR technology for learners with visual impairment. The AI powered OCR systems demonstrated to be better at recognizing the text, provide support to different text formats, and be linked with other assistive tools, thereby promoting the accessibility and inclusivity in the sphere of education. These innovations enable visual impairments students to have a greater range of learning resources and take better part in the learning processes.

2.4 Enhanced Engagement and Comprehension

a. **Audiobooks:** Text-to-speech has the potential to convert written content, e.g. classic literature, textbooks, and supplementary reading materials, into audiobook formats (Yang & Taele, 2025). This will provide a different medium that is appropriate to those students that learn more by ear. Audiobooks are particularly beneficial in the areas where ample reading is necessary or to learners who like to listen than to read.

b. **Interactive Textbooks:** The interactive digital textbooks can take advantage of text-to-speech (TTS) technology to provide passages of text in audio form and explain complicated concepts and comment on interaction with students verbally. Combining TTS with other multimedia features, e.g., video and interactive visualisations, one promotes multiple learning strategies, thus, improving the overall knowledge.

2.5 Case Studies and Real World Application of AI in for Visually Impaired Students in World and in India

Several schools and educational institutions across the world have been able to incorporate AI devices to facilitate the learning process among the visually impaired learners, making it more enjoyable and easier to access.

Figure 9: Few Examples of AI integration in to Education for Visually Impaired Students

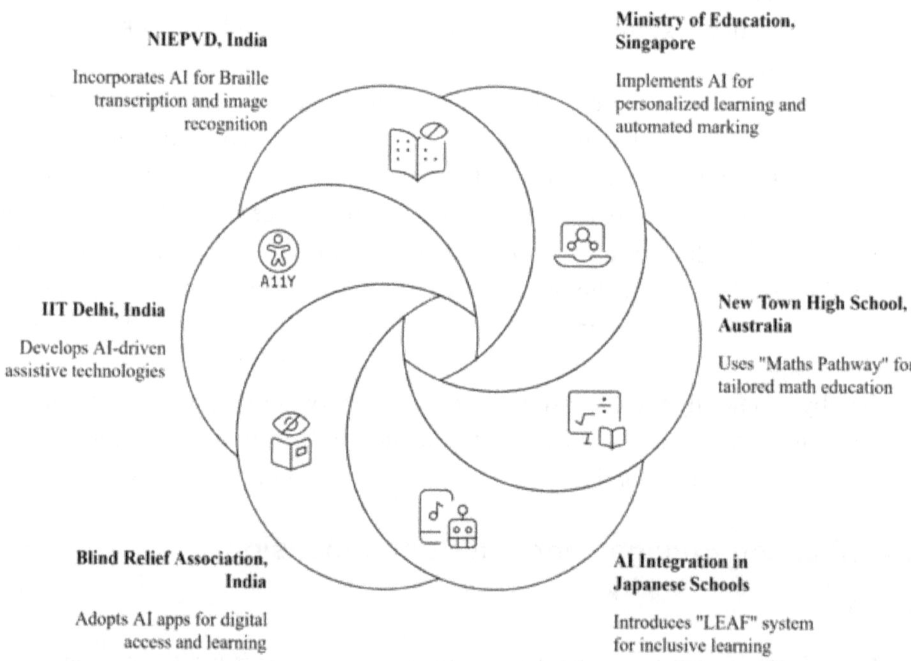

The figure 9 illustrates key milestones in the global integration of artificial intelligence (AI) into educational systems supporting visually impaired students. The timeline highlights initiatives from Australia, India, and Japan and are discussed below

1. **Ministry of Education (MoE), Singapore**: The MoE has implemented different AI driven solutions across various schools to address the challenge of providing personalized learning experiences in a heterogenous classroom setup. The con-

ventional teaching methods are generally aimed to cater the needs of average students in a heterogenous classroom structure thus leading the gifted students without any challenge and educationally backward students struggling to keep up. One of the solutions among different solutions to address the above problem is the implementation of automated English marking systems for primary and secondary levels students. Thess AI driven platform are designed to evaluate the performance of the students by adopting open ended questions, short answer questions, and essays, focusing on grammar, spelling and syntax errors, giving the ability to teachers to focus on higher level of thinking and how to make such content more creative.

2. **New Town High School (Australia)**: The school wants to improve the problem solving skills, creativity, analytical skills, the level of engagement and learning in Science, Technology, Engineering and Mathematics (STEM) subjects, in which students generally feel difficulties with complicated ideas and no individualized assistance due to large class size. To address the above problems, the school adopted an AI driven platform called "*Maths Pathway*", which uses machine learning to tailor math education according to each student's learning pace and style. These platform continuous evaluates the student's progress and modifies the material, accordingly and offers personalized modules and real time feedback to students.

3. **AI Integration in Japan Schools:** In Japan, to address the problem of enhancing the inclusivity and personalized learning particularly with disabled students, is being addressed by adopting AI technologies in their teaching and learning. The conventional educational systems have been found in capable of accommodating the various learning styles and learning rates of students particularly those who needs special educational support. To create an inclusive process of learning in the schools, Japan has introduced the ***LEAF*** system, that consists of tools like ***BookRoll*** and ***LogPalette.*** *BookRoll* can be used to browse through digital learning materials and allows some features like highlighting of the text using a mouse in a book and memo annotations, where as *LogPalette* takes the data provided by the *Bookroll* and visualizes it to provide insights on how student are using the materials and what they understand.

In India, some learning institutions made notable efforts to incorporate AI technology to empower the visually impaired students. The following are some of the examples:

1. The Blind Relief Association (BRA), New Delhi, India: The BRA is a non-profit organization was founded on February 26, 1944 located in New Delhi

with aim to empowering the visually impaired in psychological, physical and economically for more than seventy years. The BRA adopts the use of different AI powered application in their education, training and rehabilitation procedures that include screen readers, voice recognition and so on. These technologies help students to get access to digital learning resources and improvise their learning processes.

2. **Indian Institute of Technology (IIT) Delhi:** IIT Delhi is taking part in AI driven assistive technology development projects to support visually impaired students. This involves the creation of vehicles with real time *text-to-speech support, image scanning and navigation support.*
3. **National Institute for the Empowerment of Persons with Visual Disabilities (NIEPVD) Dehradun, India:** NIEPVD incorporates AI applications (such as automated Braille transcription systems (NCERT and AI driven image recognition software) into their curriculum under the New Education Policy (NEP 2020). AI was also a choice made by the institution in addition to the Information Technology (IT) and the sports as part of the skill development program.

2.6 AI in Braille Translation

Automated Braille transcription tools.

Automated Braille conversion systems transform digital content into Braille format, thereby enhancing accessibility for the blind and visually impaired. These tools streamline the conversion process by leveraging a range of technologies, including Optical Character Recognition and Text-to-Braille translation.

1. Text Extraction:
   a. **Digital Text:** Tools that can extract text from a different forms of digital files, including Word documents, PDFs, and electronic books (eBooks). These tools generally work with multiple file formats and use an algorithm to analyse and edit the text.
   b. **OCR Integration:** This technology is made up of to recognise and extract text from scanned documents, images, and physical documents. The text that has been extracted is then translated into braille.
2. Braille Translation:
   a. **Text-to-Braille Conversion:** The retrieved text by using different platforms is transformed into braille using predefined codes. Braille is a lettering system comprised of raised dots that making use of letters, numbers and punctuation printing higher than the level of paper so the visually impaired

can read by touching on them. The text is mapped with these patterns of dots to the word using a process known as translation.

3. Output Production:
    a. **Braille Embossing:** Some programmes can generate files compatible with Braille embossers, which make a physical braille document by using the embossing technique in a physical device.
    b. **Digital Braille:** The tools can also create digital braille files, allowing for display of the information on braille displays or alternative displays.

2.7 Popular Automated Braille Transcription Tools

1. Duxbury Braille Translator (DBT):

The DBT is a leading software developed for both sighted and blind users by Duxbury Systems with a modern and flexible user interface for translating text into braille. It supports over 180 languages including contracted and uncontracted braille and can handle various document formats, including Microsoft Word, Open Office, and Excel files. DBT is widely used by braille publishers and transcribers (it can print both ink and braille on the same page, which is useful for proof reading), educators, and transcribers to produce accurate braille for school books (Mathematics & Science Textbooks), teaching materials, and office memos.

2. Braille2000:

Braille2000 is a comprehensive software tool designed for producing braille documents. It is fully *Internet aware,* making it easy to send braille documents to production centers, schools, blind students, or fellow transcribers with just a click. The ***"Talking Edition"*** of Braille2000 is self voicing, which means it can read aloud the content, aiding users who are visually impaired and it is compatible with Windows 7, 8, 8.1, 10 & 11 Versions. The latest version 2 of Braille 2000 has additional features for handling National Instructional Materials Accessibility Standards (NIMAS) source which authors publishing educational materials follow in the K-12 level. Braille 2000 has the capabilities to be used both by sighted and blind users, with a modern and flexible user interface. It has a library of videos, together with instructive tutorials.

SECTION 3: AI ASSISTED NAVIGATION AND WEARABLE DEVICES

3.1 AI Tools of Navigation:

The AI-based navigation apps, **Aira** and **Be My Eyes**, have greatly contributed to the mobility and independence of visually impaired persons, considering the availability of timely assistance for indoor and outdoor navigation (Ricci et al., 2024) .

3.1.1 AI Powered Aira app:

Aira app can be a valuable visual interpreting service that provides on demand assistance for visually impaired students by connecting to trained visual interpreters. This app is available for both iOS and Android devices. Here's how it can be used:

1. **On Campus Navigation**: Students can use Aira app to navigate campus easily. Visual interpreters can help to locate classrooms, libraries, cafeterias, and other facilities.
2. **Access to Learning Materials**: Aira app can assist in reading the printed materials, such as textbooks and handouts, by providing verbal descriptions.
3. **Participation in Class**: Students can use Aira app to actively engage in formal teaching learning process, particularly during visual presentations.
4. **Study Assistance**: Aira app can help students in finding available study spaces in the library or describe bulletin boards and other visual information.
5. **Daily Activities**: The Aira app can assist the students in their daily activities like shopping, travelling, and social gatherings, increasing independence, self-respect and confidence.

3.1.2 AI Powered Be My Eyes:

Be My Eyes is an innovative, volunteer based app that connects blind or low vision persons with sighted volunteers through live video calls. This application has a good number of functions and few are listed below.

1. **Volunteer Assistance:** Users can initiate video calls to connect with sighted volunteers who assist with various tasks, for instance reading labels, matching colours, navigating unfamiliar environments to prepare dinner, or identifying objects. The app has a huge base of volunteers across the globe and thus, different language support and is always available.

2. **Indoor and Outdoor Assistance:** Volunteers play a very important role in both indoor and outdoor settings. They help the users in identifying landmarks, finding transport, and guiding them through the streets. In addition, they assist in packing groceries, reading instructions or navigating indoors such as houses and offices.
3. **AI Integration:** The application seamlessly integrates AI technology, thereby enhancing the service provided by volunteers. The application integrates AI with the "Visual Assistance" feature, wherein AI recognizes objects, text, and colours, thereby providing volunteer support. The feature helps users seek immediate assistance for work
4. **User Friendly Interface:** Be My Eyes has a friendly and user-friendly interface that seeks to make users comfortable when using it. Specifically, Be My Eyes allows users to easily request assisters and receive such support in no time, making it perfect and user-friendly.
5. **Community and Support:** Be My Eyes has a powerful supportive community of volunteers who aim at helping those in need. This is a feeling of community that offers both practical assistance and a network of understanding and experience.

By leveraging both human compassion and highly advanced AI technology, ***Be My Eyes*** can greatly improve the quality of life of visually impaired people, making them feel more confident and independent in navigating the world they live in.

3.2. Smart Canes and AI driven Wearable Devices. (CRDP Article 26 & SDG 8)

Smart canes and AI driven wearable devices are important new assistive technologies for visually impaired people. These devices use artificial intelligence and other technologies to improve navigation, safety, and mobility. Here's an overview of these devices:

1. **Smart Canes**: Smart canes are technologically advanced versions of the ordinary white cane, with different types of sensors like ultrasonic, radar, GPS, etc to provide more sensory feedback and guide services to the blind.
2. **Obstacle Detection**: Smart canes have sensors such as ultrasonic or radar sensors which identify obstacles in the way of the cane. Such sensors have the capacity of detecting items at different heights and distances thus warn the user of possible hazards. Depending on the user, vibrations, sounds, or haptics can be used to provide feedback to the user which gives them knowledge of obstacles and helps them navigate through them.

3. **GPS Integration:** Smart canes that include the help of GPS can navigate the user to a particular destination or specific routes, thus helping the visually impaired locate specific locations or walk specific routes.
4. **Geofencing:** More evolved models can set up virtual (Mina et al., 2023; Walle et al., 2022) boundaries sending the user notifications if the boundaries have been violated or if the user has entered an illegal zone.
5. **Emergency Features:** Smart canes often come equipped with emergency features that allow the user to send alerts to those who are supposed to care for them.
6. **Smartphone Connectivity:** Smartphone Connectivity: Smart canes can also be connected to smartphone applications, which provide extra functionality such as route-planning capabilities, real-time location sharing, and custom settings. There are also some applications that are capable of recording travel data and providing information on user patterns and performance.

Examples of Smart Canes:

a. **Sunu Band:** The Sunu Band is a wearable smart device that can be worn on the wrist or as a belt. It uses echolocation ultrasonic technology to sensor the user's surroundings and can detect object objects 5 meters away. It works on the principle of sonar, where it sends out sound waves and sound pulse and waits for those to bounce off objects and return. So that it can detect how far away these objects are. It uses haptic feedback to alert the user about the objects. The interesting thing about this device is that as the user gets closer to an object, the vibrations intensify and speed up all the way to a steady vibration when the user is right in front of the object. It has indoor mode and outdoor mode options (Muhsin et al., 2023).

b. **We WALK Smart Cane**: The We WALK Smart Cane is a technologically advanced assistive device used by visually impaired people. The difference is evident as it is embedded with technology, yet it still looks like a white cane. The We WALK Smart Cane delivers haptic feedback for obstacle detection, voice-based guidance, precise navigation, integration with navigation guides, real-time public transport information, and options for exploring nearby points of interest. The device is accessible through a smartphone, thus catering to people with visual impairments.

3.3 AI Driven Wearable Devices:

AI-driven wearable devices for visually impaired people apply artificial intelligence in the enhancement of their mobility, navigation, and interaction with the surrounding environment. These devices range from smart glasses and wearable cameras to other sensors that make use of AI to provide real-time assistance in the best possible manner.

Examples of AI Driven Wearable Devices:

a. **OrCam My Eye**: This is a wearable camera clipped onto eyeglasses that uses AI for the purpose of supplying audio descriptions in real time about text, faces, and objects. Key functionalities include reading texts, facial recognition, object identification, and integration with smartphones for additional features.
b. **e-Sight Eyewear:** These glasses have high definition cameras and AI to provide augmented vision to people with low vision. The glasses will provide real time image enhancement, magnification, variable contrast, brightness, and zoom settings, which will give real time visual information to the wearers via the wearable display.
c. **Xenoma e-skin:** Xenoma e-skin is a smart wearable clothing that uses embedded sensors to monitor movements and give feedback on navigation and interaction. It has haptic feedback that provide directional guidance and environmental awareness and can be combined with other assistive technologies.

SECTION 4: ETHICAL, AND SOCIAL CHALLENGES IN AI DRIVEN ASSISTIVE TECHNOLOGY

The rapid growth of AI based assistive technologies is creating possibilities that have never existed before to students with visual impairment. At the same time opportunities are accompanied with challenges of ethical and social complexity. The challenges of AI-based assistive technologies become more central and central as more attention is given to digital ecologies within educational systems and thus connects with the rights, dignity, and inclusion of learners with disabilities (Mager et al., 2025).

4.1 Ethical Challenges:

Generally visual impairment oriented AI systems operates on high volumes of data, ongoing data gathering and decision making algorithms. These processes provoke some serious ethical issues linked with ***privacy, data protection***, and ***informed consent.*** Numerous visually impaired students rely on screen readers, voice recognition tools, and real time recognition programs which store sensitive personal data, such as voice records, behavioural records, and learning behaviour (Suresh et al., 2025). In the absence of strong protective measures, such information may be transmitted improperly or exposed to unauthorised access.

Another important ethical concern is the issue of algorithmic bias. AI systems that are trained with non-inclusive datasets can fail to understand visual images, may falsely recognize objects or give flawed feedback, which is more likely to impact the visually impaired users disproportionately. These biases may only strengthen the already existing inequalities especially to students who belong to underrepresented linguistic, cultural, or social demographic. To keep the trust and obligation, it is necessary to make sure that AI systems are transparent in the decisions that they make, and that users can interpret decisions made or question them.

4.2 Social Challenges

Although AI technologies are more independent and participatory, they do not enjoy a uniform distribution of their benefits. Access to digital infrastructure is influenced by social differences, including the income level, geographic location, gender, and availability of digital infrastructure. In most low and middle income countries, the visually impaired students have poor access to quality internet, affordable gadgets, or trained teachers who can assist in the utilisation of assistive technologies (Barbieri et al., 2025). This digital divide would be a threat to increasing the prevailing inequalities in education instead of mitigating them.

The adoption of AI tools is also affected by culture about disability. Some communities stigmatize visual impairment, which discourages the use of assistive devices among learners, or it could decrease institutional readiness to invest in inclusive technologies. Moreover, the trend to the AI mediated learning environment can have the unintended effect of minimizing human interaction, which, in turn, may impact the social and emotional growth of visually impaired students depending on interpersonal support.

SECTION 5: FUTURE DIRECTIONS OF AI IN SPECIAL EDUCATION

Along with the further development of AI based assistive technologies, the future of special education, particularly visually impaired students will be defined by the innovations that will mitigate the existing restrictions but widen the opportunities of individually designed, inclusive, and equitable learning. Continuing on the implementation issues found above, the future directions should deal with the reinforcement of infrastructure, development of teacher capacity (Barbieri et al., 2025), and the introduction of ethical and inclusive design principles at each level of technological development (Kooli & Chakraoui, 2025).

5.1 Advancing Inclusive AI Design and Ethical Governance

The future AI systems should be designed to have more commitments to transparency, fairness, and accessibility. This involves development of algorithms, which are trained on a variety of databases that capture linguistic, cultural, and disability based realities of learners across the world. The ethical governance structures will also have to change in such a way that the visually impaired students will have control over their data, they will be aware of how the AI systems work, and they will enjoy technologies that do not infringe upon their autonomy and dignity. To establish trust and accountability, the following generation of AI tools must include explainable AI (XAI), and privacy preserving architectures, and user controlled data settings.

5.2 Strengthening Infrastructure for Scalable Implementation

Improved digital infrastructure should be of focus to make the most out of AI in the special education sector. This involves the provision of affordable high speed internet, availability of learning management systems and interoperable assistive devices that can operate among platforms as well as languages (Kooli & Chakraoui, 2025). Cloud based AI services, affordable hardware, and offline capable tools will be necessary in the realization of underserved regions especially those in low and middle income countries. Long term strategies of investment will be required by governments and institutions to make sure the AI technologies are updated, sustainable, and accessible to many people.

5.3 Empowering Educators Through Continuous Professional Development

Teacher readiness is crucial to the future of AI in the special education field. The shift towards professional development should not be a single training session but sustained, competency-based learning trajectories that will help educators develop the professional skills to implement AI tools in any meaningful way in pedagogy (Daher, 2025). A teacher assist system may be developed based on AI to facilitate lesson planning, accessibility checks and individualized instructions (Devaki et al., 2025). Joint training designs that incorporate teachers, technologists, and disability specialists in coming up with learning experiences will be instrumental in making sure that AI supplements and does not substitute human knowledge (Barbieri et al., 2025).

5.4 Personalized and Multisensory Learning Environments

Increasingly, AI will allow the creation of extremely customized learning processes, which are responsive to their speed, sensory preferences, and profile of thinking. In the case of visually impaired students, the systems of the future can incorporate the development of tactile graphic representation, real time haptic feedback, sophisticated speech interfaces and multimodal learning analytics. The new Immersive environment made available through extended reality (XR) environment augmented, virtual, and mixed reality will provide language learning, mobility training, and conceptual understanding. Such multisensory ecosystems will assist in closing the gaps in the traditional instruction and allow more profound involvement.

5.5 Policy Innovation and Cross Sector Collaboration

The development of the future will need powerful policy frameworks that can be in line with international commitments like the CRPD, Marrakesh Treaty and SDGs. There should be policies that deal with procurement standards, accessibility compliance, data governance and long term funding models. Intergovernmental, cross-sector cooperation among governments, universities, NGOs, technology firms, and disability groups will be necessary to scale innovations and make AI solutions culturally accessible, affordable, and based on lived experiences of visually impaired students.

5.6 Toward a Human Centered AI Ecosystem

Finally, to support the future of AI in special education, the focus should be on developing a human centered ecosystem where technology will enhance but not destroy the relationship, creativity and emotional support that are essential in meaningful learning. AI must serve as an empowering collaborator that contributes to increased independence, broader access and the ability of the visually impaired student to engage in academic and social life. An AI tool combining ethical design, inclusive policy and sustainable implementation can be used to create an educational system in which all learners can flourish in the next generation.

CONCLUSION

The incorporation of AI powered assistive technologies is one of the significant changes in the ways visually impaired students' access, interact with, and engage in learning. Scalability and accessibility of solutions in visual impairment and the continued inequity in educational access have become necessary in an ever increasing global context. As discussed in this chapter, AI-powered systems like state of the art screen readers, real-time recognition, tactile interfaces and multisensory learning are all vigorously transforming the concept of accessibility. The technologies provide individualised and dynamic learning experiences that have never been offered by traditional methods. Nevertheless, AI applications in special education will require a conscious and responsible effort. Issues connected to data privacy, algorithm discrimination, digital marginalization, educator readiness and infrastructural constraints should be tackled using rights-based approaches. The Convention on the Rights of Persons with Disabilities and the Sustainable Development Goals provide an excellent insight on the need to focus on equity, accessibility and full inclusion of persons with disabilities. Moving forward, the future of AI in special education will be based on the ability to invest in inclusive design, strong policy formulation, inter-sectoral cooperation, and lifelong professional growth of educators. AI can potentially do better than improve the learning outcomes when used ethically and strategically. It can enable the visually impaired students to be independent, confident and self-directed learners in both academic and social learning. This chapter concludes by asserting the fact that technology is a potent tool, however, it is only with an ethically oriented mind set and educational justice that it can be used to create a truly non-discriminatory future of all learners.

REFERENCES

Alimović, S. (2024). Benefits and challenges of using assistive technology in the education and rehabilitation of Individuals with visual impairments. *Disability and Rehabilitation. Assistive Technology*, *19*(8), 3063–3070. DOI: 10.1080/17483107.2024.2344802 PMID: 38685705

Anokye, G. O., Price-Sanchez, C., Yong, A. C., Ali, M., Tate, C., Graham, R., & Chan, V. F. (2025). School-based eye health interventions for improving eye care and spectacles compliance in children in low- and middle-income countries: A scoping review. *AJO International*, *2*(2), 100126. DOI: 10.1016/j.ajoint.2025.100126

Baguma, R., & Wolters, M. K. (2021). Making Virtual Learning Environments Accessible to People with Disabilities in Universities in Uganda. *Frontiers of Computer Science*, *3*, 638275. DOI: 10.3389/fcomp.2021.638275

Barbieri, M., Pennazio, V., Sabatini, S. P., & Gori, M. (2025). Through their eyes: Enhancing teacher awareness of visual impairments via extended reality simulations (REALTER). *Frontiers in Education*, *10*, 1634253. DOI: 10.3389/feduc.2025.1634253

Daher, R. (2025). Integrating AI literacy into teacher education: a critical perspective paper. *Discover Artificial Intelligence 2025 5:1*, *5*(1), 217-. DOI: 10.1007/s44163-025-00475-7

Devaki, V., Suresh, C., & Boopathi, L. (2025). Building Teacher Skills for Effective Integration of Technology in the Classroom. Https://Services.Igi-Global.Com/Resolvedoi/Resolve.Aspx?Doi=10.4018/979-8-3373-0771-8.Ch012, 269–302. DOI: 10.4018/979-8-3373-0771-8.ch012

Dong, W., Pan, D., & Kim, S. (2024). Exploring the integration of IoT and Generative AI in English language education: Smart tools for personalized learning experiences. *Journal of Computational Science*, *82*, 102397. Advance online publication. DOI: 10.1016/j.jocs.2024.102397

Dumitru, C., Abdulsahib, G. M., Khalaf, O. I., & Bennour, A. (2026). Integrating artificial intelligence in supporting students with disabilities in higher education: An integrative review. *Technology and Disability*, *38*(1), 3–24. Advance online publication. DOI: 10.1177/10554181251355428

Elshaer, I. A., AlNajdi, S. M., & Salem, M. A. (2025). Sustainable AI Solutions for Empowering Visually Impaired Students: The Role of Assistive Technologies in Academic Success. *Sustainability 2025, Vol. 17*, *17*(12). DOI: 10.3390/su17125609

Ferri, D., & Donnellan, K. (2022). The Implementation of the Marrakesh Directive: A Comparative Analysis across Six EU Member States. SSRN *Electronic Journal.* https://doi.org/DOI: 10.2139/SSRN.4406281

Ferri, D., & Rossello, G. (2023). The Role of the Marrakesh Treaty in Supporting Access to Printed Material for People Who Are Blind or Visually Impaired: A Critical Discussion of the Results of an Empirical Study Conducted in Six European Countries. *Disabilities 2023, Vol. 3, Pages 147-164, 3*(2), 147–164. DOI: 10.3390/disabilities3020011

Fitas, R. (2025). Inclusive education with AI: supporting special needs and tackling language barriers. *AI and Ethics 2025 5:6, 5*(6), 5729–5757. DOI: 10.1007/s43681-025-00824-3

Girish, A., & Vaidyanathan, S. (2021). Visually Impaired Persons and Access to Copyrighted Works: The Indian Roadmap. *Indonesian Journal of International Law, 18*(4), 501–522. DOI: 10.17304/ijil.vol18.4.821

Hamideh Kerdar, S., Bächler, L., & Kirchhoff, B. M. (2024). The accessibility of digital technologies for people with visual impairment and blindness: a scoping review. *Discover Computing 2024 27:1, 27*(1), 24-. DOI: 10.1007/s10791-024-09460-7

Hassan, A. H., Ahmed, E. M., Hussien, J. M., Sulaiman, R., Abdulhak, M., & Kahtan, H. (2025). A cyber physical sustainable smart city framework toward society 5.0: Explainable AI for enhanced SDGs monitoring. *Research in Globalization, 10*, 100275. DOI: 10.1016/j.resglo.2025.100275

Kathiria, P., Mankad, S. H., Patel, J., Kapadia, M., & Lakdawala, N. (2024). Assistive systems for visually impaired people: A survey on current requirements and advancements. *Neurocomputing, 606*, 128284. DOI: 10.1016/j.neucom.2024.128284

Kooli, C., & Chakraoui, R. (2025). AI-driven assistive technologies in inclusive education: Benefits, challenges, and policy recommendations. *Sustainable Futures : An Applied Journal of Technology, Environment and Society, 10*, 101042. DOI: 10.1016/j.sftr.2025.101042

Lee, D., Arnold, M., Srivastava, A., Plastow, K., Strelan, P., Ploeckl, F., Lekkas, D., & Palmer, E. (2024). The impact of generative AI on higher education learning and teaching: A study of educators' perspectives. *Computers and Education: Artificial Intelligence, 6*, 100221. DOI: 10.1016/j.caeai.2024.100221

Mager, A., Eitenberger, M., Winter, J., Prainsack, B., Wendehorst, C., & Arora, P. (2025). Situated ethics: Ethical accountability of local perspectives in global AI ethics. *Media Culture & Society, 47*(5), 1028–1041. DOI: 10.1177/01634437251328200

McIntyre, N. A. (2022). Access to online learning: Machine learning analysis from a social justice perspective. *Education and Information Technologies 2022 28:4, 28*(4), 3787–3832. DOI: 10.1007/s10639-022-11280-5

Milde, N., Schmidt, D. C., Larsen, A., & Kessel, L. (2024). Which rehabilitation initiatives can effectively improve participation in an educational setting for visually impaired and blind adolescents? A systematic review. *BMC Ophthalmology 2023 24:1, 24*(1), 10-. DOI: 10.1186/s12886-023-03267-8

Mina, P. N. R., Solon, I. M., Sanchez, F. R., Delante, T. K., Villegas, J. K., Basay, F. J., Andales, J., Pasko, F., Estrera, M. F. R., Samson, R.Jr, & Mutya, R. (2023). Leveraging Education through Artificial Intelligence Virtual Assistance: A Case Study of Visually Impaired Learners. *International Journal of Educational Innovation and Research, 2*(1), 10–22. DOI: 10.31949/ijeir.v2i1.3001

Muhsin, Z. J., Qahwaji, R., Ghanchi, F., & Al-Taee, M. (2023). Review of substitutive assistive tools and technologies for people with visual impairments: recent advancements and prospects. *Journal on Multimodal User Interfaces 2023 18:1, 18*(1), 135–156. DOI: 10.1007/s12193-023-00427-4

Pamuji, Nerri, I. A., & Niratama, F. (2023). *Literature Review: Enhancing Education Accessibility: The Role of Assistive Technology in Promoting Equality for the Visually Impaired.* 1159–1171. DOI: 10.2991/978-2-38476-152-4_118

Panda, S., & Kaur, Dr. N. (2024). Quality Education for Visually Impaired: Achieving Sustainable Development Goal 04 through Web Accessibility Measures. *SSRN Electronic Journal.* DOI: 10.2139/ssrn.4857711

Phutane, M., Jung, C., Chen, N., & Azenkot, S. (2023). Speaking with My Screen Reader: Using Audio Fictions to Explore Conversational Access to Interfaces. *ASSETS 2023 - Proceedings of the 25th International ACM SIGACCESS Conference on Computers and Accessibility.* https://doi.org/DOI: 10.1145/3597638.3608404;PAGE:STRING:ARTICLE/CHAPTER

Prakash, S., Agrawal, K., Singh, S., Aggarwal, G., & Dosaj, S. (2023). *Voice Based Email System for the Visually Challenged.* DOI: 10.21203/rs.3.rs-2982553/v1

Pundlik, S., Shivshanker, P., & Luo, G. (2024).. . *Impact of Apps as Assistive Devices for Visually Impaired Persons., 55*, 9. DOI: 10.1146/annurev-vision-111022

Que, L., Zhu, Q., Jiang, C., & Lu, Q. (2025). An analysis of the global, regional, and national burden of blindness and vision loss between 1990 and 2021: The findings of the Global Burden of Disease Study 2021. *Frontiers in Public Health, 13*, 1560449. DOI: 10.3389/fpubh.2025.1560449 PMID: 40365429

Reiss, M. J. (2021). The use of AI in education: Practicalities and ethical considerations. *London Review of Education, 19*(1), 1–14. DOI: 10.14324/LRE.19.1.05

Ricci, F. S., Liguori, L., Palermo, E., Rizzo, J.-R., & Porfiri, M. (2024). Navigation Training for Persons With Visual Disability Through Multisensory Assistive Technology: Mixed Methods Experimental Study. *JMIR Rehabilitation and Assistive Technologies, 11*(1), e55776. DOI: 10.2196/55776 PMID: 39556804

Suresh, C., Mahammad Ali, S., & Devaki, V. (2025). Perception About Usage of GAI Tools in Teaching and Research by Teachers and Students in Higher Education Institutions. Https://Services.Igi-Global.Com/Resolvedoi/Resolve.Aspx?Doi=10.4018/979-8-3693-8191-5.Ch015, 381–412. DOI: 10.4018/979-8-3693-8191-5.ch015

Walle, H., Serres, B., Gilles, V., de Runz, C., De Runz, C., Serres, B., & Venturini, G. (2022). A Survey on Recent Advances in AI and Vision Based Methods for Helping and Guiding Visually Impaired People. *Applied Sciences, 2022*(5). https://doi.org/DOI: 10.3390/app12052308ï

Wang, J., Wang, S., & Zhang, Y. (2023). Artificial intelligence for visually impaired. *Displays, 77*, 102391. Advance online publication. DOI: 10.1016/j.displa.2023.102391

Yan, W., Li, B., & Lowell, V. L. (2025). Integrating Artificial Intelligence and Extended Reality in Language Education: A Systematic Literature Review (2017–2024). *Education Sciences 2025, Vol. 15, 15*(8). DOI: 10.3390/educsci15081066

Yang, C., & Taele, P. (2025). AI for Accessible Education: Personalized Audio-Based Learning for Blind Students. *Proceedings of Augmented Educators and AI: Shaping the Future of Human-AI Collaboration in Learning on CHI 2025 Workshop (Augmented Educators and AI(CHI 2025 Workshop)), 1*. https://arxiv.org/pdf/2504.17117

Zaraii Zavaraki, E. (2024). Artificial Intelligence for People with Special Educational Needs. In *Artificial Intelligence for Quality Education* [Working Title]. IntechOpen., DOI: 10.5772/intechopen.1004158

Chapter 5

AI as Emerging Assistive Technology in Higher Education:

Opportunities, Tensions, and Critical Perspectives Under a Universal Design for Learning Framework

Filipe T. Moreira
http://orcid.org/0000-0002-3461-9827
InED, Escola Superior de Educação, Instituto Politécnico do Porto, Portugal

Pedro Simões
ICNOVA, Instituto Politécnico da Guarda, Portugal

Paulo M. Barroso
http://orcid.org/0000-0001-7638-5064
ICNOVA, Instituto Politécnico de Viseu, Portugal

Alexandre Figueiredo
http://orcid.org/0000-0002-6021-8779
ICNOVA, Instituto Politécnico de Portalegre, Portugal

Deepak Gupta
http://orcid.org/0000-0003-3929-1362
Institute of Technology and Management, Gwalior, India

DOI: 10.4018/979-8-2600-2716-5.ch005

2027, IGI Global Scientific Publishing. Copying or distributing in print or electronic forms without written permission of IGI Global Scientific Publishing is prohibited. Use of this chapter to ative artificial intelligence (AI) technologies is expressly prohibited. The publisher reserves all rights to license its use for generative AI training and machine learning model development.

ABSTRACT

The integration of Artificial Intelligence in higher education has generated considerable interest, yet its potential as an assistive technology remains undertheorised within the Universal Design for Learning framework. This chapter examines AI as an emerging assistive technology capable of reducing barriers for a wide range of learners, including students with disabilities, those working in a second language, and any student whose needs fall outside what traditional structures serve. Drawing on UDL and emerging research, it maps the opportunities AI presents and the tensions it introduces: data privacy, educator surveillance, algorithmic bias, cognitive autonomy, and the irreplaceable human dimension of teaching. A framework for responsible integration is built around six principles: inclusion as design, transparency, informed consent, complementarity, professional development, co-design, and ongoing evaluation.

1 INTRODUCTION

Technology has always been a defining feature of human civilisation. Long before the digital age, tools, writing systems, and mechanical devices shaped how societies organised themselves, communicated, and transmitted knowledge. What distinguishes each technological revolution from the previous one is not merely the nature of the artefact, but the scale and depth of the transformation it provokes. The printing press did not simply make books cheaper; it restructured how knowledge was produced, legitimised, and distributed across social hierarchies. The industrial revolution did not merely accelerate production; it fundamentally reorganised labour, urban life, and economic relations. In this sense, technology is never neutral: it carries within it the potential to reconfigure the conditions under which people live, work, and learn (Nemorin et al., 2023).

Arriving at a new technological paradigm always entails a period of disruption, adaptation, and renegotiation of what was previously taken for granted. This is particularly evident when a technology reaches beyond a single domain and begins to reshape multiple areas of human activity simultaneously. The more pervasive its reach, the more profound and often unsettling the transformation it triggers. Artificial Intelligence is precisely this kind of technology. Its applications span healthcare, law, creative industries, scientific research, and education, among many others, making it one of the most cross-cutting technological developments of our time. This breadth is not merely a question of utility; it raises fundamental questions about authorship, accountability, expertise, and the nature of human agency itself.

It would be a mistake, however, to treat Artificial Intelligence as a sudden arrival. The theoretical foundations of the field were laid in the mid-twentieth century, and the term itself was coined by John McCarthy in 1956. The decades that followed saw sustained progress in machine learning, natural language processing, and computational reasoning (Nemorin et al., 2023). What has changed is not the existence of AI, but its visibility and accessibility. The release of large language models and generative AI tools to the general public, most prominently from 2022 onwards, marked a qualitative shift in the relationship between ordinary users and intelligent systems. For the first time, a significant portion of the population could interact directly with AI, generating text, images, code, and other artefacts in a matter of seconds, without any specialised technical knowledge. This democratisation of access brought with it both remarkable possibilities and equally serious concerns.

Generative AI has intensified debates that were already present in the field but had not yet reached mainstream urgency. Questions about the reliability of AI-produced content, the risks of misinformation, the opacity of algorithmic decision-making, and the ethical implications of training data collection have moved from academic conferences into policy forums, newsrooms, and classroom discussions (Uygun, 2024). At the same time, the speed with which generative tools can produce new outputs such as texts, analyses, lesson plans, and assessments has attracted enormous interest from educators, institutions, and technology developers alike. The tension between this productive potential and the ethical challenges it creates has become one of the defining conversations of contemporary education.

It is within this broader context that the present chapter situates itself. Education has historically been one of the domains most sensitive to technological change, not only because it is the primary institutional site for the formation of future citizens, but because the values it embodies, among them equity, access, critical thinking, and human development, are precisely those most at stake when powerful technologies are introduced without adequate reflection. In higher education particularly, where students are expected to engage in independent inquiry and to develop sophisticated cognitive and professional competencies, the arrival of AI raises questions that go well beyond classroom management or academic integrity. It invites a fundamental rethinking of what learning means, what assessment measures, and what kind of support genuinely serves students in all their diversity.

This chapter examines Artificial Intelligence as an emerging assistive technology in higher education, understood through the lens of Universal Design for Learning (UDL). Rather than offering a catalogue of tools or a straightforward endorsement of AI adoption, it seeks to engage critically with both the possibilities and the tensions that AI introduces in this context, from its potential to reduce barriers for students with disabilities or linguistic challenges, to the cognitive, ethical, and privacy-related questions it necessarily raises. The aim is not to resolve these tensions but to map them honestly, in the belief that a clear-eyed understanding of what is at stake is the necessary starting point for any responsible integration of AI in educational practice. To pursue this aim with the necessary rigour, the chapter draws on a critical narrative review of the literature, whose scope and procedures are described in the section that follows. The discussion then turns to the conceptual reframing of AI as assistive technology, before examining in turn the opportunities AI presents, the tensions it introduces, the evidence emerging from current practice, and the principles that might guide its responsible integration.

2 A CRITICAL NARRATIVE REVIEW

This chapter is grounded in a critical narrative review of the literature. This methodological choice is appropriate for a conceptually driven inquiry that seeks to synthesise a heterogeneous body of evidence, develop a theoretical argument, and identify tensions that cut across the findings of individual studies. Unlike systematic reviews, which prioritise exhaustiveness and replicability through strict protocols applied to a bounded empirical question, narrative reviews allow for the interpretive and analytical work that a chapter of this kind requires. The aim is not to aggregate effect sizes or to produce a comprehensive inventory of the field, but to map a set of interrelated questions — about AI, assistive technology, inclusion, and higher education — and to develop a critical framework for thinking through them. As González-Calatayud et al. (2021) note in their own systematic review of AI for student assessment, the field is still in an early and rapidly evolving stage, which itself justifies approaches that prioritise conceptual clarity and critical orientation over premature quantitative synthesis.

The literature informing this chapter was identified through searches conducted in Web of Science, Scopus, ERIC, and Google Scholar, using search terms drawn from three conceptual domains: the technology domain, including terms such as "artificial intelligence," "generative AI," and "large language models"; the educational context domain, including "higher education," "university," and "tertiary education"; and the inclusion and accessibility domain, including "assistive technology," "Universal Design for Learning," "UDL," "inclusive education," and "disability." Searches were not restricted by country of origin and covered publications from 2013 to 2025, with particular attention to work published after 2019 to capture developments in AI-enhanced education, while also including foundational work on UDL and assistive technology that predates the widespread availability of generative AI tools.

Sources were selected for inclusion on the basis of four criteria: relevance to the chapter's central concerns at the intersection of AI, assistive technology, inclusive pedagogy, and higher education; methodological transparency and scholarly rigour; the quality and specificity of the contribution to the arguments developed here; and availability in full text. Studies addressing AI in education exclusively in primary or secondary contexts were included only where their findings offered direct conceptual relevance to higher education. Studies that were purely technical in orientation, without educational analysis, were excluded. The selection process was purposive rather than exhaustive, which is consistent with the narrative review methodology: the goal is analytical adequacy rather than comprehensive coverage.

Throughout the chapter, a deliberate effort is made to distinguish between findings that are empirically grounded in the reviewed studies, conclusions that represent emerging but still limited evidence, and arguments that are conceptual or normative in nature. This distinction is treated as a methodological obligation. The evidence base for AI specifically as assistive technology in higher education remains limited, and a substantial proportion of the relevant literature addresses either AI in education more broadly or assistive technology outside higher education contexts. Where such studies are cited, their contextual distance from the chapter's specific focus is acknowledged, and the claims drawn from them are calibrated accordingly. The narrative synthesis is organised thematically, following the structure of the chapter's argument, from the conceptual reframing of AI as assistive technology through the opportunities and tensions its integration presents, to the evidence from emerging practice and the principles for responsible integration.

3 AI AS ASSISTIVE TECHNOLOGY: A CONCEPTUAL REFRAMING

Before the opportunities and tensions of AI in higher education can be examined, the central claim of this chapter, that AI can function as a form of assistive technology, requires conceptual scrutiny rather than mere assertion. Assistive technology has traditionally been understood as any device, software, or system designed to help individuals with disabilities perform tasks that might otherwise be difficult or impossible. Screen readers, speech-to-text software, alternative communication devices, and captioning tools are among the most familiar examples. This conception, while important, has tended to frame assistive technology as a compensatory resource, something provided to a specific population to bridge a gap defined by limitation. The Universal Design for Learning framework challenges this framing by proposing that the design of learning environments should anticipate diversity from the outset, rather than retrofitting accommodations after the fact (Dalton et al., 2019). When the two perspectives are brought together, they point toward a broader and more inclusive understanding of what assistive technology can be and for whom it is intended.

It is necessary, however, to be precise about what is being claimed when AI is described as assistive technology, since the term carries legal, pedagogical, disability-related, and design-specific meanings that should not be conflated. In the strict, formal sense recognised in disability legislation and accessibility standards, assistive technology refers to purpose-built tools designed and certified to address specific functional limitations. General-purpose AI systems such as large language models do not meet this definition, and this chapter does not claim that they do. The argument advanced here is narrower and more specific: that such tools can perform an assistive function when they are used, in a given context, to reduce a barrier to participation that a learner would otherwise face. The distinction matters. A large language model is not an assistive technology in the way a screen reader is, but it may serve an assistive purpose for a particular student engaged in a particular task. Throughout this chapter, the phrase "AI as assistive technology" should be understood in this functional sense, as a description of what AI can do under certain conditions, not as a claim about the formal classification of the tools themselves.

Artificial Intelligence, understood in this functional sense, fits within the broader reconceptualisation of assistive technology in significant ways. What distinguishes AI from earlier generations of educational technology is not simply its computational power, but its capacity to respond to the individual user in real time, adapting content, format, feedback, and pace to meet needs that are rarely identical across learners. This responsiveness aligns directly with UDL's three foundational principles: providing multiple means of representation, of action and expression, and of engagement (Saborío-Taylor & Rojas-Ramírez, 2024). An AI system that can present information in different formats, offer explanations at varying levels of complexity, or generate alternative representations of the same concept is not merely a convenience; it may, for some learners and in some contexts, constitute a meaningful reduction of barriers to participation.

In higher education, the population of students who might benefit from this kind of adaptive support is considerably broader than the category of students formally registered with disability services. Students navigating learning in a second or third language, students managing attention difficulties that have never been formally diagnosed, students returning to education after years in the workforce, and students from educational backgrounds where certain academic conventions were never explicitly taught all encounter barriers that traditional university structures rarely address with flexibility. The conventional lecture, the standardised written assignment, and the fixed-duration examination were not designed with this diversity in mind. AI tools capable of generating personalised study materials, reformulating complex academic texts, providing immediate and targeted feedback on writing, or converting spoken language to text open possibilities for these learners that may, in functional terms, amount to a form of assistive support. Whether they actually do so in practice depends on conditions that the following sections examine with care, rather than on the capabilities of the tools alone.

It is worth noting that the most widely accessible AI tools currently available, including large language models such as Claude and Gemini, are not purpose-built assistive technologies. They are general-purpose systems whose assistive potential emerges from the flexibility and breadth of what they can do. A student with dyslexia might use them to have a complex reading reformulated in simpler language. A student with motor difficulties might use voice interaction to produce written work. A student struggling with academic writing conventions might receive scaffolded guidance that a lecturer with thirty students simply does not have the time to provide individually. Beyond supporting individual learners, these tools also allow educators to develop differentiated digital learning resources with a speed and degree of personalisation that was previously impractical, generating adapted texts, quizzes, visual summaries, or accessible versions of course materials tailored to the specific needs of a given group (Alkan, 2024). These are possibilities rather than established outcomes, and the distinction between the two is one that this chapter takes seriously.

This productive dimension of AI, its capacity not only to assist consumption but to support the creation of pedagogical resources, deserves particular attention in the context of higher education. Lecturers working with diverse cohorts can use AI to develop materials that anticipate different entry points, offer multiple explanations of the same concept, or present content in formats suited to different sensory or cognitive preferences. In this sense, AI may function as an assistive resource not only for students but for educators seeking to implement inclusive practices under conditions of limited time and institutional support. The potential is being explored in many institutions, even if the theoretical frameworks for understanding it, and the empirical evidence for evaluating it, remain underdeveloped.

None of this, however, is straightforward. Framing AI as assistive technology raises questions that the field of assistive technology has long grappled with, and that take on new dimensions in the context of intelligent systems. Who decides what constitutes a barrier and what constitutes appropriate support? What happens when the tool designed to assist also collects data, makes inferences, and shapes the learning experience in ways that are not transparent to the user? What is the relationship between the support AI provides and the development of the cognitive capacities that higher education is supposed to cultivate? These questions do not invalidate the assistive potential of AI, but they insist that potential cannot be evaluated in isolation from the conditions under which it is realised. The following sections take up these tensions directly, beginning with the opportunities AI presents and then turning, with equal seriousness, to the challenges it poses.

4 OPPORTUNITIES IN HIGHER EDUCATION: PERSONALISATION, ACCESS, AND INCLUSION

The promise of personalised learning has accompanied educational technology for decades. From early computer-assisted instruction to adaptive learning platforms, the aspiration has remained remarkably consistent: that technology might allow each student to learn at their own pace, in their own way, following a path shaped by their individual needs and prior knowledge. What AI brings to this long-standing ambition is not merely greater computational power, but a qualitatively different kind of responsiveness. Rather than selecting from a pre-defined set of paths, AI systems can generate new content, reframe existing explanations, and adapt their outputs dynamically to the specific moment and the specific learner. This distinction matters, because it shifts personalisation from a catalogue of options to something closer to genuine dialogue (González-Calatayud et al., 2021).

Before these possibilities are explored, an important qualification must frame the entire discussion. The opportunities described in this section are, for the most part, possibilities supported by emerging evidence rather than outcomes established by robust empirical research. Much of the available evidence consists of small-scale studies, often conducted over short periods and in specific disciplinary or linguistic contexts, and the gap between what AI tools can do in principle and what they reliably achieve across diverse student populations remains substantial. This section therefore describes opportunities, not guarantees, and the conditions under which those opportunities are realised, or fail to be realised, are as important as the opportunities themselves.

It is important to resist the assumption that personalisation in this sense is only relevant for students who carry a formal diagnosis or a registered disability. The premise of Universal Design for Learning is precisely that variability is not the exception but the rule: every learner brings a distinct combination of prior knowledge, cognitive preferences, linguistic background, motivational patterns, and life circumstances that shape how they engage with academic content (Bray et al., 2024). A student who processes information more effectively through visual representation than through extended prose is not, in any clinical sense, a student with a special need. Yet the traditional lecture, with its dependence on sustained verbal exposition and note-taking, may serve that student poorly. AI tools capable of generating diagrams, summaries, alternative explanations, or interactive representations of the same concept respond to this kind of variability without requiring that it be named, categorised, or formally accommodated. In this sense, AI as assistive technology is not a provision for the few but a potential structural support for the many.

For students who do experience specific learning differences, the potential is more immediate and, in some reported cases, considerable. Students with dyslexia can use AI to have dense academic texts reformulated in clearer language, to receive feedback on their own writing that identifies patterns they may not perceive, or to convert spoken ideas into structured written form. Students with attention difficulties can work with AI to break complex tasks into manageable steps, receive immediate confirmation of progress, or return to explanations as many times as needed without the social exposure that asking a lecturer the same question repeatedly can entail. Students who are deaf or hard of hearing benefit from AI-powered transcription and captioning tools that have improved significantly in accuracy and speed. Students with motor impairments can interact through voice, reducing dependence on keyboard input (Massola, 2023). It must be acknowledged, however, that these uses have not been subjected to the kind of disability-specific user testing, accessibility auditing, or comparative evaluation against established assistive technologies that would be needed to establish them as verified interventions. A student with dyslexia who relies on AI to reformulate a text is depending on a system that may also introduce errors, alter meaning, or produce fluent but inaccurate output, and the consequences of such failures for a learner who cannot easily detect them are not trivial. The promise is real, but so is the need for caution.

The linguistic dimension of inclusion deserves equal attention, and equal care. Higher education is increasingly international, and many students are studying in a language that is not their first, sometimes not even their second. The cognitive load of processing complex disciplinary content while simultaneously managing a second language is substantial, and it affects comprehension, performance, and confidence in ways that are rarely visible to those teaching the course. AI tools can assist these students by clarifying terminology, offering explanations in simpler syntactic structures, or providing translations that aim to preserve disciplinary precision. Whether they succeed in preserving it is a genuine and underexamined question. Translation and linguistic simplification by AI can distort disciplinary meaning in ways that a student working in a second language may be least equipped to detect, and there is a further risk that habitual reliance on AI linguistic smoothing allows a student to produce competent-sounding text without developing their own academic voice in the target language. The support is valuable, but it is not without cost, and the cost falls precisely on the dimension, independent linguistic competence, that higher education in a second language is partly meant to develop (Segura-Castillo & Quirós-Acuña, 2019).

The Material Conditions of Access

A chapter concerned with inclusion cannot discuss the opportunities AI offers without attending to the material conditions under which inclusion either happens or fails. The assistive potential described above is not distributed equally, and the factors that determine access are precisely those that tend to track existing patterns of advantage and disadvantage. To present AI as an equalising force without examining these conditions would be to reproduce the very inequalities that an inclusive analysis is meant to expose.

The most capable AI tools are increasingly offered through paid subscription models, with the most advanced capabilities reserved for those who can afford them. A student who can pay for a premium subscription has access to a materially different tool from one who relies on a free tier or who cannot pay at all. Where institutions provide licensed access, the inequality may be mitigated, but institutional licensing is uneven, often partial, and shaped by budgetary pressures that fall hardest on under-resourced institutions serving the most disadvantaged students. The result is a real risk that AI, far from levelling the field, introduces a new axis of stratification that maps onto socioeconomic position.

Access is not only a question of cost. Reliable internet connectivity, suitable devices, and the digital literacy required to use AI tools effectively are unevenly distributed, both between and within countries. A student without dependable connectivity cannot rely on cloud-based AI tools, and a student who has never been taught how to prompt, evaluate, and critically interrogate AI outputs is poorly positioned to benefit from them even when access is available. Digital literacy, in this sense, is not a uniform background condition but a competence that is itself unequally distributed, and one that institutions cannot assume their students possess. The students most likely to lack it are frequently those whom inclusive education is most concerned to support.

Finally, the reliability of the tools themselves imposes a material limit on their assistive value. Large language models are prone to generating plausible but incorrect information, a phenomenon commonly described as hallucination, and they can do so with a fluency and confidence that makes errors difficult to detect. For a student using AI to understand a difficult concept, to check their own reasoning, or to receive feedback on disciplinary content, an undetected error is not a minor inconvenience but a potential source of genuine misunderstanding. The students least equipped to identify such errors, those new to a discipline, those working in a second language, those without strong prior preparation, are often the same students for whom the assistive promise of AI is most attractive. This convergence of vulnerability and risk is one that any honest account of AI's opportunities must hold in view.

Educators and Inclusive Course Design

Beyond supporting individual learners, AI also expands what educators can practically offer in terms of inclusive course design. Developing genuinely differentiated materials has always been desirable in principle and difficult in practice, because it demands time that most lecturers in higher education do not have. AI changes this equation. A lecturer can use tools such as Claude or Gemini to generate accessible versions of a reading, produce a visual summary of a lecture, create a set of questions pitched at different levels of complexity, or design an alternative assessment format in a fraction of the time these tasks would previously require. This is not a replacement of pedagogical judgement; it is an amplification of the educator's capacity to act on values of inclusion that they may already hold but have lacked the resources to fully realise. This amplification, however, is conditional on the educator's capacity to evaluate AI outputs critically, since the same reliability limitations that affect students apply with equal force to materials generated for teaching, and an error embedded in a widely distributed resource can propagate further than one encountered by a single learner (Saborío-Taylor & Rojas-Ramírez, 2024).

Real-time feedback is another dimension of AI's potential that carries particular significance in higher education. Formative feedback is consistently identified in the research literature as one of the most powerful influences on learning outcomes, yet it is also one of the resources most unevenly distributed across student populations (González-Calatayud et al., 2021). Students with greater cultural capital, stronger prior academic preparation, or more access to informal networks of support tend to receive more feedback, more often, and in more actionable forms. AI tools that provide immediate responses to a student's work introduce a form of feedback that is, in principle, available to every student regardless of their social position or their confidence in approaching a tutor. This equalising potential, however, should be stated carefully rather than asserted confidently, since it depends on precisely the conditions of access discussed above. Where access is stratified by cost, connectivity, and digital literacy, AI feedback may widen rather than narrow the very gaps it appears to address. The potential is genuine, but its realisation is contingent, and the contingency is not a detail but the heart of the matter.

Taken together, these possibilities suggest that AI occupies a meaningful and largely undertheorised position at the intersection of assistive technology, inclusive pedagogy, and educational equity. The argument is not that AI solves the structural problems of higher education, or that personalisation through technology is a substitute for the human relationships that learning depends on. Nor is it that the opportunities described here are established beyond doubt; they are, as this section has repeatedly stressed, possibilities whose realisation depends on conditions that are frequently absent. It is, more modestly, that AI may extend the reach of inclusive practice in ways that matter for real students navigating real institutions, provided that the material and pedagogical conditions for doing so are deliberately created. Understanding those possibilities clearly, together with the conditions they depend on, is the precondition for also understanding, as the following section attempts to do, where they reach their limits and what risks accompany them.

5 THE CRITICAL PERSPECTIVE: ETHICAL, COGNITIVE, AND INSTITUTIONAL TENSIONS

The opportunities described in the previous section are real, and they deserve to be taken seriously. But they do not exist in a vacuum. Every expansion of AI in educational settings brings with it a set of tensions that are equally real, and that a responsible analysis cannot afford to minimise. These tensions are not simply technical problems awaiting better engineering; many of them are structural, rooted in the conditions under which AI systems are developed, deployed, and used within institutions that carry their own histories of inequality and their own competing interests. Engaging with them honestly is not a reason to reject AI in higher education, but it is an indispensable condition for introducing it well.

Privacy, Surveillance, and the Rights of Educators

Among the most immediate concerns raised by the integration of AI in higher education is the question of data. AI systems of the kind discussed in this chapter depend, at every level, on the collection, processing, and analysis of information. When a student interacts with an AI tool to receive feedback on their writing, data about that interaction is generated and, in most cases, retained. When an AI system monitors engagement patterns across a course, it produces a continuous record of student behaviour that may persist well beyond the duration of any single assessment. The sensitivity of this data is considerable: it can reveal learning difficulties, emotional states, periods of difficulty or crisis, and patterns of academic struggle that students may not have chosen to disclose through formal channels (Uygun, 2024). The question of who owns this data, who can access it, for what purposes, and under what conditions it might be shared is not a peripheral concern. It is central to any honest accounting of what AI adoption in higher education actually involves.

These concerns apply not only to students but also to educators, and this dimension has received considerably less attention in the literature. When AI tools are introduced into teaching environments, whether through automated transcription of lectures, AI-assisted monitoring of classroom interaction, or institutional platforms that analyse teaching patterns, they generate data about educators as well. A lecturer who has not consented to having their pedagogical choices recorded, analysed, and potentially evaluated by an algorithmic system is in a position that raises serious questions about professional autonomy and dignity. The right not to be surveilled in one's own professional practice is not a trivial matter, and it becomes especially fraught when the institution deploying the AI is also the employer. Higher education institutions moving towards AI-enhanced teaching environments have an obligation to develop clear, transparent, and genuinely consensual frameworks for data governance that protect all members of the educational community, not only students (Alkan, 2024).

Algorithmic Bias and the Reproduction of Inequality

A further concern, and one that sits at the heart of any discussion of AI in inclusive education, is the risk that AI systems reproduce or amplify the very inequalities they are intended to address. AI models are trained on data, and that data reflects the world as it is, including its patterns of exclusion, its dominant linguistic norms, its cultural assumptions, and its historical biases. A system trained predominantly on texts produced within particular academic traditions may perform less accurately for students whose linguistic backgrounds, rhetorical conventions, or cultural references fall outside those traditions. An AI that assesses writing quality, evaluates the coherence of an argument, or infers a student's level of understanding is not making culturally neutral judgements; it is applying criteria that have been shaped by the data on which it was trained and the choices made by those who designed it (Alkan, 2024).

The irony here is pointed. An AI tool introduced to reduce barriers for students from underrepresented backgrounds may, if not carefully evaluated, function in practice to reinforce the disadvantages those students already face. This does not mean that the risk is inevitable, but it does mean that the deployment of AI in higher education requires ongoing critical scrutiny of outcomes across different student populations, not merely the measurement of aggregate satisfaction or average performance gains. Equity cannot be assumed; it must be demonstrated, and demonstrating it requires the kind of disaggregated, longitudinal analysis that institutions rarely prioritise (González-Calatayud et al., 2021).

Cognitive Dependency and the Development of Independent Thinking

Perhaps the most complex tension concerns not what AI does to students' data or to their representation within algorithmic systems, but what it does to their thinking. Higher education has always been, among other things, a site for the development of cognitive capacities: the ability to tolerate ambiguity, to construct an argument from uncertain evidence, to revise one's understanding in response to criticism, to sustain attention through difficulty. These capacities are not simply transmitted through content; they are developed through the struggle of engaging with problems that resist easy resolution. The concern that AI, by providing immediate answers, reformulated explanations, and polished versions of students' own drafts, may short-circuit precisely this developmental process is one that deserves careful attention rather than dismissal (Chan & Hu, 2023).

This is not an argument against feedback, against scaffolding, or against reducing unnecessary barriers to access. It is an argument about the difference between support that enables a student to do something they could not otherwise do, and support that does the thing for them. The distinction is not always easy to draw, and it will look different depending on the student, the task, and the stage of learning. But it is a distinction that educators and students alike need to keep in view when integrating AI into academic work. A student who uses AI to understand a concept they were struggling with, and then constructs their own argument from that understanding, is using it very differently from one who submits a lightly edited AI-generated text as their own thinking. The first use is educationally defensible; the second raises serious questions not only about academic integrity but about whether the student is actually developing the capacities that a degree is supposed to certify (Burkhard, 2022).

There is also a broader dimension to this concern that extends beyond individual assessment. If AI tools become the default mediator of students' encounters with difficulty, there is a risk that the tolerance for cognitive struggle, which is itself a learnable disposition, is progressively eroded. Students who have always had access to an intelligent system capable of resolving their uncertainties on demand may find themselves less equipped to function in professional and social contexts where that resource is not available or not appropriate. This is speculative, and the evidence base on long-term cognitive effects of AI assistance remains thin. But it is a question that higher education institutions and researchers have a responsibility to take seriously before patterns of use become entrenched.

The Human Dimension of Teaching and Learning

Underlying all of these concerns is a more fundamental question about what education is for and what it requires. Learning is not only a cognitive process; it is a relational one. The relationship between a student and an educator involves dimensions of trust, recognition, challenge, and care that no AI system currently replicates and that are not incidental to learning but constitutive of it. When a lecturer notices that a student who has been engaged suddenly becomes withdrawn, when a tutor recognises the anxiety behind a question that is ostensibly about citation format, when a supervisor senses that a doctoral student's writing difficulty is connected to something larger than technique, they are exercising a form of professional attentiveness that depends on human presence and human relationship. AI can complement this attentiveness in valuable ways, freeing educators from certain repetitive tasks and providing students with support between human interactions. It cannot replace it (Elder Hinshaw & Sakalli Gumus, 2013).

This is not a romantic argument for keeping technology out of the classroom. It is a structural argument about what teaching and learning require, and about the risk of allowing efficiency gains to be treated as equivalents of educational quality. The introduction of AI in higher education should be evaluated not only by what it enables students to do, but by what it changes about the texture of the learning environment, the nature of the relationships it mediates, and the values it implicitly prioritises. Where AI genuinely extends what educators and students can accomplish together, it deserves a place. Where it substitutes for the human engagement that learning depends on, it demands critical resistance.

6 AI AS ASSISTIVE TECHNOLOGY IN HIGHER EDUCATION: EVIDENCE AND EMERGING PRACTICE

The theoretical case for AI as assistive technology in higher education is strengthened, but also complicated, by what is beginning to emerge from research and from institutional practice. The evidence base remains relatively young, and much of what has been published either focuses on primary and secondary education, or addresses AI in higher education without the specific lens of assistive function or inclusive design. Nevertheless, a growing body of work allows some tentative observations about how students and educators in higher education are actually engaging with AI tools, what they find useful, and where the difficulties arise.

Research on students' perceptions of generative AI in higher education has revealed a broadly positive orientation, accompanied by significant ambivalence. Chan and Hu (2023), in a study of university students' perceptions of generative AI technologies including ChatGPT, found that students recognised the potential of these tools for personalised learning support, assistance with writing and academic research, and the organisation of complex information. At the same time, the same students expressed concerns about accuracy, privacy, and the effects of AI use on their own intellectual development and long-term capacities. This combination of appreciation and unease is consistent across a number of studies and reflects something important: students are not passive recipients of AI tools but active agents who bring their own judgements about what learning is for and what it requires of them. This reflexivity is itself educationally significant, and it suggests that students, far from being uncritical enthusiasts for AI assistance, are often better positioned than institutional rhetoric allows to think carefully about the conditions under which it serves them well (Chan & Hu, 2023).

The question of writing support has attracted particular attention, and for good reason. Writing is, across disciplines, one of the primary modes through which students in higher education demonstrate understanding, construct arguments, and develop voice. It is also one of the areas where the gap between what students can do and what is expected of them is most visible, and where support has historically been most unevenly distributed. Studies examining the use of AI writing assistants in higher education contexts have found that students generally experience them as useful for identifying gaps in their argumentation, improving clarity, and receiving feedback at a level of detail that tutors cannot routinely provide. Burkhard (2022) found that students held differentiated attitudes towards AI writing tools, with some using them thoughtfully as instruments of reflection and revision, and others approaching them with scepticism or without the metacognitive strategies needed to use them productively. This variation points to something that simple adoption metrics obscure: the educational value of an AI tool is not a property of the tool itself but of the relationship between the tool, the student's existing capacities, and the pedagogical context in which it is introduced (Burkhard, 2022).

The assistive dimension becomes particularly clear in studies focused on students with specific learning differences or those working in a second language. Gayed et al. (2022), in a study using an AI-based writing assistant with adult learners of English as a foreign language, found that the tool was especially valuable for learners who needed more structured guidance than traditional word processors provided. The immediacy of the feedback, its specificity to the student's actual text, and the absence of the social dimension that can make asking a human tutor for help feel exposing all contributed to a more engaged and sustained revision process. These findings resonate with what has been observed in other contexts: that AI support is often most valuable not because it is more sophisticated than human support, but because it is available at the moment when the student needs it, without the barriers of scheduling, status, or social anxiety that mediate access to human expertise (Gayed et al., 2022).

AI-Generated Educational Resources and Inclusive Course Design

One dimension of AI's role in higher education that remains underexplored in the research literature, but that is rapidly becoming significant in practice, is the use of AI by educators to develop more inclusive and differentiated course materials. The capacity of large language models to generate accessible versions of complex texts, produce summaries at different levels of abstraction, create alternative explanations of the same concept, or design assessment tasks in multiple formats has not yet been systematically studied in higher education contexts. But the implications for inclusive pedagogy are considerable, and they deserve attention that the field has not yet fully given them.

Consider a common scenario in higher education: a lecturer teaching a mixed cohort that includes students with dyslexia, students whose first language is not the language of instruction, students with strong visual-spatial processing but weaker verbal working memory, and students with highly developed prior knowledge in some areas of the course and significant gaps in others. Designing materials that genuinely serve this range of learners, rather than targeting a notional average student, has always been the aspiration of inclusive course design. In practice, it has rarely been achievable within the time constraints of academic work. AI changes this calculus. A lecturer who can produce five differentiated versions of a core reading, each pitched at a different level of linguistic complexity and accompanied by a visual summary, in the time it would previously have taken to produce one, is not abandoning pedagogical judgement but augmenting the capacity to act on it (Bray et al., 2024).

The production of digital educational resources is another area where AI's contribution is beginning to be felt. Tools such as Claude and Gemini can assist educators in generating interactive exercises, formative quizzes, case studies, or scenario-based learning activities that would otherwise require significant time and, in some cases, technical skills that lecturers do not possess. This is not merely a question of efficiency. When an educator can quickly generate a quiz that tests the same concept in multiple formats, or a case study that contextualises abstract material within a cultural setting relevant to a particular group of students, the result is a richer and more responsive learning environment. The AI does not determine the pedagogical intention; it expands the range of what that intention can produce (Vittorini et al., 2021).

It is important to note that this productive use of AI by educators is not without its own complexities. Questions arise about the accuracy of AI-generated content, particularly in specialist disciplinary areas where errors may be subtle and consequential. Questions arise about the ownership of AI-assisted materials and the intellectual labour that goes into directing, evaluating, and refining AI outputs. And questions arise about the risk that the ease of generating materials leads to a proliferation of content without a corresponding increase in coherence or pedagogical intentionality. These are real risks, and they reinforce the argument that AI in higher education requires active professional engagement rather than passive deployment. The educator who uses AI well is not the one who accepts its outputs uncritically, but the one who brings disciplinary expertise and pedagogical judgement to bear on what the AI produces, using it as a starting point rather than a finished product.

Student Autonomy, Self-Regulation, and the Role of AI Feedback

A recurring theme in the emerging literature on AI in higher education is the relationship between AI assistance and the development of student autonomy. This relationship is more complex than it might initially appear, and it resists the simple framing that positions AI support and independent learning as opposites. Research on formative assessment and feedback consistently shows that well-designed feedback does not undermine student agency; it supports the development of self-regulatory capacities by giving students the information they need to monitor their own progress, identify gaps in their understanding, and adjust their learning strategies accordingly (González-Calatayud et al., 2021). The question is whether AI-generated feedback can serve this function, and under what conditions.

The evidence suggests that it can, but with important qualifications. Studies examining students' use of AI feedback on written work have found that students are generally able to engage critically with AI suggestions, accepting some, rejecting others, and using the feedback as a prompt for reflection rather than simply implementing it mechanically. This critical engagement is not automatic; it depends on how the use of AI feedback is framed within the course, whether students have been given explicit guidance on how to evaluate AI outputs, and whether the broader pedagogical environment supports reflective practice. Where these conditions are in place, AI feedback can function as a genuine scaffold for the development of self-regulation. Where they are absent, there is a real risk that students treat AI outputs as authoritative rather than as one perspective among several, and that the feedback loop short-circuits rather than supports independent thinking (Sumakul et al., 2022).

This has implications for how higher education institutions design AI-integrated courses. It suggests that the introduction of AI tools needs to be accompanied by explicit pedagogical attention to AI literacy, understood not simply as the ability to use AI tools, but as the capacity to evaluate their outputs critically, to understand their limitations, and to make informed decisions about when and how to rely on them. This is a form of metacognitive education that higher education has always valued in principle. The arrival of AI makes it more urgent and more specific in its demands. Students who leave university able to use AI tools fluently but uncritically are not well-prepared for the professional and civic contexts they will enter. Students who leave with the capacity to engage AI as a resource while maintaining their own analytical independence are considerably better equipped (Yi, 2021).

Institutional Responses and the Gap Between Policy and Practice

The institutional response of higher education to the emergence of AI has been, in most cases, reactive rather than proactive, and more focused on risk management than on the development of coherent pedagogical frameworks. Many universities moved quickly, following the public release of ChatGPT in late 2022, to update their academic integrity policies to address AI-generated work. This was a necessary response, but it was also a partial one, because it framed AI primarily as a threat to assessment rather than as a complex set of tools whose educational implications extend well beyond the integrity of individual assignments.

A more adequate institutional response would attend to several dimensions simultaneously: the development of guidelines for the ethical and pedagogically sound use of AI by both students and educators; the provision of professional development support to help lecturers understand the capabilities and limitations of AI tools and integrate them thoughtfully into their teaching; the creation of governance frameworks for data privacy that protect students and educators from the surveillance risks that AI deployment can introduce; and the establishment of ongoing processes for evaluating the equity implications of AI use across different student populations. Few institutions have yet managed to address all of these dimensions coherently, and the gap between policy statements and lived practice remains wide in most higher education contexts (Uygun, 2024).

This gap matters particularly for students from marginalised backgrounds, who are most likely to encounter AI in its least thoughtful forms and least likely to have the social and cultural capital to navigate its limitations critically. An institution that deploys AI-powered feedback tools without ensuring that all students understand how to engage with them critically, or that introduces AI-assisted monitoring of student engagement without adequate transparency about what is being measured and why, is not serving the values of equity and inclusion that inclusive education requires. The technology, in such cases, does not reduce the inequality it was intended to address; it adds a new layer to it. Avoiding this outcome requires institutional intentionality of a kind that is still, in most places, more aspiration than reality (González-Calatayud et al., 2021).

7 TOWARDS A FRAMEWORK FOR RESPONSIBLE INTEGRATION: PRINCIPLES FOR AI AS ASSISTIVE TECHNOLOGY IN HIGHER EDUCATION

The analysis developed in this chapter points toward a framework for integrating AI as assistive technology in higher education. The six principles presented in Table 1 are not offered as novel ethical insights, since their normative content is shared with much of the responsible-AI literature, but as an attempt to translate that content into an operational form specific to the assistive use of AI in higher education. Each principle is therefore paired with an indicator that allows its presence or absence to be assessed, and an implementation step that institutions can act on. The principles were derived from the three sources that structure the chapter as a whole: the UDL framework, the empirical literature reviewed, and the critical analysis of tensions developed above. They are presented as a coherent set rather than a ranked list, because in practice they constrain and qualify one another.

Table 1. Six Principles for the Responsible Integration of AI as Assistive Technology in Higher Education, with Indicators and Implementation Steps

Principle	Indicator	Implementation step
Inclusion by design	Equity outcomes are disaggregated by disability, language, and socioeconomic status before and after adoption	Require an equity impact assessment, with affected students involved, prior to any institutional AI deployment
Transparency & consent	Students and staff can state what data is collected, by whom, and for what purpose	Publish an accessible AI data statement per tool; secure opt-in consent for any monitoring of educators
Complementarity	AI is introduced alongside, not in place of, human contact hours and tutor feedback	Prohibit AI adoption justified primarily by staffing reduction; document the pedagogical rationale
Professional development	Proportion of teaching staff trained in AI capabilities, limits, and bias detection	Provide recurring, not one-off, development with time allocated within workload
Co-design	Students and educators, including from marginalised groups, sit on adoption decisions	Establish a standing co-design body with genuine decision rights, not advisory status
Ongoing evaluation	Differential and longitudinal outcomes are tracked and acted upon	Commit in advance to revising or withdrawing tools that fail equity or learning criteria

Inclusion by design

The first principle responds directly to the risk, examined earlier, that AI improves average outcomes while widening the gap between student groups. The chosen indicator, disaggregated equity outcomes measured before and after adoption, is deliberately more demanding than the satisfaction surveys and aggregate performance gains that institutions typically rely on, because those measures are precisely the ones that conceal differential effects. An equity impact assessment conducted before deployment, with the students most likely to face barriers involved in defining what counts as an acceptable outcome, shifts the question from whether a tool works on average to whether it works for those it is meant to help (Bray et al., 2024).

Transparency and informed consent

The tension this principle addresses is twofold, concerning both students whose interaction data reveals more than they may realise, and educators whose professional practice may be recorded and analysed without meaningful consent. The indicator is intentionally concrete: if students and staff cannot articulate what data a tool collects and to what end, the transparency requirement has not been met, regardless of what institutional policy documents claim. The implementation step distinguishes the two populations, since students may reasonably be required to accept certain data uses as a condition of enrolment, whereas the monitoring of educators raises questions of professional autonomy that warrant a genuine right to decline (Alkan, 2024).

Complementarity rather than substitution

This principle exists to name and resist a specific risk: that AI is adopted not to enrich what educators and students do together but to reduce the human contact that learning depends on. The indicator looks at whether AI is added alongside human contact or used to replace it, and the implementation step makes the institution document a pedagogical rationale rather than a financial one. The distinction matters most under conditions of resource pressure, which is exactly when the substitution of cheaper automated support for more expensive human engagement becomes most tempting and most damaging (Elder Hinshaw & Sakalli Gumus, 2013).

Professional development as a structural requirement

Because the assistive value of AI depends on the educator's capacity to evaluate its outputs, and because the reliability limits discussed earlier make uncritical use actively harmful, professional development cannot be treated as optional. The indicator, the proportion of staff trained not merely to use AI but to recognise its errors and biases, captures a competence that one-off workshops rarely build. Allocating time within workload, rather than expecting development to happen in addition to a full teaching load, is the step that determines whether the requirement is real or nominal (Ayanwale et al., 2022).

Co-design with students and educators

The contextual knowledge needed to integrate AI well, knowledge of what actually happens in learning and where barriers arise, resides with educators and students rather than with managers or technology vendors. The indicator therefore asks whether those groups, and specifically those from marginalised backgrounds, are present in adoption decisions. The implementation step insists on decision rights rather than advisory status, because consultation that can be overridden reproduces the very exclusion that co-design is meant to counter, enacting a commitment to student agency in form while denying it in substance (Saborío-Taylor & Rojas-Ramírez, 2024).

Ongoing evaluation and willingness to revise

Given how rapidly the tools are developing and how thin the long-term evidence remains, no adoption decision should be treated as final. The indicator looks for differential and longitudinal tracking, the kind that can detect effects on cognitive development and on equity that short-term measures miss, and the implementation step requires a prior commitment to act on what evaluation reveals. An evaluation with no possibility of reversing the decision it assesses is a ritual rather than a safeguard, and the willingness to withdraw a tool that fails its criteria is what gives the whole framework its force (Nemorin et al., 2023).

Two features distinguish this framework from a generic statement of principles. The first is the insistence on disaggregated and longitudinal indicators rather than aggregate measures, so that a tool which raises average performance while widening group gaps is recognised as a failure. The second is the requirement that each principle carry a consequence: a co-design body without decision rights, a consent process without the option to decline, or an evaluation without a commitment to act would satisfy the letter of the framework while defeating its purpose. The framework does not assume uniform application; institutions differ, and the indicators will need adaptation rather than mechanical transfer. What should not be adapted away is the underlying requirement that the assistive use of AI be judged by whether it actually reduces barriers for the students who face the most, rather than by the convenience or cost savings it offers the institution. This is precisely the orientation that an inclusive, UDL-informed approach to technology integration demands (Saborío-Taylor & Rojas-Ramírez, 2024).

8 CONCLUSION: NAVIGATING UNCERTAINTY WITH CARE

Any honest conclusion to a chapter about AI in higher education must begin by acknowledging what we do not yet know. Despite the volume and intensity of the conversation surrounding artificial intelligence in education since the public emergence of generative tools, the evidence base for confident claims about long-term outcomes remains, as Nemorin et al. (2023) observe, still developing. The narrative review that informs this chapter has confirmed the unevenness of that base: much of the relevant work consists of small-scale studies conducted over short periods in specific contexts, and a substantial proportion addresses AI in education broadly rather than the assistive use of AI in higher education specifically. We have early findings and promising indications, but not yet the longitudinal, large-scale, methodologically diverse research that would allow us to speak with confidence about what AI integration actually produces over time, for whom, and under what conditions. This is not a reason for paralysis, but it is a reason for the caution that has shaped the argument throughout.

What this chapter has tried to do, rather than resolve these uncertainties, is map them with precision. The conceptual work of section three matters here: AI is not assistive technology in the formal sense that a screen reader is, but it can perform an assistive function for a particular learner engaged in a particular task. Holding to that distinction allows the genuine possibilities to be stated without overstatement. For students who have historically encountered barriers in higher education, whether arising from disability, language background, or ways of processing knowledge that traditional assessment does not accommodate, the adaptive and immediately available support that AI can offer is worth taking seriously. As Dalton et al. (2019) argue in the context of UDL, the question is never whether to support diverse learners but how, and AI opens new answers to that question, provided the conditions for realising them are deliberately created.

Those conditions, examined in section four, are where caution becomes most concrete. The assistive potential of AI is not distributed equally, and the factors that govern access, subscription cost, institutional licensing, connectivity, and digital literacy, track existing patterns of advantage in ways that can turn an apparently equalising tool into a new axis of stratification. The reliability limits of the tools compound the problem, since the students least able to detect a confident but incorrect output are frequently those for whom the assistive promise is most attractive.

An inclusive analysis cannot treat these material conditions as background detail; they are, as the chapter has argued, the heart of the matter.

The critical perspective developed in section five resists the technological solutionism that often accompanies new tools in education. AI does not arrive as a neutral instrument. It carries the biases of its training data, the commercial interests of its developers, the surveillance capacities that data collection enables, and the risk that its accessibility leads to forms of use that substitute for, rather than develop, the cognitive capacities higher education exists to cultivate. The implications for educators deserve particular emphasis, since much of the debate focuses on students while the prospect of AI being used to monitor and constrain professional judgement, rather than support it, receives less attention than it warrants. Both Alkan (2024) and Uygun (2024) point to this ethical complexity, the latter documenting how privacy and ethical apprehensions accompany even broadly favorable views of AI among educators, and their concerns are central rather than peripheral to any responsible account.

On the question of cognitive development, the chapter has deliberately refrained from confident claims in either direction. It is too early to know whether sustained reliance on AI erodes students' tolerance for intellectual difficulty or their capacity for independent reasoning. Chan and Hu (2023) found that students themselves hold nuanced and self-aware views about these risks, which is itself significant: it suggests that students are not passive recipients of AI's effects but reflective agents who can, with appropriate support, navigate the tensions that AI assistance creates. What that support looks like in practice is among the questions that future research most urgently needs to address.

The operational framework proposed in section seven is offered in this spirit of grounded caution rather than confident prescription. Its principles are not original in their normative content, but their translation into indicators and implementation steps is intended to make responsible integration assessable rather than merely aspirational. The framework's insistence that each principle carry a consequence, and that the assistive use of AI be judged by whether it reduces barriers for the students who face the most, is its central claim. Whether the framework proves useful is itself a matter for the kind of evaluation it calls for, and it is offered as a contribution to be tested rather than a settled solution.

Future research is not a formulaic closing gesture here but a genuine necessity. Studies that follow student populations over time, that disaggregate outcomes across diverse groups, that attend to the quality of learning rather than only its measurable proxies, and that involve students and educators as participants rather than subjects, are what the field needs to move beyond its current mixture of enthusiasm, anxiety, and speculation. Research focused specifically on higher education matters, given how much existing work derives from school settings where the dynamics of autonomy and institutional power differ. And research that examines AI as assistive technology, rather than as a general-purpose tool, has the potential to contribute something distinctive: a way of thinking that centres access and participation rather than efficiency and performance.

What seems clear, even without the research that would permit firmer conclusions, is that the arrival of AI in higher education is not a passing disruption to be managed with updated integrity policies and a few training sessions. It is a sustained transformation of the conditions under which learning and teaching take place, raising questions about equity, autonomy, professional dignity, and the nature of knowledge that universities have a responsibility to engage seriously. AI may be part of the answer to the question that should animate all of higher education, namely what conditions genuinely allow all students to learn, develop, and participate fully. It is unlikely to be the whole of it, and it will be none of it if introduced without the care, the critical scrutiny, and the sustained commitment to equity that the stakes demand. Beginning from that recognition is, at this still-early moment, the most honest and most useful place to start.

REFERENCES

Alkan, A. (2024). Artificial intelligence: Its role and potential in education. İnsan ve Toplum Bilimleri Araştırmaları Dergisi, 13(1), 483–497. DOI: 10.15869/itobiad.1331201

Ayanwale, M. A., Sanusi, I. T., Adelana, O. P., Aruleba, K. D., & Oyelere, S. S. (2022). Teachers' readiness and intention to teach artificial intelligence in schools. *Computers and Education: Artificial Intelligence, 3*, 100099. DOI: 10.1016/j.caeai.2022.100099

Bray, A., Devitt, A., Banks, J., Sanchez Fuentes, S., Sandoval, M., Riviou, K., Byrne, D., Flood, M., Reale, J., & Terrenzio, S. (2024). What next for Universal Design for Learning? A systematic literature review of technology in UDL implementations at second level. *British Journal of Educational Technology*, *55*(1), 113–138. DOI: 10.1111/bjet.13328

Burkhard, M. (2022). Student perceptions of AI-powered writing tools: Towards individualized teaching strategies. In *Proceedings of the 19th International Conference on Cognition and Exploratory Learning in Digital Age (CELDA 2022)* (pp. 73–81). IADIS Press. DOI: 10.33965/CELDA2022_202207L010

Chan, C. K. Y., & Hu, W. (2023). Students' voices on generative AI: Perceptions, benefits, and challenges in higher education. *International Journal of Educational Technology in Higher Education, 20*(1), 43. DOI: 10.1186/s41239-023-00411-8

Dalton, E. M., Lyner-Cleophas, M., Ferguson, B. T., & McKenzie, J. (2019). Inclusion, universal design and universal design for learning in higher education: South Africa and the United States. *African Journal of Disability*, *8*, a519. DOI: 10.4102/ajod.v8i0.519 PMID: 31392169

Elder Hinshaw, R., & Sakalli Gumus, S. (2013). Universal Design for Learning principles in a hybrid course: Perceptions and practice. *SAGE Open*, *3*(1), 2158244013480789. Advance online publication. DOI: 10.1177/2158244013480789

Gayed, J. M., Carlon, M. K. J., Oriola, A. M., & Cross, J. S. (2022). Exploring an AI-based writing assistant's impact on English language learners. *Computers and Education: Artificial Intelligence, 3*, 100055. DOI: 10.1016/j.caeai.2022.100055

González-Calatayud, V., Prendes-Espinosa, P., & Roig-Vila, R. (2021). Artificial intelligence for student assessment: A systematic review. *Applied Sciences (Basel, Switzerland)*, *11*(12), 5467. DOI: 10.3390/app11125467

Massola, G. (2023). Curriculum and technology: Use of digital devices to promote inclusion and autonomy in learning. Seven Editora. https://sevenpublicacoes.com.br/editora/article/view/672

Nemorin, S., Vlachidis, A., Ayerakwa, H. M., & Andriotis, P. (2023). AI hyped? A horizon scan of discourse on artificial intelligence in education (AIED) and development. *Learning, Media and Technology*, *48*(1), 38–51. DOI: 10.1080/17439884.2022.2095568

Saborío-Taylor, S., & Rojas-Ramírez, F. (2024). Universal design for learning and artificial intelligence in the digital era: Fostering inclusion and autonomous learning. International Journal of Professional Development. *Learners and Learning*, *6*(2), ep2408. Advance online publication. DOI: 10.30935/ijpdll/14694

Segura-Castillo, M. A., & Quirós-Acuña, M. (2019). Desde el Diseño Universal para el Aprendizaje: El estudiantado al aprender se evalúa y al evaluarle aprende. *Review of Education*, •••, 643–655. DOI: 10.15517/revedu.v43i1.28449

Sumakul, D. T. Y. G., Hamied, F. A., & Sukyadi, D. (2022). Students' perceptions of the use of AI in a writing class. In Proceedings of the 67th TEFLIN International Virtual Conference & the 9th ICOELT 2021 (Advances in Social Science, Education and Humanities Research, Vol. 624, pp. 52–57). Atlantis Press. DOI: 10.2991/assehr.k.220201.009

Uygun, D. (2024). Teachers' perspectives on artificial intelligence in education. *Advances in Mobile Learning Educational Research*, *4*(1), 931–939. DOI: 10.25082/AMLER.2024.01.005

Vittorini, P., Menini, S., & Tonelli, S. (2021). An AI-based system for formative and summative assessment in data science courses. *International Journal of Artificial Intelligence in Education, 31*(2), 159–185. DOI: 10.1007/s40593-020-00230-2

Yi, Y. (2021). Establishing the concept of AI literacy: Focusing on competence and purpose. Jahr – European. *Journal of Bioethics*, *12*(2), 353–368. DOI: 10.21860/j.12.2.8

Chapter 6
A Conceptual Framework for Assistive Microlearning in Higher Education

I Komang Mertayasa
http://orcid.org/0000-0002-4753-8268
Institut Agama Hindu Negeri Tampung Penyang, Indonesia

Putu Cory Candra Yhani
https://orcid.org/0009-0009-5404-6403
Institut Agama Hindu Negeri Tampung Penyang, Indonesia

Putu Wisnu Saputra
http://orcid.org/0009-0004-6482-1913
Institut Agama Hindu Negeri Tampung Penyang, Indonesia

ABSTRACT

This chapter proposes a conceptual framework for Assistive Microlearning in Higher Education that integrates cognitive theory, artificial intelligence, learning analytics, and adaptive systems within a recursive pedagogical architecture. Moving beyond tool-centered and accessibility-driven approaches, the framework reconceptualizes assistive technologies as epistemic mediators embedded in structured microlearning design. Grounded in Cognitive Load Theory, Self-Regulated Learning, and reflective practice, the model articulates a multi-layered system linking learner diagnostics, adaptive micro-segmentation, data-informed feedback, and progressive competency development. Its application in teacher education demonstrates how AI-supported

DOI: 10.4018/979-8-2600-2716-5.ch006

2027, IGI Global Scientific Publishing. Copying or distributing in print or electronic forms without written permission of IGI Global Scientific Publishing is prohibited. Use of this chapter to ative artificial intelligence (AI) technologies is expressly prohibited. The publisher reserves all rights to license its use for generative AI training and machine learning model development.

microteaching can transform episodic rehearsal into iterative professional formation. The framework offers a scalable and ethically grounded paradigm for sustainable technological integration in higher education.

INTRODUCTION

Higher education institutions are currently facing increasingly complex learning challenges, particularly related to time constraints, cognitive load, diverse learner needs, and rising demands for professional competencies. Students often experience academic pressure due to a packed class schedule, closely spaced assignment deadlines, and other responsibilities outside of learning, which can lead to stress, decreased engagement, and academic performance (Alias & Razak, 2023; Le & Nguyen, 2025). The limitation of instructional time also restricts opportunities for in-depth study, practice, and ongoing reflection (Birtwistle & Wagenaar, 2020; Holbert, 2025).

In a digital learning environment, cognitive load becomes an important issue. Students are faced with an overwhelming flow of information, digital distractions, and complex learning materials, which can disrupt their ability to process, store, and evaluate knowledge (Pang et al., 2025; Wang et al., 2025). These challenges are increasingly evident in professional education, including teacher education, as prospective teachers must integrate theoretical understanding, pedagogical skills, reflection, adaptability, and decision-making in dynamic learning situations (Valero, 2022).

In that context, assistive technology gains new relevance. Traditionally, assistive technology has been closely associated with accessibility and accommodations for students with disabilities. However, the development of mobile applications, wearable technologies, immersive technologies, AI-supported tools, and learning analytics has expanded their role as pedagogical resources that can support all learners (Martinez-Hernandez et al., 2021; Singh et al., 2025). Mobile applications can provide flexible and just-in-time learning access, and wearable technologies can support performance monitoring and real-time feedback, while virtual reality and augmented reality can deliver interactive and contextual learning simulations (Bedard & Zhang, 2025; Poggianti et al., 2025).

This development indicates the need for a shift from a reactive accessibility model to a proactive learning optimisation model. Technology can no longer be understood merely as an additional tool after learning barriers arise but must be designed from the outset as part of pedagogy and curriculum. Thus, technology can function as scaffolding that helps learners access materials, manage cognitive load, receive feedback, reflect, and gradually develop competencies.

In line with that, microlearning has emerged as a relevant learning strategy to address time constraints and cognitive complexity. Through concise, focused, and directed learning units, microlearning can help reduce cognitive load as well as enhance engagement and learning retention (Alhebaishi et al., 2025; Susilana et al., 2022). Based on cognitive load theory, self-directed learning, and constructivist pedagogy, microlearning not only shortens the material but also organises the learning experience to be more structured, flexible, and adaptive (Zambrano Verdesoto & Caicedo, 2025).

Nevertheless, the relationship between assistive technology and microlearning has not yet been extensively developed conceptually. Many digital learning initiatives focus on the use of tools or platforms, while microlearning is often understood merely as the delivery of brief content. This gap indicates the need for a conceptual framework that connects learners' needs, technology affordances, microlearning design, learning processes, and multidimensional outcomes.

This chapter develops the conceptual framework of Assistive Microlearning in higher education, with teacher education and microteaching as the main application contexts. This framework positions assistive technology as a pedagogical and cognitive mediator, and microlearning as a learning architecture to support the development of competencies in an inclusive, adaptive, reflective, and sustainable manner.

Reframing Assistive Technologies in Higher Education

Assistive technology has historically been understood within a compensatory framework, that is, as devices or systems that help individuals overcome certain functional limitations. In this perspective, assistive technology is positioned as a tool to restore, replace, or support abilities that face obstacles, such as mobility aids, alternative communication devices, cognitive support applications, or environmental control systems (Esleen et al., 2024; Mahmoudi-Dehaki et al., 2025). In education, assistive technology is also often associated with increased access to learning materials and participation of students with special educational needs (Pradeep, 2023; Shaheen, 2025).

Although the function of accessibility remains important, a narrow understanding can place assistive technology in a reactive position, meaning it is only used after learning barriers arise. Contemporary higher education requires a more proactive perspective, as the challenges are not only related to disabilities or physical access but also to cognitive load, time constraints, the diversity of learner profiles, and the complexity of professional competencies. Therefore, assistive technology needs to be repositioned as part of a learning optimisation strategy that helps learners manage information, focus attention, receive feedback, reflect, and gradually develop competencies.

This repositioning marks a shift from a reactive accessibility model to a proactive learning optimisation model. In this model, technology is not only used to tailor learning for specific groups but is designed from the outset as a scaffolding mechanism for all learners. Technology can help structure learning experiences, reduce unnecessary cognitive load, provide immediate feedback, and enhance reflective engagement.

The development of digital technology expands those functions. Mobile-based learning applications can provide short modules, formative quizzes, study reminders, reflection guides, and quick access to materials. Wearable technology can record performance data, such as activity patterns, practice duration, or engagement indicators. Immersive technologies such as virtual reality and augmented reality allow learners to practise in complex, safe, and repeatable simulated situations (Bedard & Zhang, 2025; Poggianti et al., 2025). Additionally, artificial intelligence and learning analytics can help analyse learning patterns, identify difficulties, provide personalised recommendations, and display competency development through learning dashboards.

However, the integration of assistive technology should not stop at the use of devices or applications in isolation. Technology needs to be integrated into curriculum design to ensure it has purpose, continuity, and relevance to learning outcomes. At the micro level, technology can support daily learning activities, such as short modules, targeted exercises, quick feedback, and individual reflection. At the meso level, technology can help organise development within a single course through competency maps and formative assessments. At the macro level, technology can be used to monitor the development of competencies across semesters or programmes, especially in professional education such as teacher education.

In teacher education and microteaching, this repositioning becomes very important. Microteaching emphasises the practice of specific skills, repetitive practice, feedback, and reflection. Assistive technology can enhance this process through short preparation modules, virtual class simulations, performance recordings, data-based feedback, and reflection guides after practice. For example, prospective teachers practising questioning skills can study microlearning modules through a mobile application, conduct recorded microteaching practices, and then use performance data to reflect on variations in questions, wait times, and follow-up responses.

Thus, repositioning assistive technology in higher education means shifting the perspective from a compensatory tool to a pedagogical mediator. Assistive technology needs to be understood as part of the learning system that helps manage cognitive load, supports personalisation, strengthens reflection, and enables gradual competency development. However, technology must still be chosen based on pedagogical needs, not merely because of its novelty or sophistication.

Microlearning as Cognitive Architecture and Assistive Learning Strategy

Microlearning should not be understood merely as a method of delivering content in a short duration. Conceptually, microlearning refers to the design of learning that presents learning units concisely, focused, and directed towards specific learning outcomes (Cronin & Durham, 2024; Monib et al., 2025). The main value of microlearning does not solely lie in the brevity of the material, but rather in its ability to organise the learning experience to be more structured, cognitively manageable, and aligned with the needs of the learners. Thus, microlearning can be positioned as cognitive architecture, which is a learning design that helps organise the information load, focus attention, provide feedback, and support the gradual development of competencies.

In higher education, this approach is relevant because learners often face complex material, heavy academic demands, and limited time for in-depth study, practice, and reflection. Learning that is too long, dense, and unsegmented can increase the risk of cognitive overload. On the other hand, microlearning allows complex material or competencies to be broken down into small, meaningful, and interconnected units. This segmentation helps learners gradually move from basic understanding to more complex mastery without losing the coherence of learning.

From the perspective of cognitive load theory, the effectiveness of microlearning can be explained through its ability to manage three types of cognitive load: intrinsic load, extraneous load, and germane load. Intrinsic load relates to the inherent complexity of the material or skills being learned. In microlearning, this load is managed by breaking down large competencies into smaller sub-competencies. For example, classroom management skills in teacher education can be broken down into skills for opening lessons, managing transitions, giving instructions, responding to student behaviour, and closing lessons.

Extraneous load refers to the additional cognitive load resulting from inefficient learning design, such as unclear instructions, overly dense material, or confusing learning displays. Microlearning can reduce this load through focused material presentation, brief instructions, relevant visualisations, formative quizzes, short videos, and immediate feedback. Meanwhile, germane load is related to cognitive efforts that support the formation of schemas and meaningful understanding. Microlearning can enhance germane load through brief reflections, targeted exercises, repeated feedback, and the application of concepts in different contexts.

Table 1. Cognitive Load Types and the Role of Microlearning

Type of Cognitive Load	Meaning	Role of Microlearning
Intrinsic load	The cognitive load caused by the inherent complexity of the material or competency being learned	Breaks complex competencies into smaller and more manageable learning units
Extraneous load	The additional cognitive load caused by inefficient instructional design, unclear instructions, or irrelevant information	Reduces unnecessary information, clarifies instructions, and focuses learning activities on essential objectives
Germane load	The cognitive effort used to construct schemas, deepen understanding, and support meaningful learning	Strengthens reflection, guided practice, feedback, and progressive understanding

In addition to being rooted in cognitive load theory, microlearning is also in line with self-directed learning and adult learning. In higher education, learners need flexibility to manage their time, pace, and learning strategies. Microlearning supports this need through modular materials that can be accessed as needed and are suitable for just-in-time learning situations (Corbeil et al., 2023; Zambrano Verdesoto & Caicedo, 2025). Learners can access specific materials before practice, while completing assignments, or after receiving feedback from the instructor.

That flexibility gives microlearning an assistive function. In this context, the term 'assistive' does not only refer to support for students with special needs but also to a learning structure that helps all students manage learning demands more effectively. Microlearning serves as scaffolding that helps learners understand concepts, develop skills, monitor progress, and reflect on the learning process. This function can be enhanced through technology such as mobile applications, automated quizzes, digital journals, video playback, learning analytics, and AI-based feedback. However, microlearning also has its limitations. One of the main criticisms is the risk of knowledge fragmentation. If the learning units are organised without clear connections, microlearning can turn into a collection of shallow information snippets that do not form a coherent conceptual understanding (Blinov et al., 2022; Ilic, 2024). Therefore, microlearning should not be understood as an excessive simplification, but rather as a segmentation strategy that maintains continuity between learning units. Each unit needs to have clear objectives, connections with other units, relevant activities, and feedback mechanisms that support the development of learners.

In teacher education and microteaching practice, the function of microlearning as a cognitive architecture and assistive strategy becomes very important. Teaching skills are a complex competence that involves mastery of the material, instructional communication, classroom management, question usage, student response, and time management. Through microlearning, these skills can be broken down into smaller, more manageable units for training. For example, one unit focuses on instruction-giving techniques, the next unit on questioning skills, and another unit on strategies for responding to student behaviour.

For example, prospective teachers practising questioning skills can study microlearning modules on closed questions, open questions, and higher-order questions. After that, the prospective teachers practise it in microteaching. The practice sessions can be recorded and analysed to observe variations in questions, wait times, interaction distribution, and the quality of follow-up responses. Based on that feedback, the prospective teacher reflects and repeats the practice with better strategies. In this cycle, microlearning serves as the initial structure, technology as the feedback mediator, and reflection as the professional development mechanism.

Thus, microlearning has a dual role: as a cognitive architecture that helps organise the complexity of learning and as an assistive strategy that provides structured, flexible, and adaptive support. This perspective serves as the foundation for the development of the assistive microlearning conceptual framework in higher education.

Literature Synthesis, Research Gaps, and Methodological Basis for Framework Development

The literature on assistive technology, microlearning, artificial intelligence, learning analytics, and teacher education shows significant developments in higher education. However, these five domains are still often discussed separately. Assistive technology is often placed within the discourse of accessibility and accommodation for students with special needs. Microlearning is more often studied as a strategy for delivering concise and flexible content. AI and learning analytics are generally associated with personalisation, learning diagnostics, and progress monitoring. Meanwhile, teacher education and microteaching are more often discussed within the framework of practice, feedback, and professional reflection. This separation indicates the need to develop a conceptual framework that can more systematically connect these various domains.

In the literature on assistive technology, technology is understood as a means to expand access, enhance participation, and help learners overcome learning barriers. Various studies position assistive technology as supportive devices for learners with disabilities or special educational needs, for example, through communication aids, cognitive applications, environmental control systems, or mobility support devices (Esleen et al., 2024; Mahmoudi-Dehaki et al., 2025; Pradeep, 2023; Shaheen, 2025). However, this approach still tends to be compensatory because technology is used primarily after obstacles arise. The development of mobile applications, wearable technologies, immersive technologies, AI-supported tools, and learning analytics shows that assistive technology can function more broadly as a pedagogical mediator that helps all learners access materials, receive feedback, monitor progress, and reflect on the learning process (Bedard & Zhang, 2025; Martinez-Hernandez et al., 2021; Poggianti et al., 2025; Singh et al., 2025). The gap lies in the lack of a strong explanation of how these technologies are systematically integrated into learning design.

The literature on microlearning emphasises that short, focused, and flexible learning can help learners manage their study time, increase engagement, and support knowledge retention (Alias & Razak, 2023; Cronin & Durham, 2024; Monib et al., 2025; Susilana et al., 2022). Microlearning is also relevant in digital environments because it can be integrated with multimedia, short quizzes, gamification, and mobile-based learning (Silva et al., 2025; Yadav et al., 2025; Zambrano Verdesoto & Caicedo, 2025). However, some literature still views microlearning as a format for delivering short content. This understanding risks reducing microlearning to short videos or fragmented mini-modules. Criticism of microlearning indicates that microlearning can become superficial if not structured with the principles of coherence and competency progression (Blinov et al., 2022; Ilic, 2024). Therefore, microlearning needs to be understood as a cognitive architecture that helps manage the learning load, organise competency stages, and maintain the interconnection between learning units.

Meanwhile, AI and learning analytics offer opportunities to enhance adaptive learning. AI-based systems can analyse learning patterns, provide feedback, adjust the sequence of materials, and recommend activities according to the needs of learners (Almuqhim & Berri, 2025; Yadav et al., 2025). Learning analytics can help educators and learners monitor engagement, achievement, and competency development in a more measurable way. However, the integration of AI and learning analytics risks becoming merely tool-driven if not linked to pedagogical design, reflection, and data usage ethics. In the context of teacher education, microteaching has long been used to develop teaching skills through focused practice, observation, feedback, and reflection (Iliasova et al., 2025; Jaiwant & Kureethara, 2024). However, conventional microteaching practices are often still episodic, rely on subjective feedback, and do not always systematically document competency development.

Based on this synthesis, the main gap addressed in this chapter is the lack of a conceptual framework that explicitly integrates assistive technology and micro-learning as an adaptive learning architecture in higher education, particularly in teacher education and microteaching. These gaps encompass three aspects. First, conceptually, assistive technology and microlearning are still often discussed as two separate domains. Second, pedagogically, it has not been sufficiently explained how technology supports segmentation, feedback, reflection, and competency development. Third, methodologically, a foundation for framework development is needed to show how various theories and literature findings are synthesised into a coherent model.

Table 2. Literature Synthesis and Research Gaps

Literature Domain	Main Contribution	Limitation	Implication for the Proposed Framework
Assistive technologies	Support accessibility, participation, and learning accommodation	Still predominantly understood as compensatory tools	Repositioned as pedagogical and cognitive mediators
Mobile, wearable, and immersive technologies	Provide flexible access, performance monitoring, and simulation-based learning	Often discussed in terms of technological functions rather than pedagogical integration	Used to support microlearning, feedback, and reflection
Microlearning	Provides short, flexible, and focused learning experiences	Risks being reduced to fragmented short-form content	Understood as a cognitive architecture and assistive learning strategy
Cognitive Load Theory	Explains the importance of managing cognitive load in learning	Not always operationally connected with assistive technologies	Serves as the basis for segmentation, instructional design, and feedback
AI and learning analytics	Support diagnosis, personalization, and learning monitoring	Risk becoming tool-driven and insufficiently reflective	Positioned within cycles of diagnosis, feedback, reflection, and improvement
Teacher education and microteaching	Support skill rehearsal, observation, feedback, and reflection	Practices are often episodic and insufficiently data-informed	Provide the application context for assistive microlearning

The conceptual framework in this chapter is developed through an integrative conceptual synthesis approach. This approach is used because the chapter's goal is not to empirically test a hypothesis but rather to build a theoretical understanding that connects assistive technology, microlearning, cognitive load theory, AI, learning analytics, and competency development in higher education. Thus, the framework development method is conceptual, systematic, and literature-based.

The process of developing the framework is carried out through four main steps. First, the identification of relevant literature domains was conducted, namely assistive technology, microlearning, cognitive load theory, self-directed learning, AI-supported learning, learning analytics, teacher education, and microteaching. Second, the main concepts from each domain are mapped, such as accessibility, scaffolding, segmentation, intrinsic load, extraneous load, germane load, personalisation, feedback, reflection, and professional competence. Third, the relationships between concepts are analysed based on their pedagogical functions. At this stage, technology is understood as a mediator of learning, microlearning as a cognitive structure, and AI learning analytics as a supporter of diagnosis and feedback. Fourth, these concepts are abstracted into five main components of the framework, namely the needs of learners, the affordance of assistive technology, the architecture of microlearning design, the learning process, and multidimensional outcomes.

Table 3. Stages of Developing the Assistive Microlearning Conceptual Framework

Stage	Focus	Outcome
Literature identification	Assistive technologies, microlearning, Cognitive Load Theory, AI, learning analytics, and teacher education	Identification of the main conceptual domains relevant to the chapter
Concept mapping	Accessibility, scaffolding, segmentation, cognitive load, feedback, and reflection	Development of a conceptual map of assistive learning supported by microlearning
Relational analysis	Relationships among learner needs, technologies, instructional design, learning processes, and outcomes	Identification of functional relationships among framework components
Conceptual abstraction	Formulation of the main framework components	Development of five components of the Assistive Microlearning framework

With that methodological basis, the assistive microlearning framework is not positioned as a simple combination of several concepts but rather as a conceptual synthesis that connects theory, technology, and learning design. This framework positions learners as the starting point of design, technology as a pedagogical mediator, microlearning as a cognitive structure, reflection as a development mechanism, and learning outcomes as multidimensional results. Because it is still conceptual, this framework requires empirical validation through quasi-experimental research, mixed-methods design-based research, or longitudinal studies to assess its impact on cognitive load, learning engagement, reflection quality, self-efficacy, and professional competence development.

Conceptual Framework of Assistive Microlearning in Higher Education

Based on the synthesis of literature and previous methodological foundations, this chapter proposes the conceptual framework of assistive microlearning in higher education. This framework is developed to integrate assistive technology, microlearning, cognitive load management, adaptive feedback, reflection, and competency development into a coherent learning system. Technology is not positioned as an external addition but as part of the pedagogical architecture that helps learners access materials, manage complexity, receive feedback, and gradually develop competencies.

This framework is built on the assumption that the challenges of higher education cannot be solved merely by adding digital devices to the learning process. Cognitive load, time constraints, learner diversity, and professional competency demands require a design that connects learning needs, technology functions, learning activities, reflection, and competency achievements. Therefore, assistive microlearning is understood as a system consisting of five main components: learner needs, affordance of assistive technology, microlearning design architecture, learning process, and multidimensional outcomes.

The first component is the needs of the learners. In this framework, the needs of the learners become the starting point of the design. These needs not only encompass accessibility but also time constraints, cognitive load, motivation, academic readiness, digital literacy, and professional competency demands. In teacher education, these needs can manifest as difficulties in managing the classroom, asking questions, giving instructions, using media, or reflecting on teaching practices. These needs can be identified through diagnostic assessments, observations, self-reflection, task results, digital learning data, or feedback from lecturers and peers.

The second component is the affordance of assistive technology. Assistive technology is understood as a pedagogical mediator that helps learners access, process, practise, and reflect on learning. Mobile applications can provide brief materials, formative quizzes, study reminders, and quick reflections. Wearable technologies can monitor activities, responses, or interaction patterns. Immersive technologies such as VR and AR can provide safe and repeatable simulations. AI-supported tools and learning analytics can analyse learning patterns, provide adaptive feedback, and recommend the next learning path.

The third component is the architecture of microlearning design. Microlearning is not reduced to short videos or quick quizzes but is understood as a cognitive structure that organises the segmentation of material, the sequence of competencies, brief activities, feedback, reflection, and learning progression. Referring to Cognitive Load Theory, microlearning helps manage intrinsic load by breaking down complex competencies, reducing extraneous load through focused design, and reinforcing germane load through practice, reflection, and repeated feedback.

The fourth component is the learning process, which includes cognitive regulation, self-regulation, feedback, reflection, and iteration. This process occurs when learners study a microlearning unit, practise, receive feedback, reflect on their performance, and then improve their learning or practice strategies for the next time. In microteaching, for example, prospective teachers can study a short module on questioning skills, practise them, receive video-based or analytics feedback, and then repeat the practice with better strategies.

The fifth component is multidimensional achievement. The success of learning is not only seen from the mastery of the material but also from cognitive, professional, motivational, and reflective development. In teacher education, these achievements are evident in the increased ability to design lessons, manage classrooms, give instructions, build interactions, and reflect on teaching practices. This achievement is not final but serves as a foundation for identifying new needs and adjusting future learning.

Table 4. Main Components of the Assistive Microlearning Framework

Component	Main Function	Example in Teacher Education
Learner needs	Serve as the basis for identifying learning problems and competency targets	Preservice teachers experience difficulty managing classroom transitions
Assistive technology affordances	Provide support for access, simulation, feedback, and monitoring	Mobile applications, video playback, VR simulation, learning analytics, and AI feedback
Microlearning architecture	Segments competencies and manages cognitive load	Short modules on questioning techniques or giving clear instructions
Learning processes	Activate regulation, feedback, reflection, and iteration	Microteaching practice and data-informed reflection
Multidimensional outcomes	Support cognitive, professional, motivational, and reflective development	Improved classroom readiness, self-efficacy, and reflective ability

Visually, the relationships between the components are illustrated in Figure 1. This framework shows that learning occurs recursively: learners' needs determine the selection of technology and microlearning design; the design activates the learning process; learning outcomes are then reused to adjust subsequent support.

Figure 1. Conceptual Framework of Assistive Microlearning in Higher Education.

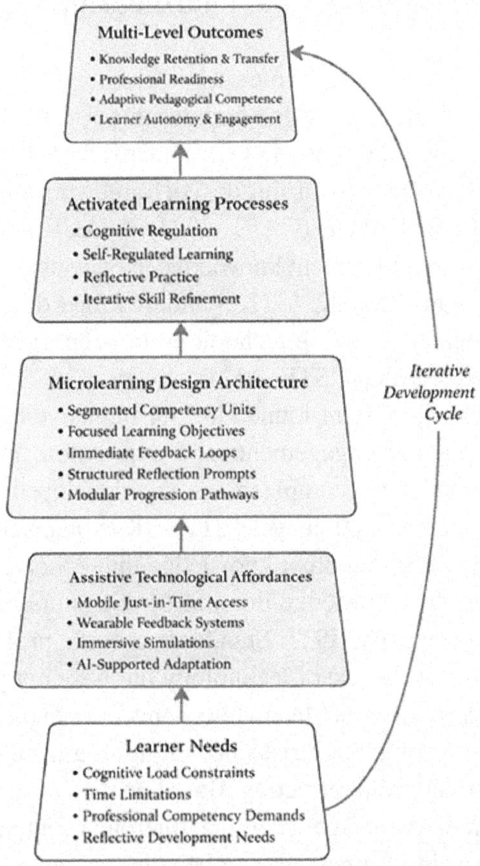

This framework illustrates the dynamic relationships between learners' needs, the affordance of assistive technology, microlearning architecture, the learning process, and multidimensional outcomes. The recursive arrows indicate that learning outcomes, development data, and reflections are reused to adjust the next learning design.

The conceptual contributions of this framework lie in three aspects. First, assistive technology is repositioned from an accessibility tool to a pedagogical and cognitive mediator. Second, microlearning is expanded from a brief learning format to a cognitive architecture for competency development. Third, the needs of learners, technology, instructional design, reflective processes, and competency achievements are interconnected within a single adaptive and sustainable design system.

Differentiation Framework of UDL, TPACK, ISTE Standards, and Conventional Microlearning

The assistive microlearning framework is closely related to several established models, particularly Universal Design for Learning (UDL), Technological Pedagogical Content Knowledge (TPACK), ISTE Standards for Educators, and conventional microlearning. UDL refers to a learning design framework aimed at optimising access and participation for all learners (CAST, 2024). TPACK explains the integration of technology, pedagogy, and content knowledge in educator competencies (Mishra & Koehler, 2006). Meanwhile, the ISTE Standards for Educators provide standards for the role of educators in using technology to support impactful, collaborative, and learner-centred learning (ISTE, 2024).

UDL provides an important foundation for inclusive learning through various means of representation, engagement, and expression. However, UDL has not specifically explained how competencies are developed through micro-stages, adaptive feedback, and reflection cycles. TPACK explains the relationship between technology, pedagogy, and content knowledge that educators need to possess, but it focuses more on the knowledge domain of educators rather than the learning experiences of students. The ISTE Standards provide professional orientation on the role of educators in the use of technology but have not yet detailed the mechanisms of microlearning design. Meanwhile, conventional microlearning emphasises short and flexible learning, but it risks becoming fragmented if not connected with competency progression and reflection. Based on the conceptual positions of UDL, TPACK, ISTE Standards, and conventional microlearning, the comparison with the Assistive Microlearning framework can be summarised as follows (CAST, 2024; ISTE, 2024; Mishra & Koehler, 2006).

Table 5. Comparison of UDL, TPACK, ISTE Standards, Conventional Microlearning, and the Assistive Microlearning Framework

Model/ Framework	Main Focus	Limitation	Position of the Assistive Microlearning Framework
Universal Design for Learning	Accessibility, flexibility, and diverse ways of learning	Does not specifically explain competency segmentation and adaptive feedback in detail	Extends inclusion through microlearning, Cognitive Load Theory, and staged reflection
TPACK	Integration of technological, pedagogical, and content knowledge by educators	Focuses more on teachers' knowledge domains than learners' cognitive experiences	Shifts the focus toward learners' technology-mediated learning experiences
ISTE Standards	Professional roles of educators in technology-enhanced education	Normative in nature and not yet operationalized at the microlearning design level	Operationalizes the roles of designer, facilitator, and analyst in learning design
Conventional microlearning	Short and flexible learning units	Risks becoming fragmented short-form content	Repositions microlearning as a cognitive and assistive learning architecture
Assistive Microlearning	Integration of learner needs, technologies, microlearning, feedback, reflection, and outcomes	Requires empirical validation	Serves as an integrative framework for inclusive, adaptive, and recursive learning

Epistemologically, this framework rejects the instrumental view that understands technology merely as a neutral tool. Technology is understood as a mediator that shapes the way learners access information, process knowledge, receive feedback, and build understanding. Ontologically, learning is viewed as a recursive process, not a linear path from material delivery to final assessment. Needs diagnosis, microlearning, practice, feedback, reflection, and improvement occur as a continuous cycle.

Thus, the Assistive Microlearning framework does not replace UDL, TPACK, ISTE Standards, or conventional microlearning but rather extends and operationalises the key ideas of these models. Its main value lies in design coherence: technology is used not for its novelty, but for its contribution to managing cognitive load, personalisation, reflection, and competency development.

Integration with AI, Learning Analytics, and Adaptive Systems

AI, learning analytics, and adaptive systems play a crucial role in operationalising the assistive microlearning framework. If microlearning provides a segmented learning structure, then AI and analytics enhance the system's ability to read learners' needs, provide feedback, adjust learning paths, and monitor competency development. In this framework, AI does not replace educators but rather becomes a system that supports pedagogical decision-making.

The first function of AI is to assist in diagnosing learning needs. Through data such as quiz results, access time, module completion, participation, and practical performance, the system can help identify students who are experiencing difficulties. However, this data still needs to be interpreted by educators, as low scores or slow task completion do not always indicate inability; they can also be influenced by motivation, fatigue, access to technology, or other contextual factors.

The second function is to support feedback and reflection. Learning analytics can display learning progress, module completion rates, areas of competence that are still weak, or patterns of student engagement. In assistive microlearning, feedback not only indicates right or wrong but also helps learners understand what they have mastered, what needs improvement, and what steps can be taken next. Data becomes meaningful when connected with reflection, rubrics, and pedagogical guidance.

The third function is to create adaptive learning pathways. The system can adjust the sequence of materials or difficulty levels or recommend microlearning units based on the learners' performance. In teacher education, prospective teachers who are weak in questioning skills can be directed to additional units on types of questions, probing techniques, and wait time. Prospective teachers who struggle with classroom management can be directed to simulations on managing transitions or responding to student behaviour.

The fourth function is to accelerate AI-supported feedback in learning practices. In microteaching, for example, the system can help analyse recordings of teaching practice, such as speaking duration, question variation, interaction frequency, or media usage patterns. The results of the analysis do not replace the lecturer's assessment but provide initial data that enriches reflection and guidance. In addition, gamification can be used in a limited way to enhance motivation through progress bars, badges, or competency levels, as long as it remains linked to learning outcomes and not just score acquisition.

Table 6. Functions of AI, Learning Analytics, and Adaptive Systems in Assistive Microlearning

Technology Component	Function	Example of Application
AI-driven diagnostics	Identifies learners' needs and learning difficulties	The system detects learning difficulties based on quiz results and learning time
Learning analytics dashboard	Displays learning progress and competency achievement	The dashboard shows areas of competency that still need improvement
Adaptive learning pathway	Adjusts the sequence and level of learning difficulty	Learners are directed to reinforcement micro-units based on their performance
AI-supported feedback	Provides initial and timely feedback	The system analyzes reflections or microteaching performance
Gamified progression	Visualizes learning progress and competency development	Badges or progress bars are awarded based on competency achievement

Conceptually, the integration of AI in assistive microlearning occurs in a cycle where learning data is collected, needs are analysed, microlearning units are selected, feedback is provided, reflection is conducted, and learning paths are adjusted. This cycle is illustrated in Figure 2.

Figure 2. AI–Microlearning Integration Loop.

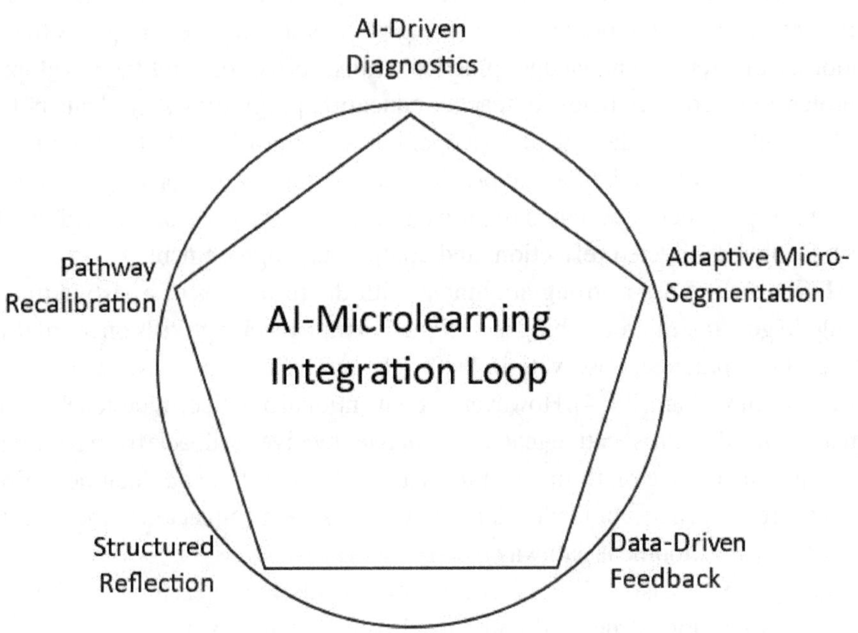

This cycle depicts the recursive relationship between learning data collection, AI-based diagnosis, microlearning unit selection, adaptive feedback, learner reflection, and learning path adjustment. Each learning outcome serves as a basis for improving the design and support of subsequent learning.

Nevertheless, the integration of AI and learning analytics needs to consider ethical and institutional aspects. Student data must be managed transparently, securely, and responsibly. Students need to know what data is being collected, for what purpose it is used, and who can access it. Adaptive systems must also be free from algorithmic bias and narrow labelling of students' abilities. Therefore, quantitative indicators need to be complemented with qualitative reflections, educator observations, and pedagogical dialogues.

Thus, the integration of AI in assistive microlearning is not merely about automation or efficiency but about pedagogical coherence. AI and analytics are valuable when they help connect diagnosis, microlearning design, feedback, reflection, and competency development. The centre of learning remains on the learners and pedagogical relationships, while technology serves as an enhancer of an inclusive, adaptive, and sustainable learning system.

Application of Framework in Teacher Education and Microteaching

Teacher education is a relevant context for applying the Assistive Microlearning framework because the process of forming prospective teachers requires the integration of theoretical knowledge, practical skills, reflection, and the development of professional competencies. In teacher education programmes, students not only need to understand pedagogical concepts but also must be able to apply them in complex, dynamic, and often unpredictable learning situations. Therefore, the learning of prospective teachers requires a design that allows for focused practice, quick feedback, directed reflection, and continuous improvement.

Microteaching has a strong alignment with the principles of assistive microlearning. In general, microteaching is designed to train teaching skills on a small scale through brief practice, observation, feedback, and reflection (Iliasova et al., 2025; Jaiwant & Kureethara, 2024). However, in conventional practice, microteaching often remains episodic. Prospective teachers practise, receive feedback from lecturers or peers, and then move on to the next activity without systematic documentation of their progress. As a result, feedback has not always been connected to the long-term competency development pathway.

Through the Assistive Microlearning framework, microteaching can be reconstructed into a more structured and data-driven learning cycle. This cycle begins with identifying the needs of prospective teachers, followed by the provision of relevant microlearning units, brief teaching practice, technology-based feedback, directed reflection, and re-practice. In this way, microteaching not only becomes a teaching demonstration activity but evolves into a process of gradually, reflectively, and recursively developing professional competencies.

Figure 3. Operational Cycle of Assistive Microlearning in Microteaching Contexts

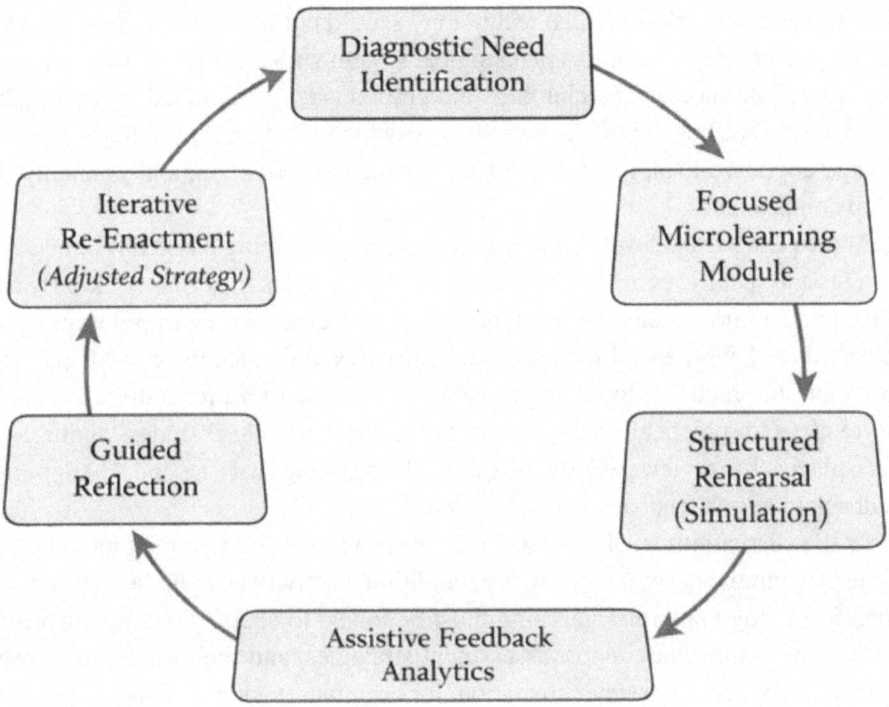

This image shows the operational cycle of implementing Assistive Microlearning in microteaching. The cycle begins with the diagnosis of prospective teachers' needs, followed by the provision of microlearning units, microteaching practice, technology-based feedback, directed reflection, and re-practice. The cycle arrows indicate that the results of practice and reflection are reused to improve the next learning strategy, so the microteaching process proceeds gradually, adaptively, and sustainably.

The cycle shows that the application of Assistive Microlearning in microteaching does not stop at providing brief materials or using digital technology. Moreover, this framework emphasises the interconnection between needs diagnosis, targeted practice, feedback, reflection, and practice repetition. Thus, microteaching can serve as a space for the development of professional competencies that are more systematic, adaptive, and data-driven.

Pedagogical, Curriculum, and Institutional Implications

The Assistive Microlearning Framework has important implications for learning design, curriculum development, and institutional readiness in higher education. This framework emphasises that technology should not be used as a separate addition but rather integrated into a pedagogical system with clear goals, structure, and evaluation. The success of technology integration is not determined by the number of devices used, but rather by the extent to which the technology helps learners manage cognitive load, receive feedback, engage in reflection, and gradually develop competencies.

At the pedagogical level, lecturers need to design learning based on the needs of students and specific competency achievements. Complex materials or skills can be broken down into smaller, focused, and interconnected microlearning units. Each unit needs to have clear objectives, brief activities, quick feedback, and space for reflection. In practice, mobile applications can be used for preparatory materials, short videos for practical examples, formative quizzes to check understanding, and video playback to review performance, as well as learning analytics and AI-supported feedback to enrich feedback and reflection.

At the curriculum level, assistive microlearning needs to be integrated as part of the programme design, not just as an additional activity in a single learning session. Technology and microlearning must be linked to course learning outcomes, programme competency maps, assessment strategies, and the longitudinal development of learners. In teacher education, for example, teaching competence can be developed gradually starting from basic pedagogical understanding, instructional communication skills, microteaching practice, and data-based reflection to field practice. In this way, the development of competencies occurs longitudinally and is not limited to a specific course.

At the institutional level, the implementation of assistive microlearning requires support in infrastructure, policies, and faculty capacity development. Institutions need to provide a stable learning platform, adequate technology access, technical support, and a secure data management system. Lecturers also require training that is not only technical but also pedagogical, especially in designing microlearning units, reading learning data, interpreting analytical results, and guiding student reflections.

In addition, the use of AI and learning analytics demands clear ethical governance. Institutions need to ensure transparency regarding what data is collected, for what purposes the data is used, who can access it, and how the data affects learning decisions. Student data should not be used to narrowly label their abilities but should be directed towards providing more precise support. Thus, the integration of technology in assistive microlearning requires alignment between pedagogy, curriculum, institutional policies, and data usage ethics.

CONCLUSION AND FUTURE RESEARCH DIRECTIONS

This chapter has developed a conceptual framework of assistive microlearning in higher education as a response to contemporary learning challenges, particularly high cognitive load, limited study time, diverse learner needs, and the complexity of professional competencies. This framework positions assistive technology not merely as an accessibility tool or an additional device but as a pedagogical and cognitive mediator that supports access, cognitive load management, feedback, reflection, and gradual competency development.

The main contribution of this chapter lies in the integration of assistive technology, microlearning, cognitive load theory, AI, learning analytics, and reflective practices into a coherent learning architecture. In this framework, microlearning is not understood merely as the delivery of brief content but as a cognitive structure that organises the segmentation of competencies, learning progression, feedback, and reflection. Thus, assistive microlearning offers the perspective that effective learning is not only digital or flexible but must also be directed, adaptive, inclusive, and competency-oriented.

In the context of teacher education and microteaching, this framework provides a concrete application model. Microteaching can be reconstructed from episodic practice activities into a more structured, reflective, and data-driven process of professional competence development. Prospective teachers can be trained through microlearning units that focus on specific sub-competencies, such as questioning skills, giving instructions, managing the classroom, using media, and closing lessons. Through technological support, the training process can be complemented with performance recordings, quick feedback, learning analytics, and directed reflection.

Nevertheless, the Assistive Microlearning framework developed in this chapter remains conceptual. Therefore, future research needs to be directed towards empirical validation in various higher education contexts. Quasi-experimental research can be used to test the influence of this framework on cognitive load, knowledge retention, learning engagement, and academic achievement. Mixed methods research can combine quantitative data from learning analytics with qualitative data from reflections, interviews, or practice observations. Meanwhile, design-based research and longitudinal studies can be used to develop, test, and refine the implementation of assistive microlearning in real learning environments.

In teacher education, further research can examine the impact of this framework on the quality of microteaching, depth of reflection, self-efficacy of prospective teachers, teaching readiness, and development of pedagogical competence. In addition, ethical aspects, fairness, and data governance also need to be critically examined so that the use of AI and learning analytics does not result in bias, narrow labelling, or automated decisions that overlook the human context.

Thus, Assistive Microlearning can be understood not only as an instructional innovation but also as a learning design paradigm that connects technology, pedagogy, curriculum, and competency development. In the era of higher education marked by complexity, diversity, and technological acceleration, this framework offers a conceptual foundation for building more inclusive, adaptive, reflective, and sustainable learning.

REFERENCES

Alhebaishi, S., Stone, R., & Ameen, M. (2025). Emotional Engagement and Teaching Innovations for Deep Learning and Retention in Education: A Literature Review. *International Journal of Advanced Computer Science and Applications, 16*(3), 35–45. DOI: 10.14569/IJACSA.2025.0160304

Alias, N. F., & Razak, R. A. (2023). Exploring The Pedagogical Aspects of Microlearning in Educational Settings: A Systematic Literature Review. *Malaysian Journal of Learning and Instruction, 20*(2), 267–294. DOI: 10.32890/mjli2023.20.2.3

Almuqhim, S., & Berri, J. (2025). AI-Driven Personalized Microlearning Framework for Enhanced E-Learning. *Computer Applications in Engineering Education, 33*(3), e70040. Advance online publication. DOI: 10.1002/cae.70040

Bedard, A., & Zhang, Q. (2025). Highlighting Opportunities for Inclusive Education Using Virtual Reality: Exploring New Learning Pathways for People with Disabilities. In S. C., A. M., N. S., & S. G. (Eds.), *Communications in Computer and Information Science: Vol. 2524 CCIS* (pp. 37–46). Springer Science and Business Media Deutschland GmbH. DOI: 10.1007/978-3-031-94156-6_4

Birtwistle, T., & Wagenaar, R. (2020). Re-thinking an educational model suitable for 21st century needs. In *European Higher Education Area: Challenges for a New Decade* (pp. 465–482). Springer International Publishing., DOI: 10.1007/978-3-030-56316-5_29

Blinov, V. I., Sergeev, I. S., & Rodichev, N. F. (2022). The Microlearning-From Business to Education: A Promising Direction For The Development of Didactics. *Obrazovanie i Nauka, 24*(9), 43–68. DOI: 10.17853/1994-5639-2022-9-43-68

CAST. (2024). *Universal Design for Learning Guidelines version 3.0. CAST.* https://udlguidelines.cast.org/

Corbeil, J. R., Tufan, D., & Corbeil, M. E. (2023). The effect of microlearning and multimedia design on knowledge and skills acquisition of students in e-courses. *Issues in Information Systems, 24*(1), 342–355. DOI: 10.48009/1_iis_2023_129

Cronin, J., & Durham, M. L. (2024). Microlearning: A Concept Analysis. *CIN -. Computers, Informatics, Nursing, 42*(6), 413–420. DOI: 10.1097/CIN.0000000000001122 PMID: 38483251

Esleen, K. B., Hemalata, V., & Zety, M. Z. A. (2024). Assistive technology for the special needs people. In N. C., S. S.K., Y. L.C., C. A.C.H., P. S.K.S., & T. V. (Eds.), *AIP Conference Proceedings* (Vol. 3161, Issue 1). American Institute of Physics. DOI: 10.1063/5.0229697

Holbert, R. M. G. (2025). Course Calendars and Routine Review to Support College Student Achievement. *College Teaching*, 1–3. Advance online publication. DOI: 10.1080/87567555.2025.2488840

Iliasova, L., Nekrasova, I., Mena, J., & Estrada-Molina, O. (2025). Microteaching on pre-service teachers' education: Literature review. *Frontiers in Education*, *10*, 1562975. Advance online publication. DOI: 10.3389/feduc.2025.1562975

Ilic, P. (2024). Optimizing education through micro-lessons: Engaging and adaptive learning strategies. In *Optimizing Education Through Micro-Lessons: Engaging and Adaptive Learning Strategies*. IGI Global., DOI: 10.4018/979-8-3693-0195-1

ISTE. (2024). *International Society for Technology in Education Standards*. ISTE. https://iste.org/standards

Jaiwant, S. V., & Kureethara, J. V. (2024). Evaluating the impact of microlearning and micro-lessons and implications for general education. In *Global Perspectives on Micro-Learning and Micro-Credentials in Higher Education* (pp. 159–173). IGI Global., DOI: 10.4018/979-8-3693-0343-6.ch010

Le, T. T. T., & Nguyen, N. T. T. (2025). Exploring psychological challenges in higher education: Prevalence, causes, and impacts on student well-being and academic performance. *International Journal of Education and Practice*, *13*(4), 1246–1257. DOI: 10.18488/61.v13i4.4405

Mahmoudi-Dehaki, M., Nasr-Esfahani, N., & Vasan, S. (2025). The Transformative Role of Assistive Technology in Enhancing Quality of Life for Individuals With Disabilities. In *Assistive Technology Solutions for Aging Adults and Individuals with Disabilities* (pp. 45–72). IGI Global., DOI: 10.4018/9798369363089.ch003

Martinez-Hernandez, U., Metcalfe, B., Assaf, T., Jabban, L., Male, J., & Zhang, D. (2021). Wearable assistive robotics: A perspective on current challenges and future trends. *Sensors (Basel)*, *21*(20), 6751. Advance online publication. DOI: 10.3390/s21206751 PMID: 34695964

Mishra, P., & Koehler, M. J. (2006). Technological pedagogical content knowledge: A framework for teacher knowledge. *Teachers College Record*, *108*(6), 1017–1054. DOI: 10.1111/j.1467-9620.2006.00684.x

Monib, W. K., Qazi, A., & Apong, R. A. (2025). Microlearning beyond boundaries: A systematic review and a novel framework for improving learning outcomes. *Heliyon, 11*(2), e41413. Advance online publication. DOI: 10.1016/j.heliyon.2024.e41413 PMID: 39882484

Pang, H., Jin, X., & Zhang, W. (2025). Deciphering the underlying repercussions of cognitive overload on university students' fatigue, frustration and academic productivity: Implementation of stimulus–organism–response model. *Acta Psychologica, 260*, 105469. Advance online publication. DOI: 10.1016/j.actpsy.2025.105469 PMID: 40885176

Poggianti, C., Chessa, S., Pelagatti, S., & Kocian, A. (2025). Immersive Technologies for Inclusive Digital Education: A Systematic Survey. *Human Behavior and Emerging Technologies, 2025*(1). DOI: 10.1155/hbe2/8888303

Pradeep, A. (2023). Empowering Special Education Through Information Technology. *Proceedings of the International Conference on Circuit Power and Computing Technologies, ICCPCT 2023*, 31–34. DOI: 10.1109/ICCPCT58313.2023.10245240

Shaheen, H. R. A. (2025). The Role of Assistive Technology in Enhancing Learning Outcomes for Students with Educational Disabilities: Teachers' Perceptions in Amman Schools. *Journal of Educational and Social Research, 15*(6), 208–217. DOI: 10.36941/jesr-2025-0209

Silva, E. S., Costa, W. P. D., Lima, J. C. D., & Ferreira, J. C. (2025). Contribution of Microlearning in Basic Education: A Systematic Review. *Education Sciences, 15*(3), 302. Advance online publication. DOI: 10.3390/educsci15030302

Singh, S., Srivastava, N., Gupta, S., Singh, A., & Kalpana, K. (2025). Evolution of assistive technology applications featuring innovative solution "Harmony Assist." In T. M., S. S.K., S. P., K. S., & K. D. (Eds.), *AIP Conference Proceedings* (Vol. 3297, Issue 1). American Institute of Physics. DOI: 10.1063/5.0285926

Susilana, R., Dewi, L., Rullyana, G., Hadiapurwa, A., & Khaerunnisa, N. (2022). Can microlearning strategy assist students' online learning? *Cakrawala Pendidikan, 41*(2), 437–451. DOI: 10.21831/cp.v41i2.43387

Valero, M. (2022). Challenges, Difficulties and Barriers for Engineering Higher Education. *Journal of Technology and Science Education, 12*(3), 551–566. DOI: 10.3926/jotse.1696

Wang, X., Zhao, X., & Yu, C. (2025). The influence of information and social overload on academic performance: The role of social media fatigue, cognitive depletion, and self-control. *Revista de Psicodidáctica, 30*(2). Advance online publication. DOI: 10.1016/j.psicod.2025.500164

Yadav, M., Kanwal, P., & Dang, T. T. (2025). Microlearning for the masses: Empowerment of geographically dispersed teams. In *Navigating the Global Workforce Through Bold Workplace Learning and Professional Development* (pp. 319–346). IGI Global., DOI: 10.4018/979-8-3693-3338-9.ch012

Zambrano Verdesoto, G. J., & Caicedo, M. F. (2025). The Importance of Microlearning in Higher Education. *European Public and Social Innovation Review, 10*, 1–14. DOI: 10.31637/epsir-2025-2075

Chapter 7
Secondary Teachers Integrating Generative AI to Support EAL Students:
Evidence of Impact on Student Learning in Mainstream Classes

Karen Mary Dean
http://orcid.org/0009-0004-0355-4671
Latrobe University, Australia

Melissa Barnes
http://orcid.org/0000-0003-3090-2585
Latrobe University, Australia

Bingqing Li
Latrobe University, Australia

ABSTRACT

As global migration to English-speaking countries increases, more students with English as an Additional Language (EAL) are educated in mainstream classrooms, where responsibility for language support is often placed on non-specialist, frequently monolingual teachers with limited training in second language development. These teachers must address EAL learners' linguistic needs while meeting curriculum demands and responding to expectations to integrate generative AI (GenAI) into teaching. This systematic literature review examines GenAI as an emerging assistive technology in mainstream classrooms and its impact on EAL learning. Across 11 peer-reviewed studies (2010–2025), findings indicate that GenAI can improve reading and writing, reduce language anxiety, support metacognition, and promote learner

DOI: 10.4018/979-8-2600-2716-5.ch007

027, IGI Global Scientific Publishing. Copying or distributing in print or electronic forms without written permission of IGI Global Scientific Publishing is prohibited. Use of this chapter to tive artificial intelligence (AI) technologies is expressly prohibited. The publisher reserves all rights to license its use for generative AI training and machine learning model development.

autonomy, particularly when combined with explicit scaffolding and linguistically informed pedagogy. However, limited longitudinal and classroom-based evidence highlights the need for further research into effective pedagogical integration.

1. INTRODUCTION

According to the OECD (2021), government-led, educational programs driven by GenAI are expanding globally, reshaping education systems through funding, regulation, and digital infrastructure. In Australia, for example, in 2025, one in five schools reported increased use of GenAI technologies (Williams, 2025). Such growth reflects education systems' recognition of GenAI's potential to strengthen learning outcomes, while also confirming its position as a transformative force within the education sector (Kilian et al., 2023). GenAI technologies, capable of producing text, images, explanations, and personalised feedback, have become increasingly integrated into classroom teaching as an assistive technology as more schools explore their ability to support differentiation, scaffolded learning, and improve student engagement and learning outcomes (Chiu et al., 2024).

In this chapter, assistive technology is defined as any equipment, product, or software that supports students to improve their functional capabilities to improve engagement, personalise learning experiences, and improve students' integration into mainstream classes (Saabi et al., 2025). In this review, GenAI is understood as a form of assistive technology to support EAL students due to its capacity to provide access to language, curriculum content, and classroom participation through translation, rephrasing, modelling, guided practice, and immediate feedback (Gibbons, 2014; Kasneci et al., 2023). By providing inclusive, accessible, and adaptive support that responds to individual language needs, GenAI aligns with the broader aims of assistive technology and holds meaningful potential for facilitating EAL students' engagement in mainstream educational contexts.

This review aligns with the broader theme of emerging assistive technologies that extend learning beyond the classroom (Holmes et al., 2019). Within this learning environment, GenAI is perceived as a complementary assistive technology that provides adaptive, language-focused support in real time (Kasneci et al., 2023). For EAL students, GenAI works alongside a range of digital technologies that enable more accessible and personalised learning experiences (Godwin-Jones, 2022). This integration allows students to receive continuous language support and guided interaction (Gibbons, 2014).

Recent research suggests that GenAI can support language learning in targeted and pedagogical ways, particularly through personalised feedback, and the provision of immediate examples that assist students' self-directed learning (Chiu et al., 2023). These functions can directly assist EAL students by making texts more comprehensible, supporting vocabulary and grammar development, modelling language structures, and providing effective feedback that improves language (Gibbons, 2014) with digital technologies supporting these processes (Godwin-Jones, 2022).

GenAI also has the potential to promote creative language use and multimodal expression, with tools that encourage students to work across images, text, audio, and translation to build deeper linguistic understanding (Hafner & Ho, 2020; Lin et al., 2025; Woo et al., 2023; Woo et al., 2024). Studies on GenAI-assisted writing highlight its capacity to support students' writing development through automated feedback, translation, paraphrasing, and transcription, as well as GenAI-enabled writing tools and personalised support systems (Godwin-Jones, 2022; Kasneci et al., 2023). In other words, GenAI can create meaningful language learning opportunities and support more adaptive and creative approaches to language and literacy teaching.

However, the use of GenAI technologies within mainstream secondary classrooms is not straightforward. Effective integration requires teachers to balance the operational, contextual, critical, and creative dimensions of technology within their everyday practice (Tour et al., 2025). Tour et al. (2025) argue that GenAI literacy comprises four interrelated domains that shape how individuals understand, evaluate, and engage with GenAI technologies. The operational domain refers to how individuals use GenAI tools, while the contextual domain refers to how GenAI is used and understood considering its social and educational contexts. They also emphasise the importance of the critical domain, which includes evaluating GenAI's accuracy, bias, and ethics. In addition, the creative domain focuses on understanding how GenAI generates and transforms ideas and supports the development of new ideas.

While substantial research has examined how teachers use GenAI in higher education language classrooms (Belkina et al., 2025; Kasneci et al., 2023; Mesquita & Carnaz, 2024; Popenici et al., 2023) far less is known about its implementation in mainstream secondary settings, particularly in relation to supporting the language development of EAL students. This gap is significant, given that EAL students often require targeted support to access curriculum content and develop the language skills needed to participate fully in classroom learning (Gibbons, 2014). Consequently, mainstream teachers are increasingly expected to use assistive technology to support EAL students' learning, despite limited empirical evidence outlining what constitutes effective pedagogical integration in these contexts.

Empirical scholarly evidence also suggests that teachers' use of GenAI remains largely introductory, efficiency-driven, and low-risk, with teachers relying on GenAI for simple content generation, administrative shortcuts, and other low-stakes tasks, rather than supporting students to delve deeper into pedagogically rich learning experiences (Barnes & Tour, 2025; Godwin-Jones, 2022; Mancusi, 2024; Shaikh et al., 2023). This aligns with Prestridge's analysis of teachers' use of technology, which suggests that digital tools are being implemented by teachers in ways that copy existing pedagogical practices rather than enabling transformative teaching (Prestridge, 2024). Consequently, while decisions about how, when, and why GenAI is used in classrooms are largely made by teachers, these decisions are shaped by limited training, variable confidence, and ongoing uncertainty about GenAI's role in language learning (Barnes & Tour, 2025).

The need for GenAI literacy training for teachers is a recurring theme across current research (Walter, 2024). Teachers require explicit professional learning that strengthens their technical, pedagogical, and critical GenAI literacies so they can integrate GenAI safely and meaningfully into classroom practice (Fawns, 2022; Prestridge, 2024). At the same time, students need structured opportunities to develop GenAI literacy skills, such as evaluating GenAI-generated outputs, identifying inaccuracies, and engaging critically with GenAI tools, to ensure these technologies improve rather than undermine language learning (Kasneci et al., 2023; Smith & Downes, 2023).

With a growing number of EAL students in mainstream classrooms who present diverse linguistic, pedagogical, cultural, and curriculum needs (Gibbons, 2014; Smith & Downes, 2023), GenAI technologies can be utilised by teachers to differentiate mainstream curriculum for EAL learners (Smith & Downes, 2023) and explicitly teach the GenAI literacies, and capabilities required for inclusive, responsible, and meaningful use (Fawns, 2022; Godwin-Jones, 2022; Prestridge, 2024). As a result, the use of GenAI technologies in the classroom creates opportunities for students to practice and develop GenAI capabilities in learning contexts, such as interpreting GenAI feedback, evaluating GenAI-generated content, engaging in multimodal composition, and applying GenAI tools critically and creatively (Fawns, 2022; Godwin-Jones, 2022; Kasneci et al., 2023).

GenAI has become a significant instructional tool in education, offering new possibilities to support EAL students' writing development by providing guided and modelled examples of English language use, and feedback during the writing process (Woo et al., 2024). As schools increasingly adopt GenAI-enabled tools, there is growing interest in understanding how these technologies can be pedagogically implemented to support the creativity, learning, and language development of EAL students (Lin et al., 2025). Evidence emphasises that meaningful student outcomes are dependent on teachers' pedagogical decision-making, professional confidence, and understanding of how to effectively integrate GenAI within classroom practices (Chiu et al., 2023; Tai & Chen, 2024; Khan et al., 2024; Woo et al., 2024). Teachers play a central role in shaping how EAL students engage with GenAI tools, ensuring safe, purposeful, and culturally responsive use. Despite these insights, most existing literature focuses on higher education, with limited attention on mainstream secondary classrooms, where EAL students face distinct linguistic, academic, cultural and curriculum challenges (Barnes & Tour, 2025; Kasneci et al., 2023; Mancusi, 2024).

The review identifies GenAI as an assistive technology that supports EAL students by improving language access, providing structured scaffolding, enabling adaptive task support, and delivering real-time feedback. However, there is limited empirical evidence demonstrating how these approaches are effectively implemented in mainstream secondary classrooms (Gibbons, 2014; Kasneci et al., 2023). In addition, further research is needed to examine how GenAI can be purposefully and pedagogically integrated to support EAL students in mainstream classroom environments. Consequently, this review identifies a significant gap in the literature, specifically the lack of research examining how mainstream secondary teachers integrate GenAI as an assistive technology for EAL students, and the limited evidence regarding how the integration influences student learning outcomes, language development, and curriculum access.

Figure 1. GenAI as Assistive Technology for EAL Learning in Mainstream Classes

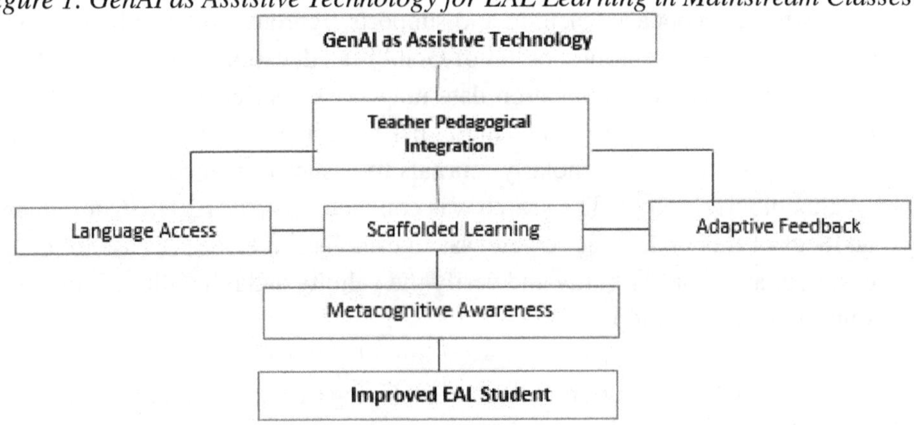

This systematic review further explores the complex ways in which secondary teachers integrate GenAI technologies as an emerging type of assistive technologies to support EAL students in mainstream classes, alongside examining available evidence of its impact on student learning. The review seeks to examine how teachers use GenAI to enhance student learning for EAL students, including language development and curriculum engagement. It also examines the role teachers play in identifying the limitations and challenges they experience when implementing these technologies. By investigating teachers' experiences across diverse educational contexts, the review aims to provide deeper insights into how GenAI can address existing challenges, strengthen instructional practices, and improve learning outcomes for EAL students.

2. METHODS

A systematic review methodology was selected to ensure the rigour and reliability of the study's conclusions and to guarantee that the review process was conducted methodically and transparently without bias or identifiable flaws (Gough, 2017). To further promote transparency, accuracy, and a comprehensive account of findings (Page et al., 2021), the Preferred Reporting Items for a Systematic Reviews and Meta-Analysis (PRISMA) framework was adopted to investigate the questions, "How do secondary mainstream teachers integrate GenAI into their teaching practices to support EAL students?" and "What evidence exists regarding GenAI's impact on student learning?".

The process commenced by searching peer-reviewed articles in three electronic databases: ProQuest Education, Scopus, and EBSCOhost (ERIC). All databases were considered relevant for this research because they provide access to a broad range of peer-reviewed literature across relevant areas in education. This ensured comprehensive coverage of empirical studies related to GenAI, EAL instruction, and mainstream secondary teaching and supports rigorous evidence base for this research. Given the recent integration of GenAI in education, and the availability of relevant research, this publication date range was restricted to the last decade (2015-2025). Only studies published in English were included. The review was also restricted to peer-reviewed scholarly journals to ensure formal academic scrutiny and methodological rigour. The search was conducted in April 2025. Consequently, the focus of this systematic review was to establish an evidence base to inform the design of an empirical study and verify the validity and reliability of studies in relevant to the research topic.

Two search-strategy frameworks were initially considered to ensure rigour in this research: PICO (Population, Intervention, Comparison, Outcome) and SPIDER (Sample, Phenomenon of Interest, Design, Evaluation, Research type). After due consideration and given its key components are better suited to qualitative and mixed methods research (Cooke et al., 2012), the SPIDER framework was selected to guide the development of keywords and search terms for the review questions. The search was restricted to article titles, abstracts, and keywords to ensure more targeted results by selecting the "noft" (no full text) field. The following search terms were used: noft (teacher* OR educator*) AND noft (student* OR learner*) AND noft (secondary school* OR high school*) AND (English language learner* OR English as an additional language* OR English as a second language*) AND noft (artificial intelligence*)

Table 1. SPIDER

Sample (S)	**Secondary teachers instructing EAL students in mainstream secondary classes**	**(teacher* OR educator*) AND (student* OR learner*) AND (secondary school* OR high school*)**
Phenomenon of Interest (P I)	Teachers' integration of GenAI in classrooms to support EAL students	(artificial intelligence*)
Design (D)	Semi-structured interviews, questionnaires, documented evidence	e.g., interviews OR questions OR documented evidence
Evaluation (E)	Evidence of impact on student learning, engagement, comprehension, and teachers' perceptions of integration of GenAI	(English language learner* OR English as an additional language* OR English as a second language*)
Research Type (R)	Qualitative and mixed methods (e.g., case studies, teacher reflection, and action research)	e.g., interviews OR questions OR documented evidence

The initial database search yielded a total of 563 articles relevant to the research topic (see PRISMA flow diagram in Figure 1). The next step was shortlisting the articles by reviewing the titles and abstracts to assess their suitability for inclusion. Inclusion criteria specify the characteristics that studies must meet to be included in a review, resulting in clarifying the scope of the review and ensuring transparency and replicability (Stern et al., 2014).

To identify those studies for inclusion, a three-step screening process was undertaken. The first step involved an initial review of the titles and abstracts of all retrieved articles to determine their relevance based on predefined inclusion and exclusion criteria (see Table 2). These criteria were developed by the lead author and guided by established recommendations for trustworthy and influential systematic reviews (Weeks et al., 2023).

Figure 2. PRISMA 2020 flow diagram of the study selection process.

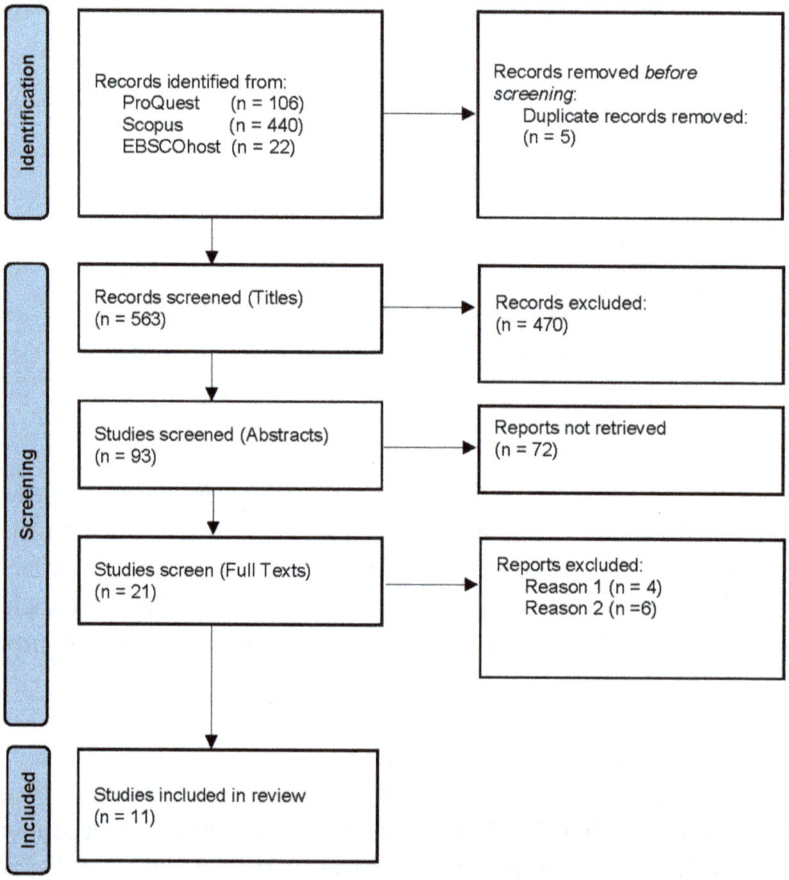

Adapted from Page et al. (2021). The PRISMA 2020 statement: An updated guideline for reporting systematic reviews. BMJ, 372, n71. https://doi.org/10.1136/bmj.n71.

This work is licensed under CC BY 4.0. To view the license, visit https://creativecommons.org/licenses/by/4.0/

The database-specific breakdown of the initial search was as follows: ProQuest (n = 106), Scopus (n = 440), and EBSCOhost (ERIC) (n = 22). During the first round of screening, all authors independently reviewed the titles and abstracts. After removing five duplicate records, 465 articles were excluded based on irrelevance or failure to meet the inclusion criteria (refer to Table 3) leaving 93 articles for further review.

The second step of screening involved two additional authors who independently assessed the remaining 93 titles and abstracts for inclusion. This process led to the following distribution of potentially eligible studies: ProQuest (n = 9), Scopus (n = 5), and EBSCOhost (ERIC) (n = 7), resulting in a total of 21 articles. Articles excluded in the titles and abstract screening did not address the key criteria for understanding how secondary teachers effectively use GenAI to enhance the learning of EAL students. Minor discrepancies emerged between the reviewers during this phase, primarily between the lead author and the other two co-authors, which were resolved through discussion. The lead author reviewed the articles again to ensure accuracy and consistency.

The three reviewers noted concerns regarding the high number of exclusions, noting that many studies focused on tertiary education contexts, which suggested that the remaining number of studies might be limited for inclusion. We considered broadening the scope to include tertiary students, however, this was later rejected to retain the review's primary focus on mainstream secondary classrooms.

Table 2. Inclusion and Exclusion Criteria

Inclusion	**Exclusion**
Studies must focus on secondary school contexts where mainstream classroom teachers are actively involved in the instruction of EAL students.	Studies focusing on *higher education, adult learning, or primary education* were excluded, as were those not explicitly situated within *classroom-based secondary instruction* involving EAL students.
Studies must reflect the perspectives, practices, or lived experiences of mainstream teachers.	Research conducted outside the *mainstream school environment* or not involving direct instruction.
Studies must examine teaching strategies, classroom applications, or the lived experiences of teachers as they relate to the integration of GenAI tools.	Studies with a primarily theoretical, technical, or programmatic evaluation focus such as those emphasising GenAI system development, large-scale program evaluation, or measurement frameworks without clear classroom application.
A clear and explicit connection to the use or implementation of GenAI tools in educational contexts is required, particularly in ways that support differentiated instruction, language acquisition, or student engagement.	Studies that do not explicitly mention or explore the *use of GenAI tools* in practical classroom settings, or that lack relevance to *language learning* or *EAL instruction.*
Only empirical research studies (qualitative, quantitative, or mixed methods) were considered, provided they include data collection and analysis directly tied to teaching and learning in classroom settings.	Systematic reviews, feasibility studies, conceptual papers, quasi-experimental designs, *and* technical research *that did not involve empirical data directly connected to classroom instruction.*

The final step involved full-text screening of the 21 articles, which were read in their entirety to determine if they presented empirical data and explicitly addressed the research objectives. Of these, several articles were excluded at the full-text stage for defined reasons (see Table 3). The main reasons for excluding the articles were that the articles addressed broader policy perspectives, theoretical and ethical discussions, and organisational approaches rather than focusing on the direct impact of teachers' classroom experiences or the empirical evidence to the integration of

GenAI on the learning of EAL students (e.g., Grieve et al., 2024; Haim et al., 2022; Pourdana & Tavassoli, 2022).

Additional exclusions occurred where articles referred to digital tools or GenAI in a broad sense, without a clear reference to the specific application of GenAI or its practical use in classrooms (e.g., Agustín-Llach, 2024; de Jong, et al., 2022). In the remaining articles, rather than focusing on the experiences of classroom teachers and EAL students, the emphasis was on abstract or theoretical themes not aligned with the inclusion criteria (e.g., Agustín-Llach, 2024; Shang et al., 2024; Çöltekin & Rama, 2023; Mirzaeian & Oskoui, 2023). Finally, some articles were excluded because they did not include secondary school students (e.g., Almawadeh, 2025; Bangeni, 2024; Javaid, Chen, & Ramzan, 2024) and others were excluded because they did not include EAL students (e.g., Ch'en, 2025; Jere, 2025; Shankar, et al., 2025).

Table 3. Exclusion Criteria

Code	Reason for Exclusion
Studies must focus on the lived experiences of teachers and the impact of GenAI on EAL students	The remaining articles emphasise system-level analysis, storytelling, or institutional strategies rather than individual perspectives.
Lack of specific focus on EAL learners	Articles discuss general learners or GenAI in education without targeting EAL students.
Insufficient relevance to GenAI	Articles refer to digital tools or GenAI broadly but lack suitable links using GenAI for classroom application.
Thematic misalignment	Articles fail to align with the research goal of understanding practical and lived classroom experiences.

Notably, only 11 of the 21 shortlisted articles selected presented empirical data that provided sufficient evidence to address the research problem. The final selection of articles comprises ProQuest (n = 6), Scopus (n = 1), and EBSCOhost (ERIC) (n = 4). These studies examined student learning outcomes using GenAI (Mageira et al. 2022; Woo et al., 2024; Woo et al., 2024) and the role of teachers in GenAI-supported instruction (Chiu et al., 2023; Khan et al., 2024; Mancusi, 2024).

The eleven articles were analysed using a narrative synthesis approach to integrate findings from multiple studies that relied primarily on text and qualitative data sources (Popay et al., 2006). Thematic analysis was used to systematically examine, analyse, and interpret the patterns or themes across studies (Braun et al., 2006). Together, these methods enabled the synthesis of diverse forms of qualitative data to support a coherent understanding of the evidence. In this review, the narrative synthesis followed several key steps:

1. A synthesis table was created to summarise the selected studies, including analysis of the research design, participant groups and sample sizes, data collection methods, and key findings (see Table 4).
2. The articles were grouped, clustered, and categorised in multiple ways, for example, by key findings, context, participant groups, and evidence of impact.
3. The data then underwent thematic analysis, where codes (e.g., teaching practices, teacher beliefs and capabilities; student learning outcomes) were identified and then organised into themes:

Theme 1: Teacher Pedagogy
Theme 2: Teacher Knowledge and Beliefs
Theme 3: Factors Influencing EAL Students' Use of GenAI

The thematic analysis was informed by the research question, "How do mainstream secondary teachers integrate GenAI into their teaching practices to support EAL students, and what evidence exists regarding GenAI's impact on student learning?"

Following this process, the thematic analysis generated three key findings across 11 peer-reviewed studies:

a) GenAI can effectively improve EAL student learning, engagement and confidence;
b) Teachers play a critical role in determining the success of GenAI integration;
c) GenAI tools support EAL students in developing reflective thinking skills and greater student independence.

3. FINDINGS

This section presents a narrative synthesis of the three key themes generated from the analysis of 11 peer-reviewed studies (five mixed-methods, three quasi-experimental, three qualitative) conducted in Taiwan, Hong Kong, Indonesia, Greece, Afghanistan, and Canada. Collectively, these studies provided contextual evidence on how teachers integrated GenAI to support EAL students.

3.1 Teacher Pedagogy

Several of the studies revealed that their participating teachers made purposeful decisions about when and how best to use GenAI, scaffolding students' use of the tools and differentiating classroom tasks according to diverse student needs (Chiu et al., 2023; Hsiao & Chang, 2023; Lin et al., 2025; Mancusi, 2024; Tai & Chen, 2024). Firstly, many teachers intentionally designed opportunities for students to learn with GenAI by providing appropriate scaffolding within classroom tasks, guiding students' use of tools and supporting meaningful engagement (Chiu et al., 2024; Mancusi, 2024; Woo et al., 2024).

In Hong Kong, for example, Chiu et al. (2023) reported that teachers scaffolded students' use of chatbots by modelling how to ask questions and interpret responses. Structured prompts were used to guide intervention, provide feedback on students' use of the tool, and clarify responses to ensure understanding. As students became more confident, teachers gradually withdrew support to promote autonomy rather than dependence.

Several studies reported on the ways in which teachers modelled and scaffolded GenAI use in their classrooms (Lin et al., 2025; Mancusi, 2024; Woo et al., 2024). For example, Woo et al. (2024) described how teachers scaffolded students' understanding of prompt sequencing, supporting students to sequence GenAI prompts in a way that managed their cognitive load. According to Woo et al. (2024), teachers introduced prompt writing through a step-by-step instructional approach, breaking it down into smaller and easier to understand sections. Teachers modelled sample prompts, demonstrated how to improve questions for clarity and purpose, and guided students in evaluating GenAI-generated responses. This deliberate scaffolding supported students to engage meaningfully with the GenAI tools while reducing cognitive load. In other words, the intentional structure and scaffolding provided to students supported their engagement with GenAI, allowing the technology to be used to enhance their learning rather than overwhelm it. As a result, students' motivation and satisfaction when using GenAI increased.

Similarly, Mancusi (2024) used a teacher-directed vocabulary building exercise to model how students could use GenAI applications to build vocabulary. Lin et al. (2025) found that GenAI played a collaborative role in supporting students in creating Digital Multimodal Composition (DMC) texts. When teachers intentionally modelled and embedded the use of GenAI in the creation of DMC tasks, EAL students displayed greater levels of creativity, engagement, and critical thinking. Rather than prescribing every step, the participating teachers created an opportunity for students to explore and make decisions, demonstrating how teachers could scaffold students' use of GenAI.

Providing students with the opportunity to choose how they engaged with GenAI, as illustrated by Lin et al. (2025), aligned with the findings of Chiu et al. (2023) and Woo et al. (2024). Students benefited most when teachers paired structured choices with explicit guidance. This enabled students to exercise independence while maintaining clarity and direction in their learning. Conversely, when teacher support was absent or minimal, GenAI tools risked contributing to cognitive overload and limiting the scope of effective learning (Chiu et al., 2023; Woo et al., 2024). Together, these studies identified the significant role that teacher expertise and professional judgement played in transforming GenAI from a technological aid into a tool that improves differentiated, self-directed and effective learning.

In addition to scaffolding student learning by modelling the use of GenAI and providing opportunities to use GenAI with support, this review also highlighted how teachers intentionally used GenAI to meet the diverse needs of students (Mancusi, 2024; Tai & Chen, 2024; Wiyaka et al., 2024; Woo et al., 2024). For example, Mancusi (2024) illustrated how curriculum-aligned GenAI prompts, used in writing, reading, speaking, and listening practice, promoted differentiation and allowed students of various ability levels to engage with the content and address diverse linguistic and learning needs. Wiyaka et al. (2024) similarly connected differentiated instruction with skill development and affective support, showing that students who received level-appropriate tasks demonstrated higher levels of confidence and motivation. In Tai and Chen's (2024) study, tasks were tailored to the needs of diverse EAL learners. This was achieved by aligning Intelligent Personal Assistant (IPA) with curriculum specifications, ensuring that students engaged with familiar and meaningful tasks, tailored IPA interactions to suit students' comprehension and processing abilities. These initiatives resulted in measurable improvements in writing, vocabulary, and grammar accuracy, demonstrating that teachers used GenAI to differentiate instruction while maintaining curriculum alignment.

Despite using GenAI tools for teacher-led discussions and student practice, the reviewed studies highlighted different focal outcomes. For example, Hsiao and Chang (2023) and Tai and Chen (2024) emphasised improvements in reading, writing, and speaking skills; Woo et al. (2023) documented improvements in creativity, and Chiu et al. (2023) drew attention to increased student motivation and engagement. Across these studies, teachers employed a range of GenAI tools, however, consistent pedagogical practices were evident regardless of the specific technology used. These findings suggested that GenAI could be integrated into classrooms when teachers purposefully planned lessons, provided well-designed scaffolding, implemented differentiation, and delivered considered feedback while maintaining a balance between student autonomy and guided support.

Teachers' deliberate use of structured prompting and sequenced learning tasks enabled GenAI to function as a learning resource rather than a passive support tool. In other words, pedagogy drove technology rather than technology driving pedagogy.

3.2 Teacher Knowledge and Beliefs

While empirical evidence directly examining teachers' knowledge and beliefs about GenAI was limited, patterns across the studies indicated that teachers recognised GenAI's potential to support language learning, differentiation, creative pursuits, and EAL student engagement.

Across the studies, teachers were positioned as facilitators who guided EAL students' learning while incorporating GenAI as a supportive tool. Rather than substituting teacher expertise, GenAI was viewed as a pedagogical tool that improved instruction when embedded in teacher-led pedagogy (Lin et al., 2025; Tai & Chen, 2024; Woo et al., 2023). In other words, technology was not perceived as replacing teachers' expertise. Teachers modelled its use, guided student engagement, and scaffolded technological learning to build students' confidence and competence (Lin et al., 2025; Mageira et al., 2022; Wiyaka et al., 2024).

Teachers also understood GenAI's potential to scaffold writing, assist with vocabulary and grammar development, and facilitate multimodal literacy tasks. For example, Woo et al. (2023) revealed how teachers modelled writing with natural language generation (NLG) tools, while Lin et al. (2025) reported teachers using GenAI to support vocabulary development, grammar feedback, and multimodal literacy tasks. Although the extent of teacher expertise in GenAI varied, these findings indicated that many teachers in the reviewed studies displayed emerging technological and pedagogical knowledge that enabled them to design GenAI-mediated learning experiences. However, the evidence did not suggest that this capability was consistent across all studies.

Teachers' beliefs about GenAI were generally optimistic, particularly regarding the potential of GenAI to improve motivation, reduce cognitive load, and promote inclusive learning environments. For example, Tai and Chen (2024) found that teachers recognised the role of multimodal GenAI feedback in reducing cognitive barriers for EAL learners. Chiu et al. (2023), guided by Self-Determination Theory (SDT), demonstrated teacher awareness of how motivation interacted with technology. Teachers in Lin's (2025) study found that GenAI fostered creativity, student agency, and intercultural competence when embedded within structured instructional design. Similarly, Wiyaka et al. (2024) reported that teachers recognised GenAI's value in reducing student anxiety and supporting self-paced language practice, particularly through chatbot formative assessment.

Conversely, issues around teachers' pedagogical confidence when designing GenAI-integrated language tasks varied across contexts and depended on access to professional learning. For example, Mageira et al. (2022) found that teachers in Greece lacked sufficient preparation to integrate cultural content and language learning through GenAI-supported content and language integrated learning (CLIL) activities, while Khan et al. (2024) emphasised the need for collaborative professional development to build collective expertise. Together with capability concerns, teachers also questioned the reliability, accuracy, and trustworthiness of GenAI content (Chiu et al., 2023; Hsiao, 2023), highlighting the need for both technical knowledge and ongoing professional development.

Where teachers possessed a strong understanding of language pedagogy and confidence with technology, GenAI served as a tool to enhance creativity, motivation, and differentiated learning. Conversely, limited pedagogical or technical expertise, coupled with insufficient professional support, hindered productive use of GenAI and risked undermining learning outcomes (Chiu et al., 2023; Khan et al., 2024; Lin et al., 2025; Mageira et al., 2022; Mancusi, 2024; Woo et al., 2024). These findings suggest that teachers' knowledge and beliefs play a central role in the meaningful integration of GenAI in EAL classrooms.

3.3 Factors Influencing EAL Students' Use of GenAI

Affective factors, such as emotions, motivation, and psychological needs, fundamentally shaped how EAL students engaged with learning (Ryan & Deci, 2000). The reviewed studies indicated that these factors remained central when GenAI was integrated into classroom practice.

Wiyaka et al. (2024) found that GenAI chatbot–assisted instruction improved Indonesian secondary students' reading performance by lowering reading anxiety. Mageira et al. (2022) reported that low-stress, AI-supported environments increased students' willingness to learn, while Tai and Chen (2024) demonstrated that multimodal intelligent pronunciation assessment (IPA) feedback improved speaking confidence and enjoyment. Tai and Chen (2024) also found that GenAI promoted autonomy by reducing dependence on direct teacher instruction, suggesting that well-designed GenAI feedback supported self-regulated learning and motivation.

These findings revealed that GenAI's affective benefits stemmed primarily from its capacity to support students' emotional and motivational development, rather than from the technology itself. Across studies, students experienced reduced anxiety and increased confidence when interacting with GenAI tools in supportive, learning environments. Empirical evidence from Chiu et al. (2023) and Woo et al. (2023) indicated that students reported that immediate GenAI feedback improved EAL students' perceived control, competence, and engagement in reading, speaking, and language learning. Similarly, Tai and Chen (2024) and Wiyaka et al. (2024) found that low-anxiety and supportive instructional contexts fostered students' persistence and motivation, enabling them to develop stronger cognitive and intrapersonal capabilities such as self-regulation, resilience, and confidence in language use.

Extending beyond these affective outcomes, GenAI also strengthened key intrapersonal capabilities, such as self-regulation, persistence, and resilience, enabling students to manage challenges and sustain learning (Dweck, 2006). Across the reviewed studies, these capabilities emerged when GenAI was embedded in thoughtfully scaffolded learning tasks that balanced technological support with teacher guidance. For example, Khan et al. (2024) found that GenAI-assisted vocabulary activities promoted both emotional and academic resilience, encouraging students to persist through difficulties. Automated feedback, personalised suggestions, and corrective responses helped students regulate their own progress and remaining committed to vocabulary development.

Collectively, the findings emphasised that GenAI's educational value lay not solely in the technology itself, but in the teachers' pedagogical principles, scaffolding practices, and adaptive teaching strategies that guided its implementation. In EAL contexts, teacher expertise, rather than technological capability, was the decisive factor that shaped meaningful language learning outcomes. Moreover, the findings suggest that teachers integrate GenAI to support students through intentional pedagogical approaches, which is informed through teachers' knowledge and beliefs about GenAI as well as student affective and intrapersonal factors.

4. DISCUSSION

Teacher decision-making continues to dominate how GenAI, as an emerging type of assistive technologies, is integrated in classroom tasks in an inclusive, adaptive and meaningful manner (Barnes & Tour, 2025; Chiu et al., 2023; Godwin-Jones, 2022; Khan et al., 2024; Lin et al., 2025; Mancusi, 2024; Shaikh et al., 2023). As revealed by this review and supported by the wider literature, without explicit instruction and modelling, EAL students are at risk of engaging with GenAI in superficial and unsupported ways that may reinforce misunderstandings, reduce_meaningful language-learning opportunities, and widen existing learning inequities (Barnes & Tour, 2025; Chiu et al., 2023; Fawns, 2022; Gibbons, 2014; Khan et al., 2024; Lin et al., 2025; Mancusi, 2024; Mageira et al., 2022; Smith & Downes, 2023; Prestridge, 2024; Woo et al., 2023). These findings suggest that both students' understanding of GenAI, and teachers' instructional approaches are still emerging in classroom contexts and require further investigation.

Research on scaffolding and EAL pedagogy demonstrates that insufficient instruction, or poorly structured teaching, can reinforce misconceptions, restrict opportunities for meaningful language use, and widen learning inequities (Fawns, 2022; Gibbons, 2014; Smith & Downes, 2023).

More recent GenAI-focused studies indicate that when teachers do not, or cannot, explicitly teach GenAI-related literacies or model purposeful use, EAL students face increased barriers to accessing feedback, developing academic language, and engaging autonomously with GenAI tools (Barnes & Tour, 2025; Chiu et al., 2023; Khan et al., 2024; Lin et al., 2025; Mancusi, 2024; Mageira et al., 2022; Prestridge,

2024; Woo et al., 2023). Therefore, this review responds directly to a significant gap in understanding how GenAI can be effectively integrated to support EAL students in mainstream secondary classrooms, where empirical evidence has so far been limited.

Although the potential of GenAI in education is widely acknowledged, it remains far from fully realised in practice. GenAI technologies demonstrate a clear capacity to support EAL students by providing scaffolding (Hsiao & Chang, 2023; Woo et al., 2023), differentiation (Huang et al., 2023; Lin et al., 2025; Tai & Chen, 2024), and targeted language support (Nazari et al., 2021; Xia et al., 2022), enabling improved access to curriculum content and the development of proficiency. However, the extent to which students benefit from these opportunities depends on teachers' pedagogical knowledge (Chiu et al., 2023), instructional approaches (Chiu et al., 2023; Fawns, 2022; Gibbons, 2014; Smith & Downes, 2023; Prestridge, 2024), digital competence (Mancusi, 2024; Khan et al., 2024), and confidence in using GenAI responsibly and accurately (Lin et al., 2025). Without these capabilities, GenAI risks reinforcing rather than reducing existing inequalities, particularly for EAL students who require carefully scaffolded, linguistically informed support. This highlights inconsistencies between GenAI's pedagogical potential to improve language learning, and the realities of classroom practice, where limited teacher confidence, insufficient training, restrict meaningful implementation.

Students bring differing levels of English proficiency, technological understanding, and prior learning experiences to their use of GenAI, which shapes how effectively they can engage in GenAI-supported tasks (Smith & Downes, 2023). Without guidance, many EAL students may struggle to understand GenAI outputs, create effective prompts, or identify inaccuracies (Fawns, 2022; Kasneci et al., 2023). Developing students' GenAI literacies, specifically their ability to use GenAI critically, ethically, and purposefully, is therefore essential to ensure equitable and meaningful learning opportunities (Prestridge, 2024; Woo et al., 2023).

This systematic review addresses two key questions: "How do secondary mainstream teachers integrate GenAI into their teaching practices to support EAL students?" and "What evidence exists regarding GenAI's impact on EAL student learning? The aim of this review was to identify and characterise the range of reported outcomes while critically examining the evidence surrounding GenAI's impact on teaching practices and student learning.

This review demonstrates that the value of GenAI for EAL students lies in the pedagogical decisions made by teachers. The reviewed studies reveal that GenAI supported language development, student engagement, and autonomy only when teachers scaffolded its use and aligned it with curriculum goals. When these conditions were absent, GenAI provided limited educational benefit for students, and in some cases, risked reinforcing existing inequalities for EAL students. This review, therefore, highlights the need for teacher-focused professional development and empirically grounded classroom research that addresses the linguistic, cognitive, and pedagogical needs of EAL students. These findings highlight the central role of teacher expertise in meaningfully shaping GenAI-supported learning for EAL students.

5. CONCLUSION

The review identifies GenAI as an assistive technology that supports EAL students by improving language access, providing explicit structured scaffolding, enabling adaptive task support, and delivering real-time feedback. The findings indicate that when classroom teachers purposefully integrate GenAI into their teaching, it has the potential to improve EAL students' language acquisition, strengthen literacy skills, and promote more inclusive, flexible, and adaptive learning. However, many studies highlight teachers' limited digital literacy, lack of confidence, and reliance on GenAI for low-level tasks. Although several studies suggest that GenAI can support differentiation, scaffolding, and adaptive language learning, few have examined which specific pedagogical approaches, including scaffolding, and prompting strategies, are most effective for EAL students. Given that EAL students require explicit linguistic and cognitive support, future research should explore how GenAI can be aligned with established EAL pedagogical frameworks to improve learning outcomes.

This review is constrained by the small number of empirical studies conducted in mainstream secondary EAL classrooms. This gap between empirical research and practical classroom practice highlights the need for further research into everyday classroom practice and the development of evidence-based pedagogical strategies that assist teachers in effectively integrating GenAI. Another limitation relates to the rapidly evolving nature of GenAI, and the narrow methodological approaches used across the reviewed studies. Most studies relied on teacher perceptions rather than direct measures of student learning, restricting the applicability of findings to Australian mainstream schools. Additionally, much of the research focused on basic GenAI applications, such as translation and grammar correction, rather than deeper pedagogical uses. As a result, there remains limited understanding of how GenAI may support language development, differentiation, or subject-specific learning, leaving a gap in evidence regarding its potential to improve technological, linguistic, and academic outcomes.

At the same time, this review highlights opportunities for future research to systematically document the evidence of GenAI's as an assistive technology for EAL students, and its impact on mainstream teachers' instructional practices. Pedagogical integration is central to transforming GenAI from a general technological tool into an effective assistive resource. This requires purposeful use to meet the diverse linguistic and cognitive needs of EAL students. Further research is needed to investigate teachers' experiences and decision-making to develop a deeper understanding of how GenAI shapes classroom practice and student outcomes.

The findings of this review suggest that GenAI can be meaningfully and effectively integrated into mainstream classrooms when teachers are supported through targeted professional learning, clearly defined pedagogical frameworks, and opportunities for ongoing collaborative inquiry. From a practical perspective, the development of mainstream teachers' GenAI pedagogical knowledge, together with ethical, critical, and responsible use of GenAI, should be embedded into teachers' ongoing professional practice. Such an approach ensures that GenAI, as an assistive technology, enhances rather than replaces effective teaching practices and supports the linguistic, cognitive, and learning needs of EAL students.

Table 4. Summary of 11 studies

Author/ Year	Context	Initiatives	Focus (Participants/ Data)	Main Themes/ Evidence of evaluation	Findings
Woo, D.J., & Susanto, H. (2024)	Hong Kong	Prompt engineering with GenAI	Secondary EFL students; qualitative	Student activities using GenAI	Students developed metacognitive strategies through prompt engineering, Understanding students' prompting can help teachers scaffold AI integrated learning and engagement and creativity were enhanced.
Wiyaka et al. (2024)	Indonesia	GenAI chatbot-assisted assessment	Secondary EFL students; empirical/ quant	GenAI chat-assisted assessments reduce anxiety when reading English and improves reading anxiety.	GenAI chatbot use reduced reading anxiety and improved comprehension and performance among EFL students and created a more relaxed environment for students.
Khan et al. (2024)	Afghanistan	GenAI-assisted vocabulary assessment	Junior secondary; empirical/quant	Using GenAI significantly assisted students and impacts their emotional resilience.	GenAI-supported vocabulary assessment contributed to high levels of student resilience and highlighted the importance of teacher/parent support.

continued on following page

Table 4. Continued

Author/ Year	Context	Initiatives	Focus (Participants/ Data)	Main Themes/ Evidence of evaluation	Findings
Mancusi, L. (2024)	USA	Teacher-led GenAI vocabulary building	Secondary; qualitative	Teacher implementation of GenAI for vocabulary instruction	Teacher-directed GenAI applications helped multilingual learners improve vocabulary; GenAI assisted feedback helped students build autonomy and improved motivation, engagement, and linguistic accuracy.
Mageira et al. (2022)	Greece	Educational GenAI chatbots	Secondary; mixed methods	Content and language learning support using chatbot in CLIL learning	GenAI chatbots supported integrated learning of content and language, improving content retention and improves autonomous learning. Improved student engagement and learning outcomes.

continued on following page

Table 4. Continued

Author/ Year	Context	Initiatives	Focus (Participants/ Data)	Main Themes/ Evidence of evaluation	Findings
Woo et al. (2024)	Hong Kong	ChatGPT in writing instruction	Secondary; mixed methods	Student motivation, and assessing the cognitive load, satisfaction with the learning process	Use of ChatGPT improved students' motivation and writing satisfaction; GenAI complemented the work of teachers but not recommended to replace their role.
Tai & Chen (2024)	Taiwan	Intelligent assistants for speaking	Secondary EFL; mixed methods	Speaking proficiency; classroom impact using intelligent personal assistants	EFL learners showed improved speaking proficiency; intelligent assistants were effective when integrated with classroom instruction.
Chiu et al. (2023)	Hong Kong	GenAI chatbot and teacher support	Secondary; quantitative/ experimental	Teacher role in Gen AI effectiveness	Teacher support significantly moderated the effectiveness of GenAI chatbots, improving student motivation and learning outcomes.

continued on following page

Table 4. Continued

Author/ Year	Context	Initiatives	Focus (Participants/ Data)	Main Themes/ Evidence of evaluation	Findings
Hsiao & Chang (2023)	Taiwan	GenAI tools in online EFL course	Secondary; mixed methods	Integration for reading and writing; learning outcomes	GenAI tools enhanced reading and writing skills in online EFL settings; students showed positive perceptions and learning gains.
Woo, Wang, & Guo (2023)	Hong Kong	Natural Language Generation tools in creative writing	Secondary; qualitative	Idea generation; strategies; evaluation	Students used NGL tools to generate diverse creative ideas; positive attitude toward GenAI-assisted writing; evaluation strategies varied.
Lin et al. (2025)	Hong Kong	Gen AI in digital multimodal composition	Secondary; mixed methods	EAL students benefit from integration of GenAI	GenAI facilitated digital composition, with students improving in vocabulary, grammar, and structural tasks with the use of IDEA framework

Note from Publisher

Correction Notice: A correction to this manuscript has been published

Reason: Image Replacement

After publication, one of the authors requested that one of the figures be replaced with a better representation. The image was replaced with one provided by an author.

Correction Date: 8th July 2026

REREFENCES

Almawadeh, N. S. (2025). Using cartoon video-based instruction for developing oral fluency of Jordanian grade 4 EFL pupils. *Theory and Practice in Language Studies*, *15*(2), 647–655. DOI: 10.17507/tpls.1502.34

Bangeni, B. (2024). Reading (in) law: A critical appraisal of the impact of language on disciplinary novices' cognitive reading strategies. *Language & Communication*, *94*, 69–84. DOI: 10.1016/j.langcom.2023.12.001

Barnes, M., & Tour, E. (2025). Teacher knowledge for navigating generative AI in schools: Pedagogical, ethical, and practical considerations. *Australian Educational Researcher*. Advance online publication. DOI: 10.1007/s13384-024-00726-1

Belkina, M., Daniel, S., Nikolic, S., Haque, R., Lyden, S., Neal, P., Grundy, S., & Hassan, G. M. (2025). Implementing generative AI (GenAI) in higher education: A systematic review of case studies. *Computers and Education: Artificial Intelligence*, *8*, 100407. DOI: 10.1016/j.caeai.2025.100407

Braun, V., & Clarke, V. (2006). Using thematic analysis in psychology. *Qualitative Research in Psychology*, *3*(2), 77–101. DOI: 10.1191/1478088706qp063oa

Ch'en, P. Y., Day, W., Pekson, R. C., Barrientos, J., Burton, W. B., Ludwig, A. B., Jariwala, S. P., & Cassese, T. (2025). GPT-4 generated answer rationales to multiple choice assessment questions in undergraduate medical education. *BMC Medical Education*, *25*(1), 333. Advance online publication. DOI: 10.1186/s12909-025-06862-z PMID: 40038669

Chiu, T. K. F., Moorhouse, B. L., Chai, C. S., & Ismailov, M. (2024). Teacher support and student motivation to learn with artificial intelligence (AI) based-chatbot. *Interactive Learning Environments*, *32*(7), 3240–3256. DOI: 10.1080/10494820.2023.2172044

Çöltekin, Ç., & Rama, T. (2023). What do complexity measures measure? Correlating and validating corpus-based measures of morphological complexity. *Linguistics Vanguard : Multimodal Online Journal*, *9*(1), 27–43. DOI: 10.1515/lingvan-2021-0007

Cooke, A., Smith, D., & Booth, A. (2012). Beyond PICO: The SPIDER tool for qualitative evidence synthesis. *Qualitative Health Research*, *22*(10), 1435–1443. DOI: 10.1177/1049732312452938 PMID: 22829486

de Jong, C., Peter, J., Kühne, R., & Barco, A. (2022). Children's intention to adopt social robots: A model of its distal and proximal predictors. *International Journal of Social Robotics*, *14*(4), 875–891. DOI: 10.1007/s12369-021-00835-0

Dweck, C. S. (2006). *Mindset: The new psychology of success* (1st ed.). Random House.

Fawns, T. (2022). An entangled pedagogy: Looking beyond the pedagogy–technology dichotomy. *Postdigital Science and Education*, *4*(3), 711–728. DOI: 10.1007/s42438-022-00302-7 PMID: 40477872

Gibbons, P. (2014). *Scaffolding language, scaffolding learning: Teaching English language learners in the mainstream classroom* (2nd ed.). Heinemann.

Godwin-Jones, R. (2022). Partnering with AI: Intelligent writing assistance and instructed language learning. *Language Learning & Technology*, *26*(2), 5–24. DOI: 10.64152/10125/73474

Gough, D. (2017). *An introduction to systematic reviews* (Gough, D., Oliver, S., & Thomas, J., Eds.; 2nd ed.). SAGE Publications. DOI: 10.4135/9781036234942

Grieve, A., Rouhshad, A., Petraki, E., Bechaz, A., & Dai, D. W. (2024). Nursing and midwifery students' ethical views on the acceptability of using AI machine translation software to write university assignments: A deficit-oriented or translanguaging perspective? *Journal of English for Academic Purposes*, *70*, 101397. DOI: 10.1016/j.jeap.2024.101379

Hafner, C. A., & Ho, W. Y. J. (2020). Assessing digital multimodal composing in second language writing: Towards a process-based model. *Journal of Second Language Writing*, *47*, 100710. DOI: 10.1016/j.jslw.2020.100710

Haim, O., Orland-Barak, L., & Goldberg, T. (2022). The role of linguistic and cultural repertoire in novice bilingual and multilingual EFL teachers' induction period. *International Journal of Multilingualism*, *19*(1), 63–84. DOI: 10.1080/14790718.2020.1715412

Holmes, W., Bialik, M., & Fadel, C. (2019). *Artificial intelligence in education.* Center for Curriculum Redesign.

Hsiao, J.-C., & Chang, J. S. (2023). Enhancing EFL reading and writing through AI-powered tools: Design, implementation, and evaluation of an online course. *Interactive Learning Environments, 32*(9), 4934–4949. DOI: 10.1080/10494820.2023.2207187

Huang, A. Y. Q., Lu, O. H. T., & Yang, S. J. H. (2023). Effects of artificial intelligence-enabled personalized recommendations on learners' learning engagement, motivation, and outcomes in a flipped classroom. *Computers & Education, 194,* 104684. DOI: 10.1016/j.compedu.2022.104684

Javaid, Z. K., Chen, Z., & Ramzan, M. (2024). Assessing stress causing factors and language related challenges among first-year students in higher institutions in Pakistan. *Acta Psychologica, 248,* 104356. Advance online publication. DOI: 10.1016/j.actpsy.2024.104356 PMID: 38885578

Kasneci, E., Sessler, K., Küchemann, S., Bannert, M., Dementieva, D., Fischer, F., Gasser, U., Groh, G., Gunnermann, S., Hüllermeier, E., Krusche, S., Kutyniok, G., Michaeli, T., Nerdel, C., Pfeffer, J., Poquet, O., Sailer, M., Schmidt, A., Seidel, T., & Kasneci, G. (2023). ChatGPT for good? On opportunities and challenges of large language models for education. *Learning and Individual Differences, 103,* 102274. DOI: 10.1016/j.lindif.2023.102274

Khan, M. A., Kurbonova, O., Abdullaev, D., Radie, A. H., & Basim, N. (2024). Is AI-assisted assessment liable to evaluate young learners? Parents' support, teacher support, immunity, and resilience are in focus in testing vocabulary learning. *Language Testing in Asia, 14*(1), 48. DOI: 10.1186/s40468-024-00324-x

Kilian, K. A., Ventura, C. J., & Bailey, M. M. (2023). Examining the differential risk from high-level artificial intelligence and the question of control. *Futures, The Journal of Policy. Futures, 151,* 103182. DOI: 10.1016/j.futures.2023.103182

Lin, C.-H., Zhou, K., Li, L., & Sun, L. (2025). Integrating generative AI into digital multimodal composition: A study of multicultural second-language classrooms. *Computers and Composition, 75,* 102895. DOI: 10.1016/j.compcom.2024.102895

Mageira, K., Pittou, D., Papasalouros, A., Kotis, K., Zangogianni, P., & Daradoumis, A. (2022). Educational AI chatbots for content and language integrated learning. *Applied Sciences (Basel, Switzerland), 12*(7), 3239. DOI: 10.3390/app12073239

Mancusi, L. (2024). Using AI applications to lead teacher-directed vocabulary-building activities for multilingual learners. *The ORTESOL Journal, 41,* 49–52.

Mirzaeian, V. R., & Oskoui, K. (2023). Google Translate in foreign language learning: A systematic review. *Applied Research on English Language, 12*(2), 51–84. DOI: 10.22108/are.2023.134264.1949

Nazari, N., Shabbir, M. S., & Setiawan, R. (2021). Application of artificial intelligence powered digital writing assistant in higher education: Randomized controlled trial. *Heliyon, 7*(5), e07014. DOI: 10.1016/j.heliyon.2021.e07014 PMID: 34027198

OECD. (2023). Digital education outlook 2021: Pushing the frontiers with AI, blockchain and robots. https://doi.org/10.1787/589b283f-en

Page, M. J., McKenzie, J. E., Bossuyt, P. M., Boutron, I., Hoffmann, T. C., Mulrow, C. D., Shamseer, L., Tetzlaff, J. M., Akl, E. A., Brennan, S. E., Chou, R., Glanville, J., Grimshaw, J. M., Hróbjartsson, A., Lalu, M. M., Li, T., Loder, E. W., Mayo-Wilson, E., McDonald, S., … Moher, D. (2021). The PRISMA 2020 statement: An updated guideline for reporting systematic reviews. *International Journal of Surgery, (London, England), 88*, 105906. https://doi.org/DOI: 10.1016/j.ijsu.2021.105906

Popay, J., Roberts, H., Sowden, A., Petticrew, M., Arai, L., Rodgers, M., Britten, N., Roen, K., & Duffy, S. (2006). *G*uidance on the conduct of narrative synthesis in systematic reviews: *A product from the ESRC methods programme Version* 1(1), b92.

Popenici, S., Rudolph, J., Tan, S., & Tan, S. (2023). A critical perspective on generative AI and learning futures. An interview with Stefan Popenici. *Journal of Applied Learning & Teaching, 6*(2), 311–331. DOI: 10.37074/jalt.2023.6.2.5

Pourdana, N., & Tavassoli, K. (2022). Differential impacts of e-portfolio assessment on language learners' engagement modes and genre-based writing improvement. *Language Testing in Asia, 12*(1), 7. Advance online publication. DOI: 10.1186/s40468-022-00156-7

Prestridge, S. (2024). *Pedagogical beliefs matter: Technologies "more" in the age of disruptive technologies*. In *SITE 2024: 35th International Conference of the Society for Information Technology and Teacher Education*. Association for the Advancement of Computing in Education. *Research Highlights in Technology & Teacher Education 2024: 35th Anniversary Edition*. Association for the Advancement of Computing in Education (AACE).

Ryan, R. M., & Deci, E. L. (2000). Self-determination theory and the facilitation of intrinsic motivation, social development, and well-being. *The American Psychologist, 55*(1), 68–78. DOI: 10.1037/0003-066X.55.1.68 PMID: 11392867

Saabi, N., Chlioui, I., & Radgui, M. (2025). A Review of Assistive Technology in Special Education. *Engineering Proceedings, 112*(1), 45. DOI: 10.3390/engproc2025112045

Shaikh, S., Yayilgan, S. Y., Klimova, B., & Pikhart, M. (2023). Assessing the usability of ChatGPT for formal English language learning. *European Journal of Investigation in Health, Psychology and Education, 13*(9), 1937–1960. DOI: 10.3390/ejihpe13090140 PMID: 37754479

Shang, F., Duan, W., & Xu, L. (2024). *Enhancing intercultural communication skills: The impact of drama in Chinese language teaching*. Language Teaching Research. LTR., DOI: 10.1177/13621688241266941

Shankar, S. K., Pothancheri, G., Sasi, D., & Mishra, S. (2025). Bringing teachers in the loop: Exploring perspectives on integrating generative AI in technology-enhanced learning. *International Journal of Artificial Intelligence in Education, 35*(1), 155–180. DOI: 10.1007/s40593-024-00428-8

Smith, J., & Downes, K. (2023). Implications for initial teacher education (ITE) programs in preparing mainstream teachers for culturally and linguistically diverse classrooms. *TESOL in Context, 32*(1), 97–108. DOI: 10.21153/tesol2023vol32no1art1827

Stern, C., Jordan, Z., & McArthur, A. (2014). Developing the review question and inclusion criteria: The first steps in conducting a systematic review. *The American Journal of Nursing, 114*(4), 53–56. DOI: 10.1097/01.NAJ.0000445689.67800.86 PMID: 24681476

Tai, T.-Y., & Chen, H. H.-J. (2024). The impact of intelligent personal assistants on adolescent EFL learners' speaking proficiency. *Computer Assisted Language Learning, 37*(5-6), 1224–1251. DOI: 10.1080/09588221.2022.2070219

Tour, E., Pegrum, M., & Macdonald, S. (2025). AI literacy practices. In *The Palgrave encyclopedia of computer-assisted language learning* (pp. 1–6). Springer Nature Switzerland., DOI: 10.1007/978-3-031-51447-0_93-2

Walter, Y. (2024). Embracing the future of Artificial Intelligence in the classroom: The relevance of AI literacy, prompt engineering, and critical thinking in modern education. *International Journal of Educational Technology in Higher Education, 21*(1), 15. Advance online publication. DOI: 10.1186/s41239-024-00448-3

Weeks, J., Cuthbert, A., & Alfirevic, Z. (2023). Trustworthiness assessment as an inclusion criterion for systematic reviews—What is the impact on results? *Cochrane Evidence Synthesis and Methods, 1*(10), e12037-n/a. https://doi.org/DOI: 10.1002/cesm.12037

Williams, A. (2025). Integrating artificial intelligence into higher education assessment. *Intersection: A Journal at the Intersection of Assessment and Learning, 6*(1), 128–154.

Wiyaka, W., Silitonga, L. M., Sunardi, S., & Pramudi, Y. T. C. (2024). From nervous to fluent: The impact of AI chatbot-assisted assessment on English reading anxiety and performance in Indonesian secondary school pupils. *Theory and Practice in Language Studies, 14*(12), 3851–3860. DOI: 10.17507/tpls.1412.20

Woo, D. J., Wang, D., Guo, K., & Susanto, H. (2024). Teaching EFL students to write with ChatGPT: Students' motivation to learn, cognitive load, and satisfaction with the learning process. *Education and Information Technologies, 29*(18), 24963–24990. DOI: 10.1007/s10639-024-12819-4

Woo, D. J., Wang, Y., Susanto, H., & Guo, K. (2023). Understanding English as a foreign language students' idea generation strategy for creative writing with natural language generation tools. *Journal of Educational Computing Research, 61*(7), 1464–1482. DOI: 10.1177/07356331231175999

Xia, Q., Chiu, T. K. F., Lee, M., Sanusi, I. T., Dai, Y., & Chai, C. S. (2022). A self-determination theory (STD) design approach for inclusive and diverse artificial intelligence (AI) K-12. *Computers & Education, 189*, 104582. Advance online publication. DOI: 10.1016/j.compedu.2022.104582

Chapter 8
PIPE as a Design-Based Assistive Framework for AI-Enhanced Pragmatic Instruction

Maria Shobeiry
http://orcid.org/0000-0002-2499-0366
University of Tehran, Iran

ABSTRACT

This chapter proposes the Present–Interpret–Provoke–Experience (PIPE) framework—a theoretically grounded, design-based architecture operationalizing AI as assistive technology to cultivate pragmatic competence in EFL education. Viewing pragmatics as probabilistic, context-sensitive knowledge beyond deterministic rules, PIPE fosters recursive engagement with communicative ambiguity via four stages: multimodal input (Present), metapragmatic reflection (Interpret), scenario destabilization (Provoke), and low-risk simulation (Experience). Grounded in quantum-inspired cognition, post-method pedagogy, and inclusive technology paradigms, it reframes pragmatic deficits as accessibility barriers, harnessing AI affordances for epistemic access without normativity or teacher displacement. Mixed-methods evidence from a blended EFL program shows gains in contextual sensitivity, strategies, and confidence, modeling scalable AI integration for equitable inclusion.

DOI: 10.4018/979-8-2600-2716-5.ch008

2027, IGI Global Scientific Publishing. Copying or distributing in print or electronic forms without written permission of IGI Global Scientific Publishing is prohibited. Use of this chapter to ative artificial intelligence (AI) technologies is expressly prohibited. The publisher reserves all rights to license its use for generative AI training and machine learning model development.

INTRODUCTION: AI, ASSISTIVE TECHNOLOGIES, AND THE PEDAGOGICAL PROBLEM OF PRAGMATICS

Over the past decade, the concept of assistive technology in education has undergone a significant transformation. Traditionally associated with compensatory tools designed to address physical, sensory, or cognitive impairments, assistive technologies are now increasingly understood as pedagogical systems that support access, participation, and meaning-making across diverse learner populations (Ayon & Dillon, 2021; Shobeiry, 2026; Zdravkova, 2022).This conceptual shift reflects a broader movement in educational research away from deficit-based models of learning toward inclusive frameworks that foreground variability, agency, and contextual sensitivity. Within this evolving landscape, emerging digital technologies—including mobile, immersive, and artificial intelligence (AI)–based solutions—have been positioned as key enablers of inclusive educational design when they are embedded within sound pedagogical principles rather than deployed as isolated technical interventions (Zdravkova, 2022). Among these technologies, AI occupies a particularly contested position (Das et al., 2025). On the one hand, AI-based systems promise unprecedented levels of adaptivity, personalization, and responsiveness, offering new possibilities for supporting learners who experience difficulty navigating complex learning environments. On the other hand, critical scholars have cautioned against technologically deterministic narratives that frame AI as a neutral or autonomous solution to pedagogical problems, warning that such framings risk marginalizing teacher expertise and oversimplifying the social nature of learning (Das et al., 2025). The challenge, therefore, is not whether AI should be used in education, but how it can be designed and integrated in ways that genuinely function as assistive technologies—supporting learners' engagement with complexity rather than obscuring it.

This chapter addresses this challenge through the lens of pragmatic competence in English as a foreign language (EFL) education. Pragmatic competence refers to learners' ability to use language appropriately in relation to context, interlocutor relationships, communicative intent, and sociocultural norms (Ahmed et al., 2023; Chinpakdee & Gu, 2024 ; Mokoro, 2024). Unlike grammatical accuracy or lexical knowledge, pragmatic appropriateness cannot be reduced to rule-based mastery; it is inherently probabilistic, context-sensitive, and often ambiguous. Learners must make interpretive judgments under conditions of uncertainty, drawing on incomplete information and negotiating meaning dynamically in interaction (Mokoro, 2024; Taguchi & Roever, 2017). These characteristics make pragmatics a particularly revealing domain for examining the pedagogical potential—and limits—of AI as an assistive educational technology (Zdravkova, 2022).

Despite its centrality to communicative participation, pragmatic competence has historically occupied a marginal position in formal language instruction, especially in EFL contexts. Curricula tend to prioritize structural aspects of language that are more easily codified, assessed, and standardized, while pragmatic development is often assumed to emerge implicitly through exposure or left to learners to acquire outside the classroom (Mokoro, 2025). This marginalization has significant implications for inclusion and accessibility. Learners who lack pragmatic competence may experience repeated communicative breakdowns, social misalignment, or perceptions of rudeness or inappropriateness, even when their grammatical proficiency is high (Ahmed et al., 2023; Chinpakdee & Gu, 2024). Such experiences can undermine confidence, restrict participation, and limit access to academic, professional, and intercultural opportunities (House & Kádár, 2024).

From an inclusive education perspective, pragmatic difficulty can thus be understood as a form of hidden accessibility barrier—one that is not tied to visible disability but nonetheless constrains learners' ability to participate fully in communicative practices (Chinpakdee & Gu, 2024, Shobeiry, 2021). Addressing this barrier requires pedagogical approaches that do not merely transmit correct forms but actively support learners in navigating uncertainty, variability, and contextual interpretation. This requirement poses a challenge for conventional instructional models, which often rely on linear explanations and fixed norms that fail to capture the fluidity of real-world communication.

It is precisely at this intersection of uncertainty, interpretation, and pedagogical complexity that AI-based assistive technologies may offer meaningful support—provided they are conceptualized appropriately (Zdravkova, 2022). Rather than positioning AI as a source of authoritative answers or prescriptive norms, this chapter advances the view that AI can function as a mediational scaffold that supports learners' engagement with pragmatic ambiguity. Such a view aligns with sociocultural and post-method perspectives on pedagogy, which emphasize the role of mediation, teacher agency, and contextual responsiveness in learning (Kumaravadivelu, 2012; Bastidas, 2022; Moreira et al., 2024). Within this framework, AI is not an instructor but a design resource that can amplify pedagogical intent by providing adaptive input, contextualized prompts, and opportunities for guided reflection.

The theoretical grounding for this approach draws on probabilistic models of cognition, which challenge deterministic accounts of human reasoning and language use. Research in quantum cognition and related probabilistic frameworks has demonstrated that human decision-making and interpretation often violate classical logical assumptions, instead reflecting context-dependent, non-linear patterns of thought (Bruza et al., 2015; Gao, 2021; Pothos & Busemeyer, 2022). Pragmatic interpretation, in particular, involves managing multiple potential meanings simultaneously and resolving ambiguity through interaction rather than rule application. From this perspective, effective pragmatics instruction must support learners in developing tolerance for uncertainty and flexibility in interpretation—capacities that are poorly served by rigid instructional scripts.AI-based systems, when designed as assistive technologies, are uniquely positioned to support this kind of learning (Zdravkova, 2022). Through adaptive feedback, scenario variation, and simulated interaction, AI can help learners encounter pragmatic variability in structured yet flexible ways. Importantly, this support does not require AI to "understand" pragmatics in a human sense; rather, it requires thoughtful pedagogical design that leverages AI's capacity to generate, vary, and mediate input while leaving interpretive authority with learners and teachers. This distinction is critical for avoiding the reification of norms and for maintaining an inclusive orientation that acknowledges multiple legitimate ways of meaning-making, particularly in English as a lingua franca contexts.

The present chapter builds on these theoretical and pedagogical foundations by presenting the Present–Interpret–Provoke–Experience (PIPE) framework as an instructional architecture for AI-assisted pragmatics instruction. The PIPE framework was developed by Shobeiry (2024) in response to the need for a structured yet flexible approach that can accommodate the complexity of pragmatic learning while remaining pedagogically transparent and teacher-mediated. Rather than treating pragmatics as an add-on skill, PIPE integrates pragmatic development into the core of instructional design, guiding learners through cycles of exposure, interpretation, destabilization, and experiential engagement.

Crucially, the chapter does not advance PIPE as a purely conceptual model. Instead, it grounds the framework in an extended, empirically informed case narrative derived from a mixed-methods study conducted in a blended EFL context. The case study is not presented as a separate methodological unit but is woven throughout the chapter as illustrative and evidentiary support for the theoretical claims advanced. In aligning with the aims of this book, the chapter contributes to ongoing discussions on emerging assistive technologies by offering a domain-specific, theory-driven account of AI integration in education. While much of the literature on assistive technologies has focused on mobile, wearable, or immersive solutions, AI-based pedagogical mediation remains under-theorized, particularly in relation to socially situated aspects of learning (Zdravkova, 2022; Zhao & Yang, 2022). By focusing on pragmatics, the chapter foregrounds the social, interpretive, and ethical dimensions of assistive technology design, highlighting the importance of pedagogical intentionality in shaping how technologies are experienced by learners.

THEORETICAL FOUNDATIONS

Pragmatic Competence, Probabilistic Cognition, and Assistive AI

Understanding how artificial intelligence may function as an assistive technology for pragmatic development requires a careful re-examination of what pragmatic competence entails and why it presents persistent pedagogical challenges. Unlike grammatical competence, which lends itself to formal description and rule-based instruction, pragmatic competence is fundamentally relational and context-sensitive (Chinpakdee & Gu, 2024, Mokoro, 2024). It emerges through interaction, interpretation, and negotiation of meaning rather than through the accumulation of stable linguistic forms (Ahmed et al., 2023; Mokoro, 2024). This distinction has profound implications for instructional design, assessment, and the role of technology in supporting learning.

Pragmatic Competence as Contextual and Probabilistic Knowledge

Pragmatic competence is commonly defined as the ability to use language in ways that are appropriate to a given social, cultural, and interactional context (Mokoro, 2024). It involves sensitivity to factors such as power relations, social distance, communicative intent, and the expectations of interlocutors (Chinpakdee & Gu, 2024). Importantly, pragmatic appropriateness is rarely absolute. Utterances are not simply "correct" or "incorrect" but are evaluated along continua of felicity, politeness, and contextual fit. The same linguistic form may be interpreted differently depending on subtle contextual cues, making pragmatic meaning inherently unstable and negotiable.

From a cognitive perspective, this instability reflects the probabilistic nature of pragmatic reasoning (Riguzzi, 2023). Speakers and listeners operate under conditions of partial information, making inferences about intent and meaning that are always provisional. As Mokoro (2024) argues, pragmatic interpretation relies on abductive reasoning processes that weigh multiple possible meanings rather than selecting from a fixed set of rules. This feature distinguishes pragmatics from other domains of language knowledge and complicates attempts to formalize it pedagogically.

In EFL contexts, the challenge is further amplified by limited exposure to diverse communicative situations. Learners often encounter pragmatics through decontextualized textbook dialogues or prescriptive norms that obscure variability and mask the social negotiation involved in meaning-making. As a result, learners may achieve high levels of grammatical proficiency while continuing to experience pragmatic difficulty, particularly in spontaneous interaction. Such difficulties are not merely linguistic but social, as pragmatic misalignment can lead to misunderstanding, perceived impoliteness, or exclusion from interactional communities (House & Kádár, 2024). These challenges, from an inclusive education perspective, can be reframed as accessibility issues. Pragmatic norms are often tacit, unevenly distributed, and culturally embedded, making them less accessible to learners who lack insider knowledge or opportunities for guided participation. Addressing pragmatic competence, therefore, requires instructional approaches that make implicit norms visible while simultaneously acknowledging variability and resisting the reification of a single "correct" way of speaking.

Probabilistic and Quantum-Inspired Models of Cognition

The difficulty of capturing pragmatic reasoning within deterministic instructional frameworks has led researchers to explore alternative cognitive models that better reflect the dynamics of human interpretation. Probabilistic approaches to cognition, including those inspired by quantum theory, have gained traction as ways of modeling decision-making processes that are context-dependent, non-linear, and sensitive to ambiguity (Bruza et al., 2015; Pothos & Busemeyer, 2022).

Quantum cognition does not suggest that the brain operates according to physical quantum mechanics. Rather, it offers a conceptual framework for understanding how human reasoning often violates classical logical assumptions (Gao, 2021;Pothos & Busemeyer, 2022). In pragmatic interpretation, for example, meanings may exist in a state of superposition, with multiple potential interpretations coexisting until contextual cues or interactional moves "collapse" them into a more stabilized understanding. This perspective resonates strongly with empirical observations of pragmatic processing, where meaning is frequently negotiated over time rather than determined instantaneously.Such models challenge pedagogical approaches that assume learners can be taught pragmatic rules that apply uniformly across contexts. Instead, they suggest that instruction should focus on developing learners' capacity to navigate uncertainty, tolerate ambiguity, and adapt interpretations dynamically. This shift has important implications for the design of assistive technologies. Rather than providing definitive answers, assistive systems should support exploratory engagement with pragmatic possibilities, enabling learners to compare interpretations, reflect on contextual variables, and experience the consequences of different pragmatic choices.

Post-Method Pedagogy and Teacher Agency

The need for flexible, context-sensitive instruction aligns closely with post-method pedagogy, which emerged as a response to the limitations of prescriptive teaching methods. Post-method pedagogy emphasizes teacher autonomy, principled pragmatism, and sensitivity to local contexts, arguing that effective instruction cannot be reduced to the implementation of universal techniques (Kumaravadivelu, 2012). Within this framework, teachers are positioned as reflective practitioners who design instruction in response to learners' needs, institutional constraints, and sociocultural realities.

In the context of pragmatics instruction, post-method principles are particularly salient. Because pragmatic norms vary across communities and situations, teachers must make pedagogical decisions about which norms to foreground, how to represent variability, and how to support learners in developing pragmatic awareness rather than rote conformity. Bastidas (2022) highlights that teacher agency is crucial for mediating between global models of language use and local communicative practices, especially in multilingual and English as a lingua franca settings. The integration of AI into such pedagogical contexts raises important questions about agency and control. If AI systems are designed as autonomous instructors that deliver content or evaluate performance according to fixed norms, they risk undermining the very flexibility that pragmatics instruction requires. Conversely, when AI is embedded as a design resource that supports teacher-led pedagogy, it can enhance instructional capacity without displacing professional judgment. This distinction underpins the conceptualization of AI in the present chapter as an assistive, rather than directive, technology.

AI as Assistive Mediation in Education

Within the broader literature on educational technology, AI has increasingly been framed as a mediational tool that can support learning by augmenting human capacities rather than replacing those (Zdravkova, 2022). Assistive AI systems are characterized by their responsiveness to learner input, their capacity to adapt to variability, and their integration into pedagogical workflows (Das et al., 2025). Importantly, such systems are most effective when their functions are transparent and aligned with instructional goals.

In the context of pragmatics instruction, AI offers several affordances that are particularly relevant. First, AI can facilitate access to diverse and context-rich input, enabling learners to encounter pragmatic variation beyond what is feasible in traditional classrooms. Second, AI can support metapragmatic reflection by providing prompts, annotations, or alternative interpretations that encourage learners to think critically about meaning. Third, AI can enable low-risk experiential learning through simulated interaction, allowing learners to experiment with pragmatic choices without the social costs of real-world failure. However, these affordances do not automatically translate into effective pedagogy. As Zdravkova (2022) cautions, educational technologies are never neutral; their design reflects particular assumptions about learning, knowledge, and authority. Without careful pedagogical integration, AI systems may reinforce normative biases, oversimplify pragmatic complexity, or privilege certain varieties of language use over others. For this reason, the design of AI-assisted pragmatics instruction must be guided by explicit theoretical commitments to inclusivity, variability, and learner agency.Taken together, the theoretical perspectives reviewed in this section point toward a conception of pragmatics instruction that is probabilistic, context-sensitive, and learner-centered. They also suggest that AI, when appropriately designed and integrated, can function as an assistive technology that supports such instruction. Crucially, this support must be mediated through pedagogical frameworks that articulate clear instructional goals, roles, and processes.

The PIPE framework elaborated in the next section emerges from this theoretical synthesis. PIPE operationalizes probabilistic and post-method principles into a coherent instructional architecture that structures learners' engagement with pragmatic meaning while leaving space for interpretation, variability, and teacher mediation (Shobeiry, 2024). By embedding AI support within each stage of the framework, PIPE exemplifies how emerging assistive technologies can be harnessed to address one of the most persistent challenges in language education: supporting learners in making sense of meaning under conditions of uncertainty.

PIPE Framework: From Theory to Assistive Practice

The theoretical perspectives outlined in the preceding section converge on a central pedagogical insight: pragmatic competence cannot be effectively developed through linear, rule-based instruction alone. Because, as Mokoro (2024) argues, pragmatic meaning is probabilistic, context-sensitive, and socially negotiated, instruction must be designed to support learners' engagement with uncertainty rather than to eliminate it. At the same time, such engagement requires structure, mediation, and scaffolding, particularly in formal educational settings where exposure to authentic interaction is constrained. The PIPE framework was developed to address this tension by offering a principled instructional architecture that integrates probabilistic cognition, post-method pedagogy, and assistive AI design into a coherent pedagogical system (Shobeiry, 2024).

Rather than functioning as a method in the traditional sense, PIPE operates as an instructional architecture—a flexible yet structured design that guides pedagogical decision-making while remaining adaptable to local contexts (Shobeiry, 2024). This distinction is crucial. Methods prescribe techniques; architectures organize learning processes (Salama et al., 2025). PIPE does not dictate specific classroom activities or technological tools. Instead, it articulates a sequence of pedagogical orientations that structure how learners encounter, interpret, destabilize, and ultimately experience pragmatic meaning. In doing so, it provides a design logic within which AI-based tools can function as assistive mediators rather than autonomous instructors.

Rationale for an Architectural Approach

The choice to conceptualize PIPE as an instructional architecture reflects both theoretical and practical considerations. From a post-method perspective, pedagogical effectiveness depends on teachers' capacity to adapt instruction to learners' needs, institutional constraints, and sociocultural contexts (Kumaravadivelu, 2012). Rigid methods risk oversimplifying pragmatic complexity and undermining teacher agency. An architectural approach, by contrast, offers a principled structure that supports pedagogical coherence while leaving room for contextual adaptation (Moreira et al., 2024; Salama et al., 2025).

From a cognitive standpoint, the architectural metaphor aligns with probabilistic models of learning. If pragmatic meaning emerges through iterative cycles of interpretation and re-interpretation, instruction must be designed to revisit concepts from multiple angles rather than progressing linearly toward mastery. PIPE operationalizes this recursive logic by organizing instruction into stages that are sequential yet dynamically interconnected (Shobeiry, 2024). Learners move through the stages not to arrive at definitive answers, but to develop increasingly sophisticated ways of managing pragmatic uncertainty. Within this architecture, AI-based tools are positioned as assistive supports that enhance access, reflection, and experiential learning. Their role is not to replace teacher mediation or learner interpretation, but to extend pedagogical capacity by enabling forms of input variation, feedback, and simulation that would otherwise be difficult to sustain in classroom settings.

The Present Stage in PIPE: Structured Exposure and Accessible Input

The Present stage constitutes learners' initial encounter with pragmatic phenomena. Unlike traditional presentation stages that focus on explicit explanation of rules, the Present stage in PIPE emphasizes structured exposure to contextualized language use. Learners are introduced to pragmatic instances through multimodal input—such as video clips, scripted interactions, or authentic communicative samples—that foreground contextual variables without immediately prescribing interpretation.

From an assistive technology perspective, AI plays a critical role in enhancing accessibility at this stage. AI-supported systems can curate input based on learner proficiency, provide adaptive replay options, and offer multimodal supports such as captions, glosses, or visual annotations. These affordances are particularly important for learners who may struggle with processing speed, working memory, or unfamiliar sociocultural cues. By lowering perceptual and cognitive barriers, AI functions as an assistive scaffold that enables all learners to engage meaningfully with complex input. Pedagogically, the Present stage is deliberately non-evaluative. Learners are not asked to judge appropriateness or produce language; instead, they are encouraged to observe, notice, and attend to contextual features. This orientation aligns with inclusive design principles by reducing anxiety and allowing learners to engage with pragmatic phenomena without fear of immediate failure.

The Interpret Stage in PIPE: Guided Metapragmatic Reflection

The Interpret stage shifts the instructional focus from exposure to meaning-making. Here, learners are guided to reflect on pragmatic intent, contextual factors, and potential interpretations of the input encountered in the Present stage. This stage operationalizes the insight from probabilistic cognition that meaning is not inherent in linguistic forms but emerges through interpretation.

AI-assisted tools support this reflective process by providing prompts, guiding questions, and alternative interpretive pathways. For example, annotation systems may highlight differences in tone, politeness strategies, or relational positioning across similar utterances, encouraging learners to compare and contrast pragmatic effects. Importantly, these tools do not supply definitive answers. Instead, as Verschueren (2022) argues, they support metapragmatic awareness by making interpretive dimensions visible and discussable. At this stage, teacher mediation remains central. The instructor orchestrates discussion, validates multiple interpretations, and situates learners' insights within broader pragmatic patterns. AI functions as an assistive resource that amplifies this mediation by offering structured support for reflection, particularly in large or blended classes where individualized feedback would otherwise be limited.

The Provoke Stage in PIPE: Destabilization and Productive Uncertainty

The Provoke stage represents a distinctive feature of the PIPE framework. Drawing directly on probabilistic and quantum-inspired models of cognition, this stage is designed to destabilize learners' emerging interpretations by confronting them with pragmatic variability and ambiguity. Learners are exposed to scenarios that challenge initial assumptions, such as interactions where similar forms yield different pragmatic effects or where expectations based on prior knowledge are violated. At this stage, AI plays a particularly powerful assistive role by enabling the systematic generation and manipulation of scenarios. Through AI-supported variation, learners can encounter multiple realizations of a pragmatic function across contexts, interlocutors, or communicative goals. This exposure highlights the non-deterministic nature of pragmatic meaning and encourages learners to tolerate uncertainty rather than seeking fixed rules.

Pedagogically, provocation is not intended to confuse learners but to deepen understanding. By experiencing the limits of rule-based reasoning, learners begin to appreciate pragmatics as a dynamic process of negotiation. This experience is especially valuable in English as a foreign language contexts, where pragmatic norms are co-constructed rather than inherited. The Provoke stage thus supports inclusive pedagogy by validating diversity and resisting normative simplification.

The Experience Stage in PIPE: Low-Risk Pragmatic Engagement

The Experience stage provides learners with opportunities to enact pragmatic choices in simulated or semi-authentic interactions. This stage operationalizes the insight that pragmatic competence develops through use and feedback rather than observation alone. However, real-world interaction carries social risks that may inhibit experimentation, particularly for learners who lack confidence or fear pragmatic failure.

AI-assisted environments offer a solution by enabling low-risk experiential learning. Conversational agents, role-play simulations, or scenario-based tasks allow learners to test pragmatic strategies and observe outcomes without the interpersonal consequences of real-world miscommunication. Feedback at this stage is designed to be formative and reflective, emphasizing consequences and alternatives rather than correctness. Crucially, experiential learning within PIPE is not isolated from earlier stages. Learners draw on observations from the Present stage, interpretive insights from the Interpret stage, and uncertainty tolerance developed in the Provoke stage. The architecture thus supports cumulative learning, where experience reinforces reflection rather than replacing it.

PIPE as Assistive Technology Design

Viewed holistically, PIPE exemplifies how AI can be integrated into pedagogy as an assistive technology. Each stage addresses a different dimension of accessibility: perceptual access to input, cognitive access to interpretation, affective access to uncertainty, and social access to interaction. AI-based tools are embedded strategically to support these dimensions without dictating learning trajectories or outcomes. This design aligns with contemporary definitions of assistive technology that emphasize support for participation rather than remediation of deficits. By scaffolding learners' engagement with pragmatic complexity, PIPE enables access to communicative practices that might otherwise remain opaque or exclusionary. At the same time, the framework preserves teacher agency by positioning instructional design—not technology—as the primary driver of learning.

The following section of the chapter moves from conceptual development to empirical grounding. Rather than presenting the case study as a discrete methodological unit, the chapter now introduces an extended case narrative that illustrates how AI-assisted PIPE instruction unfolded in practice within a blended EFL context. Through this narrative, quantitative outcomes and qualitative insights are woven into the broader argument, demonstrating how the architectural principles articulated here translate into observable learning processes and outcomes.

AN ILLUSTRATIVE CASE: AI-ASSISTED PIPE IN A BLENDED EFL CONTEXT

Program Context and Participants

To illustrate how the PIPE framework functions in practice, this section draws on observations from a 14-week blended EFL program implemented in a private language institute in Tehran, Iran, during summer 2025. The program involved 64 intermediate-level adult learners (ages 19–34; 38 female, 26 male) enrolled in a communicative English course. Within this context, some learners experienced instruction organized around the PIPE stages with AI-supported tools, while others followed standard communicative activities without systematic pragmatics focus. The following narrative draws on learner reflections, interaction logs, classroom observations, and patterns observed in pre- and post-program assessments to illuminate how learners engaged with the framework. These illustrative materials are presented not as evidence of generalizable effectiveness, but as a grounded exploration of how the architectural principles of PIPE translate into practice.

Enacting PIPE in Practice

Implementation of PIPE unfolded as a recursive rather than strictly linear process. Across units targeting common pragmatic functions—requests, refusals, apologies, complaints, and stance-taking—learners revisited the four stages at increasing levels of complexity.

In the **Present** stage, learners were exposed to pragmatically rich, contextualized input through short video clips of naturally occurring or semi-scripted interactions, audio recordings, and written dialogues. AI-supported features embedded in the online platform facilitated accessibility by allowing flexible replay, optional captioning, and non-evaluative annotations, enabling learners to attend to contextual details at their own pace without immediate performance pressure.

The **Interpret** stage shifted attention to guided metapragmatic reflection. Learners explored possible intentions, contextual influences, and interpretive variations through teacher-mediated discussion. AI tools contributed prompts and highlighted salient features (e.g., degrees of indirectness, mitigation strategies, or relational cues), encouraging multiple legitimate readings rather than converging on a single "correct" interpretation.

The **Provoke** stage introduced deliberate destabilization by presenting contrasting scenarios that challenged emerging generalizations—for instance, similar linguistic forms yielding different pragmatic effects across power relations or identical intentions realized through divergent strategies. AI-assisted generation and variation of scenarios made systematic exploration of such contrasts feasible, helping learners confront the inherently probabilistic and context-dependent nature of pragmatic meaning.

Finally, the **Experience** stage provided opportunities for low-risk enactment through simulated conversational interactions and structured role-plays. AI-based conversational agents offered formative, consequence-oriented feedback that emphasized alternatives and interpretive possibilities rather than prescriptive evaluation, allowing learners to experiment safely with pragmatic choices.

Emerging Patterns and Learner Experiences

Across the five targeted pragmatic functions, patterns of improvement were observed in learners' pragmatic appropriateness from pre- to post-program assessments. Scores on discourse completion tasks and role-plays suggested meaningful shifts, with the most substantial gains noted in the area of requests and more gradual change in the pragmatically complex area of complaints. Learners who experienced the PIPE stages showed stronger patterns of improvement compared to those following standard communicative activities, though these observations remain preliminary and context-bound.

Qualitative insights from learner interviews, interaction logs, and classroom observations illuminated three interconnected themes that help explain how learners engaged with the framework.

First, learners demonstrated increased tolerance for ambiguity. In interviews, several participants described how repeated engagement with the Provoke stage normalized uncertainty. One participant reflected:

"At first I wanted clear rules for every situation, but seeing how much things could change depending on context made me realize that uncertainty is just part of real conversations." (Participant #12)

Another noted that encountering contrasting scenarios helped her move beyond seeking single correct answers:

"I used to think there was one polite way to say something. Now I see it depends on who you're talking to and what's happening." (Participant #8)

Second, participants reported reduced communication anxiety, particularly valuing the low-stakes environment of the Experience stage. The opportunity to experiment with AI-simulated interactions before real-world communication appeared to build confidence:

"Trying different ways of saying things in the online interactions helped me see what might work better without worrying about making mistakes in front of people." (Participant #7)

"In the simulations, I could try things I wasn't sure about and see what happened. That made me braver in real conversations." (Participant #3)

Third, analysis of interviews and interaction logs revealed a discernible shift from rule-seeking toward interpretive flexibility. Learners increasingly articulated multiple possible meanings and considered contextual variables when making pragmatic choices. This was evident in both their reflections and their interactions with the AI tools during the Experience stage. One participant explained:

"Before, I just memorized phrases. Now I think about whether the situation is formal or casual, or whether I'm talking to a friend or a stranger. I have more options." (Participant #15)

By comparison, learners in the standard communicative condition—who did not experience the PIPE stages—tended to rely more heavily on familiar, formulaic expressions and continued to express hesitation in less predictable scenarios. One learner from this group noted:

"If I haven't practiced exactly what to say, I get nervous. I wish I had more chances to practice different situations." (Comparison participant, interview dataset, 2025)

These observations, while illustrative rather than generalizable, offer insight into how AI-assisted PIPE instruction may support pragmatic development when embedded within coherent pedagogical design. The qualitative themes, in particular, illuminate *how* learners experienced the framework and what dimensions of learning—tolerance for ambiguity, reduced anxiety, interpretive flexibility—appeared to shift through engagement with the four stages.

DISCUSSION

What the Case Illustrates About AI, Inclusion, and Pedagogical Design

The illustrative case offers a situated lens through which broader questions about AI, assistive technologies, and pedagogical design can be interrogated. Rather than treating the observed patterns as evidence of technological effectiveness per se, this discussion interprets them in light of the chapter's central claim: that the pedagogical value of AI in education lies not in automation or optimization, but in its capacity to function as an assistive mediator within carefully designed instructional architectures. The case thus invites reflection on how AI might reshape access to learning, how inclusion can be enacted at the level of pedagogy rather than policy, and how probabilistic domains such as pragmatics challenge dominant models of AI-enhanced instruction.

Rethinking Effectiveness: From Skill Acquisition to Epistemic Access

One of the implications that emerges from this illustrative case concerns how learning gains might be conceptualized. The patterns of development observed among learners in this implementation suggest that pragmatic development, when supported through the PIPE architecture, may not be adequately captured by traditional skill-acquisition models. Unlike grammatical accuracy or lexical expansion, pragmatic development does not involve the accumulation of discrete, transferable rules. Instead, as the learner reflections suggest, it involves expanding capacity to interpret, evaluate, and respond to communicative situations under conditions of uncertainty (Ahmed et al., 2023; Mokoro, 2024).In this implementation, the technology did not function as a source of authoritative knowledge; rather, it facilitated epistemic access to pragmatic complexity by enabling learners to encounter variation, reflect on alternatives, and experience consequences in structured ways. In this sense, AI served as a catalyst for epistemic engagement rather than a transmitter of content.

This reconceptualization aligns with broader critiques of outcome-driven models of educational technology, which often prioritize efficiency and measurability over depth of understanding. The case invites consideration of whether effectiveness in AI-assisted learning might be evaluated not only in terms of performance gains, but also in terms of how learners' relationships to knowledge domains are transformed.

Assistive Technology as Pedagogical Mediation

The case also offers a lens through which to consider ongoing debates about what constitutes assistive technology in educational contexts. Assistive technologies are frequently associated with remediation or accommodation for learners with diagnosed needs (Zdravkova, 2022). However, the patterns observed here suggest a broader interpretation: assistive technologies might support all learners by reducing barriers inherent in the learning task itself. In pragmatics instruction, such barriers include limited exposure to authentic interaction, difficulty perceiving subtle contextual cues, and anxiety associated with communicative risk.

Within the PIPE framework, AI-based tools addressed these barriers not by simplifying pragmatic content, but by scaffolding learners' engagement with it. Features such as adaptive input presentation, guided annotation, scenario variation, and simulated interaction expanded learners' access to pragmatic phenomena that would otherwise remain opaque. Importantly, these supports were temporary and dynamic, designed to facilitate learning processes rather than replace them.This mediational role distinguishes assistive AI from instructional automation. Rather than directing learner behavior or evaluating performance against fixed benchmarks, AI functioned as a flexible support that amplified pedagogical intent. The teacher remained central as a designer, mediator, and interpreter, while technology extended the reach and depth of instructional practice. This configuration aligns with inclusive design principles that emphasize participation, agency, and adaptability.

Inclusion Beyond Accommodation: Addressing Invisible Barriers

A key contribution of the case lies in how it illustrates one way inclusion might be reframed in language education. Pragmatic difficulty is rarely recognized as an accessibility issue, yet it disproportionately affects learners who lack exposure to target-language communities or who operate across linguistic and cultural boundaries. These learners may possess high levels of grammatical competence while remaining marginalized in communicative practice due to pragmatic uncertainty.

In the AI-assisted PIPE framework, this invisible barrier was addressed by making pragmatic complexity visible and discussable. Learners were not positioned as deficient for failing to meet native-speaker norms; instead, they were invited to explore how meaning is negotiated across contexts and interlocutors. The Provoke stage, in particular, challenged deficit-oriented assumptions by highlighting variability and legitimizing multiple interpretations. From an inclusion standpoint, this approach shifts the focus from individual accommodation to pedagogical redesign. Rather than adapting instruction for particular learners, the architecture itself was designed to accommodate diversity in interpretation, experience, and communicative goals. AI-supported tools enhanced this inclusivity by enabling differentiated access to input and reflection without stigmatization.

AI and Probabilistic Domains of Learning

The case also speaks to a broader theoretical challenge in AI-enhanced education: how to support learning in domains characterized by indeterminacy. Many AI-based educational systems are optimized for deterministic domains where correct answers can be clearly specified. Pragmatics, by contrast, resists such specification. Meaning is contingent, negotiable, and context-bound, rendering rule-based feedback insufficient. The ways learners engaged with AI-assisted PIPE instruction in this context suggest that AI can contribute meaningfully to probabilistic domains when its role is reimagined. Rather than providing evaluative judgments, AI-supported tools facilitated exploration, comparison, and reflection. By generating varied scenarios and prompting metapragmatic inquiry, AI helped learners experience the non-deterministic nature of pragmatic meaning firsthand. This observation has implications beyond pragmatics. Other educational domains—such as ethical reasoning, intercultural communication, and professional judgment—share similar characteristics. The present case thus offers a transferable design logic for integrating AI into learning contexts where ambiguity is not a problem to be solved, but a condition to be navigated.

Ethical Dimensions of AI-Assisted Pragmatics Instruction

The integration of AI into pragmatics instruction raises critical ethical considerations that must be addressed for the PIPE framework to remain genuinely assistive and inclusive. First, data privacy and learner surveillance demand robust governance frameworks: AI systems that capture learner interactions during simulated practice generate records of pragmatic choices, including potentially face-threatening attempts, which could be repurposed for institutional monitoring or algorithmic profiling if not protected by transparent policies and informed consent protocols. Second, algorithmic bias poses particular risks in pragmatics instruction, as AI trained on corpora reflecting dominant cultural norms may reinforce native-speaker ideologies and marginalize legitimate alternatives from English as a lingua franca contexts; mitigation requires selecting tools with transparent training data, fine-tuning on locally relevant corpora, and designing feedback mechanisms that surface alternatives rather than prescribe correctness. Third, learner autonomy must be preserved through explicit discussion of pedagogical rationale, enabling students to understand why they are asked to tolerate uncertainty during the Provoke stage, with alternative pathways available for those who experience sustained distress. Fourth, the very technologies enabling PIPE's assistive functions may reproduce digital divides, requiring blended implementations that incorporate low-tech alternatives and ensure AI-supported activities do not disadvantage learners already marginalized by unequal access to devices or connectivity. These ethical dimensions underscore that assistive technologies are never neutral; their integration must be accompanied by ongoing critical reflection, institutional accountability, and participatory design processes that center the voices of learners and teachers, ensuring that AI functions as a tool for epistemic access rather than a source of new exclusionary barriers.

Pedagogical Innovation and Teacher Agency

An often-overlooked dimension of AI integration is its impact on teacher agency. Technologies that automate instruction risk marginalizing teachers by constraining pedagogical choice. In contrast, the PIPE framework positioned teachers as active designers of learning experiences. AI tools were selected and configured to serve pedagogical goals articulated by the instructor, rather than dictating instructional pathways.

The case illustrates how architectural frameworks can empower teachers to integrate emerging technologies without surrendering control over pedagogical meaning. By providing a clear design logic, PIPE enabled coherent integration of AI tools while allowing adaptation to contextual constraints. This balance between structure and flexibility is particularly important in institutional settings where teachers face competing demands and limited resources. Furthermore, from a professional development perspective, the framework supported teachers' metapedagogical awareness. By explicitly articulating the purposes of each instructional stage, PIPE encouraged reflective practice and intentional use of technology. This dimension of teacher learning is a critical but often neglected aspect of sustainable innovation.

Limitations and Tensions

While the case provides a grounded illustration of the pedagogical potential of AI-assisted PIPE instruction, it also reveals important tensions. Learners' initial discomfort with uncertainty highlights the affective challenges inherent in probabilistic learning (Riguzzi, 2023). Without careful mediation, exposure to variability could exacerbate confusion rather than support development. This underscores the indispensability of teacher guidance and the limits of technology-driven solutions. Additionally, the institutional context shaped what was possible. Access to digital infrastructure, class size, and curricular flexibility all influenced implementation. These factors remind us that assistive technologies do not operate in a vacuum; their effectiveness depends on alignment with institutional realities and pedagogical values.

Beyond the specific institutional constraints noted in the illustrative case, the PIPE framework's applicability is likely to vary along several contextual dimensions that warrant explicit consideration. First, technological infrastructure represents a critical boundary condition. In low-resource settings where reliable internet access, personal devices, or AI-capable platforms are unavailable, the assistive functions described in this chapter cannot be realized. While the pedagogical architecture remains conceptually intact, its operationalization would require alternative mediational means, potentially reducing the depth and variability of learner engagement. Second, curricular and assessment pressures may constrain implementation. In educational systems where high-stakes examinations prioritize discrete grammatical knowledge, teachers may face institutional resistance to dedicating instructional time to recursive engagement with pragmatic ambiguity. The PIPE framework's emphasis on process over product, and its tolerance for multiple interpretations, may conflict with assessment regimes that demand correct answers and measurable outcomes. Third, learner characteristics and cultural orientations toward uncertainty and error shape the framework's reception. In cultural contexts where deference to authority and preference for explicit rules are strongly socialized, learners may experience the Provoke stage as distressing rather than productive, requiring extended affective scaffolding that may exceed available instructional resources. Fourth, teacher expertise and professional development constitute enabling conditions that cannot be assumed. PIPE's architectural logic demands that teachers exercise sophisticated professional judgment in selecting input, mediating interpretation, and calibrating provocation. Without adequate preparation and ongoing support, implementation may drift toward procedural compliance, undermining the framework's theoretical foundations. These limitations do not invalidate the framework but rather underscore that PIPE, like all pedagogical architectures, must be adapted to local ecologies rather than applied as a universal template.

CONCLUSION

Rethinking AI as Assistive Pedagogical Design

This chapter set out to reconceptualize the role of artificial intelligence in language education by shifting attention away from automation, efficiency, and prediction toward assistive pedagogical design. Anchored in the teaching of pragmatics—a domain characterized by uncertainty, contextuality, and social negotiation—the chapter argued that AI's educational value emerges most clearly when it is embedded within principled instructional architectures that foreground human interpretation, agency, and inclusion. Through the development and empirical grounding of the PIPE framework, the chapter has illustrated how emerging AI-based technologies can function as mediational supports that expand access to complex learning domains rather than reducing them to tractable problems.

At a conceptual level, the chapter contributes to ongoing debates about the nature of learning supported by AI. Much of the current discourse assumes that AI is most effective in domains where knowledge can be formalized and performance can be objectively evaluated. Pragmatics challenges this assumption. Meaning in pragmatic interaction is probabilistic, relational, and contingent, resisting codification into fixed rules or correct answers. The pattern observed in AI-assisted PIPE instruction in this context suggests that AI can meaningfully support learning even in non-deterministic domains, provided that its role is reframed. Rather than delivering knowledge or judging correctness, AI can assist learners by structuring exposure, supporting reflection, generating variability, and enabling low-risk experiential engagement.

The PIPE framework operationalizes this reframing by articulating a pedagogical architecture in which AI is subordinated to instructional intent. Each stage of the framework addresses a distinct dimension of accessibility: perceptual access to input, cognitive access to interpretation, affective access to uncertainty, and social access to interaction. In doing so, PIPE aligns closely with contemporary understandings of assistive technology as support for participation rather than remediation. Importantly, this support is not targeted at a narrowly defined group of learners but is designed to accommodate diversity as a normal condition of educational practice. These theoretical claims are reinforced by the illustrative case through demonstrating how AI-assisted PIPE instruction unfolded in a real educational setting. The observed gains in pragmatic competence, coupled with learners' reported shifts in metapragmatic awareness and tolerance for uncertainty, suggest that the framework supports a deeper form of learning than rule acquisition alone. Learners did not merely learn how to perform pragmatic functions more effectively; they developed new ways of understanding what pragmatic competence entails. This epistemic shift—from seeking correct forms to managing communicative choice—represents a critical outcome that is often overlooked in evaluations of educational technology.

From an inclusion perspective, the chapter highlights how pragmatic difficulty functions as an invisible barrier to participation in communicative practice. Learners who possess grammatical proficiency may nonetheless experience exclusion due to uncertainty about appropriateness, politeness, or stance. By making pragmatic complexity explicit and negotiable, AI-assisted PIPE instruction addresses this barrier at the level of pedagogical design. Inclusion, in this sense, is not achieved through accommodation after the fact, but through the intentional design of learning environments that anticipate and legitimize diversity in interpretation and use. Moreover, the chapter underscores the centrality of teacher agency in meaningful AI integration. Technologies do not become assistive by virtue of their features alone; they become assistive when they are embedded in pedagogical frameworks that reflect educational values and contextual realities. The PIPE framework positions teachers as designers and mediators, responsible for orchestrating learning processes and interpreting technological affordances. This orientation counters narratives of technological determinism and affirms the professional expertise required to integrate emerging technologies responsibly. At the same time, the chapter acknowledges the tensions inherent in this approach. Engaging learners with uncertainty requires careful scaffolding and sustained mediation. Without such support, exposure to variability may lead to frustration rather than insight. Institutional constraints—such as curricular mandates, assessment regimes, and resource availability—also shape what is possible. These limitations point to the need for continued research that examines how assistive pedagogical architectures can be adapted across contexts and scaled without losing their conceptual integrity.

Final point, this chapter argues that the future of AI in education lies not in replacing human judgment, but in assisting learners and teachers in engaging more deeply with the complexities of meaning-making. By repositioning AI as a component of pedagogical architecture rather than a standalone solution, the chapter contributes a model of innovation that is theoretically grounded, empirically informed, and aligned with inclusive educational values. In doing so, it responds directly to the aims of this volume by demonstrating how emerging assistive technologies can support pedagogical innovation across diverse learning contexts while preserving the fundamentally human character of education.

Pedagogical Implications and Recommendations

The PIPE framework's educational value depends on how teachers enact its architectural logic in specific contexts. For the Present stage, educators are recommended to curate input that reveals pragmatic variability rather than presenting normative exemplars while leveraging AI-supported multimodal features (captions, replay options, annotations) to provide differentiated access without premature explanation. During the Interpret stage, teachers are advised to orchestrate discussion that legitimizes multiple interpretations, using AI-generated annotations as prompts for inquiry rather than authoritative judgments, and connecting reflection to learners' lived experiences across linguistic and cultural repertoires. The Provoke stage requires careful calibration: introduce variability gradually, explicitly frame uncertainty as normal and valuable, and provide affective scaffolding for learners who experience discomfort, while using AI to systematically generate contrastive scenarios that expand the range of pragmatic variation beyond what traditional materials allow. In the Experience stage, design simulated interactions with clear learning goals, configure AI feedback to emphasize alternatives and consequences rather than correctness, and ensure post-activity reflection connects experiential outcomes to prior observations from earlier stages. Across all stages, position AI as a tool for extending teacher mediation rather than replacing professional judgment, develop learners' critical AI literacy alongside pragmatic competence, and adapt the framework to local constraints—in low-resource settings, approximate the four stages through carefully designed non-digital activities while maintaining commitment to recursive engagement with pragmatic complexity. Finally, advocate for institutional support including collaborative teacher planning time, transparent data governance policies, and professional development that builds architectural thinking rather than technical skills alone, enabling sustainable implementation that preserves the framework's inclusive, non-normative orientation while supporting diverse learners in navigating communicative uncertainty.

Future Directions

While the PIPE framework and its illustrative application provide a robust foundation for AI-assisted pragmatics instruction, several critical avenues warrant systematic investigation to refine, validate, and extend its theoretical and pedagogical scope. Foremost among these is the imperative for large-scale, longitudinal experimental studies to establish causal efficacy and long-term transfer effects. The preliminary case narrative, though promising, reflects a constrained institutional context; randomized controlled trials across diverse EFL settings—spanning public schools, higher education, and non-formal programs in varied geopolitical regions—would quantify pragmatic gains relative to traditional methods, while tracking persistence in authentic intercultural interactions beyond instructional cycles. Such designs should incorporate validated pragmatic assessments (e.g., discourse completion tasks, role-play evaluations) alongside learner-reported outcomes, addressing the current study's illustrative limitations and enabling meta-analytic synthesis.

A second priority involves interrogating individual learner differences in responsiveness to PIPE's probabilistic architecture. Factors such as baseline tolerance for ambiguity, intercultural exposure, cognitive flexibility, and digital literacies likely moderate AI-mediated engagement; multivariate analyses could illuminate these interactions, informing adaptive personalization within the framework. For instance, neuroimaging or eye-tracking studies might elucidate how AI-supported provocation stages recalibrate interpretive processes, aligning with quantum cognition predictions of superposition-like meaning resolution. Concurrently, affective dimensions—particularly anxiety reduction and epistemic trust in AI mediation—demand psychophysiological exploration to optimize scaffolding gradients, mitigating risks of frustration in uncertainty exposure.

Technologically, advancing PIPE necessitates integration with next-generation multimodal AI, including generative large language models and immersive XR environments, to enhance experiential fidelity without normative bias. Research should prioritize ethical algorithm design: auditing for cultural hegemony in scenario generation, embedding metapragmatic transparency, and hybridizing AI with human interlocutors for paralinguistic cues absent in current simulations. Hybrid PIPE variants could leverage wearable sensors for real-time biofeedback during Provoke/Experience stages, fostering self-regulated pragmatic adaptation in hybrid or informal settings like mobile micro-learning apps. Also, teacher professionalization emerges as another pivotal trajectory. Experimental interventions training educators in architectural pedagogy—emphasizing PIPE's recursive logic and AI orchestration—would assess impacts on implementation fidelity, agency preservation, and innovation diffusion. Longitudinal tracking of teacher metapragmatics could reveal cascading effects on classroom inclusivity, countering automation-induced deskilling.

Institutionally, scalability studies must navigate curricular inertia and equity divides, evaluating PIPE's adaptability to low-resource contexts via open-source AI toolkits. Policy-oriented research could advocate reframing pragmatics as an accessibility mandate, influencing EFL standards and assistive technology funding. Cross-disciplinary extensions to adjacent probabilistic domains—ethical decision-making, intercultural negotiation, or clinical communication—promise broader assistive Edtech applications.

Finally, critical scholarship should probe PIPE's equity implications: power asymmetries in data-driven personalization, Global South representation in training corpora, and resistance to decolonial pragmatics in English as a lingua franca paradigms. Participatory action research with learners and teachers as co-designers would ensure cultural responsiveness, transforming PIPE from EFL-specific innovation to a universalizable architecture for AI-mediated inclusion. Collectively, these directions position PIPE not as endpoint, but as catalyst for evidence-based evolution in assistive pedagogies.

Further Reading

- Macías Borrego, M. (2025). Artificial intelligence-assisted error analysis: Developing pragmatic competence in EFL learners. In *Application of AI in the teaching and learning of English as a foreign language (EFL)* (pp. 50). IGI Global. https://doi.org/10.4018/979-8-3373-0969-9.ch004. This paper explores the intersection of Artificial Intelligence, error analysis, and pragmatics to enhance pragmatic competence in English as a Foreign Language (EFL) learners. The research highlights the persistent challenge of developing pragmatic competence—the ability to use language appropriately within social and cultural contexts—especially in cross-cultural communication. It argues that AI-powered error analysis tools offer a transformative solution by providing real-time, diagnostic feedback on nuanced pragmatic errors related to politeness, speech acts, and cultural appropriateness. Leveraging advancements in Natural Language Processing (NLP), these systems can detect and correct pragmatic missteps, offering learners tailored suggestions, such as refining a direct request into a more polite form. Furthermore, the paper discusses how AI-driven platforms can create immersive environments for practicing these critical skills. While acknowledging challenges, such as encoding dynamic cultural norms and mitigating algorithmic bias, the study concludes that AI holds significant potential to revolutionize the teaching of pragmatic competence, though continued research is essential to fully realize its effectiveness and ensure cultural sensitivity.
- Rahman, G., Mudhsh, B. A., Almutairi, M., & Kouki, M. (2025). Optimizing ESL Learners' Speech Act Performance: The Role of AI-Powered Chatbots in Pragmatic Competence Development. *Theory & Practice in Language Studies (TPLS), 15*(10). https://doi.org/10.17507/tpls.1510.05. This research explores the effectiveness of AI-powered chatbots in developing the pragmatic competence of English as a Second Language (ESL) learners, with a specific focus on their ability to produce contextually appropriate speech acts such as requests, apologies, and refusals. Based on a mixed-methods study involving 50 Pakistani undergraduate students, the research implemented a four-week intervention using a Google Dialogflow chatbot to simulate real-life conversational scenarios. Quantitative findings demonstrated a statistically significant improvement in the learners' performance, with mean appropriateness scores rising substantially, with requests showing the greatest gains.

Qualitative analysis of participant feedback revealed that the AI chatbot fostered increased engagement, reduced language anxiety, and heightened learners' awareness of polite and context-sensitive language use due to its adaptive and non-judgmental nature. While acknowledging limitations, such as the chatbot's difficulty with nuanced cultural variations, the study concludes that AI-powered conversational agents are a valuable tool for pragmatic instruction. It contributes to the field by advocating for their integration into blended learning environments, particularly in underrepresented educational contexts, to effectively build socio-pragmatic skills.

- Erdogan, N., & Kitson, C. (2025). Integrating AI in language learning: Boosting pragmatic competence for young English learners. *LatIA, 3*. https://doi.org/10.62486/latia2025115. This study elaborates on the role of Artificial Intelligence (AI) tools in enhancing the pragmatic language skills of young English Learners (ELs). It begins by establishing a theoretical foundation, defining core concepts such as interlanguage pragmatics, pragmatic competence, and intercultural communicative competence, while also detailing key pragmatic elements like discourse maxims, implicatures, and speech acts. The article underscores the critical importance of sociocultural context and interaction in developing these skills within a second language. It then investigates the practical application of AI—including chatbots and dialogue systems—in creating immersive, interactive environments that teach essential pragmatic abilities, from interpreting implied meanings to applying speech acts appropriately. While highlighting AI's potential to facilitate contextual learning and practical language use, the article also addresses the inherent challenges and limitations in teaching pragmatics. It concludes by advocating for targeted future research to better understand pragmatic development in young learners and to optimize the effective integration of AI tools in this vital aspect of language acquisition.
- Tahir, R. I. (2025). The Impact of ChatGPT as a peer Interaction Partner in Enhancing Pragmatic Competence among EFL Learners Impact of ChatGPT as a peer Interaction Partner in Enhancing Pragmatic Competence among EFL Learners. *JOURNAL OF LANGUAGE STUDIES*, *9*(2), 219–233. https://doi.org/10.25130/Lang.9.2.14. This publication illuminates the impact of utilizing ChatGPT as an artificial peer interaction partner to enhance pragmatic competence among English as a Foreign Language (EFL) learners. Grounded in Vygotsky's sociocultural theory, the mixed-methods study employed pre- and post-tests, discourse analysis of learner-ChatGPT interactions, and semi-structured interviews with intermediate-level students. The findings indicate statistically significant improvements in the learners' ability to produce contextually appropriate speech acts, apply politeness strategies, and adapt lan-

guage to sociocultural contexts, corroborating earlier research on AI-assisted language practice. Qualitative data reveal that ChatGPT provided a valuable low-stakes environment for interaction and immediate feedback, consistent with technology-mediated language learning principles. However, the study also acknowledges limitations, noting that the AI cannot replicate paralinguistic cues or deeply nuanced cultural norms. Consequently, while affirming ChatGPT's utility as a supportive tool for pragmatic development, the research ultimately reinforces the indispensable role of human interlocutors in fostering comprehensive intercultural communicative competence.

REFERENCES

Ahmed, K., Akram, A., Sharif, A. S., & Tariq, A. (2023). Developing pragmatic competence through instructional intervention: Evidence from EFL contexts. *Journal of English Language and Literature Education*, *5*(1), 141–170. DOI: 10.54692/jelle.2023.0501160

Ayon, V., & Dillon, A. (2021). Assistive technology in education. *The International Journal of Information, Diversity, &. Inclusion (Washington, D.C.)*, *5*(3), 174–184. https://www.jstor.org/stable/48644451

Bastidas, J. A. (2022). Are language teaching methods really dead? Revisiting post-method pedagogy. *PROFILE Issues in Teachers'. Professional Development (Philadelphia, Pa.)*, *24*(2), 203–213. DOI: 10.15446/profile.v24n2.96952

Bruza, P. D., Wang, Z., & Busemeyer, J. R. (2015). Quantum cognition: A new theoretical approach to psychology. *Trends in Cognitive Sciences*, *19*(7), 383–393. DOI: 10.1016/j.tics.2015.05.001

Chinpakdee, M., & Gu, P. Y. (2024). The impact of explicit strategy instruction on pragmatic competence in EFL learners. *Second Language Research*, *28*(1), 296–319. DOI: 10.1177/1362168821994157

Das, S., Mutsuddi, I., & Ray, N. (2025). Artificial intelligence in adaptive education: A transformative approach. In Rahman, A. (Ed.), *Advancing adaptive education: Technological innovations for disability support* (pp. 30–59). IGI Global., DOI: 10.4018/979-8-3693-8227-1.ch002

Gao, S. (2021). Does quantum cognition imply quantum minds? *Journal of Consciousness Studies*, *28*(3-4), 100–111.

House, J., & Kádár, D. (2024). *Cross-cultural pragmatics and foreign language learning*. Edinburgh University Press., DOI: 10.1515/9781399523240

Kumaravadivelu, B. (2012). *Language teacher education for a global society: A modular model for knowing, analyzing, recognizing, doing, and seeing*. Routledge., DOI: 10.4324/9780203832530

Mokoro, E. (2024). Pragmatic competence in second language learners. *European Journal of Linguistics*, *3*(2), 15–28. DOI: 10.47941/ejl.2044

Moreira, F. T., Vairinhos, M., & Ramos, F. (2024). Teachers' perceptions about IoT technologies in school activities. *Educational Media International*, *61*(1–2), 184–197. DOI: 10.1080/09523987.2024.2358655

Pothos, E. M., & Busemeyer, J. R. (2022). Quantum cognition. *Annual Review of Psychology, 73*(1), 749–778. DOI: 10.1146/annurev-psych-033020-123501

Riguzzi, F. (2023). *Foundations of Probabilistic Logic Programming: Languages, semantics, inference and learning*. River Publishers. DOI: 10.1201/9781003427421

Salama, A. M., & Patil, M. P. (2025). The socius in architectural pedagogy: Transformative design studio teaching models. *Architecture (Washington, D.C.), 5*(3), 61. DOI: 10.3390/architecture5030061

Shobeiry, M. (2021). Pragmatic functions of formulaic expressions of embarrassment in Persian refusals: A qualitative study. *Journal of International Social Research, 14*(76), 33–41. DOI: 10.17719/jisr.11353

Shobeiry, M. (2024). *The PIPE educational model* [ ]. Academic Center for Education, Culture, and Research (ACECR). Tehran.

Shobeiry, M. (2026). Spelling Improvement and Motivation Through Gamification and Mobile Apps. In Moreira, F. T., & Teles, R. (Eds.), *Engaging Learners With Immersive Technologies and Game-Based Learning* (pp. 189–220). IGI Global Scientific Publishing., DOI: 10.4018/979-8-3373-4465-2.ch008

Taguchi, N., & Roever, C. (2017). *Second language pragmatics*. Oxford University Press.

Verschueren, J. (2022). Metapragmatics. In Verschueren, J., & Östman, J. (Eds.), *Handbook of Pragmatics: Manual* (2nd ed., pp. 948–953). John Benjamins Publishing Company., DOI: 10.1075/hop.m2.met1

Windasari, A., Syefrinando, B., Wiliyanti, V., Komikesari, H., & Yuberti, . (2024). The influence of the blended learning model on students' concept understanding ability viewed from self-confidence. *AIP Conference Proceedings, 3058*(1), 020013. Advance online publication. DOI: 10.1063/5.0206001

Zdravkova, K. (2022). The Potential of Artificial Intelligence for Assistive Technology in Education. In Ivanović, M., Klašnja-Milićević, A., & Jain, L. C. (Eds.), *Handbook on Intelligent Techniques in the Educational Process. Learning and Analytics in Intelligent Systems* (Vol. 29). Springer., DOI: 10.1007/978-3-031-04662-9_4

Zhao, Y., & Yang, L. (2022). Examining the relationship between perceived teacher support and students' academic engagement in foreign language learning: Enjoyment and boredom as mediators. *Frontiers in Psychology, 13*, 987554. DOI: 10.3389/fpsyg.2022.987554

KEY TERMS AND DEFINITIONS

Assistive Technology (Educational Context): Technological tools or systems designed to support learners' access to learning processes and participation, rather than to remediate deficits or automate instruction (Ayon & Dillon, 2021, Zdravkova, 2022).

Architectural Pedagogy: An approach to instructional design that emphasizes coherent learning structures and trajectories over isolated activities or methods (Salama et al., 2025).

Blended Learning: An instructional format that combines face-to-face teaching with online or digital learning components (Windasari et al., 2024).

Metapragmatic Awareness: Learners' conscious understanding of how pragmatic meaning is constructed, interpreted, and negotiated in interaction (Verschueren, 2022).

PIPE Framework: A pedagogical architecture consisting of four recursive stages—Present, Interpret, Provoke, and Experience—designed to support pragmatic development through structured engagement with uncertainty (Shobeiry, 2024).

Pragmatic Competence: The ability to interpret and produce language that is appropriate to context, interlocutor relationships, and communicative goals (Chinpakdee & Gu, 2024, Mokoro, 2024, Taguchi & Roever, 2017).

Probabilistic Learning Domain: A domain of learning characterized by variability, uncertainty, and the absence of fixed correct answers, such as pragmatics or ethical reasoning (Riguzzi, 2023).

Quantum Cognition: A theoretical approach that models human cognition as context-sensitive and probabilistic, drawing on mathematical principles from quantum theory (Gao, 2021; Pothos & Busemeyer, 2022).

Teacher Mediation: The active role of teachers in guiding, interpreting, and shaping learning processes, particularly in technology-enhanced environments (Zhao & Yang, 2022).

Chapter 9
Gamification and Game-Based Learning With Accessibility Considerations

Nofamataro Zebua
http://orcid.org/0009-0008-3902-2289
Universitas Nias, Indonesia

Yaredi Waruwu
http://orcid.org/0009-0008-3428-6066
Universitas Nias, Indonesia

ABSTRACT

This chapter examines the integration of gamification and game-based learning with accessibility principles as a foundation for advancing inclusive learning in the digital era. It outlines key theoretical frameworks, including motivational theory and Universal Design for Learning, and discusses the roles of assistive technologies and artificial intelligence in supporting adaptive instruction. Empirical findings on inclusive game-based practices across educational levels are reviewed to highlight their impact on engagement and learning outcomes. The chapter also addresses pedagogical, ethical, and policy challenges, emphasizing the need for interdisciplinary collaboration and equitable technology design to support diverse learners.

DOI: 10.4018/979-8-2600-2716-5.ch009

027, IGI Global Scientific Publishing. Copying or distributing in print or electronic forms without written permission of IGI Global Scientific Publishing is prohibited. Use of this chapter to tive artificial intelligence (AI) technologies is expressly prohibited. The publisher reserves all rights to license its use for generative AI training and machine learning model development.

INTRODUCTION

Gamification and game-based learning have evolved as effective pedagogical approaches to enhance students' motivation, engagement, and learning outcomes across various levels of education (Nadeem et al., 2023). This development aligns with the digital transformation of education, which demands more adaptive and learner-centered technology-based instructional innovations. However, the implementation of gamification has often not fully considered the needs of learners with diverse physical, sensory, cognitive, and socio-emotional abilities (Lamrani & Abdelwahed, 2020; López-Bouzas et al., 2024). This condition may create access gaps and reinforce exclusion within digital learning environments.

Inclusive education emphasizes the importance of providing equal learning opportunities for all learners without discrimination (UNESCO, 2020). In this context, gamification and game-based learning must be designed with accessibility principles to ensure effective use by the entire learner population. The integration of assistive technologies and universal design approaches serves as a critical foundation for the development of inclusive game-based learning environments (Gill et al., 2024; Sousa et al., 2025). Therefore, a comprehensive examination of gamification with accessibility considerations is highly relevant for the future development of educational technology.

THEORETICAL FRAMEWORK OF GAMIFICATION, GAME-BASED LEARNING, AND ACCESSIBILITY

Gamification and game-based learning (GBL) have emerged as influential approaches in contemporary educational research because of their potential to increase learner engagement, motivation, and participation across diverse educational contexts. Although these concepts are often discussed together, they represent distinct pedagogical approaches. Gamification refers to the integration of game design elements—such as points, badges, leaderboards, progress systems, and narratives—into non-game learning environments to influence learner behavior and motivation, whereas GBL uses games themselves as the primary medium through which learning and knowledge construction occur (Plass et al., 2020). The growing academic interest in these approaches is closely connected to broader educational transformations, including increased learner diversity, digitalization in education, and the global demand for more inclusive and accessible learning environments. Large-scale reviews indicate that gamification and GBL are now implemented across multiple disciplines and educational levels; however, their educational effectiveness depends substantially on the theoretical assumptions and accessibility principles underlying their design (Plass et al., 2020). Rather than functioning as universally effective strategies, gamified systems may either support or hinder inclusion depending on how motivational structures, accessibility features, and social interactions are implemented. This issue has become particularly significant in inclusive education, where poorly designed competitive systems may unintentionally marginalize learners with disabilities or learners with limited prior digital experience. Consequently, understanding the theoretical foundations that shape motivation, accessibility, and learner participation is essential for developing more rigorous and equitable gamified learning environments.

Self-Determination Theory (SDT) provides one of the most influential theoretical foundations for understanding learner motivation within gamification and GBL. According to SDT, learning environments are more likely to foster sustained engagement when they support learners' psychological needs for autonomy, competence, and relatedness (Ryan & Deci, 2020). Within gamified learning environments, these needs are often operationalized through meaningful choices, adaptive challenges, immediate feedback systems, and collaborative interaction mechanisms (Peters et al., 2018). Empirical studies suggest that gamified systems grounded in SDT principles tend to produce stronger intrinsic motivation than systems relying solely on external rewards or repetitive point accumulation. In GBL environments, immersive gameplay and exploratory learning pathways may strengthen learners' sense of competence by enabling experimentation, problem-solving, and iterative feedback processes (Peters et al., 2018; Plass et al., 2020). However, recent debates in educational technology research indicate that motivational outcomes are not universally positive. Some studies argue that excessive reliance on reward-oriented mechanics can shift learner attention away from meaningful learning toward performance optimization, thereby reducing long-term intrinsic engagement. These tensions demonstrate that motivational theory should not be treated as a supplementary framework, but rather as a critical foundation for evaluating whether gamified systems genuinely support meaningful and inclusive learning experiences.

Questions of accessibility and inclusion are most comprehensively addressed through the Universal Design for Learning (UDL) framework, which emphasizes flexibility in representation, engagement, and learner expression. UDL offers a conceptual and practical approach for designing learning environments that accommodate learner variability, including differences in cognitive processing, sensory abilities, communication styles, and physical interaction needs. Within gamified and game-based environments, UDL principles can be operationalized through multimodal content delivery, customizable interfaces, adaptive feedback systems, captioning, text-to-speech features, and alternative interaction pathways. Existing empirical research indicates that integrating UDL principles into gamified environments can improve participation, perceived accessibility, and learning outcomes for students with disabilities and other marginalized learner groups. Adaptive game mechanics, such as adjustable difficulty levels and personalized feedback modalities, have also been associated with reduced participation barriers and increased learner confidence. Nevertheless, accessibility in gamification remains an ongoing scholarly challenge rather than a fully resolved design problem. Some researchers argue that many gamified systems continue to prioritize efficiency, competition, and standardized achievement structures at the expense of accessibility and learner diversity. As a result, accessibility should not be viewed as an additional technical feature added after development, but as a foundational design principle that shapes how learners access, interpret, and engage with educational content. In this regard, UDL functions as a critical bridge connecting motivational theory with inclusive educational practice.

Social constructivist theory further expands the conceptual framework by emphasizing that learning occurs through interaction, collaboration, and socially mediated meaning-making processes. From this perspective, inclusive GBL environments can function as collaborative spaces where learners with differing abilities co-construct understanding through shared problem-solving experiences, communication, and negotiated participation (Peters et al., 2018; Plass et al., 2020). Research on collaborative educational games suggests that social mechanics such as cooperative missions, peer support systems, and differentiated player roles can strengthen social relatedness and foster a sense of belonging among learners. This aspect is especially important in inclusive education contexts, where social participation is closely connected to learner confidence and academic persistence. At the same time, critical debates remain concerning the potential risks associated with competitive gamification structures. Scholars have argued that leaderboards, performance rankings, and competitive reward systems may reinforce social hierarchies, discourage participation among lower-performing learners, and unintentionally exclude students with disabilities or learners requiring alternative pacing. These critiques highlight a broader tension within gamification research between engagement-oriented design and equitable participation. Addressing this tension requires theoretically informed design decisions that prioritize collaboration, accessibility, and learner agency rather than relying primarily on simplistic competitive mechanics.

Despite the growing body of empirical evidence supporting gamification and GBL, important theoretical and methodological gaps remain. Many existing studies continue to examine motivation, accessibility, and game-based interaction as separate constructs, resulting in fragmented explanations of how inclusive gamified learning environments actually function in practice. Longitudinal evidence examining the long-term effects of UDL-informed gamification on diverse learner populations also remains limited. Furthermore, relatively few studies integrate motivational theory, accessibility frameworks, and social learning perspectives into a unified analytical model capable of guiding both instructional design and evaluation (Peters et al., 2018). This limitation is particularly significant given the rapid expansion of adaptive technologies and AI-driven educational systems, which increasingly shape learner experiences within digital environments. Future research should therefore prioritize mixed-method, longitudinal, and design-based approaches that examine how adaptive and accessible game mechanics operate in authentic educational settings across diverse learner populations. Such research would contribute not only to stronger theoretical coherence, but also to the development of practical design principles for creating gamified learning environments that are motivating, accessible, and socially inclusive.

ASSISTIVE TECHNOLOGIES AND AI IN INCLUSIVE GAMIFICATION

Assistive technologies and artificial intelligence (AI) have become increasingly important in the development of inclusive gamification, particularly within educational contexts that seek to support learners with diverse abilities and learning needs. Inclusive gamification refers to the intentional design of game-based learning environments that are accessible, equitable, and responsive to learner variability, including the needs of students with disabilities. Within these environments, assistive technologies such as screen readers, text-to-speech systems, speech recognition tools, automatic captioning, adaptive controllers, and customizable interfaces play a critical role in reducing functional barriers that often limit participation in digital learning activities. Rather than functioning solely as technical accommodations, these technologies influence how learners access information, interact with game mechanics, communicate with peers, and engage with instructional content. This shift is significant because it reframes accessibility as a central pedagogical concern rather than an optional design enhancement.

The growing academic and policy interest in inclusive gamification is closely connected to global discussions surrounding inclusive education and digital equity. International educational agendas increasingly emphasize that all learners, including students with disabilities, should have equal opportunities to participate in meaningful and high-quality learning experiences. However, recent research suggests that gamification does not inherently guarantee inclusion. In some cases, poorly designed gamified systems may unintentionally reproduce exclusion through inaccessible interfaces, rigid interaction systems, competitive ranking structures, or algorithmic bias that disadvantages learners with diverse needs (UNESCO, 2021). These concerns have become particularly relevant as educational institutions increasingly adopt AI-supported digital learning platforms. Research in inclusive educational technology demonstrates that accessible design elements—such as adaptive feedback systems, multimodal interaction, personalized scaffolding, and flexible navigation structures—can significantly improve learner participation and engagement when intentionally integrated into gamified learning environments. Consequently, examining the relationship between assistive technologies, AI, and inclusive gamification contributes not only to educational technology research, but also to broader scholarly debates in disability studies and the learning sciences concerning accessibility, learner agency, and equity in digital education (Zebua & Ziraluo, 2026).

Several complementary learning theories provide the conceptual foundation for understanding how inclusive gamification operates in practice. Universal Design for Learning (UDL) is particularly influential because it emphasizes the importance of offering multiple means of representation, engagement, and expression in order to accommodate diverse learner profiles. Within gamified learning environments, UDL principles support the integration of accessibility features such as text-to-speech systems, multimodal feedback, customizable displays, captioning, and adaptive interaction pathways that reduce participation barriers for learners with sensory, cognitive, or motor impairments. Existing empirical studies indicate that gamified environments designed according to UDL principles can improve learner participation, engagement, and perceived accessibility among students with disabilities. At the same time, UDL also provides a broader pedagogical argument that accessibility should be embedded within instructional design from the outset rather than added as a reactive accommodation after system development. This perspective is important because it positions inclusive gamification as a proactive educational design strategy rather than merely a technological intervention.

Self-determination theory further explains why accessible and adaptive gamified systems may strengthen learner motivation and participation. According to this framework, learners are more likely to sustain engagement when educational environments support their needs for autonomy, competence, and relatedness. In inclusive gamified environments, adaptive feedback systems, flexible pacing, personalized challenges, and multiple interaction options may help learners experience greater control over their learning processes while reducing anxiety associated with inaccessible instructional structures. Empirical studies involving learners with visual impairments, autism spectrum conditions, and learning disabilities suggest that accessible gamification can improve perceived competence, strengthen participation, and increase sustained engagement when compared to more static forms of digital instruction. However, scholarly debates remain regarding the extent to which gamification genuinely promotes intrinsic motivation. Some researchers argue that excessive reliance on reward-oriented mechanics may encourage performance-driven behavior rather than meaningful learning engagement, particularly when accessibility features are treated as secondary to competitive game structures. These debates highlight the importance of grounding inclusive gamification in broader pedagogical principles rather than relying exclusively on motivational mechanics.

Constructivist learning theory offers an additional perspective by emphasizing that knowledge is actively constructed through interaction, exploration, collaboration, and social participation. From this viewpoint, assistive technologies within inclusive gamified environments are not merely supplementary tools but foundational elements that shape how learners navigate information, communicate with others, and participate in collaborative learning experiences. This perspective is particularly important in inclusive education because participation barriers often extend beyond technical accessibility to include social belonging and learner identity. Research on collaborative game-based learning environments suggests that accessible communication tools, adaptive collaborative tasks, and differentiated player roles can foster stronger social engagement and support co-construction of knowledge among learners with differing abilities. Consequently, accessibility within gamification should be understood not only in terms of technical usability, but also in relation to how digital learning environments support meaningful social participation and learner agency.

Recent advances in AI significantly expand the possibilities of inclusive gamification by enabling adaptive learning and large-scale personalization. AI-driven systems can dynamically adjust game difficulty, feedback timing, content modality, navigation complexity, and narrative progression according to learners' performance data and interaction patterns. Such adaptive mechanisms are particularly valuable for learners with diverse cognitive profiles because they allow differentiated pacing and personalized scaffolding without publicly identifying learners as needing additional support. Experimental and quasi-experimental studies indicate that AI-supported adaptive gamification can improve learner engagement and academic performance when compared to static game designs (Zhai et al., 2020). These findings suggest that AI functions as an important mediating layer between assistive technologies and pedagogical goals by enabling real-time responsiveness to learner diversity. Nevertheless, the rapid integration of AI into educational gamification has also generated significant ethical and pedagogical concerns. Scholars increasingly warn that AI systems trained on non-representative datasets may reproduce algorithmic bias and disadvantage learners with disabilities or atypical interaction patterns. Other researchers argue that excessive automation may reduce teachers' professional agency and obscure the pedagogical reasoning behind adaptive instructional decisions. Reviews conducted by Holmes et al. (2019) and Williamson and Eynon (2020) further indicate that much of the existing evidence is based on short-term interventions and relatively small participant samples, limiting the generalizability of current findings across educational contexts and disability categories. These critiques demonstrate that the integration of AI in inclusive gamification should be approached critically rather than assumed to be inherently beneficial.

Despite the growing body of empirical evidence supporting assistive technologies and AI-driven inclusive gamification, several important research gaps remain. Existing studies often focus primarily on short-term engagement outcomes while giving limited attention to the long-term effects of inclusive gamification on learner autonomy, identity development, social participation, and academic trajectories. Furthermore, many studies continue to examine accessibility, motivation, and adaptive technology as separate constructs rather than integrating them into a coherent theoretical framework. Future research should therefore adopt longitudinal, mixed-method, and participatory design approaches that involve learners with disabilities, educators, and accessibility specialists directly in the design and evaluation of gamified systems. Such approaches would allow researchers to examine not only measurable learning outcomes, but also the lived experiences and perceptions of learners navigating inclusive digital environments. Academically, advancing this field requires stronger integration between learning theory, accessibility standards, and AI ethics. Practically, the thoughtful integration of assistive technologies and AI into gamified learning environments has substantial potential to support inclusive instructional design, improve teacher decision-making, and contribute to the development of more equitable and responsive digital education systems.

EMPIRICAL STUDIES AND ACCESSIBLE GAME-BASED LEARNING PRACTICES

Game-based learning (GBL) refers to the purposeful integration of game mechanics, interactive challenges, narratives, and reward systems into educational environments to enhance learner engagement, motivation, and academic outcomes. Unlike conventional instructional approaches that often rely on passive content delivery, GBL positions learners as active participants who construct understanding through interaction, experimentation, and problem-solving. In inclusive education contexts, accessible GBL extends beyond entertainment-oriented game design by incorporating accessibility principles that enable meaningful participation for learners with diverse cognitive, sensory, physical, and social needs. These principles are closely connected to Universal Design for Learning (UDL), multimodal interaction, adaptive feedback systems, and usability-oriented design features that support equitable access to digital learning experiences. The growing relevance of accessible

GBL reflects broader concerns regarding educational equity and the limitations of traditional instructional systems in accommodating learner diversity.

Recent educational research increasingly highlights that conventional classroom practices frequently rely on standardized instructional methods and uniform assessment structures that may disadvantage students requiring alternative modes of communication, interaction, or content representation. Learners with disabilities, for example, often encounter barriers related to inaccessible instructional materials, inflexible pacing, and limited opportunities for personalized engagement. Within this context, accessible GBL has emerged as a promising pedagogical approach because it combines learner-centered interaction with adaptive and flexible learning experiences. Meyer et al. (2014) argue that accessibility-oriented instructional design can reduce participation barriers and strengthen learner engagement across both mainstream and special education settings. However, contemporary debates within educational technology research also suggest that accessibility cannot be assumed simply because digital games are interactive. Some gamified environments may unintentionally reproduce exclusion through visually complex interfaces, rapid interaction demands, or reward structures that privilege certain cognitive and behavioral profiles over others. Consequently, the effectiveness of accessible GBL depends not only on technological innovation, but also on the extent to which accessibility principles are integrated into pedagogical and design decisions from the outset.

Empirical studies further indicate that accessible GBL can support improvements in learner motivation, collaboration, problem-solving abilities, and sustained participation when accessibility features are intentionally embedded into game design. Research involving students with autism spectrum conditions, visual impairments, and learning disabilities demonstrates that features such as customizable interfaces, audio guidance, captioning systems, multimodal feedback, and adaptive difficulty levels can positively influence both academic performance and learner confidence. These findings are particularly important because they suggest that accessibility-oriented design contributes directly to instructional effectiveness rather than functioning merely as a compliance-oriented accommodation. At the same time, researchers caution that learner engagement within accessible GBL is influenced by multiple contextual factors, including prior digital literacy, instructional support, social interaction patterns, and the alignment between game mechanics and learner needs. As a result, the investigation of empirical evidence related to accessible GBL has become increasingly significant within contemporary educational technology research, especially in discussions concerning inclusive pedagogy, digital equity, and the ethical design of learning environments.

The theoretical foundations of accessible GBL are strongly informed by constructivist learning theory, self-determination theory, and Universal Design for Learning. Constructivist perspectives emphasize that learning occurs through active engagement with meaningful tasks, exploration, and social interaction, all of which are naturally facilitated through well-designed educational games. Within accessible GBL environments, learners construct understanding by experimenting with game systems, solving contextualized problems, and interacting collaboratively with peers. Self-determination theory further explains how game elements related to autonomy, competence, and relatedness can strengthen intrinsic motivation when learners are able to interact with educational content in ways aligned with their abilities and preferences (Ryan & Deci, 2020). This perspective is particularly relevant in inclusive contexts because adaptive game structures can provide learners with greater control over pacing, interaction modes, and learning pathways. UDL complements these theories by offering a systematic framework for designing games that provide multiple means of representation, engagement, and expression, thereby reducing participation barriers for learners with diverse needs (Meyer et al., 2014; Smith & Basham, 2014). Together, these theoretical perspectives position accessibility not as an additional technical feature, but as a foundational pedagogical principle shaping how learners access, interpret, and engage with educational experiences.

Empirical research conducted across educational levels provides substantial evidence that accessible GBL can enhance learning motivation, conceptual understanding, and knowledge retention among students with special needs. In higher education contexts, studies report that educational games incorporating multimodal feedback, adaptive difficulty systems, and visual scaffolding significantly improve conceptual comprehension and long-term retention among students with learning disabilities (Zainuddin et al., 2020). Similar patterns have been observed in primary and secondary education, where accessible digital games support sustained attention, engagement, and task persistence among learners with diverse cognitive profiles (Toh & Kirschner, 2020; Vlachopoulos & Makri, 2021). These findings reinforce the argument that accessibility-oriented design is closely connected to instructional quality and learner outcomes. Nevertheless, scholarly debates remain regarding the extent to which positive engagement outcomes translate into long-term academic development. Some researchers note that many interventions focus primarily on short-term motivational gains without sufficiently examining broader educational outcomes such as learner autonomy, transfer of knowledge, or social participation over time. This limitation suggests the need for more comprehensive longitudinal research examining how accessible GBL influences learners across different educational trajectories.

Case-based and design-oriented research also demonstrates the effectiveness of serious games for learners with intellectual disabilities and autism spectrum disorder. Empirical evidence indicates that games featuring simplified structures, clear visual cues, predictable navigation systems, and immediate feedback mechanisms can improve learner focus, task persistence, and social interaction skills (Connors et al., 2014). These studies consistently emphasize the importance of user-centered design approaches, particularly the involvement of learners, educators, and accessibility specialists throughout the game development process. Participatory design processes help ensure that game mechanics align with learners' cognitive, sensory, and communication needs rather than relying on generalized assumptions about accessibility. However, important methodological limitations remain within this body of research. Some scholars argue that many studies rely on relatively small participant samples, short intervention periods, and highly specific educational contexts, which limits the generalizability of findings and makes long-term impact assessment difficult (Smith & Basham, 2014; Vlachopoulos & Makri, 2021). These limitations highlight the need for stronger methodological rigor and more diverse participant representation within future accessible GBL research.

At the institutional and systemic level, Scopus-indexed studies increasingly emphasize the importance of interdisciplinary collaboration among educators, game developers, instructional designers, and assistive technology specialists in producing high-quality inclusive educational games. Such collaboration not only improves pedagogical alignment, but also supports compliance with international digital accessibility standards such as the Web Content Accessibility Guidelines (WCAG) and Universal Design for Learning frameworks (Connors et al., 2014; Meyer et al., 2014). Despite the growing body of positive evidence, several important research gaps remain unresolved, including limited longitudinal studies, insufficient cross-cultural validation, and the absence of standardized accessibility evaluation metrics within GBL research. Furthermore, relatively few studies critically examine how social, economic, and institutional inequalities influence access to accessible digital learning technologies across educational settings. Future research should therefore adopt mixed-method, participatory, and design-based approaches capable of examining both measurable learning outcomes and the lived experiences of learners navigating accessible game-based environments. Advancing this field requires stronger integration between learning theory, accessibility standards, instructional design, and ethical considerations surrounding digital inclusion. Overall, current empirical evidence strongly supports accessible game-based learning as a viable instructional strategy with significant implications for inclusive pedagogy, educational technology development, and equitable digital education.

PEDAGOGICAL, ETHICAL, AND POLICY CHALLENGES

Pedagogical Capacity and Instructional Design Constraints

The implementation of inclusive gamification in education, particularly when integrated with artificial intelligence and digital technologies, presents a complex set of pedagogical challenges that extend far beyond technical adoption alone. Inclusive gamification refers to the intentional application of game elements within learning environments designed to accommodate diverse learner needs, including differences in cognitive, sensory, social, linguistic, and cultural characteristics. Within inclusive education frameworks, gamified learning environments are expected not only to increase learner motivation and engagement, but also to ensure accessibility, differentiated instruction, and equitable participation for all students (Deterding et al., 2011; Plass et al., 2015). This expectation has become increasingly significant as educational institutions adopt digital learning systems at a larger scale while simultaneously facing growing learner diversity. However, contemporary research suggests that the integration of gamification into inclusive education remains pedagogically uneven, particularly when accessibility considerations are treated as secondary to technological innovation or motivational design. As a result, the effectiveness of inclusive gamification depends not merely on the presence of game mechanics, but on how those mechanics are aligned with broader pedagogical principles related to accessibility, learner agency, and educational equity.

One of the most significant challenges identified in current research concerns educators' limited preparedness to design and implement accessible game-based learning experiences. Effective gamification requires more than technical familiarity with digital platforms; it also demands pedagogical understanding of motivational design, formative assessment, learner variability, adaptive feedback systems, and inclusive instructional frameworks such as Universal Design for Learning (UDL). Studies conducted by Kapp (2012) and Schindler et al. (2017) demonstrate that gamified learning environments are most effective when game mechanics are intentionally aligned with pedagogical objectives and responsive to diverse learner profiles. In practice, however, many educators continue to implement gamification through superficial reward structures such as points, badges, and leaderboards without critically considering accessibility, learner diversity, or instructional relevance. This issue has generated important scholarly debates regarding whether gamification genuinely supports meaningful learning or merely increases short-term behavioral engagement. Researchers increasingly argue that reward-oriented gamification may unintentionally disadvantage learners who require alternative pacing, collaborative interaction, or differentiated pathways for demonstrating understanding. These concerns are particularly important within inclusive education settings, where competitive structures may reinforce existing educational inequalities rather than reduce them.

Research further indicates that professional development opportunities related to inclusive game design and AI-supported learning environments remain limited, particularly within teacher education programs and continuing professional training initiatives. Zainuddin et al. (2020) emphasize that without structured capacity-building programs, educators often lack the confidence and pedagogical expertise necessary to integrate gamification in ways that genuinely support accessibility and learner inclusion. Existing training initiatives frequently prioritize technical tool usage over critical pedagogical decision-making, resulting in implementations that focus on surface-level engagement rather than meaningful instructional transformation. This limitation becomes increasingly problematic as AI-driven educational technologies introduce additional layers of complexity, including adaptive feedback systems, data analytics, algorithmic personalization, and automated assessment mechanisms. While these technologies offer significant potential for differentiated instruction, they also require educators to understand issues related to algorithmic bias, accessibility ethics, learner privacy, and interpretive transparency. Consequently, pedagogical preparedness should be understood as a foundational requirement for ensuring that gamification and AI-enhanced learning environments promote educational equity rather than unintentionally reproducing disparities among learners. Future research and policy initiatives should therefore prioritize interdisciplinary professional development models that integrate inclusive pedagogy, accessibility standards, learning theory, and ethical considerations surrounding digital education.

Technological Infrastructure, Accessibility, and Digital Equity

The implementation of inclusive gamification is also shaped by substantial technological challenges that extend beyond instructional design and pedagogical readiness. Disparities in digital infrastructure, internet connectivity, device availability, and platform accessibility continue to influence whether game-based learning innovations can be implemented equitably across educational contexts. These challenges are particularly visible in developing and low-resource settings, where schools and learners may have limited access to stable internet connections, updated hardware, or digital learning ecosystems capable of supporting advanced gamified environments. Research conducted by Warschauer and Matuchniak (2010) demonstrates that digital inequality should not be understood solely in terms of physical access to technology, but also in relation to meaningful participation, digital literacy, and the ability to achieve educational outcomes through technology use. This distinction is important because learners may technically possess access to digital devices while still lacking the infrastructural and instructional support necessary to participate effectively in gamified learning environments. Consequently, the implementation of inclusive gamification is closely connected to broader issues of digital equity and educational justice.

In many educational systems, particularly within developing countries and underserved communities, infrastructure limitations significantly constrain the adoption of accessible and adaptive game-based learning platforms. Educational institutions may face unreliable internet access, limited bandwidth capacity, insufficient technical support, and restricted availability of compatible devices for students with disabilities. These limitations can reduce opportunities for participation in digital learning environments and unintentionally widen existing educational inequalities between well-resourced and under-resourced schools. Moreover, the increasing integration of AI-driven adaptive technologies into gamified systems introduces additional technological demands, including higher processing requirements, cloud-based data systems, and continuous platform updates that may not be feasible in low-resource contexts. While AI-supported gamification has the potential to personalize instruction and improve accessibility, scholars increasingly caution that such innovations may disproportionately benefit educational institutions with stronger technological infrastructures and financial resources. This tension highlights an important debate within educational technology research regarding whether digital innovation genuinely promotes inclusion or risks reproducing structural inequalities under the language of technological progress.

Another significant challenge concerns the accessibility of educational game platforms themselves. Many digital learning systems and gamified applications do not fully comply with internationally recognized accessibility standards such as the Web Content Accessibility Guidelines (WCAG), which emphasize perceivability, operability, understandability, and robustness for users with disabilities. Failure to meet these standards may create barriers for learners with visual, auditory, cognitive, or motor impairments, thereby contradicting the foundational principles of inclusive education. For example, visually complex interfaces, rapid navigation requirements, inaccessible audio content, and limited keyboard compatibility may prevent meaningful participation for students requiring alternative interaction pathways. Al-Azawei et al. (2016) argue that integrating Universal Design for Learning (UDL) principles into digital learning environments is essential for ensuring that gamified systems remain accessible to diverse learner populations. Their work further suggests that accessibility should not be treated as a secondary technical adjustment added after development, but rather as a foundational principle guiding the design of digital educational experiences from the beginning. This perspective reinforces broader scholarly arguments that accessibility is inseparable from pedagogical quality within inclusive educational environments.

Device compatibility also remains a critical concern within inclusive gamification research and practice. Many gamified learning platforms are optimized for specific operating systems, high-performance hardware, or updated software environments, limiting accessibility for students using older devices or lower-cost technologies. This issue is particularly significant in contexts where learners rely on shared family devices, outdated smartphones, or limited institutional technology resources. As a result, accessibility barriers may emerge not only from disability-related factors, but also from economic and technological inequalities that shape learners' opportunities to engage with digital education. Scholars have increasingly emphasized that technological accessibility should therefore be understood in a broader socio-technical sense that includes affordability, compatibility, usability, and contextual feasibility. Addressing these challenges requires systemic investment in digital infrastructure, institutional policy support, and accessibility-centered design practices capable of supporting diverse educational realities. Without such efforts, inclusive gamification risks becoming an innovation primarily accessible to privileged educational settings rather than a genuinely equitable instructional approach capable of supporting all learners.

Ethical Considerations, Data Governance, and Policy Frameworks

The rapid expansion of gamified learning environments, particularly those supported by artificial intelligence (AI) and learning analytics, has generated increasingly complex ethical and policy-related challenges within contemporary education. AI-driven gamification systems commonly rely on the continuous collection, analysis, and interpretation of student data in order to personalize learning experiences through adaptive difficulty adjustment, targeted feedback mechanisms, predictive analytics, and individualized learning pathways. Although these forms of personalization may enhance learner engagement and instructional responsiveness, they also raise important concerns regarding data privacy, surveillance, algorithmic transparency, and ethical governance. Holmes et al. (2019) argue that the integration of AI into educational systems must be guided by principles of transparency, accountability, fairness, and human oversight to ensure that technological innovation does not compromise learners' rights or educational equity. This concern is particularly significant in inclusive educational contexts, where vulnerable learner populations may be disproportionately affected by poorly regulated data practices or inaccessible technological systems. Consequently, ethical considerations surrounding AI-supported gamification should not be treated as secondary technical concerns, but rather as central components of responsible educational design and policy development.

One of the most widely debated issues in current research concerns the collection and governance of student data within AI-driven gamified systems. Many digital learning platforms gather extensive behavioral information, including interaction patterns, engagement duration, response accuracy, emotional indicators, and performance trajectories, often through automated learning analytics systems. While such data can support adaptive instruction and personalized learning experiences, the absence of clear regulatory oversight may expose students to risks related to data misuse, unauthorized access, commercial exploitation, or long-term digital profiling. Zawacki-Richter et al. (2019) emphasize that educational institutions and policymakers must establish transparent data governance frameworks that include informed consent procedures, ethical review mechanisms, and clear limitations regarding how learner data are collected, stored, analyzed, and shared. These concerns are especially important in educational settings involving minors and learners with disabilities, where questions of consent, autonomy, and digital vulnerability become more complex. Scholars increasingly argue that ethical AI implementation requires not only technical security protections, but also institutional accountability structures capable of ensuring that learners and educators understand how algorithmic systems influence educational experiences and decision-making processes.

Algorithmic bias represents another major ethical challenge within AI-supported gamification research. AI systems are heavily dependent on training datasets and predictive models that may unintentionally reflect existing social, cultural, linguistic, or educational inequalities. When datasets fail to represent diverse learner populations adequately, adaptive systems may generate inaccurate recommendations, unequal learning pathways, or biased performance evaluations that disadvantage certain groups of students, particularly learners with disabilities or atypical learning patterns. This issue has become a central debate within educational AI research because algorithmic systems often appear neutral while reproducing inequities embedded within underlying datasets and design assumptions. In inclusive educational contexts, biased algorithms may incorrectly interpret learner behavior, overlook accessibility needs, or reinforce deficit-oriented assumptions regarding learner capability. These concerns demonstrate that personalization alone should not be automatically equated with educational fairness or inclusion. Instead, researchers increasingly emphasize the importance of explainable AI systems, inclusive dataset development, and continuous ethical auditing processes to ensure that adaptive gamified environments remain equitable and responsive to learner diversity.

Beyond data governance and algorithmic bias, scholars have also raised concerns regarding the broader pedagogical implications of AI-supported gamification. Some researchers argue that excessive reliance on automated systems may reduce teacher agency by shifting instructional decision-making toward algorithmic recommendations and predictive analytics. In such cases, educators may become positioned primarily as facilitators of technology-driven learning environments rather than as critical pedagogical decision-makers. This tension reflects a broader debate within educational technology research concerning the balance between automation and human-centered teaching practices. While AI-driven systems can support adaptive instruction and reduce certain administrative burdens, they may also obscure the pedagogical reasoning underlying instructional decisions and limit opportunities for contextualized professional judgment. In inclusive education, where learner needs are often complex, socially situated, and highly individualized, excessive standardization through automated systems may conflict with the relational and interpretive dimensions of teaching. Consequently, many scholars advocate for human-centered AI approaches that position technology as a supportive tool rather than a replacement for teacher expertise and professional autonomy.

At the policy level, the sustainable implementation of inclusive gamification requires comprehensive and coordinated regulatory frameworks that extend beyond data protection alone. The OECD (2021) emphasizes that digital transformation in education must involve holistic policy approaches integrating technological innovation with ethical oversight, accessibility standards, infrastructure development, and equity-oriented planning. Without such policy support, gamification initiatives risk remaining fragmented, short-term interventions rather than evolving into sustainable and inclusive educational practices. Existing policy gaps are particularly visible in areas such as accessibility compliance, teacher professional development, ethical AI standards, and institutional accountability mechanisms. Furthermore, educational policies often struggle to keep pace with the rapid evolution of AI technologies and commercial educational platforms, creating uncertainty regarding governance responsibilities and implementation standards. Addressing these challenges requires collaboration among educators, researchers, policymakers, technology developers, and accessibility specialists to ensure that technological innovation aligns with broader educational values related to inclusion, equity, and learner well-being. Ultimately, the long-term viability of inclusive gamification depends not only on technological advancement, but also on the development of ethical, pedagogical, and policy frameworks capable of supporting responsible and equitable digital education systems.

FUTURE DIRECTIONS AND INTERDISCIPLINARY COLLABORATION

Interdisciplinary Foundations for Accessible Gamification and Game-Based Learning

The advancement of accessible gamification and game-based learning (GBL) in inclusive education increasingly depends on sustained interdisciplinary collaboration that integrates educational theory, human–computer interaction, learning analytics, design research, and public policy into a coherent innovation ecosystem. Interdisciplinary collaboration may be operationally defined as a structured process through which experts from multiple domains co-construct knowledge, tools, and interventions to address complex educational challenges that cannot be adequately resolved within a single disciplinary framework. In the context of accessible GBL, such collaboration allows for the alignment of pedagogical objectives with technological affordances and sociocultural realities, thereby fostering systems that are not only engaging but also equitable and responsive to diverse learner needs. Research in inclusive educational technology consistently demonstrates that collaborative design processes—particularly those involving educators, accessibility specialists, learners with disabilities, and policymakers—produce more usable and sustainable interventions compared with siloed development models (Holmes & Tuomi, 2022; Karageorgou et al., 2026). From a theoretical standpoint, this integrative approach aligns with socio-constructivist learning theory and universal design for learning (UDL), both of which emphasize the importance of flexible environments that accommodate variability in learners' cognitive, sensory, and social profiles (Meyer et al., 2014). However, while interdisciplinary collaboration is widely endorsed in policy discourse, empirical evidence suggests that institutional barriers, disciplinary language differences, and uneven resource distribution often limit the depth and continuity of such collaboration, highlighting the need for structural mechanisms that support cross-sector partnerships and shared research agendas (Voogt et al., 2015).

Accessible gamification and GBL can thus be conceptualized as socio-technical systems that require ongoing negotiation among pedagogical, technological, and ethical considerations. Gamification, defined as the application of game design elements such as feedback loops, reward systems, and progression mechanics in non-game contexts, has demonstrated potential to enhance motivation and persistence when grounded in sound instructional design and learner-centered principles (Deterding et al., 2011; Hamari et al., 2014). When accessibility is systematically embedded—through customizable interfaces, multimodal representation, and adaptive pacing—these approaches can support diverse learners, including those with sensory, cognitive, or socio-emotional differences. Nonetheless, the literature also reports mixed outcomes, with some studies indicating that gamified environments may produce short-term engagement without sustained learning gains or may overwhelm learners who are sensitive to overstimulation (Sailer et al., 2017). Such findings underscore the need for rigorous evaluation frameworks that consider not only engagement metrics but also inclusivity, well-being, and long-term learning outcomes. Interdisciplinary research–practice partnerships are therefore essential to ensure that accessible GBL systems remain pedagogically meaningful and socially responsive rather than driven solely by technological novelty or market trends.

Emerging Technologies, Equity, and Future Research Directions

Emerging technological trends further underscore the importance of interdisciplinary collaboration, particularly with the growing integration of generative artificial intelligence (AI), augmented reality (AR), and virtual reality (VR) into educational ecosystems. Generative AI systems, including adaptive tutoring platforms and automated content generation tools, have demonstrated potential to personalize learning experiences by dynamically adjusting instructional materials, feedback, and interaction modalities based on learner data (Luckin et al., 2016; Holmes et al., 2019). Similarly, immersive technologies such as AR and VR offer opportunities to create experiential learning environments that can be designed with accessibility in mind—for example, by incorporating alternative input methods, adjustable visual or auditory elements, and haptic feedback to support learners with diverse needs. A systematic review by Radianti et al. (2020) indicates that immersive environments can enhance engagement and conceptual understanding across educational levels, although accessibility features are often inconsistently implemented and remain secondary to aesthetic or entertainment-driven design priorities. This suggests that accessibility considerations must be embedded from the earliest stages of technological development rather than treated as subsequent adaptations.

Despite their promise, advanced technologies also present ethical and practical challenges that require careful scrutiny. Critical scholarship cautions against technological determinism, emphasizing that digital innovations do not inherently produce inclusive outcomes and may instead reproduce or amplify existing inequities if access, digital literacy, and cultural relevance are not addressed (Selwyn, 2019). For instance, learners from under-resourced contexts may face barriers to accessing high-bandwidth immersive environments, while AI-driven systems trained on biased datasets may inadvertently marginalize certain groups. Consequently, the development of accessible GBL must remain grounded in principles of equity, transparency, and participatory design. Future research should prioritize longitudinal and mixed-methods studies that examine how accessible gamification and immersive technologies influence academic achievement, social participation, and digital inclusion across diverse populations. In addition, policy frameworks and institutional strategies should incentivize inclusive design and interdisciplinary research collaborations, ensuring that accessibility is treated as a foundational design principle rather than a compliance requirement. Ultimately, accessible gamification and GBL represent more than technological enhancements; they constitute a strategic foundation for adaptive and inclusive educational systems capable of responding to the complexities of the digital era. Through sustained interdisciplinary collaboration, critical evaluation, and evidence-based innovation, these approaches hold substantial potential to support equitable educational transformation and to shape learning environments that are responsive to the diverse needs of all learners.

REFERENCES

Al-Azawei, A., Serenelli, F., & Lundqvist, K. (2016). Universal Design for Learning (UDL): A content analysis of peer reviewed journals from 2012 to 2015. *The Journal of Scholarship of Teaching and Learning, 16*(3), 39–56. DOI: 10.14434/josotl.v16i3.19295

Connors, E. C., Chrastil, E. R., Sánchez, J., & Merabet, L. B. (2014). Virtual environments for the transfer of navigation skills in the blind: A comparison of directed instruction vs. video game based learning approaches. *Frontiers in Human Neuroscience, 8*, 223. DOI: 10.3389/fnhum.2014.00223 PMID: 24822044

Deterding, S., Dixon, D., Khaled, R., & Nacke, L. (2011). From game design elements to gamefulness: Defining "gamification." *Proceedings of the 15th International Academic MindTrek Conference*. https://doi.org/DOI: 10.1145/2181037.2181040

Hamari, J., Koivisto, J., & Sarsa, H. (2014). Does gamification work? A literature review of empirical studies. *47th Hawaii International Conference on System Sciences*. https://doi.org/DOI: 10.1109/HICSS.2014.377

Holmes, W., Bialik, M., & Fadel, C. (2019). *Artificial Intelligence in Education: Promises and Implications for Teaching and Learning*. Center for Curriculum Redesign.

Holmes, W., & Tuomi, I. (2022). State of the art and practice in AI in education. *European Journal of Education, 3*(4), 100074. DOI: 10.1111/ejed.12533

Kapp, K. M. (2012). *The gamification of learning and instruction*. Pfeiffer.

Karageorgou, E., Adam, S., Doukakis, S., & Vlamos, P. (2026). Digital Accessibility for Students with Disabilities and Inclusive Learning in Education. In Vlamos, P. (Ed.), *GeNeDIS 2024. GeNeDIS 2024. Advances in Experimental Medicine and Biology* (Vol. 1490). Springer., DOI: 10.1007/978-3-032-03402-1_44

Luckin, R., Holmes, W., Griffiths, M., & Forcier, L. (2016). *Intelligence unleashed: An argument for AI in education*. Pearson.

Meyer, A., Rose, D. H., & Gordon, D. (2014). *Universal design for learning: Theory and practice*. CAST Professional Publishing.

OECD. (2021). *OECD Digital Education Outlook 2021: Pushing the frontiers with AI, blockchain and robots*. OECD Publishing., DOI: 10.1787/589b283f-

Peters, D., Calvo, R. A., & Ryan, R. M. (2018). Designing for Motivation, Engagement and Wellbeing in Digital Experience. *Frontiers in Psychology*, *9*, 797. Advance online publication. DOI: 10.3389/fpsyg.2018.00797 PMID: 29892246

Plass, J. L., Homer, B. D., & Kinzer, C. K. (2015). Foundations of game-based learning. *Educational Psychologist*, *50*(4), 258–283. DOI: 10.1080/00461520.2015.1122533

Plass, J. L., Mayer, R. E., & Homer, B. D. (2020). *Handbook of game-based learning*. Mit Press.

Radianti, J., Majchrzak, T. A., Fromm, J., & Wohlgenannt, I. (2020). A systematic review of immersive virtual reality applications for higher education. *Computers & Education*, *147*, 103778. DOI: 10.1016/j.compedu.2019.103778

Ryan, R. M., & Deci, E. L. (2020). Intrinsic and extrinsic motivation from a self-determination theory perspective: Definitions, theory, practices, and future directions. *Contemporary Educational Psychology*, *61*, 101860. DOI: 10.1016/j.cedpsych.2020.101860

Sailer, M., Hense, J., Mayr, S., & Mandl, H. (2017). How gamification motivates: An experimental study. *Computers in Human Behavior*, *69*, 371–380. DOI: 10.1016/j.chb.2016.12.033

Schindler, L. A., Burkholder, G. J., Morad, O. A., & Marsh, C. (2017). Computer-based technology and student engagement: A critical review. *International Journal of Educational Technology in Higher Education*, *14*(25), 25. Advance online publication. DOI: 10.1186/s41239-017-0063-0

Selwyn, N. (2019). *Should robots replace teachers? AI and the future of education.* Polity Press.

Smith, S. J., & Basham, J. D. (2014). Designing Online Learning Opportunities for Students with Disabilities. *Teaching Exceptional Children*, *46*(5), 127–137. DOI: 10.1177/0040059914530102

UNESCO. (2020). *Education for sustainable development: a roadmap*. UNESCO., DOI: 10.54675/YFRE1448

UNESCO. (2021). AI and education: Promise and implications. Guidance for policy-makers.

Voogt, J., Laferrière, T., Breuleux, A., Itow, R., Hickey, D., & McKenney, S. (2015). Collaborative design as a form of professional development. *Instructional Science*, *43*(2), 259–282. DOI: 10.1007/s11251-014-9340-7

Warschauer, M., & Matuchniak, T. (2010). New technology and digital worlds: Analyzing evidence of equity in access, use, and outcomes. *Review of Research in Education, 34*(1), 179–225. DOI: 10.3102/0091732X09349791

Williamson, B., & Eynon, R. (2020). Historical threads, missing links, and future directions in AI in education. *Learning, Media and Technology, 45*(3), 223–235. DOI: 10.1080/17439884.2020.1798995

Zainuddin, Z., Chu, S. K. W., Shujahat, M., & Perera, C. J. (2020). The impact of gamification on learning and instruction: A systematic review of empirical evidence. *Educational Research Review, 30*, 100326. DOI: 10.1016/j.edurev.2020.100326

Zawacki-Richter, O., Marín, V. I., Bond, M., & Gouverneur, F. (2019). Systematic review of research on artificial intelligence applications in higher education. *International Journal of Educational Technology in Higher Education, 16*(39), 39. Advance online publication. DOI: 10.1186/s41239-019-0171-0

Zebua, N., & Ziraluo, Y. P. B. (2026). Bridging the Gap: Integrating GenAI into Secondary Science Curricula. In *Harnessing Generative Artificial Intelligence for Science Education* (pp. 137–162). IGI Global Scientific Publishing. DOI: 10.4018/979-8-3373-2913-0.ch005

Zhai, X., Yin, Y., Pellegrino, J. W., Haudek, K. C., & Shi, L. (2020). Applying machine learning in science assessment: A systematic review. *Studies in Science Education, 56*(1), 111–151. DOI: 10.1080/03057267.2020.1735757

KEY TERMS AND DEFINITIONS

Accessible Gamification: The systematic integration of game design elements—such as points, feedback systems, levels, and challenges—into learning environments while ensuring that all features are usable by learners with diverse cognitive, sensory, and physical abilities. Accessible gamification prioritizes universal design for learning (UDL), customizable interfaces, and multimodal interaction to support equitable participation and sustained engagement in instructional contexts.

Accessible Learning: Accessible learning denotes the design of learning environments that allow all learners, including those with disabilities, to access content, participate meaningfully, and achieve learning objectives.

Adaptive Gamification: Adaptive gamification describes gamified learning systems that dynamically adjust difficulty levels, feedback, and content based on individual learner performance and needs.

AI-Based Gamification: Gamified learning systems that employ artificial intelligence to personalize learning experiences through data-driven adaptation, feedback, and performance analytics.

Algorithmic Bias: Systematic and unfair outcomes in AI-driven systems caused by biased data, design assumptions, or decision rules that may disadvantage certain groups of learners.

Artificial Intelligence (AI) in Education: Artificial intelligence in education refers to the application of intelligent algorithms and data-driven systems to support adaptive learning, personalization, and instructional decision-making.

Assistive Technologies: Assistive technologies are digital tools and systems, such as screen readers, text-to-speech, speech-to-text, and captioning, that support learners with disabilities in accessing and interacting with learning materials.

Data Privacy in Education: The ethical and legal protection of students' personal and behavioral data collected through digital learning systems, ensuring that such data are used responsibly, transparently, and securely.

Digital Equity: The condition in which all learners have fair access to digital technologies, connectivity, and learning opportunities, as well as the skills required to use them effectively for educational purposes.

Equity in Digital Learning: The principle that all learners should have fair access to high-quality digital learning experiences, resources, and outcomes regardless of ability, socioeconomic status, or technological access. Equity in digital learning requires not only accessible design but also supportive policies, infrastructure, and pedagogical practices.

Game-Based Learning (GBL): Game-based learning is an instructional approach in which games function as the primary medium for teaching and learning, enabling knowledge construction through interactive and experiential activities.

Gamification: Gamification refers to the use of game design elements such as points, badges, leaderboards, and narratives in non-game contexts to enhance motivation, engagement, and learning outcomes.

Immersive Technologies (AR and VR): Digital environments created through augmented reality (AR) and virtual reality (VR) that enable learners to interact with simulated or enhanced spaces in real time. When designed with accessibility considerations—such as adjustable sensory inputs, alternative navigation methods, and adaptive interfaces—immersive technologies can support experiential learning for diverse learners.

Inclusive Education: Inclusive education is an educational approach that ensures equal learning opportunities for all learners by recognizing and accommodating diverse abilities, needs, and backgrounds.

Multimodality: Multimodality refers to the use of multiple modes of representation, such as visual, auditory, and interactive elements, to enhance understanding and accessibility in learning environments.

Self-Determination Theory (SDT): Self-determination theory is a motivational framework that emphasizes autonomy, competence, and relatedness as essential psychological needs for effective and sustained learning.

Social Constructivism: Social constructivism is a learning theory that views knowledge as being constructed through social interaction, collaboration, and shared meaning-making.

Socio-Technical Learning Systems: Educational environments that emerge from the interaction between technological infrastructures, pedagogical practices, institutional policies, and social contexts. Accessible gamification and GBL are considered socio-technical systems because their effectiveness depends on both technological design and the social conditions in which they are implemented.

Teacher Professional Capacity: Educators' knowledge, skills, and pedagogical competencies required to design, implement, and evaluate inclusive and technology-enhanced learning environments effectively.

Universal Design for Learning (UDL): A pedagogical framework that guides the design of flexible learning environments capable of accommodating individual differences by providing multiple means of representation, engagement, and expression.

Compilation of References

Aarthi, S., Ravikumar, R. N., Khudayberganov, S., Ismailov, A., & Khujaniyozova, O. R. (2025). Using Intelligent Tutoring Systems to Enhance Student Engagement. *Advances in Computational Intelligence and Robotics Book Series*, 155–188. DOI: 10.4018/979-8-3373-1827-1.ch008

Abrar, M., Khalid, S., & Ullah, R. (2026). The intersection of artificial intelligence and assistive technologies in the diagnosis and intervention of mental health conditions. *Artificial Intelligence Review*, *59*(2), 40. DOI: 10.1007/s10462-025-11447-9

Adako, O. P., Adeusi, O. C., & Alaba, P. A. (2025). AI in autism education: A review of collaborative and longitudinal approaches. *Disability and Rehabilitation. Assistive Technology*, •••, 1–26. DOI: 10.1080/17483107.2025.2579825 PMID: 41175378

Agarwal, A. (2025). *DIKSHA-based smart classroom setups – What's missing?* iDream Education. https://www.idreameducation.org/blog/diksha-based-smart-classroom/

Ahmed, K., Akram, A., Sharif, A. S., & Tariq, A. (2023). Developing pragmatic competence through instructional intervention: Evidence from EFL contexts. *Journal of English Language and Literature Education*, *5*(1), 141–170. DOI: 10.54692/jelle.2023.0501160

Ahmed, S., Rahman, M. S., Kaiser, M. S., & Hosen, A. S. (2025). Advancing personalized and inclusive education for students with disability through artificial intelligence: Perspectives, challenges, and opportunities. *Digital*, *5*(2), 11. DOI: 10.3390/digital5020011

Ahuja, N. J., Dutt, S., Choudhary, S. L., & Kumar, M. (2025). Intelligent tutoring system in education for disabled learners using human–computer interaction and augmented reality. *International Journal of Human-Computer Interaction*, *41*(3), 1804–1816. DOI: 10.1080/10447318.2022.2124359

Akhter, E. (2025). *Ai in the classroom: evaluating the effectiveness of intelligent tutoring systems for multilingual learners in secondary education. 01*(01), 532–563. https://doi.org/DOI: 10.63125/gcq1qr39

Al Shami, A., & Nashwan, A. J. (2024). Assistive technology in rehabilitation: exploring historical models, current innovations, and emerging trends. *The Palgrave Encyclopedia of Disability*, 1-8. DOI: 10.1007/978-3-031-40858-8_415-1

Alam, A. (2023a). Media multitasking with M-learning technology in real-time classroom learning: Analysing the dynamics in formal educational settings for the future of E-learning in India. In *2023 2nd International Conference on Smart Technologies and Systems for Next Generation Computing (ICSTSN)* (pp. 1-6). IEEE. DOI: 10.1109/ICSTSN57873.2023.10151509

Alam, A. (2023b). The secret sauce of student success: Cracking the code by navigating the path to personalized learning with educational data mining. In *2023 2nd International Conference on Smart Technologies and Systems for Next Generation Computing (ICSTSN)* (pp. 1-8). IEEE. DOI: 10.1109/ICSTSN57873.2023.10151558

Alam, A., & Mohanty, A. (2022, December). Facial analytics or virtual avatars: competencies and design considerations for student-teacher interaction in AI-powered online education for effective classroom engagement. In *International Conference on Communication, Networks and Computing* (pp. 252-265). Cham: Springer Nature Switzerland. DOI: 10.1007/978-3-031-43145-6_21

Alam, A., & Mohanty, A. (2023, January). Learning on the move: a pedagogical framework for state-of-the-art mobile learning. In *International Conference on Data Management, Analytics & Innovation* (pp. 735-748). Singapore: Springer Nature Singapore. DOI: 10.1007/978-981-99-1414-2_52

Alam, A. (2022). Impact of university's human resources practices on professors' occupational performance: empirical evidence from India's higher education sector. In *Inclusive businesses in developing economies: Converging people, profit, and corporate citizenship* (pp. 107–131). Springer International Publishing., DOI: 10.1007/978-3-031-12217-0_6

Alam, A. (2023c). Intelligence unleashed: An argument for AI-enabled learning ecologies with real world examples of today and a peek into the future. In *International Conference on Innovations in Computer Science, Electronics & Electrical Engineering*-2022 (Vol. 2717, No. 1, p. 030001). AIP Publishing LLC. DOI: 10.1063/5.0129803

Alam, A., & Mohanty, A. (2024). Integrated constructive robotics in education (ICRE) model: A paradigmatic framework for transformative learning in educational ecosystem. *Cogent Education*, *11*(1), 2324487. DOI: 10.1080/2331186X.2024.2324487

Al-Azawei, A., Serenelli, F., & Lundqvist, K. (2016). Universal Design for Learning (UDL): A content analysis of peer reviewed journals from 2012 to 2015. *The Journal of Scholarship of Teaching and Learning*, *16*(3), 39–56. DOI: 10.14434/josotl.v16i3.19295

Alhebaishi, S., Stone, R., & Ameen, M. (2025). Emotional Engagement and Teaching Innovations for Deep Learning and Retention in Education: A Literature Review. *International Journal of Advanced Computer Science and Applications*, *16*(3), 35–45. DOI: 10.14569/IJACSA.2025.0160304

Alias, N. F., & Razak, R. A. (2023). Exploring The Pedagogical Aspects of Microlearning in Educational Settings: A Systematic Literature Review. *Malaysian Journal of Learning and Instruction*, *20*(2), 267–294. DOI: 10.32890/mjli2023.20.2.3

Alimović, S. (2024). Benefits and challenges of using assistive technology in the education and rehabilitation of Individuals with visual impairments. *Disability and Rehabilitation. Assistive Technology*, *19*(8), 3063–3070. DOI: 10.1080/17483107.2024.2344802 PMID: 38685705

Alkan, A. (2024). Artificial intelligence: Its role and potential in education. İnsan ve Toplum Bilimleri Araştırmaları Dergisi, 13(1), 483–497. DOI: 10.15869/itobiad.1331201

Almawadeh, N. S. (2025). Using cartoon video-based instruction for developing oral fluency of Jordanian grade 4 EFL pupils. *Theory and Practice in Language Studies*, *15*(2), 647–655. DOI: 10.17507/tpls.1502.34

Almuqhim, S., & Berri, J. (2025). AI-Driven Personalized Microlearning Framework for Enhanced E-Learning. *Computer Applications in Engineering Education*, *33*(3), e70040. Advance online publication. DOI: 10.1002/cae.70040

Al-Rashaida, M., Aishan, H., Moustafa, A., Abuwatfa, R., Mohsen, W., & Khan, A. G. Y. (2025). AI Strategies for Inclusive Education Resources and Support. In *AI in Learning, Educational Leadership, and Special Education: Innovations and Ethical Dilemmas* (pp. 349-380). IGI Global. DOI: 10.4018/979-8-3373-0573-8.ch012

Alsamh, M. H., Hawbani, A., Kumar, S., & Alsamhi, S. H. (2024). Multisensory metaverse-6G: A new paradigm of commerce and education. *IEEE Access : Practical Innovations, Open Solutions*, *12*, 75657–75677. DOI: 10.1109/ACCESS.2024.3392838

American Foundation for the Blind. (2019). *An evaluation of OrCam MyEye 2.0. AccessWorld*. https://www.afb.org/aw/19/8/15066

Amore, F., Silvestri, V., Guidobaldi, M., Sulfaro, M., Piscopo, P., Turco, S., De Rossi, F., Rellini, E., Fortini, S., Rizzo, S., Perna, F., Mastropasqua, L., Bosch, V., Oest-Shirai, L. R., Haddad, M. A. O., Higashi, A. H., Sato, R. H., Pya, Y., Daibert-Nido, M., & Markowitz, S. N. (2023). Efficacy and patients' satisfaction with the OrCam MyEye device among visually impaired people: A multicenter study. *Journal of Medical Systems*, *47*(1), 11. DOI: 10.1007/s10916-023-01908-5 PMID: 36645535

Anokye, G. O., Price-Sanchez, C., Yong, A. C., Ali, M., Tate, C., Graham, R., & Chan, V. F. (2025). School-based eye health interventions for improving eye care and spectacles compliance in children in low- and middle-income countries: A scoping review. *AJO International*, *2*(2), 100126. DOI: 10.1016/j.ajoint.2025.100126

Arias-Flores, H., Valencia-Aragón, K., Calle-Jimenez, T., & Sanchez-Gordon, S. (2025). *Artificial Intelligence and Assistive Technologies: A Systematic Review of Educational Applications for Disabilities*. 283–292. DOI: 10.1007/978-3-031-93848-1_19

Ashour, A., & Elkhawaga, G. O. (2026). Innovations in geriatric care: Leveraging technology to meet the needs of an aging world, a narrative review. *The Journal of the Egyptian Public Health Association*, *101*(1), 2. DOI: 10.1186/s42506-025-00203-0 PMID: 41677990

Assistive Technology Industry Association. (2023). *What is assistive technology?* https://www.atia.org/home/at-resources/what-is-at/

Ayanwale, M. A., Sanusi, I. T., Adelana, O. P., Aruleba, K. D., & Oyelere, S. S. (2022). Teachers' readiness and intention to teach artificial intelligence in schools. *Computers and Education: Artificial Intelligence*, *3*, 100099. DOI: 10.1016/j.caeai.2022.100099

Ayon, V., & Dillon, A. (2021). Assistive technology in education. *The International Journal of Information, Diversity, &. Inclusion (Washington, D.C.)*, *5*(3), 174–184. https://www.jstor.org/stable/48644451

Baguma, R., & Wolters, M. K. (2021). Making Virtual Learning Environments Accessible to People with Disabilities in Universities in Uganda. *Frontiers of Computer Science*, *3*, 638275. DOI: 10.3389/fcomp.2021.638275

Baheti, M., Tyagi, B., Kumar, V., Prabavathy, M., & Sharma, A. (2025, August). Learning of languages through Computer Assisted technologies & IOT enabled devices. In *2025 World Skills Conference on Universal Data Analytics and Sciences (WorldSUAS)* (pp. 1-6). IEEE. DOI: 10.1109/WorldSUAS66815.2025.11199122

Bairaqdar, M. (2025). Using Microsoft's immersive reader tool to enhance students' listening comprehension. *Dialog on Language Instruction*, 35(1).

Bangeni, B. (2024). Reading (in) law: A critical appraisal of the impact of language on disciplinary novices' cognitive reading strategies. *Language & Communication, 94*, 69–84. DOI: 10.1016/j.langcom.2023.12.001

Barbieri, M., Pennazio, V., Sabatini, S. P., & Gori, M. (2025). Through their eyes: Enhancing teacher awareness of visual impairments via extended reality simulations (REALTER). *Frontiers in Education, 10*, 1634253. DOI: 10.3389/feduc.2025.1634253

Barnes, M., & Tour, E. (2025). Teacher knowledge for navigating generative AI in schools: Pedagogical, ethical, and practical considerations. *Australian Educational Researcher*. Advance online publication. DOI: 10.1007/s13384-024-00726-1

Bastidas, J. A. (2022). Are language teaching methods really dead? Revisiting post-method pedagogy. *PROFILE Issues in Teachers'. Professional Development (Philadelphia, Pa.), 24*(2), 203–213. DOI: 10.15446/profile.v24n2.96952

Baxter, G., & Hainey, T. (2024). Using immersive technologies to enhance the student learning experience. *Interactive Technology and Smart Education, 21*(3), 403–425. DOI: 10.1108/ITSE-05-2023-0078

Beach, P., Lytle, B., Ness, N., Leung, S., Lieberman, L., & Peng, C. (2026). Navigating innovation: The lived experiences of orientation & mobility specialists using assistive technology and virtual reality. *Disability and Rehabilitation. Assistive Technology*, •••, 1–13. DOI: 10.1080/17483107.2026.2626466 PMID: 41672743

Bedard, A., & Zhang, Q. (2025). Highlighting Opportunities for Inclusive Education Using Virtual Reality: Exploring New Learning Pathways for People with Disabilities. In S. C., A. M., N. S., & S. G. (Eds.), *Communications in Computer and Information Science: Vol. 2524 CCIS* (pp. 37–46). Springer Science and Business Media Deutschland GmbH. DOI: 10.1007/978-3-031-94156-6_4

Belkina, M., Daniel, S., Nikolic, S., Haque, R., Lyden, S., Neal, P., Grundy, S., & Hassan, G. M. (2025). Implementing generative AI (GenAI) in higher education: A systematic review of case studies. *Computers and Education: Artificial Intelligence, 8*, 100407. DOI: 10.1016/j.caeai.2025.100407

Bhambri, P. (2025). Virtual and augmented reality for immersive learning experiences: Practical applications and challenges. *Architecting the digital future: Platforms, design, and application*, 17-46. DOI: 10.4018/979-8-3693-2973-3.ch002

Bi, N. B. D. N. (2025). Inclusive and equitable education with AI: Addressing the needs of diverse learners through AI solutions, ensuring quality and accessibility. *International Journal of Humanities and Social Science Invention, 14*(4), 69–74. DOI: 10.35629/7722-14046974

Birtwistle, T., & Wagenaar, R. (2020). Re-thinking an educational model suitable for 21st century needs. In *European Higher Education Area: Challenges for a New Decade* (pp. 465–482). Springer International Publishing., DOI: 10.1007/978-3-030-56316-5_29

Blinov, V. I., Sergeev, I. S., & Rodichev, N. F. (2022). The Microlearning-From Business to Education: A Promising Direction For The Development of Didactics. *Obrazovanie i Nauka, 24*(9), 43–68. DOI: 10.17853/1994-5639-2022-9-43-68

Bonanno, M., Saracino, B., Ciancarelli, I., Panza, G., Manuli, A., Morone, G., & Calabrò, R. S. (2025, July). Assistive technologies for individuals with a disability from a neurological condition: A narrative review on the multimodal integration. In *Healthcare* (Vol. 13, No. 13, p. 1580). MDPI. DOI: 10.3390/healthcare13131580

Braun, V., & Clarke, V. (2006). Using thematic analysis in psychology. *Qualitative Research in Psychology, 3*(2), 77–101. DOI: 10.1191/1478088706qp063oa

Bray, A., Devitt, A., Banks, J., Sanchez Fuentes, S., Sandoval, M., Riviou, K., Byrne, D., Flood, M., Reale, J., & Terrenzio, S. (2024). What next for Universal Design for Learning? A systematic literature review of technology in UDL implementations at second level. *British Journal of Educational Technology, 55*(1), 113–138. DOI: 10.1111/bjet.13328

Bruza, P. D., Wang, Z., & Busemeyer, J. R. (2015). Quantum cognition: A new theoretical approach to psychology. *Trends in Cognitive Sciences, 19*(7), 383–393. DOI: 10.1016/j.tics.2015.05.001

Burkhard, M. (2022). Student perceptions of AI-powered writing tools: Towards individualized teaching strategies. In *Proceedings of the 19th International Conference on Cognition and Exploratory Learning in Digital Age (CELDA 2022)* (pp. 73–81). IADIS Press. DOI: 10.33965/CELDA2022_202207L010

Carreon, A., Mosher, M., Goldman, S., Smith, S., & Smith, B. (2025). A ten-year review of the Journal of Special Education Technology: Innovations and trends for individuals with disabilities. *Journal of Special Education Technology, 01626434251349414*. Advance online publication. DOI: 10.1177/01626434251349414

CAST. (2024). *Universal Design for Learning Guidelines version 3.0. CAST*. https://udlguidelines.cast.org/

Cavender, A., Ladner, R., & Riskin, E. (2020). Automated captioning technologies and accessibility for people who are deaf or hard of hearing. *ACM Transactions on Accessible Computing*.

Ch'en, P. Y., Day, W., Pekson, R. C., Barrientos, J., Burton, W. B., Ludwig, A. B., Jariwala, S. P., & Cassese, T. (2025). GPT-4 generated answer rationales to multiple choice assessment questions in undergraduate medical education. *BMC Medical Education, 25*(1), 333. Advance online publication. DOI: 10.1186/s12909-025-06862-z PMID: 40038669

Chakraborty, D., Ray, D., & Nair, S. (2025). Ethical Considerations In Deploying AI And Data-Driven Technologies For Adaptive Education. *International Journal of Environmental Sciences*, •••, 8291–8299. DOI: 10.64252/cef9cs80

Chalkiadakis, A., Seremetaki, A., Kanellou, A., Kallishi, M., Morfopoulou, A., Moraitaki, M., & Mastrokoukou, S. (2024). Impact of artificial intelligence and virtual reality on educational inclusion: A systematic review of technologies supporting students with disabilities. *Education Sciences, 14*(11), 1223. DOI: 10.3390/educsci14111223

Chamola, V., Peelam, M. S., Mittal, U., Hassija, V., Singh, A., Pareek, R., Mangal, P., Sangwan, D., de Albuquerque, V. H. C., Mahmud, M., & Brown, D. J. (2025). Metaverse for education: Developments, challenges, and future direction. *Computer Applications in Engineering Education, 33*(3), e70018. DOI: 10.1002/cae.70018

Chan, C. K. Y., & Hu, W. (2023). Students' voices on generative AI: Perceptions, benefits, and challenges in higher education. *International Journal of Educational Technology in Higher Education, 20*(1), 43. DOI: 10.1186/s41239-023-00411-8

Chen, J., Yi, C., Du, H., Niyato, D., Kang, J., Cai, J., & Shen, X. (2024). A revolution of personalized healthcare: Enabling human digital twin with mobile AIGC. *IEEE Network, 38*(6), 234–242. DOI: 10.1109/MNET.2024.3366560

Chiew, T. K., Khoo, S., Ansari, P., & Kiruthika, U. (2024). Mobile and wearable technologies for persons with disabilities: A bibliometric analysis (2000–2021). *Disability and Rehabilitation. Assistive Technology*, *19*(3), 994–1002. DOI: 10.1080/17483107.2022.2138996 PMID: 36306172

Chinpakdee, M., & Gu, P. Y. (2024). The impact of explicit strategy instruction on pragmatic competence in EFL learners. *Second Language Research*, *28*(1), 296–319. DOI: 10.1177/1362168821994157

Chiu, T. K. F., Moorhouse, B. L., Chai, C. S., & Ismailov, M. (2024). Teacher support and student motivation to learn with artificial intelligence (AI) based-chatbot. *Interactive Learning Environments*, *32*(7), 3240–3256. DOI: 10.1080/10494820.2023.2172044

Chung-Shing, C. H. A. N., Wong, S. Y., Agapito, D., & Veleda, T. A. M. (2025). The effect of pre-trip virtual reality and on-site smart device use on accessible tourism experiences. *Sustainable Futures : An Applied Journal of Technology, Environment and Society*, *10*, 100811. DOI: 10.1016/j.sftr.2025.100811

Çöltekin, Ç., & Rama, T. (2023). What do complexity measures measure? Correlating and validating corpus-based measures of morphological complexity. *Linguistics Vanguard : Multimodal Online Journal*, *9*(1), 27–43. DOI: 10.1515/lingvan-2021-0007

Connors, E. C., Chrastil, E. R., Sánchez, J., & Merabet, L. B. (2014). Virtual environments for the transfer of navigation skills in the blind: A comparison of directed instruction vs. video game based learning approaches. *Frontiers in Human Neuroscience*, *8*, 223. DOI: 10.3389/fnhum.2014.00223 PMID: 24822044

Cooke, A., Smith, D., & Booth, A. (2012). Beyond PICO: The SPIDER tool for qualitative evidence synthesis. *Qualitative Health Research*, *22*(10), 1435–1443. DOI: 10.1177/1049732312452938 PMID: 22829486

Corbeil, J. R., Tufan, D., & Corbeil, M. E. (2023). The effect of microlearning and multimedia design on knowledge and skills acquisition of students in e-courses. *Issues in Information Systems*, *24*(1), 342–355. DOI: 10.48009/1_iis_2023_129

Creed, C., Al-Kalbani, M., Theil, A., Sarcar, S., & Williams, I. (2024). Inclusive augmented and virtual reality: A research agenda. *International Journal of Human-Computer Interaction*, *40*(20), 6200–6219. DOI: 10.1080/10447318.2023.2247614

Cronin, J., & Durham, M. L. (2024). Microlearning: A Concept Analysis. *CIN -. Computers, Informatics, Nursing*, *42*(6), 413–420. DOI: 10.1097/CIN.0000000000001122 PMID: 38483251

Cunningham, E. (2024). *Assistive technology: Ava*. IXD@Pratt. https://ixd.prattsi.org/2024/09/assistive-technology-ava/

Daher, R. (2025). Integrating AI literacy into teacher education: a critical perspective paper. *Discover Artificial Intelligence 2025 5:1, 5*(1), 217-. DOI: 10.1007/s44163-025-00475-7

Daineko, Y., & Seitnur, A. (2025). Artificial intelligence for predictive health analytics: Challenges, methods, and immersive system integration. *Procedia Computer Science, 265*, 636–641. DOI: 10.1016/j.procs.2025.07.232

Dalton, E. M., Lyner-Cleophas, M., Ferguson, B. T., & McKenzie, J. (2019). Inclusion, universal design and universal design for learning in higher education: South Africa and the United States. *African Journal of Disability, 8*, a519. DOI: 10.4102/ajod.v8i0.519 PMID: 31392169

Darrow, A. (2025). *The UX journey of reading products at Microsoft Education. UX of EdTech.* Medium.

Das, S., Mutsuddi, I., & Ray, N. (2025). Artificial intelligence in adaptive education: A transformative approach. In Rahman, A. (Ed.), *Advancing adaptive education: Technological innovations for disability support* (pp. 30–59). IGI Global., DOI: 10.4018/979-8-3693-8227-1.ch002

Dawson, K., Antonenko, P., Lane, H., & Zhu, J. (2019). Assistive technologies to support students with dyslexia. *Teaching Exceptional Children, 51*(3), 226–239. DOI: 10.1177/0040059918794027

de Jong, C., Peter, J., Kühne, R., & Barco, A. (2022). Children's intention to adopt social robots: A model of its distal and proximal predictors. *International Journal of Social Robotics, 14*(4), 875–891. DOI: 10.1007/s12369-021-00835-0

Desmarchelier, B., Djellal, F., Gallouj, F., & Gallouj, N. (2025). Beyond the reverse product cycle: An exploration of the digital, social and spatial transformation of libraries. *Research Policy, 54*(8), 105297. DOI: 10.1016/j.respol.2025.105297

Deterding, S., Dixon, D., Khaled, R., & Nacke, L. (2011). From game design elements to gamefulness: Defining "gamification." *Proceedings of the 15th International Academic MindTrek Conference.* https://doi.org/DOI: 10.1145/2181037.2181040

Devadas, V. (2025). *AI augmented education for children with special needs: A scholarly perspective.* World Journal of Advanced Engineering Technology and Sciences., DOI: 10.30574/wjaets.2025.15.3.1125

Devaki, V., Suresh, C., & Boopathi, L. (2025). Building Teacher Skills for Effective Integration of Technology in the Classroom. Https://Services.Igi-Global.Com/Resolvedoi/Resolve.Aspx?Doi=10.4018/979-8-3373-0771-8.Ch012, 269–302. DOI: 10.4018/979-8-3373-0771-8.ch012

Dewi, S. R., Fatmawati, S., & Widodo, A. (2021). Integrating Microsoft immersive reader in SMAR model to promote students' reading comprehension. *Refleksi Edukatika: Jurnal Ilmiah Kependidikan, 11*(2), 190–196. DOI: 10.24176/re.v11i2.5354

Dhouib, A., Fadi Hijab, M. H., Chemnad, K., Al-Thani, D., & Othman, A. (2025). Advancing inclusive smart learning environments: A systematic review of technologies, challenges, and best practices for students with disabilities. *Smart Learning Environments, 12*(1), 70. DOI: 10.1186/s40561-025-00416-y

Digital India. (2023). *DIKSHA: Digital infrastructure for knowledge sharing*. Government of India.

Dong, W., Pan, D., & Kim, S. (2024). Exploring the integration of IoT and Generative AI in English language education: Smart tools for personalized learning experiences. *Journal of Computational Science, 82*, 102397. Advance online publication. DOI: 10.1016/j.jocs.2024.102397

Dumitru, C., Muttashar Abdulsahib, G., Ibrahim Khalaf, O., & Bennour, A. (2026). Integrating artificial intelligence in supporting students with disabilities in higher education: An integrative review. *Technology and Disability, 38*(1), 3–24. DOI: 10.1177/10554181251355428

Dweck, C. S. (2006). *Mindset: The new psychology of success* (1st ed.). Random House.

Ebrahimian. (2025). *Empowering Inclusive Pedagogy: Teacher's Experiences with AI-Driven Assistive Technologies in Special Needs Classrooms*. DOI: 10.21203/rs.3.rs-7408910/v1

Elder Hinshaw, R., & Sakalli Gumus, S. (2013). Universal Design for Learning principles in a hybrid course: Perceptions and practice. *SAGE Open, 3*(1), 2158244013480789. Advance online publication. DOI: 10.1177/2158244013480789

Elsadig, M., Alohali, M. A., Ibrahim, A. O., & Abulfaraj, A. W. (2024). Roles of blockchain in the metaverse: Concepts, taxonomy, recent advances, enabling technologies, and open research issues. *IEEE Access : Practical Innovations, Open Solutions, 12*, 38410–38435. DOI: 10.1109/ACCESS.2024.3367014

Elshaer, I. A., AlNajdi, S. M., & Salem, M. A. (2025). Sustainable AI Solutions for Empowering Visually Impaired Students: The Role of Assistive Technologies in Academic Success. *Sustainability 2025, Vol. 17, 17*(12). DOI: 10.3390/su17125609

Esleen, K. B., Hemalata, V., & Zety, M. Z. A. (2024). Assistive technology for the special needs people. In N. C., S. S.K., Y. L.C., C. A.C.H., P. S.K.S., & T. V. (Eds.), *AIP Conference Proceedings* (Vol. 3161, Issue 1). American Institute of Physics. DOI: 10.1063/5.0229697

Fawns, T. (2022). An entangled pedagogy: Looking beyond the pedagogy–technology dichotomy. *Postdigital Science and Education*, *4*(3), 711–728. DOI: 10.1007/s42438-022-00302-7 PMID: 40477872

Ferebee, S. (2025). *AI and Accessibility: Breaking Barriers for People with Disabilities*. DOI: 10.70389/PJAI.100012

Ferri, D., & Donnellan, K. (2022). The Implementation of the Marrakesh Directive: A Comparative Analysis across Six EU Member States. SSRN *Electronic Journal*. https://doi.org/DOI: 10.2139/SSRN.4406281

Ferri, D., & Rossello, G. (2023). The Role of the Marrakesh Treaty in Supporting Access to Printed Material for People Who Are Blind or Visually Impaired: A Critical Discussion of the Results of an Empirical Study Conducted in Six European Countries. *Disabilities 2023, Vol. 3, Pages 147-164, 3*(2), 147–164. DOI: 10.3390/disabilities3020011

Fitas, R. (2025). Inclusive education with AI: Supporting special needs and tackling language barriers. *AI and Ethics*, *5*(6), 5729–5757. DOI: 10.1007/s43681-025-00824-3

Floreo. (2024). *Virtual reality learning for neurodivergent learners*.

Foisy, L. (2024). *Boosting writing skills in K-12 dyslexic students using Read&Write*. The Alt Text Project.

Fong, K. N. K., Hai, E. Y. K., Zhang, J. J., & Lam, W. W. T. (2025). Use of advanced technologies in occupational therapy. In *Occupational Therapy in East Asia* (pp. 343–364). Routledge., DOI: 10.4324/9781032721170-18

Fortiş, A. E., Gaudo, M. V., Fazendeiro, P., Exposito, E., & Pedro, N. (2025). *Inclusive education with AI: Supporting special needs and overcoming language barriers*. In *AI in early education: Integrating artificial intelligence for inclusive and effective learning* (pp. 173–200). DOI: 10.1002/9781394352821.ch11

Gao, S. (2021). Does quantum cognition imply quantum minds? *Journal of Consciousness Studies*, *28*(3-4), 100–111.

Gayed, J. M., Carlon, M. K. J., Oriola, A. M., & Cross, J. S. (2022). Exploring an AI-based writing assistant's impact on English language learners. *Computers and Education: Artificial Intelligence*, *3*, 100055. DOI: 10.1016/j.caeai.2022.100055

Gayosso Mexia, S., Servín Gómez, A., de la Paz Hernández García, L. M., & Sánchez Granados, J. M. (2024). EIPT: Innovación Tecnológica y Ética para la Transformación de la Educación Inclusiva. *Latinskaia Amerika = América Latina*, *5*(6). Advance online publication. DOI: 10.56712/latam.v5i6.3223

Gholizadeh HamlAbadi, K., Laamarti, F., & El Saddik, A.Gholizadeh HamlAbadi. (2024). Meta-review on brain-computer interface (BCI) in the metaverse. *ACM Transactions on Multimedia Computing Communications and Applications*, *20*(12), 1–42. DOI: 10.1145/3696109

Ghugar, U., Nayak, R., & Awotunde, J. B. (2025). Enabling technologies for seamless Human-Machine interaction in industry 5.0. In *Computational Intelligence for Analysis of Trends in Industry 4.0 and 5.0* (pp. 215–240). Auerbach Publications., DOI: 10.1201/9781003533023-9

Gibbons, P. (2014). *Scaffolding language, scaffolding learning: Teaching English language learners in the mainstream classroom* (2nd ed.). Heinemann.

GingerMind Technologies. (2024). *Eye-D: AI-powered assistance for visually impaired users.*

Girhe, T., Pandya, E., & Chacko, A. M. (2024, September). Sahayak: Affordable AI enabled Assistive Technology for Intellectually Disabled. In *2024 IEEE International Conference on Signal Processing, Informatics, Communication and Energy Systems (SPICES)* (pp. 1-5). IEEE. DOI: 10.1109/SPICES62143.2024.10779644

Girish, A., & Vaidyanathan, S. (2021). Visually Impaired Persons and Access to Copyrighted Works: The Indian Roadmap. *Indonesian Journal of International Law*, *18*(4), 501–522. DOI: 10.17304/ijil.vol18.4.821

Giuliano, R. (2024). From 5G-advanced to 6G in 2030: New services, 3GPP advances, and enabling technologies. *IEEE Access : Practical Innovations, Open Solutions*, *12*, 63238–63270. DOI: 10.1109/ACCESS.2024.3396361

Godwin-Jones, R. (2022). Partnering with AI: Intelligent writing assistance and instructed language learning. *Language Learning & Technology*, *26*(2), 5–24. DOI: 10.64152/10125/73474

González-Calatayud, V., Prendes-Espinosa, P., & Roig-Vila, R. (2021). Artificial intelligence for student assessment: A systematic review. *Applied Sciences (Basel, Switzerland)*, *11*(12), 5467. DOI: 10.3390/app11125467

Gough, D. (2017). *An introduction to systematic reviews* (Gough, D., Oliver, S., & Thomas, J., Eds.; 2nd ed.). SAGE Publications. DOI: 10.4135/9781036234942

Gowrishankar, R., Dhaarani, S., Sreejaruhasini, D., & Balavignesh, P. (2025, November). Smart Assistive Wearable Glasses for the Visually Impaired. In *2025 5th International Conference on Evolutionary Computing and Mobile Sustainable Networks (ICECMSN)* (pp. 1-5). IEEE. DOI: 10.1109/ICECMSN68058.2025.11383269

Granquist, C. (2021). OrCam MyEye 1 and Seeing AI: Text recognition technologies for individuals with severe visual impairment. *Journal of Visual Impairment & Blindness.*

Grieve, A., Rouhshad, A., Petraki, E., Bechaz, A., & Dai, D. W. (2024). Nursing and midwifery students' ethical views on the acceptability of using AI machine translation software to write university assignments: A deficit-oriented or translanguaging perspective? *Journal of English for Academic Purposes, 70*, 101397. DOI: 10.1016/j.jeap.2024.101379

Hafner, C. A., & Ho, W. Y. J. (2020). Assessing digital multimodal composing in second language writing: Towards a process-based model. *Journal of Second Language Writing, 47*, 100710. DOI: 10.1016/j.jslw.2020.100710

Haim, O., Orland-Barak, L., & Goldberg, T. (2022). The role of linguistic and cultural repertoire in novice bilingual and multilingual EFL teachers' induction period. *International Journal of Multilingualism, 19*(1), 63–84. DOI: 10.1080/14790718.2020.1715412

Hamari, J., Koivisto, J., & Sarsa, H. (2014). Does gamification work? A literature review of empirical studies. *47th Hawaii International Conference on System Sciences.* https://doi.org/DOI: 10.1109/HICSS.2014.377

Hamid, M. S., Abo Hamza, E. G., Bedewy, D., Elsiddig, F. M. E., AlShammari, S. A., Bakhiet, S. F., & Mohamed, N. I. A. (2025, August). Impact of digital competencies and assistive technologies on learning outcomes for students with learning disabilities in Kingdom of Saudi Arabia: a systematic review. In *Frontiers in education* (Vol. 10, p. 1640556). Frontiers Media SA. DOI: 10.3389/feduc.2025.1640556

Hamideh Kerdar, S., Bächler, L., & Kirchhoff, B. M. (2024). The accessibility of digital technologies for people with visual impairment and blindness: a scoping review. *Discover Computing 2024 27:1, 27*(1), 24-. DOI: 10.1007/s10791-024-09460-7

Hassan, A. H., Ahmed, E. M., Hussien, J. M., Sulaiman, R., Abdulhak, M., & Kahtan, H. (2025). A cyber physical sustainable smart city framework toward society 5.0: Explainable AI for enhanced SDGs monitoring. *Research in Globalization, 10*, 100275. DOI: 10.1016/j.resglo.2025.100275

Hicks, E., Park, S., Mavrovounioti, A., Du, W., Hu, J., Na, K., Serrano, N., Munoz, R. C., Ankrah, E., Min, A., Johnson, J., & Hayes, G. R. (2025). Informing the Design of Mobile and Wearable Technology for Noise Sensitivity. *Proceedings of the ACM on Human-Computer Interaction*, *9*(5), 1–26. DOI: 10.1145/3743725

Holbert, R. M. G. (2025). Course Calendars and Routine Review to Support College Student Achievement. *College Teaching*, 1–3. Advance online publication. DOI: 10.1080/87567555.2025.2488840

Holmes, W., Bialik, M., & Fadel, C. (2019). *Artificial intelligence in education.* Center for Curriculum Redesign.

Holmes, W., Bialik, M., & Fadel, C. (2019). *Artificial Intelligence in Education: Promises and Implications for Teaching and Learning*. Center for Curriculum Redesign.

Holmes, W., & Tuomi, I. (2022). State of the art and practice in AI in education. *European Journal of Education*, *3*(4), 100074. DOI: 10.1111/ejed.12533

Hong, F., Wang, L., & Li, C. Z. (2024). Adaptive mobile cloud computing on college physical training education based on virtual reality. *Wireless Networks*, *30*(7), 6427–6450. DOI: 10.1007/s11276-023-03450-1

Hong, H., Dai, L., & Zheng, X. (2025). Advances in wearable sensors for learning analytics: Trends, challenges, and prospects. *Sensors (Basel)*, *25*(9), 2714. DOI: 10.3390/s25092714 PMID: 40363153

House, J., & Kádár, D. (2024). *Cross-cultural pragmatics and foreign language learning*. Edinburgh University Press., DOI: 10.1515/9781399523240

Hsiao, J.-C., & Chang, J. S. (2023). Enhancing EFL reading and writing through AI-powered tools: Design, implementation, and evaluation of an online course. *Interactive Learning Environments*, *32*(9), 4934–4949. DOI: 10.1080/10494820.2023.2207187

Huang, A. Y. Q., Lu, O. H. T., & Yang, S. J. H. (2023). Effects of artificial intelligence-enabled personalized recommendations on learners' learning engagement, motivation, and outcomes in a flipped classroom. *Computers & Education, 194*, 104684. DOI: 10.1016/j.compedu.2022.104684

Hutson, J., & Hutson, P. (2024). Immersive technologies. In *Inclusive smart museums: Engaging neurodiverse audiences and enhancing cultural heritage* (pp. 153–228). Springer Nature Switzerland., DOI: 10.1007/978-3-031-43615-4_5

Iliasova, L., Nekrasova, I., Mena, J., & Estrada-Molina, O. (2025). Microteaching on pre-service teachers' education: Literature review. *Frontiers in Education, 10*, 1562975. Advance online publication. DOI: 10.3389/feduc.2025.1562975

Ilic, P. (2024). Optimizing education through micro-lessons: Engaging and adaptive learning strategies. In *Optimizing Education Through Micro-Lessons: Engaging and Adaptive Learning Strategies*. IGI Global., DOI: 10.4018/979-8-3693-0195-1

Initialized Capital. (2020). *Transcribing the online and offline world for the deaf and hard-of-hearing community and beyond with Ava*. https://blog.initialized.com/2020/12/transcribing-the-online-and-offline-world-for-the-deaf-hard-of-hearing-community-and-beyond-with-ava/

Irigoyen, E., Larrea, M., & Graña, M. (2024). A narrative review of haptic technologies and their value for training, rehabilitation, and the education of persons with special needs. *Sensors (Basel), 24*(21), 6946. DOI: 10.3390/s24216946 PMID: 39517844

ISTE. (2024). *International Society for Technology in Education Standards*. ISTE. https://iste.org/standards

Jagatheesaperumal, S. K., Ahmad, K., Al-Fuqaha, A., & Qadir, J. (2024). Advancing education through extended reality and internet of everything enabled metaverses: Applications, challenges, and open issues. *IEEE Transactions on Learning Technologies, 17*, 1120–1139. DOI: 10.1109/TLT.2024.3358859

Jaiwant, S. V., & Kureethara, J. V. (2024). Evaluating the impact of microlearning and micro-lessons and implications for general education. In *Global Perspectives on Micro-Learning and Micro-Credentials in Higher Education* (pp. 159–173). IGI Global., DOI: 10.4018/979-8-3693-0343-6.ch010

Javaid, Z. K., Chen, Z., & Ramzan, M. (2024). Assessing stress causing factors and language related challenges among first-year students in higher institutions in Pakistan. *Acta Psychologica, 248*, 104356. Advance online publication. DOI: 10.1016/j.actpsy.2024.104356 PMID: 38885578

Kapp, K. M. (2012). *The gamification of learning and instruction*. Pfeiffer.

Kapralos, B., Uribe-Quevedo, A., & Dubrowski, A. (2024). Immersive technologies for medical education. In *Encyclopedia of computer graphics and games* (pp. 921–928). Springer International Publishing., DOI: 10.1007/978-3-031-23161-2_130

Karageorgou, E., Adam, S., Doukakis, S., & Vlamos, P. (2024). Digital Accessibility for Students with Disabilities and Inclusive Learning in Education. In *International Genomics, Neuroscience, Therapeutics and Data Innovation Summit* (pp. 417-424). Cham: Springer Nature Switzerland. DOI: 10.1007/978-3-032-03402-1_44

Kasneci, E., Sessler, K., Küchemann, S., Bannert, M., Dementieva, D., Fischer, F., Gasser, U., Groh, G., Gunnermann, S., Hüllermeier, E., Krusche, S., Kutyniok, G., Michaeli, T., Nerdel, C., Pfeffer, J., Poquet, O., Sailer, M., Schmidt, A., Seidel, T., & Kasneci, G. (2023). ChatGPT for good? On opportunities and challenges of large language models for education. *Learning and Individual Differences*, *103*, 102274. DOI: 10.1016/j.lindif.2023.102274

Kathiria, P., Mankad, S. H., Patel, J., Kapadia, M., & Lakdawala, N. (2024). Assistive systems for visually impaired people: A survey on current requirements and advancements. *Neurocomputing*, *606*, 128284. DOI: 10.1016/j.neucom.2024.128284

Katke, S. R., & Pacharaney, U. (2024, November). Smart Solutions for Visual Impairment by AI-Based Assistive Devices. In *2024 2nd DMIHER International Conference on Artificial Intelligence in Healthcare, Education and Industry (IDICAIEI)* (pp. 1-5). IEEE. DOI: 10.1109/IDICAIEI61867.2024.10842872

Kchaou, M., Munusamy, Y., Alharthi, K. A., & Al-Mahmodi, A. F. (2025). Industry 5.0 adaptation for disability-inclusive healthcare: A review of emergent and AI technologies for assistive digital health. *Digital Health*, *11*, 20552076251395558. DOI: 10.1177/20552076251395558 PMID: 41229932

Kellems, R. O. (2025). *A systematic review of immersive virtual reality interventions for autism spectrum disorder*. Information Journal.

Khan, M. A., Kurbonova, O., Abdullaev, D., Radie, A. H., & Basim, N. (2024). Is AI-assisted assessment liable to evaluate young learners? Parents' support, teacher support, immunity, and resilience are in focus in testing vocabulary learning. *Language Testing in Asia*, *14*(1), 48. DOI: 10.1186/s40468-024-00324-x

Kilian, K. A., Ventura, C. J., & Bailey, M. M. (2023). Examining the differential risk from high-level artificial intelligence and the question of control. *Futures, The Journal of Policy. Futures*, *151*, 103182. DOI: 10.1016/j.futures.2023.103182

Kirongo, A. C., Huka, G., Bundi, D., Kitaria, D., & Muchiri, G. (2022). Implementation of AI-based assistive technologies for learners with physical disabilities in areas of innovation and special schools: A practical design thinking approach. African Journal of Science. *Technology and Social Sciences*, *1*(2), 73–76. DOI: 10.58506/ajstss.v1i2.124

Kohnke, S., & Zaugg, T. (2025). Artificial Intelligence: An Untapped Opportunity for Equity and Access in STEM Education. *Education Sciences*, *15*(1), 68. DOI: 10.3390/educsci15010068

Kooli, C., & Chakraoui, R. (2025). AI-driven assistive technologies in inclusive education: Benefits, challenges, and policy recommendations. *Sustainable Futures : An Applied Journal of Technology, Environment and Society*, *10*, 101042. DOI: 10.1016/j.sftr.2025.101042

Koranteng, U. (2025). *Designing the AI-Inclusive Framework (AIF): Integrating artificial intelligence, assistive technology, and universal design for learning in inclusive education. SSRN*. https://doi.org/DOI: 10.2139/ssrn.6088026

Krasniqi, V., Zdravkova, K., & Dalipi, F. (2022). Impact of assistive technologies on inclusive education and independent life of Down syndrome persons: A systematic literature review and research agenda. *Sustainability (Basel)*, *14*(8), 4630. DOI: 10.3390/su14084630

Kumar, P., & Rao, S. (2025). Empowering educators: Evaluating DIKSHA and SWAYAM for digital teacher training and economic inclusion in India.

Kumaravadivelu, B. (2012). *Language teacher education for a global society: A modular model for knowing, analyzing, recognizing, doing, and seeing*. Routledge., DOI: 10.4324/9780203832530

Kumar, S. (2025). AI and inclusive education: Opportunities and challenges. *International Journal of Scientific Research in Modern Science and Technology*, *4*(9), 92–100. Advance online publication. DOI: 10.59828/ijsrmst.v4i9.375

Lata, P. (2024). Towards equitable learning: Exploring artificial intelligence in inclusive education. *SSRN*, *7*, 416. DOI: 10.2139/ssrn.4987156

Lavric, A.. (2024). A comprehensive survey on emerging assistive technologies for visually impaired individuals. *Sensors (Basel)*. Advance online publication. DOI: 10.3390/s24154834

Le, R. (2025). Transformative AI Tools for Inclusive and Holistic Learning Environments. *Advances in Computational Intelligence and Robotics Book Series*, 469–492. DOI: 10.4018/979-8-3373-5097-4.ch017

Lee, D., Arnold, M., Srivastava, A., Plastow, K., Strelan, P., Ploeckl, F., Lekkas, D., & Palmer, E. (2024). The impact of generative AI on higher education learning and teaching: A study of educators' perspectives. *Computers and Education: Artificial Intelligence*, *6*, 100221. DOI: 10.1016/j.caeai.2024.100221

Le, T. T. T., & Nguyen, N. T. T. (2025). Exploring psychological challenges in higher education: Prevalence, causes, and impacts on student well-being and academic performance. *International Journal of Education and Practice*, *13*(4), 1246–1257. DOI: 10.18488/61.v13i4.4405

Liginlal, D., & Al-Emadi, S. (2026). Digital accessibility and equity: The need for stronger regulations and the imperative of innovation. *Universal Access in the Information Society*, *25*(2), 37. DOI: 10.1007/s10209-025-01305-4

Li, J., Yuyang, Y., & Xiaojun, Z. (2025). Exploring artificial intelligence in inclusive education: A systematic review of empirical studies. *Applied Sciences (Basel, Switzerland)*, *15*(23), 12624. DOI: 10.3390/app152312624

Lin, C.-H., Zhou, K., Li, L., & Sun, L. (2025). Integrating generative AI into digital multimodal composition: A study of multicultural second-language classrooms. *Computers and Composition*, *75*, 102895. DOI: 10.1016/j.compcom.2024.102895

Liu, J., Bleakney, A. W., Cheung, W. C., Yu, H., Cao, C., & Jan, Y. K. (2025). Emerging assistive technologies in paralympic sports: A systematic review. *Disability and Rehabilitation. Assistive Technology*, •••, 1–28. DOI: 10.1080/17483107.2025.2597408 PMID: 41403368

Liu, Z., He, Y., Demian, P., & Osmani, M. (2024). Immersive technology and building information modeling (BIM) for sustainable smart cities. *Buildings (Basel, Switzerland)*, *14*(6), 1765. DOI: 10.3390/buildings14061765

Li, W., Song, R., Zhang, B., & Yu, K. (2025). AI creativity and legal protection for AI-generated works in posthuman societal scenarios. *Sustainable Futures : An Applied Journal of Technology, Environment and Society*, *9*, 100749. DOI: 10.1016/j.sftr.2025.100749

Luckin, R., Holmes, W., Griffiths, M., & Forcier, L. (2016). *Intelligence unleashed: An argument for AI in education*. Pearson.

Macias Leon, H. A. (2025). *Estrategias de enseñanza basadas en inteligencia artificial para lograr un aprendizaje personalizado, inclusivo y centrado en las necesidades individuales de cada estudiante*. *4*(3), 81–93. https://doi.org/DOI: 10.64041/riidg.v4i3.50

Mageira, K., Pittou, D., Papasalouros, A., Kotis, K., Zangogianni, P., & Daradoumis, A. (2022). Educational AI chatbots for content and language integrated learning. *Applied Sciences (Basel, Switzerland)*, *12*(7), 3239. DOI: 10.3390/app12073239

Mager, A., Eitenberger, M., Winter, J., Prainsack, B., Wendehorst, C., & Arora, P. (2025). Situated ethics: Ethical accountability of local perspectives in global AI ethics. *Media Culture & Society*, *47*(5), 1028–1041. DOI: 10.1177/01634437251328200

Mahmoudi-Dehaki, M., Nasr-Esfahani, N., & Vasan, S. (2025). The Transformative Role of Assistive Technology in Enhancing Quality of Life for Individuals With Disabilities. In *Assistive Technology Solutions for Aging Adults and Individuals with Disabilities* (pp. 45–72). IGI Global., DOI: 10.4018/9798369363089.ch003

Mais, A., & Yauma, L. A. (2026). Inclusive education in the digital age: A systematic literature review on assistive technology development. *Multidisciplinary Reviews*, *9*(5), e2026223. DOI: 10.31893/multirev.2026223

Malviya, R., & Rajput, S. (2025). AI-driven innovations in assistive technology for people with disabilities. In *Advances and Insights into AI-Created Disability Supports* (pp. 61–77). Springer Nature Singapore., DOI: 10.1007/978-981-96-6069-8_4

Mancusi, L. (2024). Using AI applications to lead teacher-directed vocabulary-building activities for multilingual learners. *The ORTESOL Journal*, *41*, 49–52.

Martinez-Hernandez, U., Metcalfe, B., Assaf, T., Jabban, L., Male, J., & Zhang, D. (2021). Wearable assistive robotics: A perspective on current challenges and future trends. *Sensors (Basel)*, *21*(20), 6751. Advance online publication. DOI: 10.3390/s21206751 PMID: 34695964

Massola, G. (2023). Curriculum and technology: Use of digital devices to promote inclusion and autonomy in learning. Seven Editora. https://sevenpublicacoes.com.br/editora/article/view/672

McIntyre, N. A. (2022). Access to online learning: Machine learning analysis from a social justice perspective. *Education and Information Technologies 2022 28:4*, *28*(4), 3787–3832. DOI: 10.1007/s10639-022-11280-5

Melo-López, V. A., Basantes-Andrade, A., Gudiño-Mejía, C. B., & Hernández-Martínez, E. (2025). The impact of artificial intelligence on inclusive education: A systematic review. *Education Sciences*, *15*(5), 539. DOI: 10.3390/educsci15050539

Memisevic, H., & Hadžić, S. (2025). Assistive Technology in Inclusive Education. In *The Palgrave Encyclopedia of Disability* (pp. 1–8). Springer Nature Switzerland., DOI: 10.1007/978-3-031-40858-8_508-1

Meyer, A., Rose, D. H., & Gordon, D. (2014). *Universal design for learning: Theory and practice*. CAST Professional Publishing.

Microsoft. (2024). *Microsoft Immersive Reader overview*. Microsoft Learn.

Milde, N., Schmidt, D. C., Larsen, A., & Kessel, L. (2024). Which rehabilitation initiatives can effectively improve participation in an educational setting for visually impaired and blind adolescents? A systematic review. *BMC Ophthalmology 2023 24:1, 24*(1), 10-. DOI: 10.1186/s12886-023-03267-8

Mina, P. N. R., Solon, I. M., Sanchez, F. R., Delante, T. K., Villegas, J. K., Basay, F. J., Andales, J., Pasko, F., Estrera, M. F. R., Samson, R.Jr, & Mutya, R. (2023). Leveraging Education through Artificial Intelligence Virtual Assistance: A Case Study of Visually Impaired Learners. *International Journal of Educational Innovation and Research, 2*(1), 10–22. DOI: 10.31949/ijeir.v2i1.3001

Mirzaeian, V. R., & Oskoui, K. (2023). Google Translate in foreign language learning: A systematic review. *Applied Research on English Language, 12*(2), 51–84. DOI: 10.22108/are.2023.134264.1949

Mishra, P., & Koehler, M. J. (2006). Technological pedagogical content knowledge: A framework for teacher knowledge. *Teachers College Record, 108*(6), 1017–1054. DOI: 10.1111/j.1467-9620.2006.00684.x

Mokoro, E. (2024). Pragmatic competence in second language learners. *European Journal of Linguistics, 3*(2), 15–28. DOI: 10.47941/ejl.2044

Monib, W. K., Qazi, A., & Apong, R. A. (2025). Microlearning beyond boundaries: A systematic review and a novel framework for improving learning outcomes. *Heliyon, 11*(2), e41413. Advance online publication. DOI: 10.1016/j.heliyon.2024.e41413 PMID: 39882484

Moreira, F. T., Vairinhos, M., & Ramos, F. (2024). Teachers' perceptions about IoT technologies in school activities. *Educational Media International, 61*(1–2), 184–197. DOI: 10.1080/09523987.2024.2358655

Muhsin, Z. J., Qahwaji, R., Ghanchi, F., & Al-Taee, M. (2023). Review of substitutive assistive tools and technologies for people with visual impairments: recent advancements and prospects. *Journal on Multimodal User Interfaces 2023 18:1, 18*(1), 135–156. DOI: 10.1007/s12193-023-00427-4

Naik, A. S. (2024, June). Assistive Technology in Banking. In *2024 15th International Conference on Computing Communication and Networking Technologies (ICCCNT)* (pp. 1-6). IEEE. DOI: 10.1109/ICCCNT61001.2024.10724888

Navas-Bonilla, C. D. R., Guerra-Arango, J. A., Oviedo-Guado, D. A., & Murillo-Noriega, D. E. (2025, February). Inclusive education through technology: a systematic review of types, tools and characteristics. In *Frontiers in Education* (Vol. 10, p. 1527851). Frontiers Media SA. DOI: 10.3389/feduc.2025.1527851

Nazari, N., Shabbir, M. S., & Setiawan, R. (2021). Application of artificial intelligence powered digital writing assistant in higher education: Randomized controlled trial. *Heliyon*, *7*(5), e07014. DOI: 10.1016/j.heliyon.2021.e07014 PMID: 34027198

Nemorin, S., Vlachidis, A., Ayerakwa, H. M., & Andriotis, P. (2023). AI hyped? A horizon scan of discourse on artificial intelligence in education (AIED) and development. *Learning, Media and Technology*, *48*(1), 38–51. DOI: 10.1080/17439884.2022.2095568

OECD. (2021). *OECD Digital Education Outlook 2021: Pushing the frontiers with AI, blockchain and robots*. OECD Publishing., DOI: 10.1787/589b283f-

OECD. (2023). Digital education outlook 2021: Pushing the frontiers with AI, blockchain and robots. https://doi.org/10.1787/589b283f-en

Ogoshi, S., Ogoshi, Y., Saitoh, T., Tanaka, K., Itoh, Y., Wakamatu, M., & Nakai, A. (2023). Individual Education Support System Using ICT for Developmental Disabilities. In *Cognitive Behavioral Therapy-Basic Principles and Application Areas*. IntechOpen. DOI: 10.5772/intechopen.106065

Omosunlade, O. S. (2025). Digital inclusion in special education with AI-assisted curriculum models for Autism, Cerebral palsy, and Down syndrome. *World Journal Of Advanced Research and Reviews*, *25*(2), 2793–2804. DOI: 10.30574/wjarr.2025.25.2.0501

Opesemowo, O. A. G. (2024). Artificial Intelligence in Education, Bridging Community Gap: A Phenomenological Approach. *International Journal of Nursing Education*, *14*(14). Advance online publication. DOI: 10.24310/ijne.14.2024.20505

OrCam. (2024). *OrCam MyEye assistive technology for people with visual impairments.*

Örün, Ö., & Türk, M. (2026). Bridging the Gap: The Role of Immersive Technologies for Learners With Disabilities. In *Practical Perspectives on Inclusive and Immersive Learning Environments* (pp. 27-58). IGI Global Scientific Publishing. DOI: 10.4018/979-8-3373-5188-9.ch002

Page, M. J., McKenzie, J. E., Bossuyt, P. M., Boutron, I., Hoffmann, T. C., Mulrow, C. D., Shamseer, L., Tetzlaff, J. M., Akl, E. A., Brennan, S. E., Chou, R., Glanville, J., Grimshaw, J. M., Hróbjartsson, A., Lalu, M. M., Li, T., Loder, E. W., Mayo-Wilson, E., McDonald, S., … Moher, D. (2021). The PRISMA 2020 statement: An updated guideline for reporting systematic reviews. *International Journal of Surgery, (London, England), 88*, 105906. https://doi.org/DOI: 10.1016/j.ijsu.2021.105906

Pagliara, S. M., Bonavolontà, G., Pia, M., Falchi, S., Zurru, A. L., Fenu, G., & Mura, A. (2024). The integration of artificial intelligence in inclusive education: A scoping review. *Information (Basel), 15*(12), 774. DOI: 10.3390/info15120774

Pamuji, Nerri, I. A., & Niratama, F. (2023). *Literature Review: Enhancing Education Accessibility: The Role of Assistive Technology in Promoting Equality for the Visually Impaired.* 1159–1171. DOI: 10.2991/978-2-38476-152-4_118

Panda, S., & Kaur, Dr. N. (2024). Quality Education for Visually Impaired: Achieving Sustainable Development Goal 04 through Web Accessibility Measures. *SSRN Electronic Journal*. DOI: 10.2139/ssrn.4857711

Pang, H., Jin, X., & Zhang, W. (2025). Deciphering the underlying repercussions of cognitive overload on university students' fatigue, frustration and academic productivity: Implementation of stimulus–organism–response model. *Acta Psychologica, 260*, 105469. Advance online publication. DOI: 10.1016/j.actpsy.2025.105469 PMID: 40885176

Perry, N., Sun, C., Munro, M., Boulton, K. A., & Guastella, A. J. (2024). AI technology to support adaptive functioning in neurodevelopmental conditions in everyday environments: A systematic review. *NPJ Digital Medicine*, *7*(1), 370. DOI: 10.1038/s41746-024-01355-7 PMID: 39702672

Peters, D., Calvo, R. A., & Ryan, R. M. (2018). Designing for Motivation, Engagement and Wellbeing in Digital Experience. *Frontiers in Psychology*, *9*, 797. Advance online publication. DOI: 10.3389/fpsyg.2018.00797 PMID: 29892246

Phutane, M., Jung, C., Chen, N., & Azenkot, S. (2023). Speaking with My Screen Reader: Using Audio Fictions to Explore Conversational Access to Interfaces. *ASSETS 2023 - Proceedings of the 25th International ACM SIGACCESS Conference on Computers and Accessibility*. https://doi.org/DOI: 10.1145/3597638.3608404;PAGE:STRING:ARTICLE/CHAPTER

Pieriboni, G., Buzzi, M., & Leporini, B. (2026). Stem education and ICT-enhanced tools for students with disabilities: A five-year review. *Universal Access in the Information Society*, *25*(1), 3. DOI: 10.1007/s10209-025-01282-8

Piyathanavong, V., Huynh, V. N., Karnjana, J., & Olapiriyakul, S. (2024). Role of project management on sustainable supply chain development through Industry 4.0 technologies and circular economy during the COVID-19 pandemic. *Operations Management Research : Advancing Practice Through Research*, *17*(1), 13–37. DOI: 10.1007/s12063-022-00283-7

Plass, J. L., Homer, B. D., & Kinzer, C. K. (2015). Foundations of game-based learning. *Educational Psychologist, 50*(4), 258–283. DOI: 10.1080/00461520.2015.1122533

Plass, J. L., Mayer, R. E., & Homer, B. D. (2020). *Handbook of game-based learning*. Mit Press.

Poggianti, C., Chessa, S., Pelagatti, S., & Kocian, A. (2025). Immersive technologies for inclusive digital education: A systematic survey. *Human Behavior and Emerging Technologies, 2025*(1), 8888303. DOI: 10.1155/hbe2/8888303

Popay, J., Roberts, H., Sowden, A., Petticrew, M., Arai, L., Rodgers, M., Britten, N., Roen, K., & Duffy, S. (2006). Guidance on the conduct of narrative synthesis in systematic reviews: *A product from the ESRC methods programme Version* 1(1), b92.

Popenici, S., Rudolph, J., Tan, S., & Tan, S. (2023). A critical perspective on generative AI and learning futures. An interview with Stefan Popenici. *Journal of Applied Learning & Teaching, 6*(2), 311–331. DOI: 10.37074/jalt.2023.6.2.5

Pothos, E. M., & Busemeyer, J. R. (2022). Quantum cognition. *Annual Review of Psychology, 73*(1), 749–778. DOI: 10.1146/annurev-psych-033020-123501

Pourdana, N., & Tavassoli, K. (2022). Differential impacts of e-portfolio assessment on language learners' engagement modes and genre-based writing improvement. *Language Testing in Asia, 12*(1), 7. Advance online publication. DOI: 10.1186/s40468-022-00156-7

Pradeep, A. (2023). Empowering Special Education Through Information Technology. *Proceedings of the International Conference on Circuit Power and Computing Technologies, ICCPCT 2023*, 31–34. DOI: 10.1109/ICCPCT58313.2023.10245240

Prakash, S., Agrawal, K., Singh, S., Aggarwal, G., & Dosaj, S. (2023). *Voice Based Email System for the Visually Challenged*. DOI: 10.21203/rs.3.rs-2982553/v1

Prestridge, S. (2024). *Pedagogical beliefs matter: Technologies "more" in the age of disruptive technologies*. In *SITE 2024: 35th International Conference of the Society for Information Technology and Teacher Education*. Association for the Advancement of Computing in Education. *Research Highlights in Technology & Teacher Education 2024: 35th Anniversary Edition*. Association for the Advancement of Computing in Education (AACE).

Pundlik, S., Shivshanker, P., & Luo, G. (2024).. . *Impact of Apps as Assistive Devices for Visually Impaired Persons., 55*, 9. DOI: 10.1146/annurev-vision-111022

Que, L., Zhu, Q., Jiang, C., & Lu, Q. (2025). An analysis of the global, regional, and national burden of blindness and vision loss between 1990 and 2021: The findings of the Global Burden of Disease Study 2021. *Frontiers in Public Health, 13*, 1560449. DOI: 10.3389/fpubh.2025.1560449 PMID: 40365429

Radianti, J., Majchrzak, T. A., Fromm, J., & Wohlgenannt, I. (2020). A systematic review of immersive virtual reality applications for higher education. *Computers & Education, 147*, 103778. DOI: 10.1016/j.compedu.2019.103778

Ramalakshmi, K., Kumari, L. K., Mohan, B., Gunturi, S. K., Santhoshkumar, S. P., Krishnan, R. S., & Raj, J. R. F. (2026). Harnessing Immersive Technologies: Insights Into Augmented and Virtual Reality Applications. In *AI Applications in Instructional Education Strategies* (pp. 171-188). IGI Global Scientific Publishing. DOI: 10.4018/979-8-3373-0598-1.ch007

Ravindran, V., Osgood, M., Sazawal, V., Solorzano, R., & Turnacioglu, S. (2019). Virtual reality support for joint attention using the Floreo joint attention module: Usability and feasibility pilot study. *JMIR Pediatrics and Parenting, 2*(2), e14429. DOI: 10.2196/14429 PMID: 31573921

Reiss, M. J. (2021). The use of AI in education: Practicalities and ethical considerations. *London Review of Education, 19*(1), 1–14. DOI: 10.14324/LRE.19.1.05

Ricci, F. S., Liguori, L., Palermo, E., Rizzo, J.-R., & Porfiri, M. (2024). Navigation Training for Persons With Visual Disability Through Multisensory Assistive Technology: Mixed Methods Experimental Study. *JMIR Rehabilitation and Assistive Technologies, 11*(1), e55776. DOI: 10.2196/55776 PMID: 39556804

Richelli, A., Stocchetti, N., Gasparini, C., Montanari, S., Rozzini, L., & Gringoli, F. (2025, November). Towards Fully Accessible Digital Content: A Haptic-VR Workflow for Blind Users. In *Proceedings of the 3rd ACM Workshop on Mobile Immersive Computing, Networking, and Systems* (pp. 9-14). DOI: 10.1145/3742889.3768346

Riguzzi, F. (2023). *Foundations of Probabilistic Logic Programming: Languages, semantics, inference and learning*. River Publishers. DOI: 10.1201/9781003427421

Riyat, M. K., Kakkar, R. K., & Kakkar, A. (2025). Creating Immersive Learning Experiences in Education Domain Through Virtual and Augmented Reality. In *Enhancing Learning Experiences With Digital Tools: AI, ChatGPT, and Virtual and Augmented Reality* (pp. 123–156). IGI Global Scientific Publishing., DOI: 10.4018/979-8-3693-9811-1.ch006

Roul, R., & Mohalik, R. (2025). Quality of e-content on DIKSHA platform. *International Education and Research Journal.*

Roy, B., Ghosh, S., Sarkar, S. K., Sen, A., & Choudhury, N. R. (2025). Implications of Artificial Intelligence for Special Education Technology. In Walters, A. (Ed.), *Transforming Special Education Through Artificial Intelligence* (pp. 401–430). IGI Global Scientific Publishing., DOI: 10.4018/979-8-3693-5538-1.ch015

Ryan, R. M., & Deci, E. L. (2000). Self-determination theory and the facilitation of intrinsic motivation, social development, and well-being. *The American Psychologist*, *55*(1), 68–78. DOI: 10.1037/0003-066X.55.1.68 PMID: 11392867

Ryan, R. M., & Deci, E. L. (2020). Intrinsic and extrinsic motivation from a self-determination theory perspective: Definitions, theory, practices, and future directions. *Contemporary Educational Psychology*, *61*, 101860. DOI: 10.1016/j.cedpsych.2020.101860

Rybenská, K., Knapová, L., Janiš, K., Kühnová, J., Cimler, R., & Elavsky, S. (2024). SMART technologies in older adult care: A scoping review and guide for caregivers. *Journal of Enabling Technologies*, *18*(4), 200–222. DOI: 10.1108/JET-05-2023-0016

Saabi, N., Chlioui, I., & Radgui, M. (2025). A Review of Assistive Technology in Special Education. *Engineering Proceedings*, *112*(1), 45. DOI: 10.3390/engproc2025112045

Saborío-Taylor, S., & Rojas-Ramírez, F. (2024). Universal design for learning and artificial intelligence in the digital era: Fostering inclusion and autonomous learning. International Journal of Professional Development. *Learners and Learning*, *6*(2), ep2408. Advance online publication. DOI: 10.30935/ijpdll/14694

Sailer, M., Hense, J., Mayr, S., & Mandl, H. (2017). How gamification motivates: An experimental study. *Computers in Human Behavior*, *69*, 371–380. DOI: 10.1016/j.chb.2016.12.033

Salama, A. M., & Patil, M. P. (2025). The socius in architectural pedagogy: Transformative design studio teaching models. *Architecture (Washington, D.C.)*, *5*(3), 61. DOI: 10.3390/architecture5030061

Salendab, F. A., Cogo, D. A., Catipay, A. Z., & Millendez, G. J. T. (2025). The Role of Artificial Intelligence (AI) in Personalized Learning and Adaptive Assessments. *Advances in Computational Intelligence and Robotics Book Series*, 93–122. DOI: 10.4018/979-8-3373-2185-1.ch004

Santos, J., Vieira, M., Fernandes, D., Félix, J., Rodrigues, W., Soares, F., & Nascimento, T. H. (2025, November). Low-Cost Immersive Molecule Visualization from Hand-Drawn Smartwatch Input for Virtual Reality Learning. In *International Symposium on Visual Computing* (pp. 236-246). Cham: Springer Nature Switzerland. DOI: 10.1007/978-3-032-14495-9_18

Santos, C. M. (2025). Improving reading comprehension skills in English for Grade 4 pupils through Microsoft immersive reader. *Asia Pacific Higher Education Research Journal, 12*(1), 1–17. DOI: 10.56278/apherj.v12i1.3198

Sarkar, R., & Madhu, R. (2025). Ensuring Equity and Access for Students With Disabilities. *Advances in Computational Intelligence and Robotics Book Series*, 93–138. https://doi.org/DOI: 10.4018/979-8-3373-5097-4.ch004

Schindler, L. A., Burkholder, G. J., Morad, O. A., & Marsh, C. (2017). Computer-based technology and student engagement: A critical review. *International Journal of Educational Technology in Higher Education, 14*(25), 25. Advance online publication. DOI: 10.1186/s41239-017-0063-0

Segura-Castillo, M. A., & Quirós-Acuña, M. (2019). Desde el Diseño Universal para el Aprendizaje: El estudiantado al aprender se evalúa y al evaluarle aprende. *Review of Education*, •••, 643–655. DOI: 10.15517/revedu.v43i1.28449

Selwyn, N. (2019). *Should robots replace teachers? AI and the future of education*. Polity Press.

Shafik, W. (2025). Emerging Trends and Technological Innovations and People with Disabilities and the Marginalized. *Global Sustainable Transition with Inclusion: A Focus on the People with Disabilities and the Marginalized*, 293-325. DOI: 10.1007/978-981-96-6557-0_11

Shaheen, H. R. A. (2025). The Role of Assistive Technology in Enhancing Learning Outcomes for Students with Educational Disabilities: Teachers' Perceptions in Amman Schools. *Journal of Educational and Social Research, 15*(6), 208–217. DOI: 10.36941/jesr-2025-0209

Shaikh, S., Yayilgan, S. Y., Klimova, B., & Pikhart, M. (2023). Assessing the usability of ChatGPT for formal English language learning. *European Journal of Investigation in Health, Psychology and Education, 13*(9), 1937–1960. DOI: 10.3390/ejihpe13090140 PMID: 37754479

Shang, F., Duan, W., & Xu, L. (2024). *Enhancing intercultural communication skills: The impact of drama in Chinese language teaching*. Language Teaching Research. LTR., DOI: 10.1177/13621688241266941

Shankar, S. K., Pothancheri, G., Sasi, D., & Mishra, S. (2025). Bringing teachers in the loop: Exploring perspectives on integrating generative AI in technology-enhanced learning. *International Journal of Artificial Intelligence in Education, 35*(1), 155–180. DOI: 10.1007/s40593-024-00428-8

Shapiro, K., Ravindran, V., Downing, G., Stepensky, M. R., Mak-Parisi, S., Solorzano, R., Barbayannis, G., & Turnacioglu, S. (2025). Children with Autism Using the Floreo Virtual Reality Building Social Connections Module: A Feasibility Study. *Autism-Open Access, 15*(2), 436. DOI: 10.35248/2165-7890.25.15.436

Sharma, S., Dureja, S., Saini, D., Jose, R., Pant, R., & Singh, A. (2025). Empowering impaired learners: Technological advancements in higher education. *Technology and Disability, 37*(2), 123–136. DOI: 10.1177/10554181251313711

Shireesha, M., & Jeevan, J. (2024). The role of artificial intelligence in personalized learning: A pathway to inclusive education. *Library of Progress – Library Science, Information Technology & Computer*, 44(3).

Shobeiry, M. (2024). *The PIPE educational model* [ ]. Academic Center for Education, Culture, and Research (ACECR). Tehran.

Shobeiry, M. (2021). Pragmatic functions of formulaic expressions of embarrassment in Persian refusals: A qualitative study. *Journal of International Social Research, 14*(76), 33–41. DOI: 10.17719/jisr.11353

Shobeiry, M. (2026). Spelling Improvement and Motivation Through Gamification and Mobile Apps. In Moreira, F. T., & Teles, R. (Eds.), *Engaging Learners With Immersive Technologies and Game-Based Learning* (pp. 189–220). IGI Global Scientific Publishing., DOI: 10.4018/979-8-3373-4465-2.ch008

Silva, E. S., Costa, W. P. D., Lima, J. C. D., & Ferreira, J. C. (2025). Contribution of Microlearning in Basic Education: A Systematic Review. *Education Sciences, 15*(3), 302. Advance online publication. DOI: 10.3390/educsci15030302

Singh, S., Srivastava, N., Gupta, S., Singh, A., & Kalpana, K. (2025). Evolution of assistive technology applications featuring innovative solution "Harmony Assist." In T. M., S. S.K., S. P., K. S., & K. D. (Eds.), *AIP Conference Proceedings* (Vol. 3297, Issue 1). American Institute of Physics. DOI: 10.1063/5.0285926

Smith, J., & Downes, K. (2023). Implications for initial teacher education (ITE) programs in preparing mainstream teachers for culturally and linguistically diverse classrooms. *TESOL in Context, 32*(1), 97–108. DOI: 10.21153/tesol2023vol32no1art1827

Smith, S. J., & Basham, J. D. (2014). Designing Online Learning Opportunities for Students with Disabilities. *Teaching Exceptional Children*, *46*(5), 127–137. DOI: 10.1177/0040059914530102

Srivastava, K. (2025). *Leveraging Artificial Intelligence for Sustainable and Inclusive Education: Opportunities, Challenges, and Recommendations*. 361–376. DOI: 10.1201/9781998511471-18

Srivathsa, B. S., Pandey, H., & Naganandini, G. (2025). Future Trends in Education: The Impact of AI, Data Science, and Immersive Technologies. In *Driving Quality Education Through AI and Data Science* (pp. 139-164). IGI Global Scientific Publishing. DOI: 10.4018/979-8-3693-8292-9.ch007

Stelea, G. A., Robu, D., & Sandu, F. (2025). AccessiLearnAI: An Accessibility-First, AI-Powered E-Learning Platform for Inclusive Education. *Education Sciences*, *15*(9), 1125. DOI: 10.3390/educsci15091125

Stern, C., Jordan, Z., & McArthur, A. (2014). Developing the review question and inclusion criteria: The first steps in conducting a systematic review. *The American Journal of Nursing*, *114*(4), 53–56. DOI: 10.1097/01.NAJ.0000445689.67800.86 PMID: 24681476

Stinson, M., Elliot, L., & Kelly, R. (2020). Captioning and speech-to-text technologies in education for deaf and hard-of-hearing students. *Journal of Special Education Technology*.

Sumakul, D. T. Y. G., Hamied, F. A., & Sukyadi, D. (2022). Students' perceptions of the use of AI in a writing class. In Proceedings of the 67th TEFLIN International Virtual Conference & the 9th ICOELT 2021 (Advances in Social Science, Education and Humanities Research, Vol. 624, pp. 52–57). Atlantis Press. DOI: 10.2991/assehr.k.220201.009

Sun, J. (2024). The Impact of Artificial Intelligence on Personalized Learning in Education: A Systematic Review. *Pakistan Journal of Life and Social Sciences*, *22*(2). Advance online publication. DOI: 10.57239/PJLSS-2024-22.2.00560

Suresh, C., Mahammad Ali, S., & Devaki, V. (2025). Perception About Usage of GAI Tools in Teaching and Research by Teachers and Students in Higher Education Institutions. Https://Services.Igi-Global.Com/Resolvedoi/Resolve.Aspx?Doi=10.4018/979-8-3693-8191-5.Ch015, 381–412. DOI: 10.4018/979-8-3693-8191-5.ch015

Susilana, R., Dewi, L., Rullyana, G., Hadiapurwa, A., & Khaerunnisa, N. (2022). Can microlearning strategy assist students' online learning? *Cakrawala Pendidikan*, *41*(2), 437–451. DOI: 10.21831/cp.v41i2.43387

Svensson, I. (2021). Effects of assistive technology for students with reading and writing difficulties. *Disability and Rehabilitation. Assistive Technology*. Advance online publication. DOI: 10.1080/17483107.2019.1646821 PMID: 31418305

Taguchi, N., & Roever, C. (2017). *Second language pragmatics*. Oxford University Press.

Tai, T.-Y., & Chen, H. H.-J. (2024). The impact of intelligent personal assistants on adolescent EFL learners' speaking proficiency. *Computer Assisted Language Learning*, *37*(5-6), 1224–1251. DOI: 10.1080/09588221.2022.2070219

Tegon, R. (2021). Toward the 4th Agenda 2030 Goal. *Handbook of Research on Teaching With Virtual Environments and AI*. DOI:DOI: 10.4018/978-1-7998-7638-0.ch025

Texthelp. (2025). *Read&Write for education*. Texthelp.

Thabet, S., Ateya, A. A., ElAffendi, M., & Abo-Zahhad, M. (2025). MEC and SDN Enabling Technologies, Design Challenges, and Future Directions of Tactile Internet and Immersive Communications. *Future Internet*, *17*(11), 494. DOI: 10.3390/fi17110494

Thakur, N., Chouskey, P., Bansal, N., & Chopra, M. (2024). Systematic review of recent trends of Industry 5.0 with assistive technologies in higher education and smart healthcare. *Applied assistive technologies and informatics for students with disabilities*, 277-299. DOI: 10.1007/978-981-97-0914-4_16

Tohănean, D. I., Vulpe, A. M., Mijaica, R., & Alexe, D. I. (2025). Embedding digital technologies (AI and ICT) into physical education: A systematic review of innovations, pedagogical impact, and challenges. *Applied Sciences (Basel, Switzerland)*, *15*(17), 9826. DOI: 10.3390/app15179826

Toto, G. A., Marinelli, C. V., Cavioni, V., Di Furia, M., Traetta, L., Iuso, S., & Petito, A. (2024). What is the role of technologies for inclusive education? A systematic review. In *International conference on higher education learning methodologies and technologies online* (pp. 533-565). Springer, Cham. DOI: 10.1007/978-3-031-67351-1_36

Tour, E., Pegrum, M., & Macdonald, S. (2025). AI literacy practices. In *The Palgrave encyclopedia of computer-assisted language learning* (pp. 1–6). Springer Nature Switzerland., DOI: 10.1007/978-3-031-51447-0_93-2

Toyokawa, Y., Horikoshi, I., Majumdar, R., & Ogata, H. (2023). Challenges and opportunities of AI in inclusive education: A case study of data-enhanced active reading in Japan. *Smart Learning Environments, 10*(1), 67. DOI: 10.1186/s40561-023-00286-2

Udayakumar, D., Gopalakrishnan, S., Raghuram, A., Kartha, A., Krishnan, A. K., Ramamirtham, R., Muthangi, R., & Raju, R. (2025). Artificial intelligence-powered smart vision glasses for visually impaired individuals. *Indian Journal of Ophthalmology, 73*(Suppl 3), S492–S497. DOI: 10.4103/IJO.IJO_1621_24

UNESCO. (2020). *Education for sustainable development: a roadmap*. UNESCO., DOI: 10.54675/YFRE1448

UNESCO. (2021). AI and education: Promise and implications. Guidance for policy-makers.

UNESCO. (2021). *DIKSHA: Digital infrastructure for knowledge sharing*.

University of California. Berkeley News. (2024). *This company's mission is to make the world accessible to deaf people*. https://news.berkeley.edu/2024/11/08/this-companys-mission-is-to-make-the-world-accessible-to-deaf-people-it-all-started-at-berkeleys-big-ideas-contest/

Ursachi, T. M., Brezoaie, R. E., & Dascalu, M. I. (2025, June). Emerging Technologies in Immersive Learning: A Systematic Review of Trends, Challenges, and Opportunities. In *2025 IEEE 2nd International Conference on Blockchain, Smart Healthcare and Emerging Technologies (SmartBlock4Health)* (pp. 1-9). IEEE. DOI: 10.1109/SmartBlock4Health64843.2025.11189574

Uygun, D. (2024). Teachers' perspectives on artificial intelligence in education. *Advances in Mobile Learning Educational Research, 4*(1), 931–939. DOI: 10.25082/AMLER.2024.01.005

Valero, M. (2022). Challenges, Difficulties and Barriers for Engineering Higher Education. *Journal of Technology and Science Education, 12*(3), 551–566. DOI: 10.3926/jotse.1696

Verma, R. (2025). Access and use of DIKSHA for school teachers and students amid [*Indian Journal of Educational Technology*.]. *COVID*, •••, 19.

Verschueren, J. (2022). Metapragmatics. In Verschueren, J., & Östman, J. (Eds.), *Handbook of Pragmatics: Manual* (2nd ed., pp. 948–953). John Benjamins Publishing Company., DOI: 10.1075/hop.m2.met1

Vittorini, P., Menini, S., & Tonelli, S. (2021). An AI-based system for formative and summative assessment in data science courses. *International Journal of Artificial Intelligence in Education, 31*(2), 159–185. DOI: 10.1007/s40593-020-00230-2

Voogt, J., Laferrière, T., Breuleux, A., Itow, R., Hickey, D., & McKenney, S. (2015). Collaborative design as a form of professional development. *Instructional Science, 43*(2), 259–282. DOI: 10.1007/s11251-014-9340-7

Vortia, W. (2025). Use of AI in teaching mathematics to persons living with disabilities: The Context of the United States. *Magna Scientia Advanced Research and Reviews, 14*(2), 112–120. DOI: 10.30574/msarr.2025.14.2.0096

Walle, H., Serres, B., Gilles, V., de Runz, C., De Runz, C., Serres, B., & Venturini, G. (2022). A Survey on Recent Advances in AI and Vision Based Methods for Helping and Guiding Visually Impaired People. *Applied Sciences, 2022*(5). https://doi.org/DOI: 10.3390/app12052308ï

Walter, Y. (2024). Embracing the future of Artificial Intelligence in the classroom: The relevance of AI literacy, prompt engineering, and critical thinking in modern education. *International Journal of Educational Technology in Higher Education, 21*(1), 15. Advance online publication. DOI: 10.1186/s41239-024-00448-3

Wang, J., Wang, S., & Zhang, Y. (2023). Artificial intelligence for visually impaired. *Displays, 77*, 102391. Advance online publication. DOI: 10.1016/j.displa.2023.102391

Wang, X. (2023). Utilizing virtual reality to assist social competence in children with autism. *Computers & Education*. Advance online publication. DOI: 10.1016/j.compedu.2023.104815

Wang, X., Zhao, X., & Yu, C. (2025). The influence of information and social overload on academic performance: The role of social media fatigue, cognitive depletion, and self-control. *Revista de Psicodidáctica, 30*(2). Advance online publication. DOI: 10.1016/j.psicod.2025.500164

Wang, Z. (2024). Artificial intelligence in dance education: Using immersive technologies for teaching dance skills. *Technology in Society, 77*, 102579. DOI: 10.1016/j.techsoc.2024.102579

Warschauer, M., & Matuchniak, T. (2010). New technology and digital worlds: Analyzing evidence of equity in access, use, and outcomes. *Review of Research in Education, 34*(1), 179–225. DOI: 10.3102/0091732X09349791

Weeks, J., Cuthbert, A., & Alfirevic, Z. (2023). Trustworthiness assessment as an inclusion criterion for systematic reviews—What is the impact on results? *Cochrane Evidence Synthesis and Methods, 1*(10), e12037-n/a. https://doi.org/DOI: 10.1002/cesm.12037

Wells, M. B. (2025). Empowering non-verbal individuals through AI-driven symbolic text prediction: A metaliteracy approach to communication and inclusion. *Discover Education, 4*(1), 360. Advance online publication. DOI: 10.1007/s44217-025-00809-8

Wild, G., Nanyonga, A., Iqbal, A., Bano, S., Somerville, A., & Pollock, L. (2025). Lightweight and mobile artificial intelligence and immersive technologies in aviation. *Visual Computing for Industry, Biomedicine, and Art, 8*(1), 21. DOI: 10.1186/s42492-025-00203-z PMID: 40900374

Williams, A. (2025). Integrating artificial intelligence into higher education assessment. *Intersection: A Journal at the Intersection of Assessment and Learning, 6*(1), 128–154.

Williamson, B., & Eynon, R. (2020). Historical threads, missing links, and future directions in AI in education. *Learning, Media and Technology, 45*(3), 223–235. DOI: 10.1080/17439884.2020.1798995

Windasari, A., Syefrinando, B., Wiliyanti, V., Komikesari, H., & Yuberti, . (2024). The influence of the blended learning model on students' concept understanding ability viewed from self-confidence. *AIP Conference Proceedings, 3058*(1), 020013. Advance online publication. DOI: 10.1063/5.0206001

WIRED. (2023). *Data vulnerability concerns in India's DIKSHA platform.*

Wiyaka, W., Silitonga, L. M., Sunardi, S., & Pramudi, Y. T. C. (2024). From nervous to fluent: The impact of AI chatbot-assisted assessment on English reading anxiety and performance in Indonesian secondary school pupils. *Theory and Practice in Language Studies, 14*(12), 3851–3860. DOI: 10.17507/tpls.1412.20

Woo, D. J., Wang, D., Guo, K., & Susanto, H. (2024). Teaching EFL students to write with ChatGPT: Students' motivation to learn, cognitive load, and satisfaction with the learning process. *Education and Information Technologies, 29*(18), 24963–24990. DOI: 10.1007/s10639-024-12819-4

Woo, D. J., Wang, Y., Susanto, H., & Guo, K. (2023). Understanding English as a foreign language students' idea generation strategy for creative writing with natural language generation tools. *Journal of Educational Computing Research, 61*(7), 1464–1482. DOI: 10.1177/07356331231175999

Wood, S. G. (2017). Does use of text-to-speech and related read-aloud tools improve reading comprehension? *Journal of Learning Disabilities*. PMID: 28112580

Xia, Q., Chiu, T. K. F., Lee, M., Sanusi, I. T., Dai, Y., & Chai, C. S. (2022). A self-determination theory (STD) design approach for inclusive and diverse artificial intelligence (AI) K-12. *Computers & Education, 189*, 104582. Advance online publication. DOI: 10.1016/j.compedu.2022.104582

Xu, J., Zhai, X., Chen, N. S., Ghani, U., Istenic, A., & Xin, J. (2025). Integrating AI-Driven Wearable Metaverse Technologies into Ubiquitous Blended Learning: A Framework Based on Embodied Interaction and Multi-Agent Collaboration. *Education Sciences, 15*(7), 900. DOI: 10.3390/educsci15070900

Yadav, M., Kanwal, P., & Dang, T. T. (2025). Microlearning for the masses: Empowerment of geographically dispersed teams. In *Navigating the Global Workforce Through Bold Workplace Learning and Professional Development* (pp. 319–346). IGI Global., DOI: 10.4018/979-8-3693-3338-9.ch012

Yan, W., Li, B., & Lowell, V. L. (2025). Integrating Artificial Intelligence and Extended Reality in Language Education: A Systematic Literature Review (2017–2024). *Education Sciences 2025, Vol. 15, 15*(8). DOI: 10.3390/educsci15081066

Yang, C., & Taele, P. (2025). AI for Accessible Education: Personalized Audio-Based Learning for Blind Students. *Proceedings of Augmented Educators and AI: Shaping the Future of Human-AI Collaboration in Learning on CHI 2025 Workshop (Augmented Educators and AI(CHI 2025 Workshop)), 1*. https://arxiv.org/pdf/2504.17117

Yao, L. (2025). The role of technology in supporting communication and learning in children with autism. In *Connecting Ideas, Cultures, and Communities* (pp. 473-478). Routledge. DOI: 10.1201/9781003591511-74

Yi, Y. (2021). Establishing the concept of AI literacy: Focusing on competence and purpose. Jahr – European. *Journal of Bioethics, 12*(2), 353–368. DOI: 10.21860/j.12.2.8

Zainuddin, Z., Chu, S. K. W., Shujahat, M., & Perera, C. J. (2020). The impact of gamification on learning and instruction: A systematic review of empirical evidence. *Educational Research Review, 30*, 100326. DOI: 10.1016/j.edurev.2020.100326

Zambrano Verdesoto, G. J., & Caicedo, M. F. (2025). The Importance of Microlearning in Higher Education. *European Public and Social Innovation Review, 10*, 1–14. DOI: 10.31637/epsir-2025-2075

Zangiacomi, A., Pessot, E., Fornasiero, R., Bertetti, M., & Sacco, M. (2020). Moving towards digitalization: A multiple case study in manufacturing. *Production Planning and Control, 31*(2–3), 143–157. DOI: 10.1080/09537287.2019.1631468

Zaraii Zavaraki, E. (2024). Artificial Intelligence for People with Special Educational Needs. In *Artificial Intelligence for Quality Education* [Working Title]. IntechOpen., DOI: 10.5772/intechopen.1004158

Zawacki-Richter, O., Marín, V. I., Bond, M., & Gouverneur, F. (2019). Systematic review of research on artificial intelligence applications in higher education. *International Journal of Educational Technology in Higher Education, 16*(39), 39. Advance online publication. DOI: 10.1186/s41239-019-0171-0

Zdravkova, K. (2022). The Potential of Artificial Intelligence for Assistive Technology in Education. In Ivanović, M., Klašnja-Milićević, A., & Jain, L. C. (Eds.), *Handbook on Intelligent Techniques in the Educational Process. Learning and Analytics in Intelligent Systems* (Vol. 29). Springer., DOI: 10.1007/978-3-031-04662-9_4

Zebua, N., & Ziraluo, Y. P. B. (2026). Bridging the Gap: Integrating GenAI into Secondary Science Curricula. In *Harnessing Generative Artificial Intelligence for Science Education* (pp. 137–162). IGI Global Scientific Publishing. DOI: 10.4018/979-8-3373-2913-0.ch005

Zero Project. (2018). *OrCam MyEye: Vision device to understand texts and identify objects*. Essl Foundation. https://zeroproject.org/view/project/8b8f3fb8-9a17-eb11-a813-0022489b3a6d

Zhai, X., Yin, Y., Pellegrino, J. W., Haudek, K. C., & Shi, L. (2020). Applying machine learning in science assessment: A systematic review. *Studies in Science Education, 56*(1), 111–151. DOI: 10.1080/03057267.2020.1735757

Zhao, Y., & Yang, L. (2022). Examining the relationship between perceived teacher support and students' academic engagement in foreign language learning: Enjoyment and boredom as mediators. *Frontiers in Psychology, 13*, 987554. DOI: 10.3389/fpsyg.2022.987554

About the Contributors

Filipe T. Moreira holds a PhD in Multimedia in Education (University of Aveiro) and has a large experience in developing national and international ICT projects in Education. His interests lie in understanding how technology can influence children's learning processes and general development, and the philosophy of technology. At the moment he is Invited Professor at Polytechnic of Porto where it is part of NAID (Digital Inclusion Support Centre).

Sara Martins is a designer with experience in developing applications for education and other digital educational resources. She is currently working on her PhD project at the University of Aveiro. Her main research interests are based on environmental and sustainable-oriented mobile applications, child-computer interaction and environmental education. Sara holds a Bachelor's degree in Design from the University of Aveiro and a Master's degree in Graphic Design and Editorial Projects from the Faculty of Fine Arts at the University of Porto.

***

Ashraf Alam is currently serving as an Assistant Professor in the Department of Education at NIT Calicut, Kerala, India. He has been recognised among the *World's Top 2% Scientists* by Stanford University and Elsevier. His academic contributions include more than 80 Scopus-indexed publications and over 100 conference presentations delivered at national and international academic forums. His work has appeared in reputed research publication platforms including Elsevier, Springer, Taylor & Francis, CRC Press, Routledge, Atlantis Press, Springer Nature, Palgrave Macmillan, and IEEE. He earned his Ph.D. from IIT Kharagpur, where his research engaged with foundational concerns in educational policy, curriculum design, educational technology, philosophy of education, innovation in education, educational administration, governance, and pedagogical transformation. His work is grounded in a transdisciplinary orientation that draws from educational sciences, digital pedagogy, curriculum theory, learning analytics, sustainability education, instructional design, artificial intelligence, ethics of technology, and socio-technical studies. Dr. Ashraf's scholarship strives to interrogate and expand the boundaries of educational thought by examining the epistemological, ethical, and social dimensions of digital and post-digital pedagogies. His work critically engages with the changing nature of knowledge production, learner agency, pedagogical mediation, and institutional transformation in technologically saturated educational environments. He is particularly invested in advancing inclusive digital learning, gamified instructional strategies, AI-mediated educational ecosystems, and ethically governed technology integration in education. His research agenda is animated by the pursuit of design-oriented, ethically attuned, and contextually responsive frameworks that can support meaningful educational reform. Through his work, he seeks to contribute to the development of pedagogical models that are not only technologically innovative but also socially just, epistemically inclusive, developmentally sensitive, and aligned with the broader goals of sustainable and human-centred education.

Paulo Barroso Integrated researcher at NOVA Institute of Communication, NOVA University of Lisbon – School of Social Sciences and Humanities (Portugal) and assistant Professor at the Polytechnic Institute of Viseu (Portugal), College of Education, Department of Communication and Art, teaching Strategic Communication, Sociology of Communication, Semiotics, Theories of Communication, Ethics and Deontology; PhD in Philosophy (University of Santiago de Compostela, Spain), Post-Doctoral Researcher in Communication Sciences (University of Minho, Portugal) between 2007 and 2013. ORCID identifier number 0000-0001-7638-5064 (email address: pbarroso1062@gmail.com).

B. Lalitha Bala is a distinguished Tamil scholar and academician with over twelve years of teaching and research experience in Tamil literature, language, grammar, and education. She currently serves as Assistant Professor in the Department of Education at SASTRA University, Thanjavur, and holds a Ph.D. in Tamil Literature from Tamil University. Her academic journey includes multiple postgraduate qualifications, UGC-NET, and specialized training in manuscriptology, education, and digital competencies. Dr. Lalitha Bala has presented and published extensively at national and international forums, earning numerous awards for her contributions to Tamil research, literary criticism, pedagogy, and poetry. Known for her student-centric teaching approach, leadership, and commitment to lifelong learning, her work bridges classical Tamil traditions with contemporary educational perspectives, particularly in areas such as food culture, medicine, ethics, and society in Tamil literature.

Devaki V serves as an Assistant Professor at the Department of Education (SASHE), SASTRA Deemed to be University, Thanjavur. She holds a Master of Science in Physics from Alagappa University, Karaikudi, graduating with the distinction of second rank in the university. Additionally, she completed her Master of Education at Sri Sarada College of Education, Salem, Tamil Nadu. She qualified for the position of Assistant Professor in Physics and Education, having successfully cleared the Tamil Nadu State Eligibility Test and also passed the Central Teacher Eligibility Test. She completed her doctoral studies in the Department of Education at Bharathidasan University, Tiruchirappalli in 2025. Her research interests encompass metacognition, neurocognition, the pedagogy of science, and experiential learning.

Alexandre M. Pereira Figueiredo holds a degree in Mass Communication, postgraduate qualifications in Communication Sciences and in Information and Communication Technologies, a Master's degree in Communication Sciences, and a PhD in Communication Sciences. He is also a specialist in Audiovisual and Media Production and is currently pursuing a degree in Law. He is currently a professor at the Polytechnic Institute of Portalegre and a researcher at IC.NOVA, Techn&Art, and CIDIUM. He serves as editor of the electronic academic journal artciencia.com, is a member of the Editorial Board of the International Journal of European Studies, and sits on the Advisory Board of the Open Access Asia project. He has authored three books and published approximately 40 articles in specialized academic journals. He has organized one academic event and participated in eight others. His research and teaching activities are focused on the field of Communication Sciences. Previously, he held teaching positions at the the Polytechnic Institute of Guarda, the Polytechnic Institute of Santarém, the University of Beira Interior, the Polytechnic Institute of Castelo Branco, the Polytechnic Institu

Deepak Gupta is a globally recognized researcher and distinguished academician with over 22 years of experience in Computer Science and Engineering. He holds a Ph.D. in Computer Engineering and has an outstanding research portfolio comprising SCI/SCOPUS-indexed journal publications, conference proceedings, books, book chapters, patents, and copyrights. His research expertise includes Machine Learning, Artificial Intelligence, Data Mining, Deep Learning, and Emerging Computational Technologies. Dr. Gupta has actively contributed to the global research community as a reviewer, conference chair, editor, keynote speaker, and mentor for innovative research initiatives. He is widely recognized for promoting interdisciplinary research, academic excellence, and industry-oriented innovation.

Currently, he serves as Associate Professor and Head of the Department of CSE (Emerging Branches) at ITM Gwalior, Madhya Pradesh, India.

Manpreet Kaur is currently serving as an Assistant Professor at Guru Kashi University, Talwandi Sabo (Punjab, India). She has over 8 years of teaching and academic experience in higher education. Her expertise lies in the field of Computer Science and Artificial Intelligence, with a strong focus on research, teaching, and student mentorship. Throughout her career, Dr. Kaur has contributed to the academic community through teaching undergraduate and postgraduate students, guiding research projects, and actively participating in conferences, workshops, and faculty development programmes. She is passionate about integrating innovative pedagogical approaches in her teaching to enhance learning outcomes and inspire students to explore emerging technologies. Her dedication to academics and research makes her a valuable contributor to knowledge dissemination in higher education.

Bingqing (Bonnie) Li is a lecturer in the School of Education at La Trobe University. Her research interests lie in the areas of teacher education, where she explores the impactful world of teacher professional development and the dynamic integration of technology in teaching.

Murathoti Rajendra Nath Babu, holds a Post Graduate degree in Mathematics, Sociology, Psychology, English and Education (M.Ed.-University 1st Rank), M. Phil. and obtained Ph.D. in Education from Sri Venkateswara University. Presently he is working as an Associate Professor in the Department of Education, Nagaland University (A Central University). He has 15 years' research and teaching experience at B.Ed., M.Ed., M.A.(Education), Ph.D. levels. He has successfully guided 60 M.Ed./M.A. degree dissertations, 2 M.Phil. Degrees and 4 Ph.D. Degrees and at present 6 Ph.D. Scholars working under his guidance. He has presented more than 70 papers at national and international seminars, conferences and workshops. For his credit, from 2015, he has published 26 articles in various national and international journals including UGC Care Listed, Scopus & Web of Sciences, 9 books, 11 book chapters. He has cleared UGC NET with JRF Education in 2009 Teacher Eligibility Test (APTET) Paper-I & Paper-II in July 2011 & January 2012, AP DSC (District Selection Committee)-TRT (Teacher Recruitment) Mathematics for the Post of School Assistant in mathematics post (2nd Rank) in 2012 and also Departmental Tests Accounts Tests like Executive Officers (141), Gazetted Officers of Education Department (88,97) in 2013. He got Junior Research Fellow (UGC) award in 2009, senior research Fellow (UGC) in 2012 and in 2012 DSC. Having Administrative Experience as Teacher-in-charge, Department of Teacher Education, Warden, Ramei Men's Hostel, Convener, Nagaland State Education Common Entrance

Test (NSEDCET)-2019 & 2020. He has Completed 2 Research Projects funded by PMMMNMTT(MHRD) Scheme, Ministry of Education, New Delhi, Nagaland Education Mission Society, Government of Nagaland & 1 Research Project ongoing funded by ICSSR, New Delhi.

Jitendra Singh Rathore is an Associate Professor at the Department of Commerce and Management – WISDOM, Banasthali Vidyapith, India. He has total more than 18 years of experience in industry (5 years) and academics (more than 13 years) and teaches Marketing Management, Sales and Distribution Management and international marketing to undergraduate and postgraduate students. Prior to joining academics, he worked in the Banking, Financial Services and Insurance (BFSI) sector with organizations such as Bajaj Allianz, Kotak Securities and SBI cards in various capacities for 5 years. His areas of research interest include e-commerce, the sharing economy, Mentoring, channel and distribution management and the shopping behavior of consumers in the digital age.

Putu Wisnu Saputra was born in Ujung Pandang on November 9, 1995. He is a lecturer with a Master's degree in Hindu Religious Education. His academic interests focus on education, Hindu religious studies, and educational technology. As an academic, he actively engages in the implementation of the Tri Dharma of Higher Education, encompassing teaching, research, and community service. He is particularly interested in the integration of digital technology into educational practices, especially within the context of Hindu Religious Education. Through his academic and scholarly activities, Putu Wisnu Saputra is committed to contributing to the advancement of innovative, value-based, and technology-oriented education.

Chinna Suresh serving as Assistant Professor since July, 2018 in the Department of Education at the School of Arts, Sciences, Humanities, and Education (SASHE), SASTRA Deemed to be University, Thanjavur, Tamil Nadu, India. He earned his Ph.D. in Education from Sri Venkateswara University, Tirupati, Andhra Pradesh, in March,2018, and his M.Sc. in Mathematics from Sri Krishnadevaraya University, Anantapur, Andhra Pradesh, in 2010. His research interests include ICT in Education, Mathematics Pedagogy, Gender Studies, and Teaching Strategies.

Sonam Tripathi is a dedicated research scholar currently pursuing her PhD from Banasthali Vidyapith, the world's largest women's residential university, reaccredited A++ by NAAC and ranked among India's top 75 universities by NIRF. She holds an MBA from Banasthali Vidyapith and a Master's degree in Economics from Indira Gandhi National Open University. She has been deeply involved in research within the field of educational technology. Her academic work focuses on understanding how emerging technologies influence student engagement, learning effectiveness, and overall academic performance. With two years of teaching experience, she brings valuable practical insights into pedagogical practices, effectively bridging the gap between theory and classroom application. Her passion lies in exploring innovative technological models and digital mechanisms that enhance student engagement, personalized learning, and the effective integration of technology in educational environments. Her work reflects a strong engagement with contemporary educational transformations, particularly in the domain of digital learning and EdTech integration. Her research aims to contribute to the advancement of innovative and technology-driven educational practices. With a strong commitment to academic excellence, she is enthusiastic about contributing to the scholarly community through her research endeavors.

Samiksha Vyas is an Assistant Professor at Vivekananda Global University, Jaipur, India. She completed her PhD from Banasthali Vidyapith and holds an MBA from the same institution. She has been deeply involved in research within the field of the sharing economy. Furthermore, she gained professional experience while working in the forensic department at KPMG Gurgaon. Her passion lies in exploring innovative models and mechanisms to enhance collaboration and resource utilization in this emerging domain. Her work aims to shed light on the dynamics of this emerging area, fostering sustainable and efficient practices. With an unwavering commitment to advancing knowledge, she is delighted to contribute to the academic community through her research endeavors.

Yaredi Waruwu is an academic and education practitioner with a strong background in English language and educational science. He completed his Bachelor's degree (S-1) in English Literature at Santo Thomas Catholic University in Medan in 2005. Subsequently, he earned a Master's degree (S-2) in English Literature from the Islamic University of North Sumatra in 2015, and a Doctorate (S-3) in Educational Sciences from Padang State University in 2022. Since 2009, Yaredi Waruwu has served as a tenured faculty member at Nias University in North Sumatra and currently holds the position of Dean of the Faculty of Teacher Training and Education (FKIP). He also has academic experience as a faculty member at several universities, including Taman Siswa University in Padang and UIN Imam Bonjol in Padang. Beyond his academic work, he has professional experience in various national and international organizations, including in community empowerment and community-based economic development programs. He has also been involved in collaborative activities with government agencies. Yaredi Waruwu is active in research and scientific publications, both in national and international journals. He is also a frequent speaker at national and international seminars. Currently, he is a member of the Indonesian Association of Lecturers in Community Service (ADPI) and contributes as an editor to ISBN-registered books and reputable international journals.

Nofamataro Zebua is a young lecturer in the Biology Education Study Program at Universitas Nias (UNIAS), Indonesia. He completed his bachelor's degree in biology education from Universitas Nias Raya (UNIRAYA) and his master's degree from the Department of Biology at Universitas Negeri Malang (UM). He is a passionate researcher and writer who explores innovative topics in the field of education. His research focuses on biology, biology and science education, literacy, thinking skills, artificial intelligence (AI) for education, biodiversity, pedagogy, 21st-century skills, and ethnobiology to enhance student learning experiences and engagement. He is also actively providing valuable insights to educators, researchers, and students, as well as promoting digital literacy and environmental awareness through problem-based, project-based, and community-based approaches.

Index

A

C

D

E

G

H

I

L

M

P

R

S

T

U

V

www.ingramcontent.com/pod-product-compliance
Lightning Source LLC
LaVergne TN
LVHW081528300926
849161LV00006B/1341